A Kodansha Comics Trade Paperback Original
Hitorijime My Hero 6 copyright © 2017 Memeco Arii
English translation copyright © 2020 Memeco Arii

Published in the United States by Kodansha Comics, an imprint of Kodansha USA Publishing, LLC, New York.

Publication rights for this English edition arranged through Kodansha Ltd., Tokyo.

First published in Japan in 2017 by Ichijinsha Inc., Tokyo.

ISBN 978-1-63236-897-3

Printed in the United States of America.

www.kodansha.us

9 8 7 6 5 4 3
Translation: Julie Goniwich
Lettering: Michael Martin
Editing: Haruko Hashimoto
Kodansha Comics edition cover design by Phil Balsman

Publisher: Kiichiro Sugawara
Managing editor: Maya Rosewood
Vice president of marketing & publicity: Naho Yamada

Director of publishing services: Ben Applegate
Associate director of operations: Stephen Pakula
Publishing services managing editor: Noelle Webster
Assistant production manager: Emi Lotto

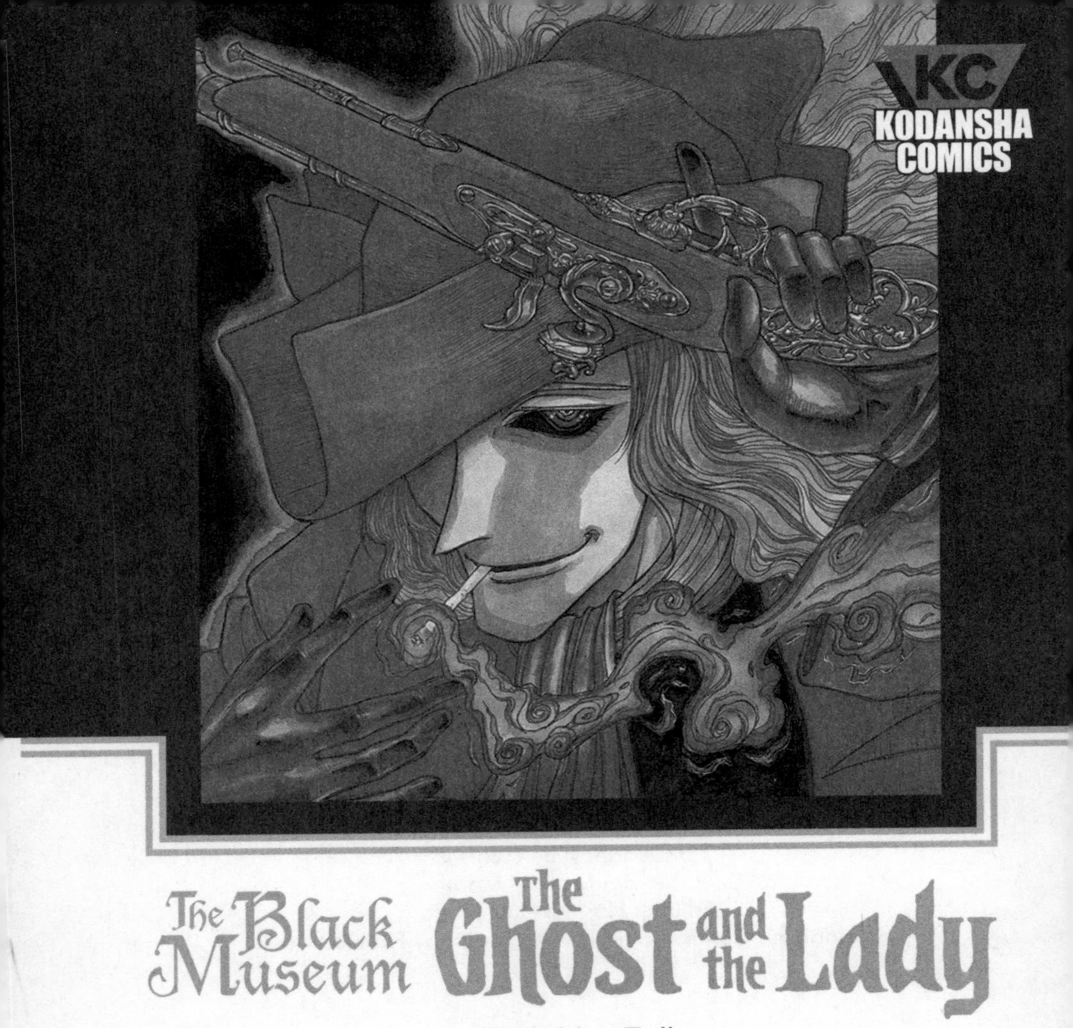

KODANSHA COMICS

The Black Museum The Ghost and the Lady

By Kazuhiro Fujita

Deep in Scotland Yard in London sits an evidence room dedicated to the greatest mysteries of British history. In this "Black Museum" sits a misshapen hunk of lead—two bullets fused together—the key to a wartime encounter between Florence Nightingale, the mother of modern nursing, and a supernatural Man in Grey. This story is unknown to most scholars of history, but a special guest of the museum will tell the tale of The Ghost and the Lady...

Praise for Kazuhiro Fujita's *Ushio and Tora*

"A charming revival that combines a classic look with modern depth and pacing... **Essential viewing both for curmudgeons and new fans alike.**" — Anime News Network

"**GREAT!** The first episode of Ushio and Tora captures the essence of '90s anime." — IGN

Magus of the Library

Mitsu Izumi

MITSU IZUMI'S STUNNING ARTWORK BRINGS A FANTASTICAL LITERARY ADVENTURE TO LUSH, THRILLING LIFE!

Young Theo adores books, but the prejudice and hatred of his village keeps them ever out of his reach. Then one day, he chances to meet Sedona, a traveling librarian who works for the great library of Aftzaak, City of Books, and his life changes forever...

KC
KODANSHA
COMICS

"An emotional and artistic tour de force! We see incredible triumph, and crushing defeat... each panel [is] a thrill!"
—Anitay

"A journey that's instantly compelling."
—Anime News Network

WELCOME TO THE BALLROOM

By Tomo Takeuchi

Feckless high school student Tatara Fujita wants to be good at something—anything. Unfortunately, he's about as average as a slouchy teen can be. The local bullies know this, and make it a habit to hit him up for cash, but all that changes when the debonair Kaname Sengoku sends them packing. Sengoku's not the neighborhood watch, though. He's a professional ballroom dancer. And once Tatara Fujita gets pulled into the world of ballroom, his life will never be the same.

KC KODANSHA COMICS

KODANSHA COMICS

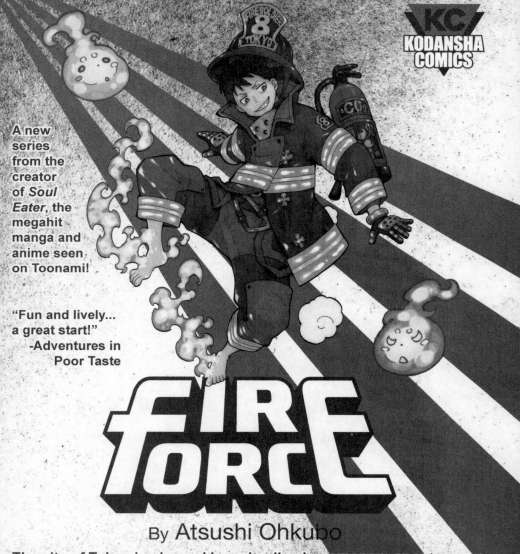

A new series from the creator of *Soul Eater*, the megahit manga and anime seen on Toonami!

FIRESOLDIER
8
TOKYO

"Fun and lively... a great start!"
-Adventures in Poor Taste

FIRE FORCE

By Atsushi Ohkubo

The city of Tokyo is plagued by a deadly phenomenon: spontaneous human combustion! Luckily, a special team is there to quench the inferno: The Fire Force! The fire soldiers at Special Fire Cathedral 8 are about to get a unique addition. Enter Shinra, a boy who possesses the power to run at the speed of a rocket, leaving behind the famous "devil's footprints" (and destroying his shoes in the process). Can Shinra and his colleagues discover the source of this strange epidemic before the city burns to ashes?

"I'm pleasantly surprised to find modern shojo using cross-dressing as a dramatic device to deliver social commentary... Recommended."

-Otaku USA Magazine

The prince in his dark days

By **Hico Yamanaka**

A drunkard for a father, a household of poverty... For 17-year-old Atsuko, misfortune is all she knows and believes in. Until one day, a chance encounter with Itaru—the wealthy heir of a huge corporation—changes everything. The two look identical, uncannily so. When Itaru curiously goes missing, Atsuko is roped into being his stand-in. There, in his shoes, Atsuko must parade like a prince in a palace. She encounters many new experiences, but at what cost…?

KC
KODANSHA
COMICS

Japan's most powerful spirit medium delves into the ghost world's greatest mysteries!

Story by Kyo Shirodaira, famed author of mystery fiction and creator of *Spiral*, *Blast of Tempest*, and *The Record of a Fallen Vampire*.

Both touched by spirits called yôkai, Kotoko and Kurô have gained unique superhuman powers. But to gain her powers Kotoko has given up an eye and a leg, and Kurô's personal life is in shambles. So when Kotoko suggests they team up to deal with renegades from the spirit world, Kurô doesn't have many other choices, but Kotoko might just have a few ulterior motives...

IN/SPECTRE

STORY BY KYO SHIRODAIRA
ART BY CHASHIBA KATASE

KC KODANSHA COMICS

In love, there are no save points.

ヲタクに恋は難しい

WOTAKOI:
LOVE IS HARD FOR OTAKU

by FUJITA

Narumi has had it rough: Every boyfriend she's had dumped her once they found out she was an otaku, so she's gone to great lengths to hide it. At her new job, she bumps into Hirotaka, her childhood friend and fellow otaku. When Hirotaka almost gets her secret outed at work, she comes up with a plan to keep him quiet. But he comes up with a counter-proposal: Why doesn't she just date him instead?

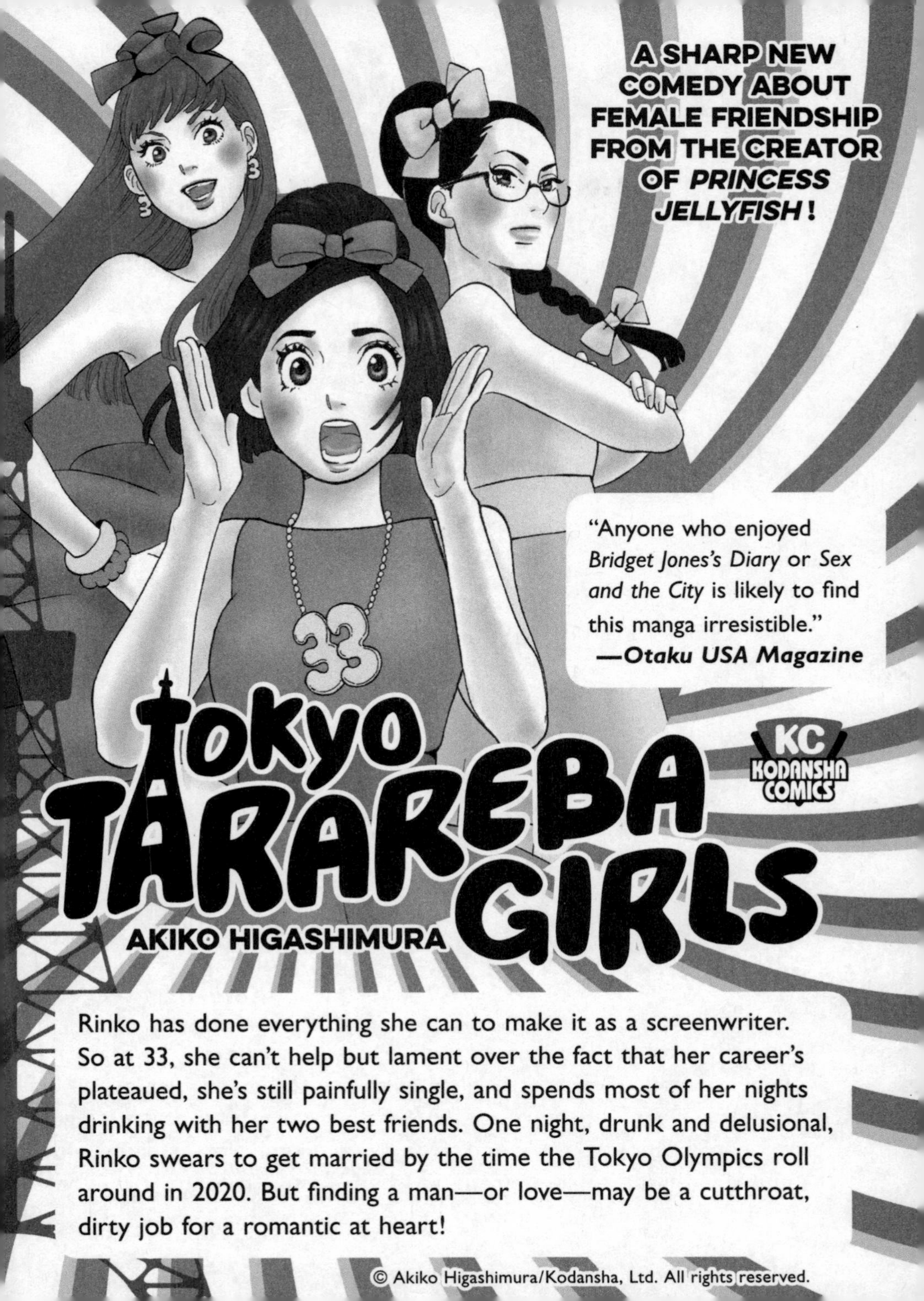
A SHARP NEW COMEDY ABOUT FEMALE FRIENDSHIP FROM THE CREATOR OF *PRINCESS JELLYFISH*!
"Anyone who enjoyed *Bridget Jones's Diary* or *Sex and the City* is likely to find this manga irresistible."
—*Otaku USA Magazine*
TOKYO TARAREBA GIRLS
AKIKO HIGASHIMURA
KC KODANSHA COMICS
Rinko has done everything she can to make it as a screenwriter. So at 33, she can't help but lament over the fact that her career's plateaued, she's still painfully single, and spends most of her nights drinking with her two best friends. One night, drunk and delusional, Rinko swears to get married by the time the Tokyo Olympics roll around in 2020. But finding a man—or love—may be a cutthroat, dirty job for a romantic at heart!
© Akiko Higashimura/Kodansha, Ltd. All rights reserved.

Princess Jellyfish

Akiko Higashimura

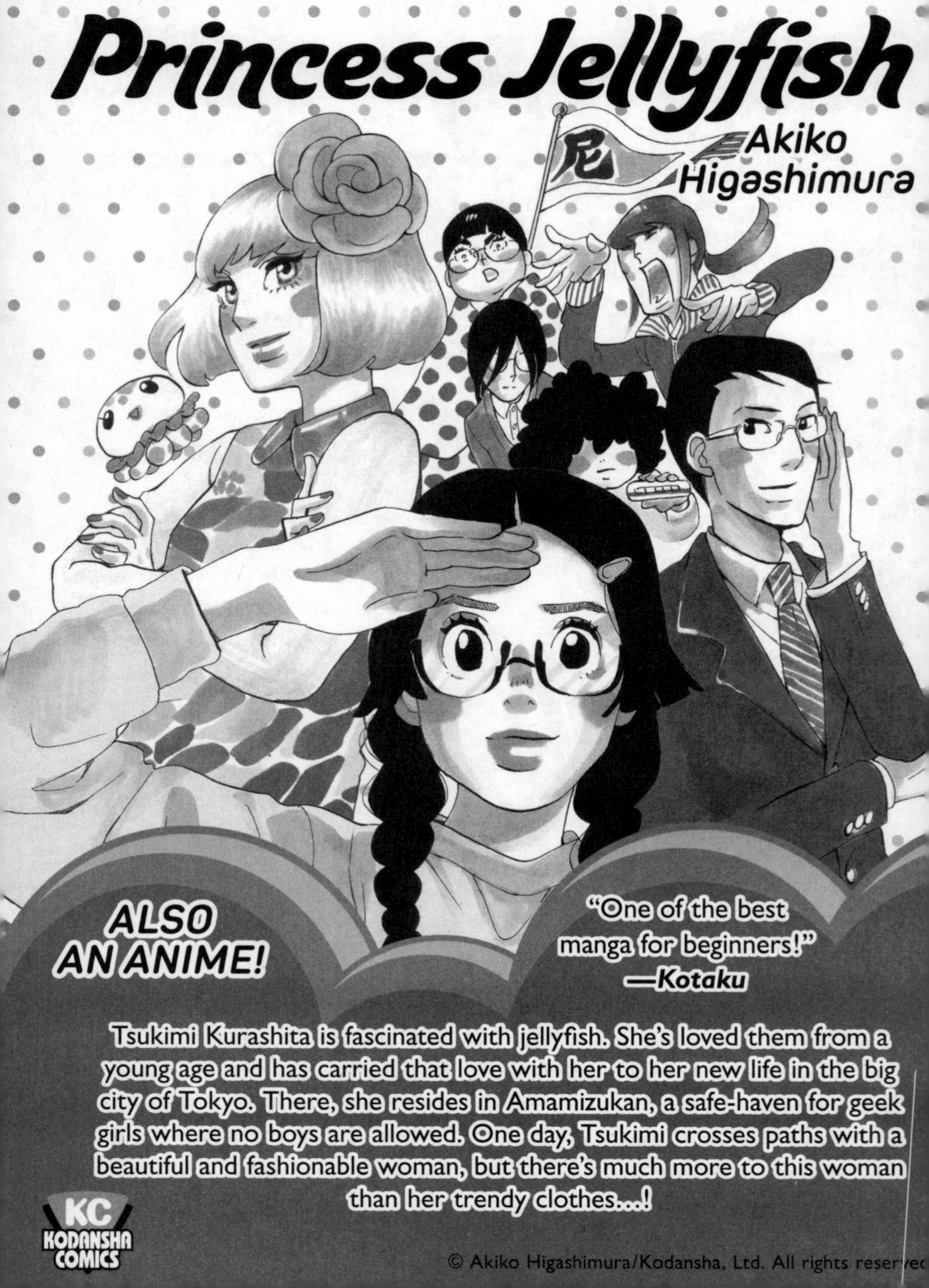

尼

ALSO AN ANIME!

"One of the best manga for beginners!"
—*Kotaku*

Tsukimi Kurashita is fascinated with jellyfish. She's loved them from a young age and has carried that love with her to her new life in the big city of Tokyo. There, she resides in Amamizukan, a safe-haven for geek girls where no boys are allowed. One day, Tsukimi crosses paths with a beautiful and fashionable woman, but there's much more to this woman than her trendy clothes...!

KC KODANSHA COMICS

Yuri Is My Job!

miman

Yuri is My Job! © Miman/Ichijinsha Inc.

Hime is a picture-perfect high school princess, so when she accidentally injures a café manager named Mai, she's willing to cover some shifts to keep her façade intact. To Hime's surprise, the café is themed after a private school where the all-female staff always puts on their best act for their loyal customers. However, under the guidance of the most graceful girl there, Hime can't help but blush and blunder! Beneath all the frills and laughter, Hime feels tension brewing as she finds out more about her new job and her budding feelings...

"A quirky, fun comedy series... If you're a yuri fan, or perhaps interested in getting into it but not sure where to start, this book is worth picking up."
— Anime UK News

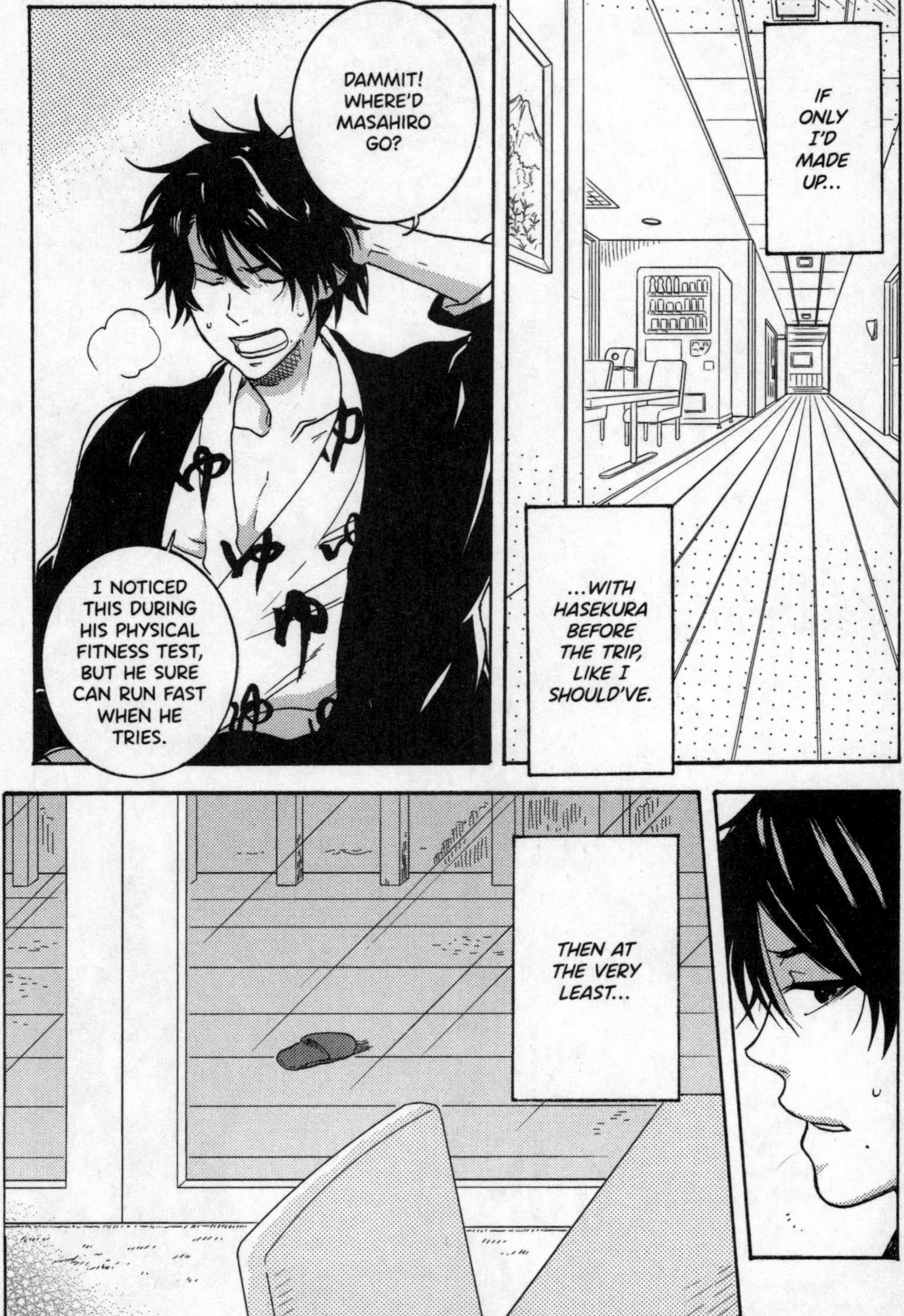

IF ONLY I'D MADE UP...
...WITH HASEKURA BEFORE THE TRIP, LIKE I SHOULD'VE.
DAMMIT! WHERE'D MASAHIRO GO?
I NOTICED THIS DURING HIS PHYSICAL FITNESS TEST, BUT HE SURE CAN RUN FAST WHEN HE TRIES.
THEN AT THE VERY LEAST...

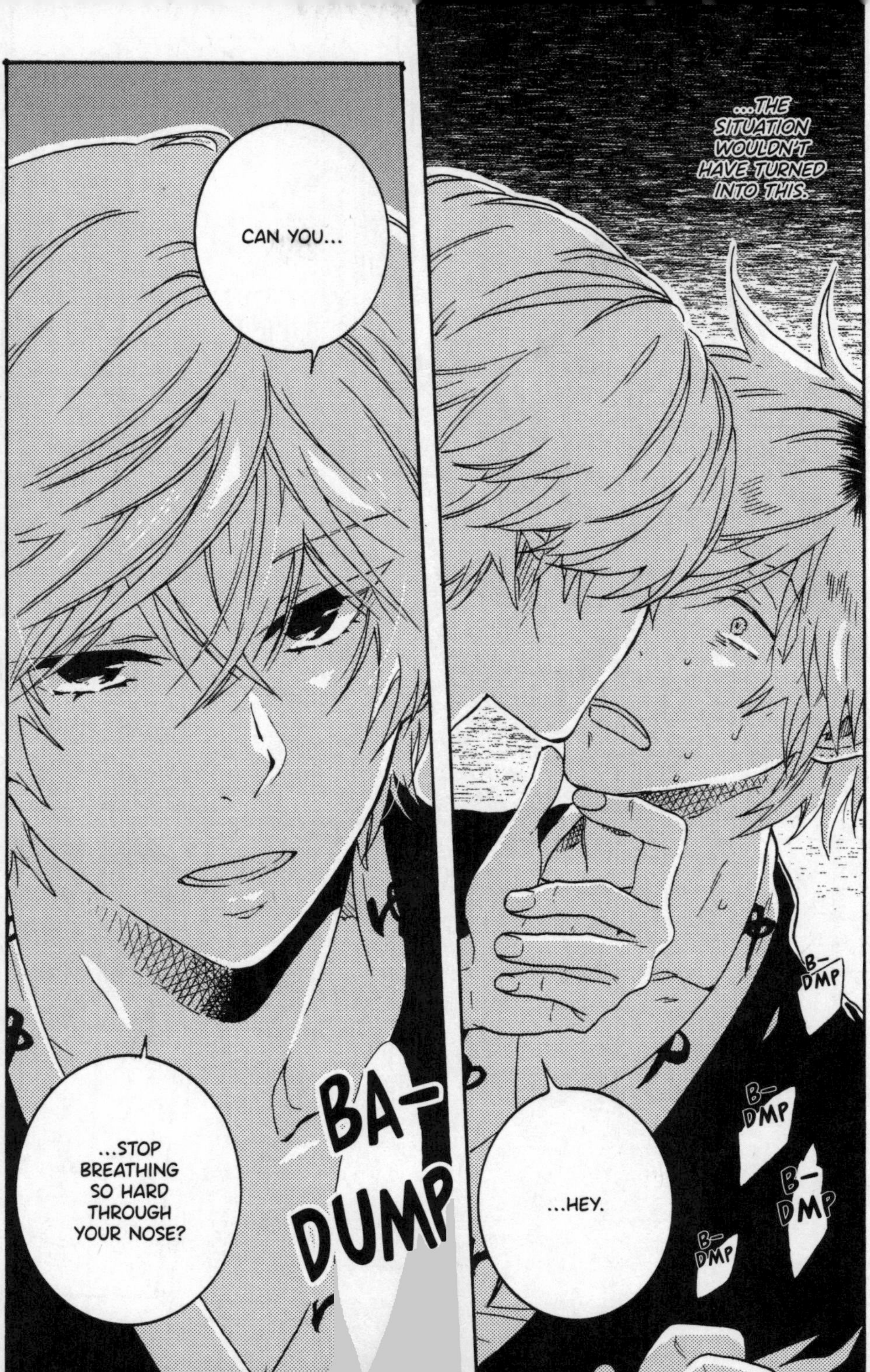

...THE SITUATION WOULDN'T HAVE TURNED INTO THIS.
B-DMP
...HEY.
B-DMP
B-DMP
B-DMP
CAN YOU...
BA-DUMP
...STOP BREATHING SO HARD THROUGH YOUR NOSE?

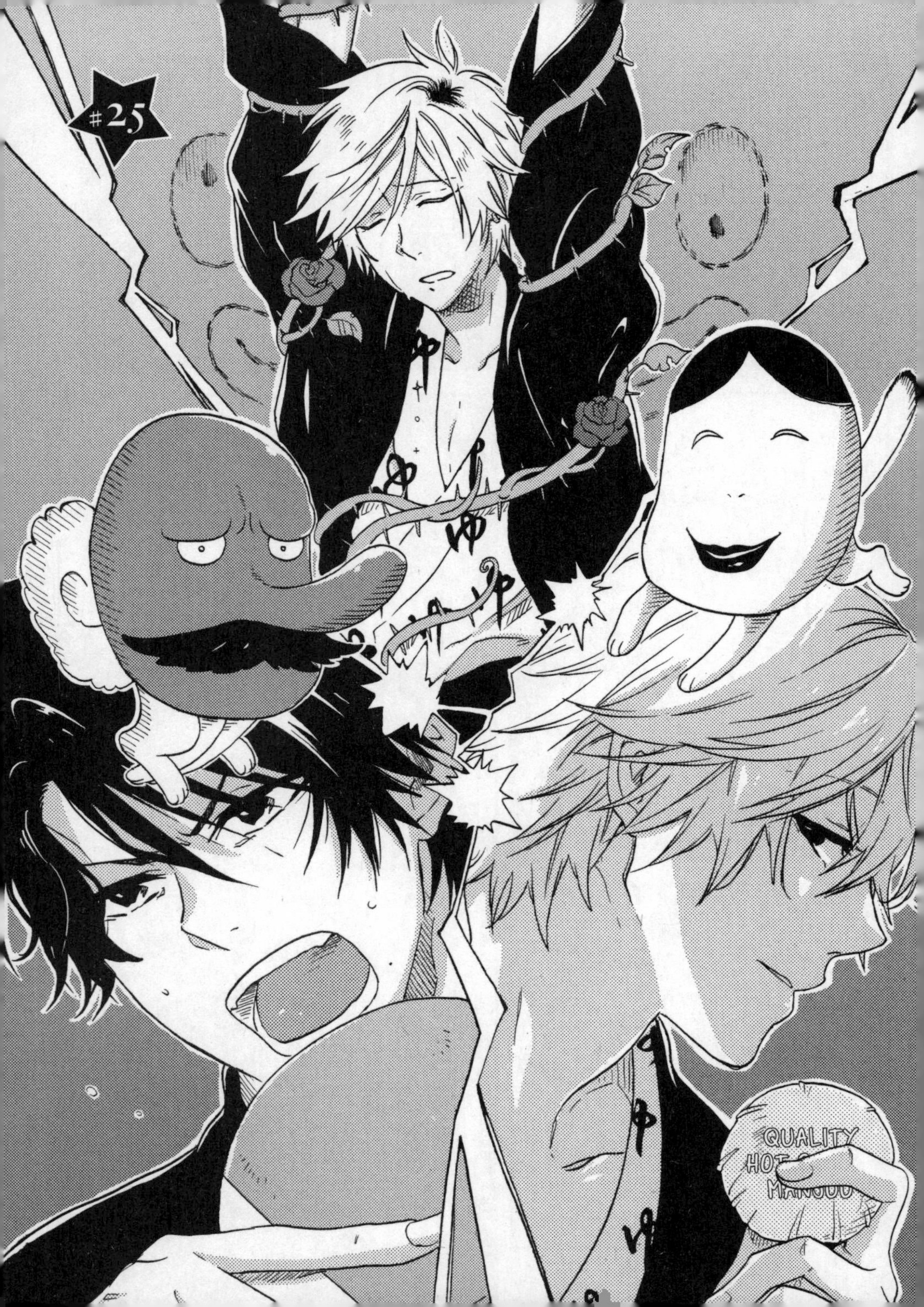
#25
QUALITY
HOT
MANJUU

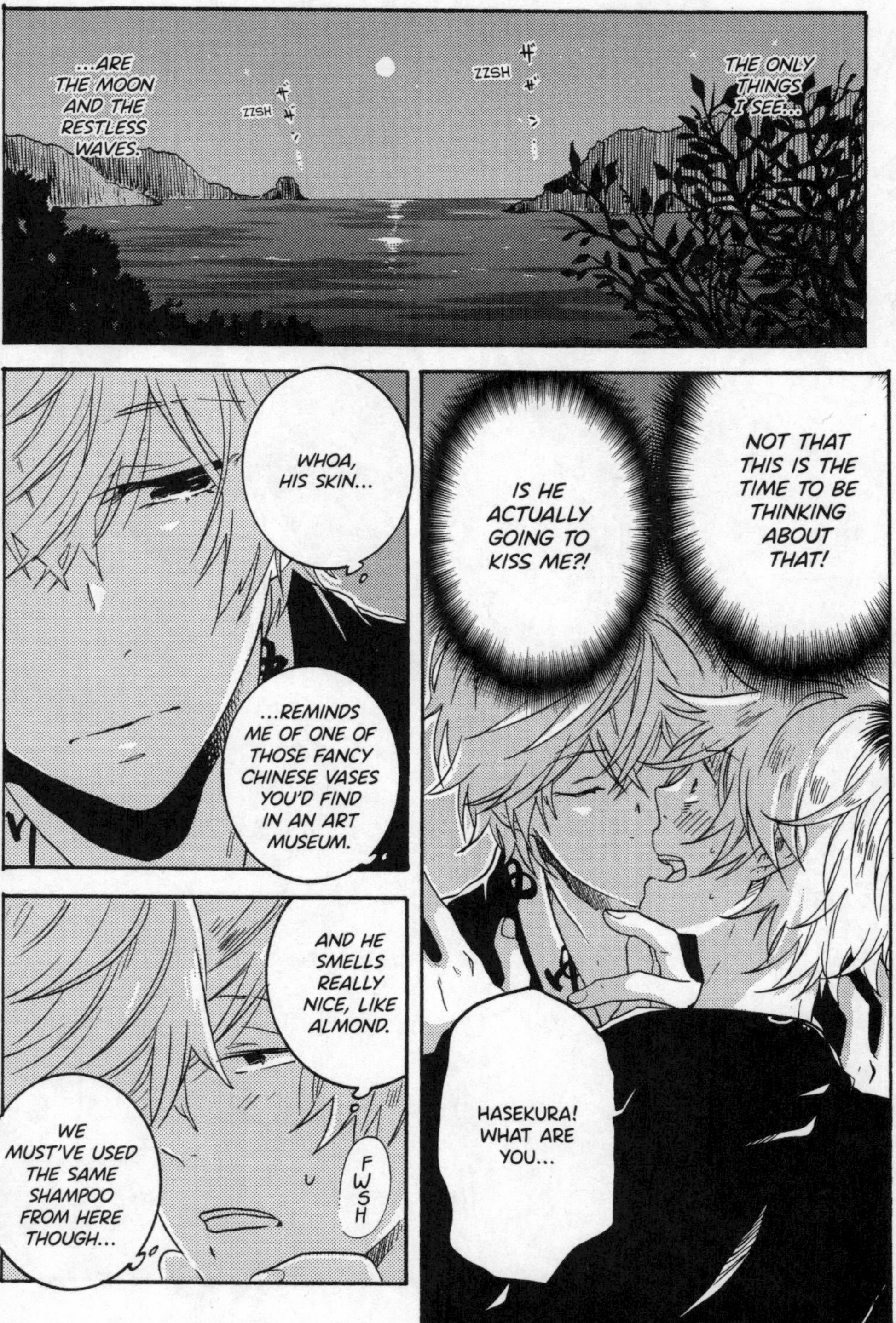
THE ONLY THINGS I SEE...
ZZSH
ZZSH
...ARE THE MOON AND THE RESTLESS WAVES.
NOT THAT THIS IS THE TIME TO BE THINKING ABOUT THAT!
IS HE ACTUALLY GOING TO KISS ME?!
HASEKURA! WHAT ARE YOU...
WHOA, HIS SKIN...
...REMINDS ME OF ONE OF THOSE FANCY CHINESE VASES YOU'D FIND IN AN ART MUSEUM.
AND HE SMELLS REALLY NICE, LIKE ALMOND.
FWSH
WE MUST'VE USED THE SAME SHAMPOO FROM HERE THOUGH...

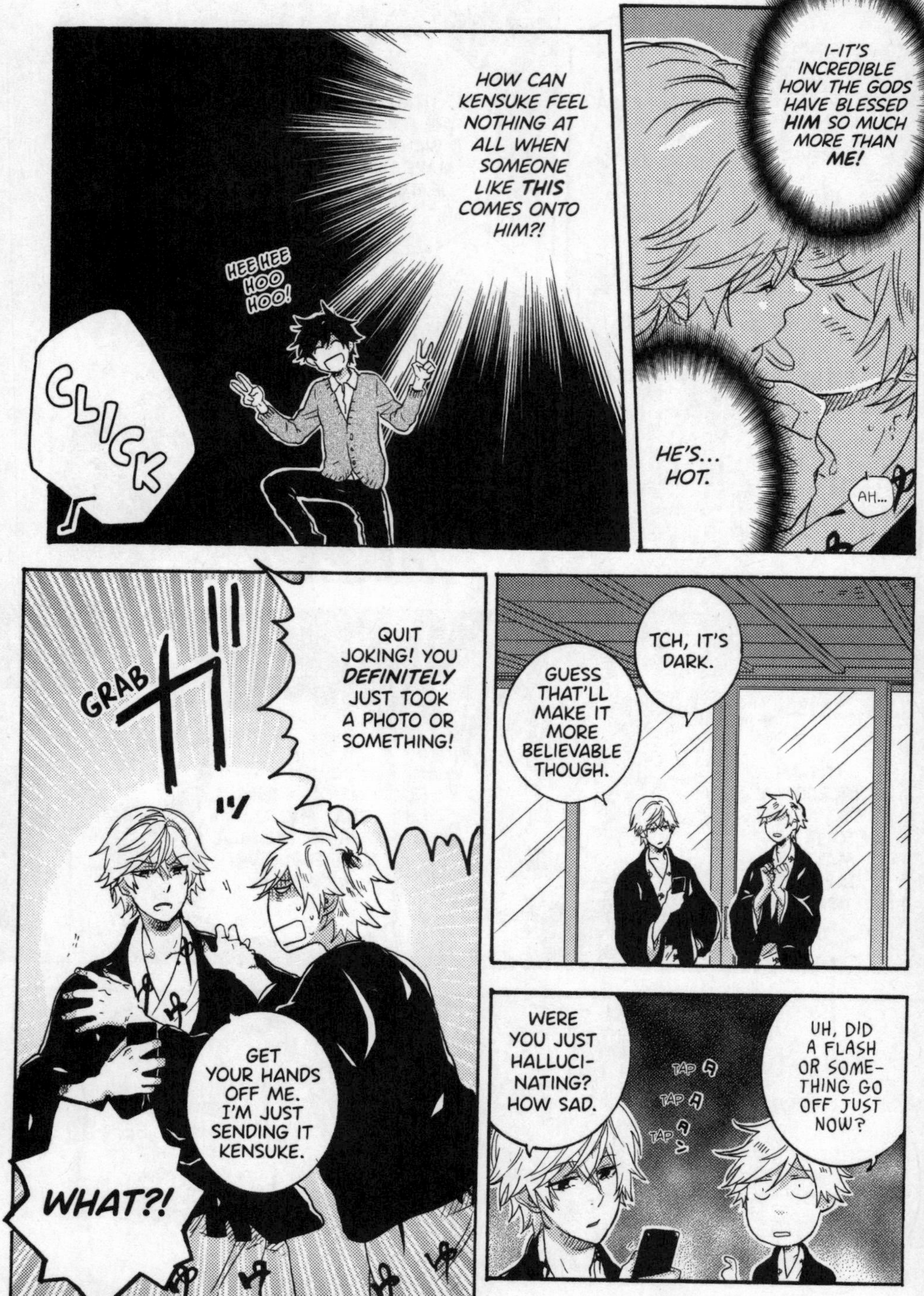

I-IT'S INCREDIBLE HOW THE GODS HAVE BLESSED HIM SO MUCH MORE THAN ME!
HE'S... HOT.
AH...
HOW CAN KENSUKE FEEL NOTHING AT ALL WHEN SOMEONE LIKE THIS COMES ONTO HIM?!
HEE HEE HOO HOO!
CLICK
TCH, IT'S DARK.
GUESS THAT'LL MAKE IT MORE BELIEVABLE THOUGH.
UH, DID A FLASH OR SOME-THING GO OFF JUST NOW?
WERE YOU JUST HALLUCI-NATING? HOW SAD.
TAP
TAP
TAP
GRAB
QUIT JOKING! YOU DEFINITELY JUST TOOK A PHOTO OR SOMETHING!
GET YOUR HANDS OFF ME. I'M JUST SENDING IT KENSUKE.
WHAT?!

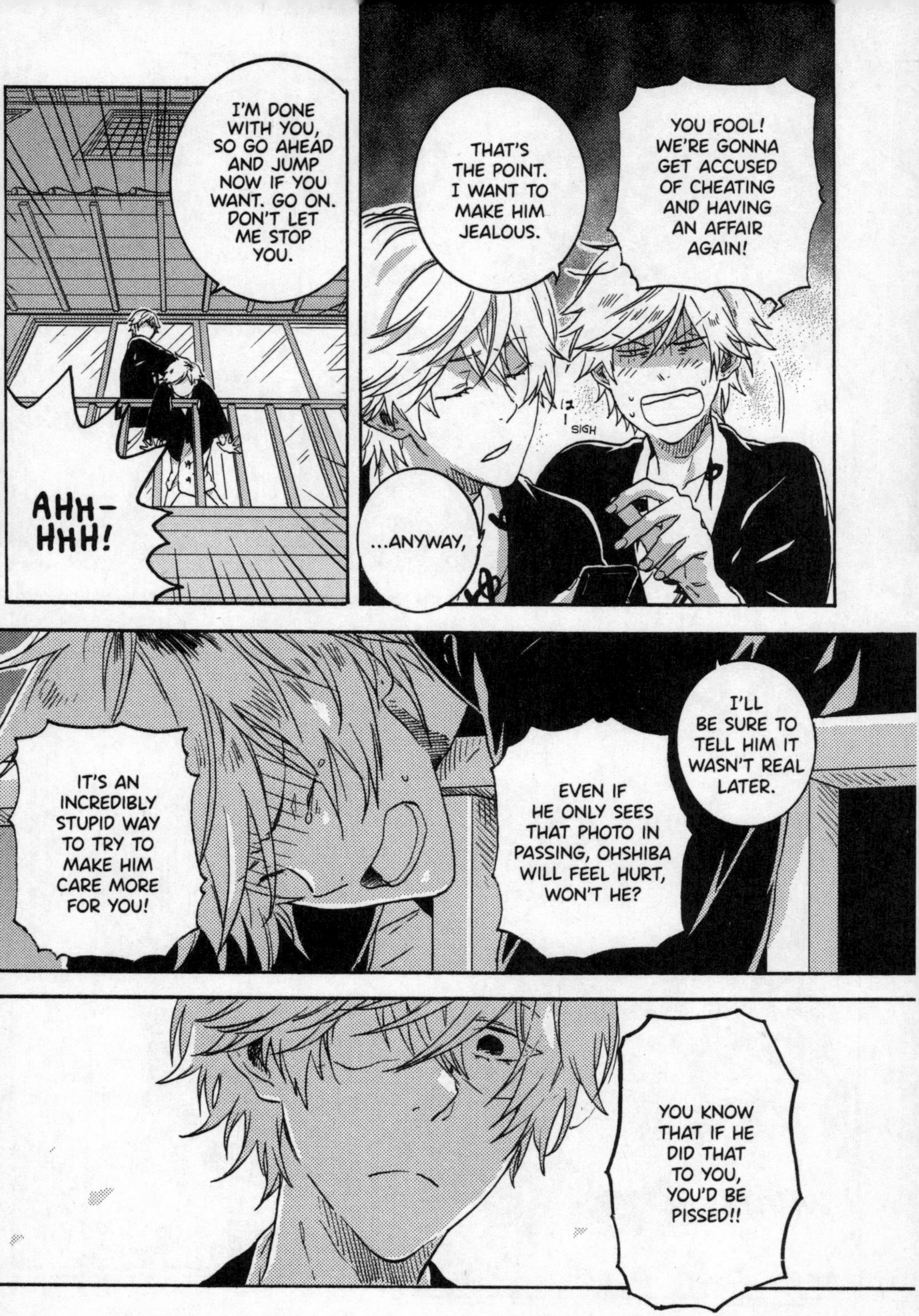
YOU FOOL! WE'RE GONNA GET ACCUSED OF CHEATING AND HAVING AN AFFAIR AGAIN!
THAT'S THE POINT. I WANT TO MAKE HIM JEALOUS.
SIGH
...ANYWAY,
I'M DONE WITH YOU, SO GO AHEAD AND JUMP NOW IF YOU WANT. GO ON. DON'T LET ME STOP YOU.
AHH-HHH!
I'LL BE SURE TO TELL HIM IT WASN'T REAL LATER.
EVEN IF HE ONLY SEES THAT PHOTO IN PASSING, OHSHIBA WILL FEEL HURT, WON'T HE?
IT'S AN INCREDIBLY STUPID WAY TO TRY TO MAKE HIM CARE MORE FOR YOU!
YOU KNOW THAT IF HE DID THAT TO YOU, YOU'D BE PISSED!!

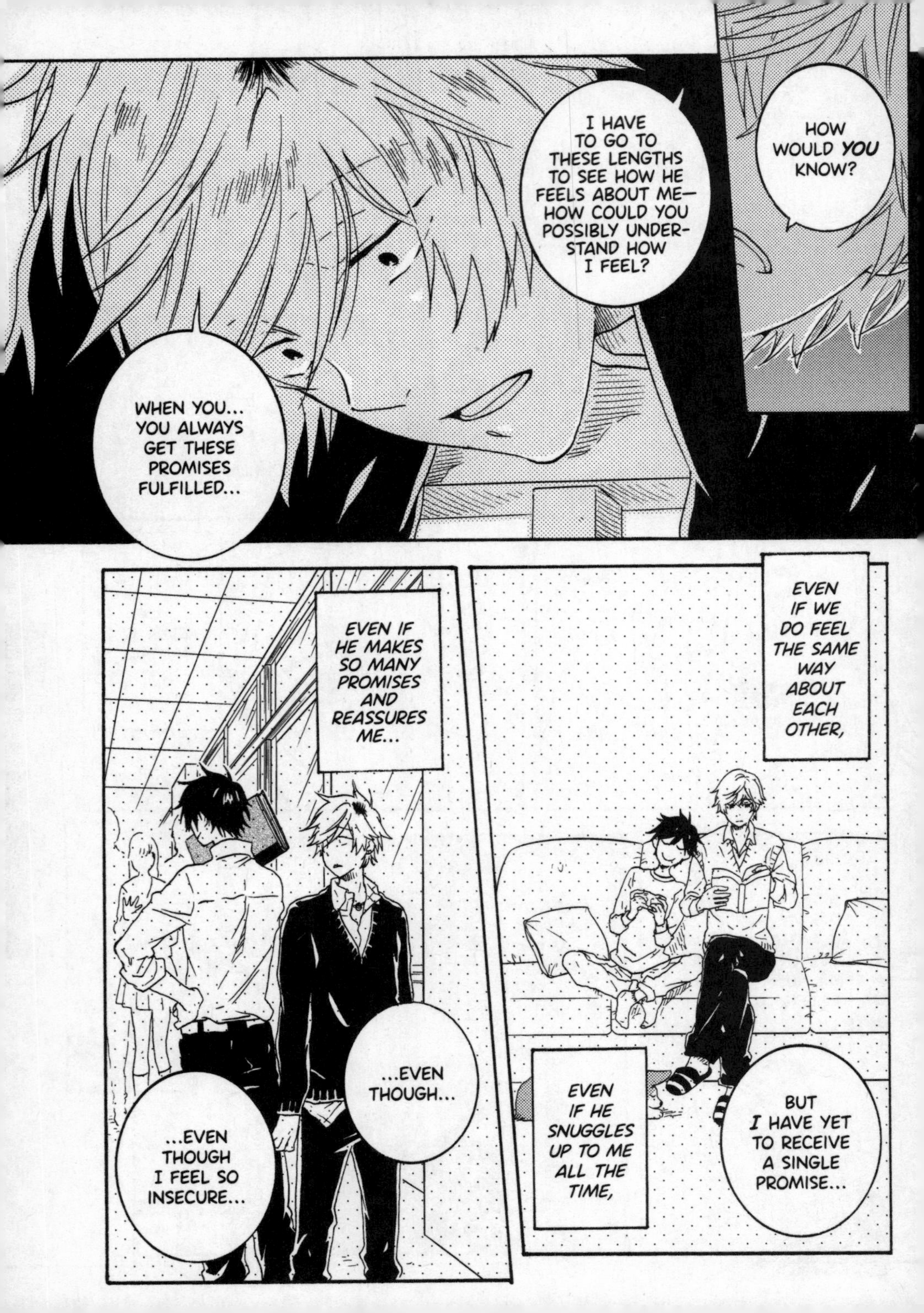
HOW WOULD *YOU* KNOW?
I HAVE TO GO TO THESE LENGTHS TO SEE HOW HE FEELS ABOUT ME—HOW COULD YOU POSSIBLY UNDER-STAND HOW I FEEL?
WHEN YOU... YOU ALWAYS GET THESE PROMISES FULFILLED...
EVEN IF WE DO FEEL THE SAME WAY ABOUT EACH OTHER,
EVEN IF HE SNUGGLES UP TO ME ALL THE TIME,
BUT *I* HAVE YET TO RECEIVE A SINGLE PROMISE...
EVEN IF HE MAKES SO MANY PROMISES AND REASSURES ME...
...EVEN THOUGH...
...EVEN THOUGH I FEEL SO INSECURE...

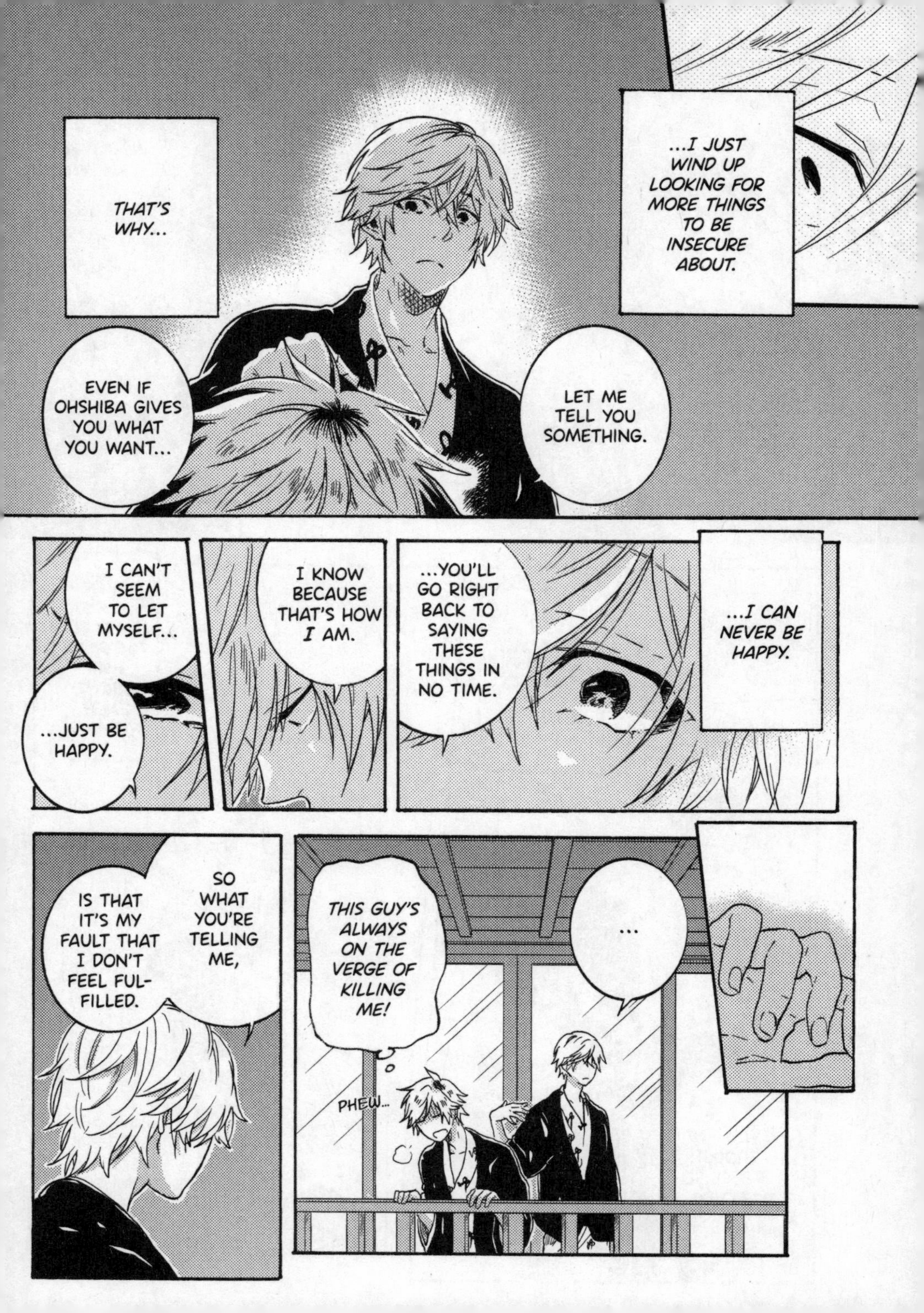
...I JUST WIND UP LOOKING FOR MORE THINGS TO BE INSECURE ABOUT.
THAT'S WHY...
LET ME TELL YOU SOMETHING.
EVEN IF OHSHIBA GIVES YOU WHAT YOU WANT...
...I CAN NEVER BE HAPPY.
...YOU'LL GO RIGHT BACK TO SAYING THESE THINGS IN NO TIME.
I KNOW BECAUSE THAT'S HOW I AM.
I CAN'T SEEM TO LET MYSELF...
...JUST BE HAPPY.
...
THIS GUY'S ALWAYS ON THE VERGE OF KILLING ME!
PHEW...
SO WHAT YOU'RE TELLING ME,
IS THAT IT'S MY FAULT THAT I DON'T FEEL FUL-FILLED.

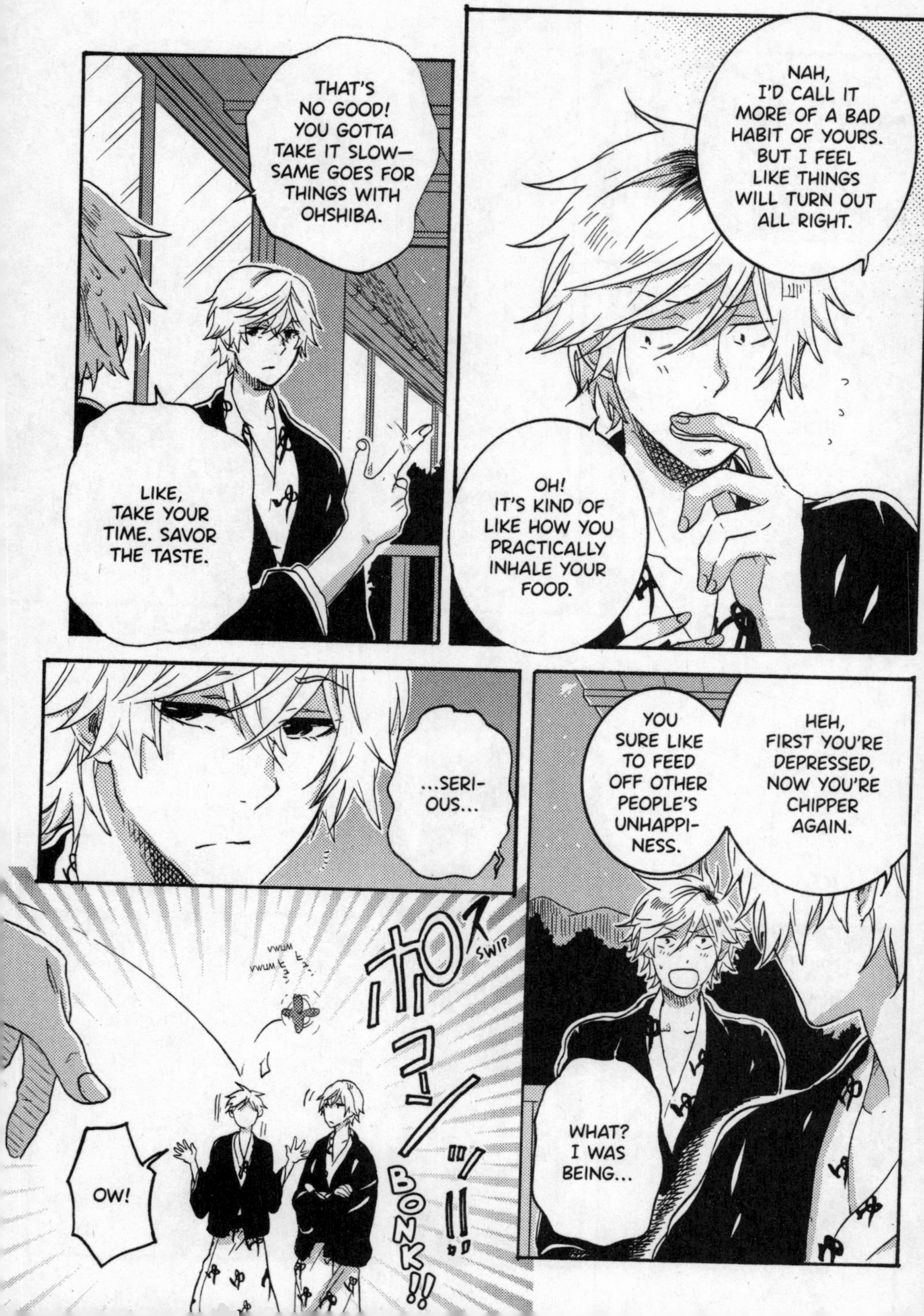
NAH, I'D CALL IT MORE OF A BAD HABIT OF YOURS. BUT I FEEL LIKE THINGS WILL TURN OUT ALL RIGHT.
OH! IT'S KIND OF LIKE HOW YOU PRACTICALLY INHALE YOUR FOOD.
THAT'S NO GOOD! YOU GOTTA TAKE IT SLOW—SAME GOES FOR THINGS WITH OHSHIBA.
LIKE, TAKE YOUR TIME. SAVOR THE TASTE.
HEH, FIRST YOU'RE DEPRESSED, NOW YOU'RE CHIPPER AGAIN.
YOU SURE LIKE TO FEED OFF OTHER PEOPLE'S UNHAPPINESS.
WHAT? I WAS BEING...
...SERI-OUS...
SWIP
VWUM VWUM
BONK!!
OW!

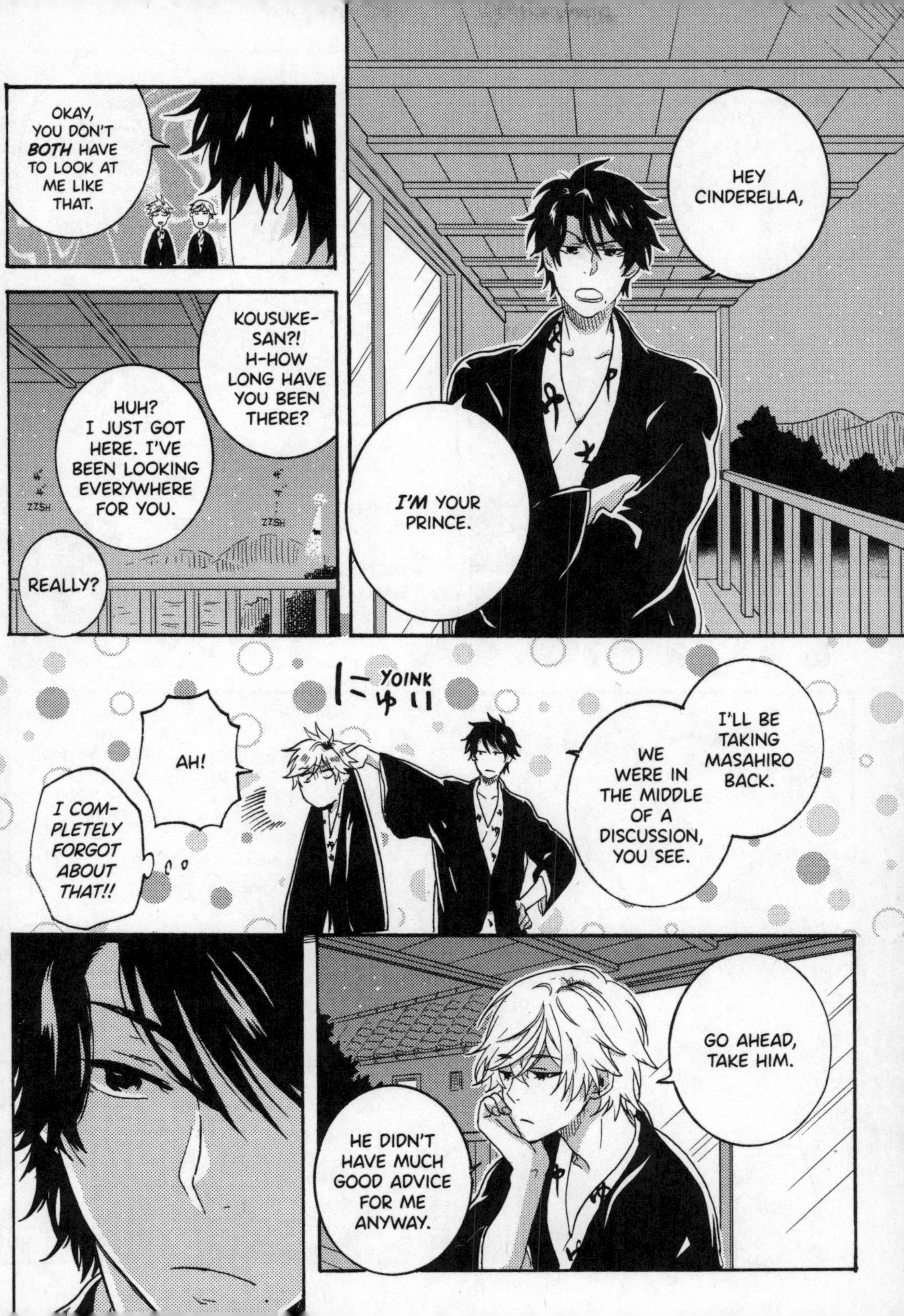
HEY CINDERELLA,
I'M YOUR PRINCE.
OKAY, YOU DON'T BOTH HAVE TO LOOK AT ME LIKE THAT.
KOUSUKE-SAN?! H-HOW LONG HAVE YOU BEEN THERE?
HUH? I JUST GOT HERE. I'VE BEEN LOOKING EVERYWHERE FOR YOU.
ZZSH
ZZSH
REALLY?
YOINK
I'LL BE TAKING MASAHIRO BACK.
WE WERE IN THE MIDDLE OF A DISCUSSION, YOU SEE.
AH!
I COMPLETELY FORGOT ABOUT THAT!!
GO AHEAD, TAKE HIM.
HE DIDN'T HAVE MUCH GOOD ADVICE FOR ME ANYWAY.

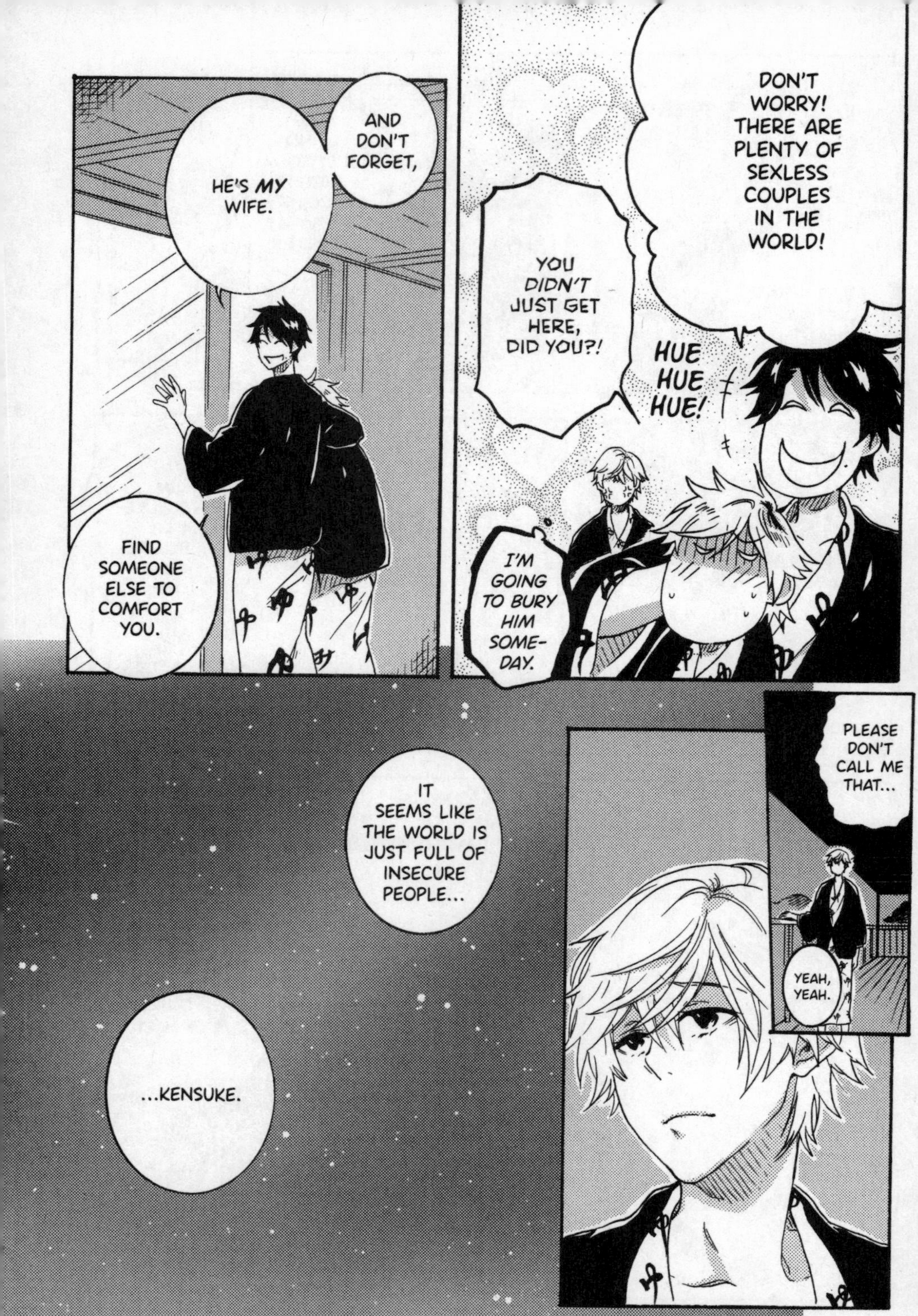
DON'T WORRY! THERE ARE PLENTY OF SEXLESS COUPLES IN THE WORLD!
YOU DIDN'T JUST GET HERE, DID YOU?!
HUE HUE HUE!
I'M GOING TO BURY HIM SOME-DAY.
AND DON'T FORGET,
HE'S MY WIFE.
FIND SOMEONE ELSE TO COMFORT YOU.
PLEASE DON'T CALL ME THAT...
YEAH, YEAH.
IT SEEMS LIKE THE WORLD IS JUST FULL OF INSECURE PEOPLE...
...KENSUKE.

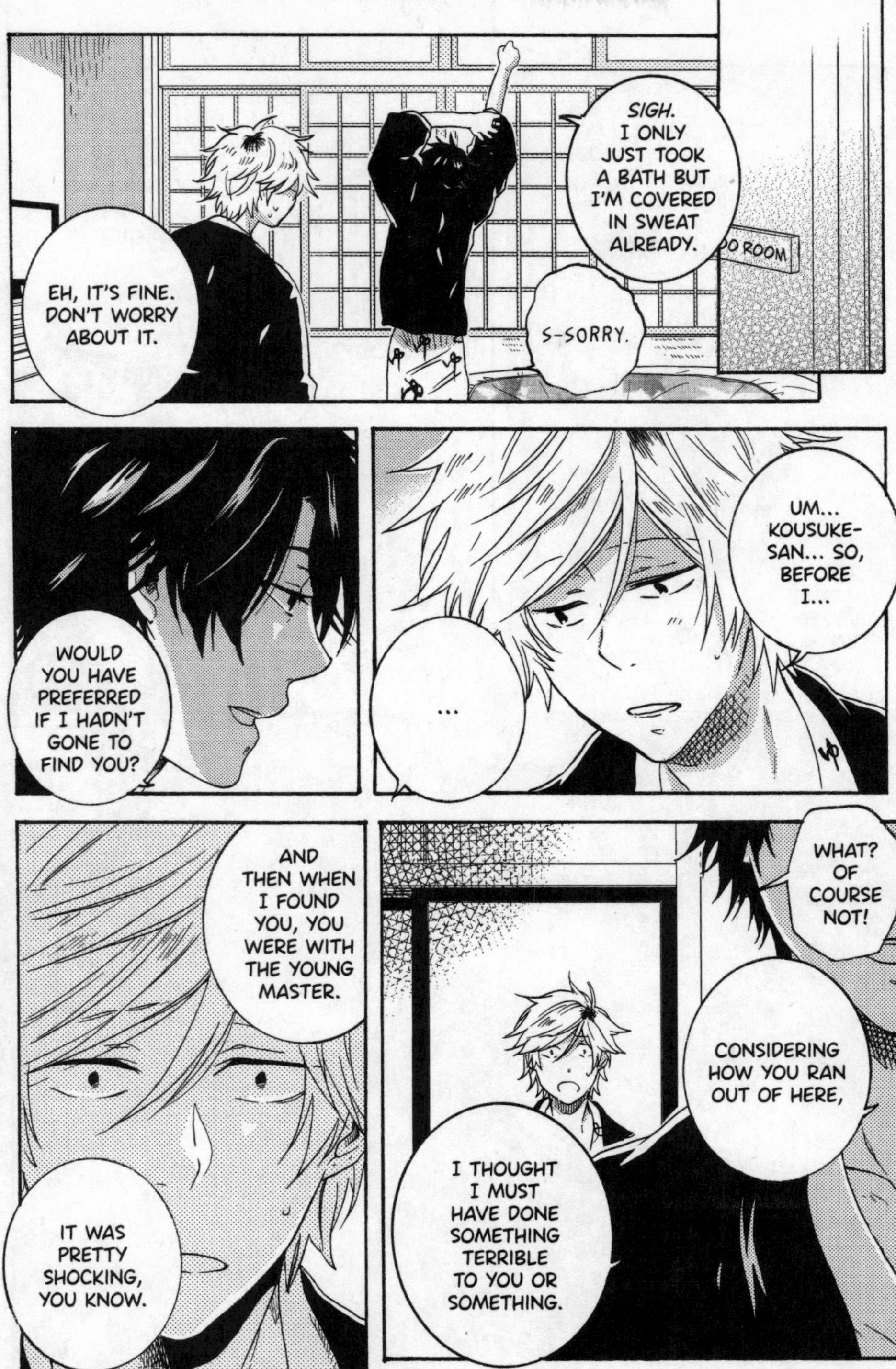
SIGH. I ONLY JUST TOOK A BATH BUT I'M COVERED IN SWEAT ALREADY.
S-SORRY.
EH, IT'S FINE. DON'T WORRY ABOUT IT.
UM... KOUSUKE-SAN... SO, BEFORE I...
...
WOULD YOU HAVE PREFERRED IF I HADN'T GONE TO FIND YOU?
WHAT? OF COURSE NOT!
CONSIDERING HOW YOU RAN OUT OF HERE,
I THOUGHT I MUST HAVE DONE SOMETHING TERRIBLE TO YOU OR SOMETHING.
AND THEN WHEN I FOUND YOU, YOU WERE WITH THE YOUNG MASTER.
IT WAS PRETTY SHOCKING, YOU KNOW.

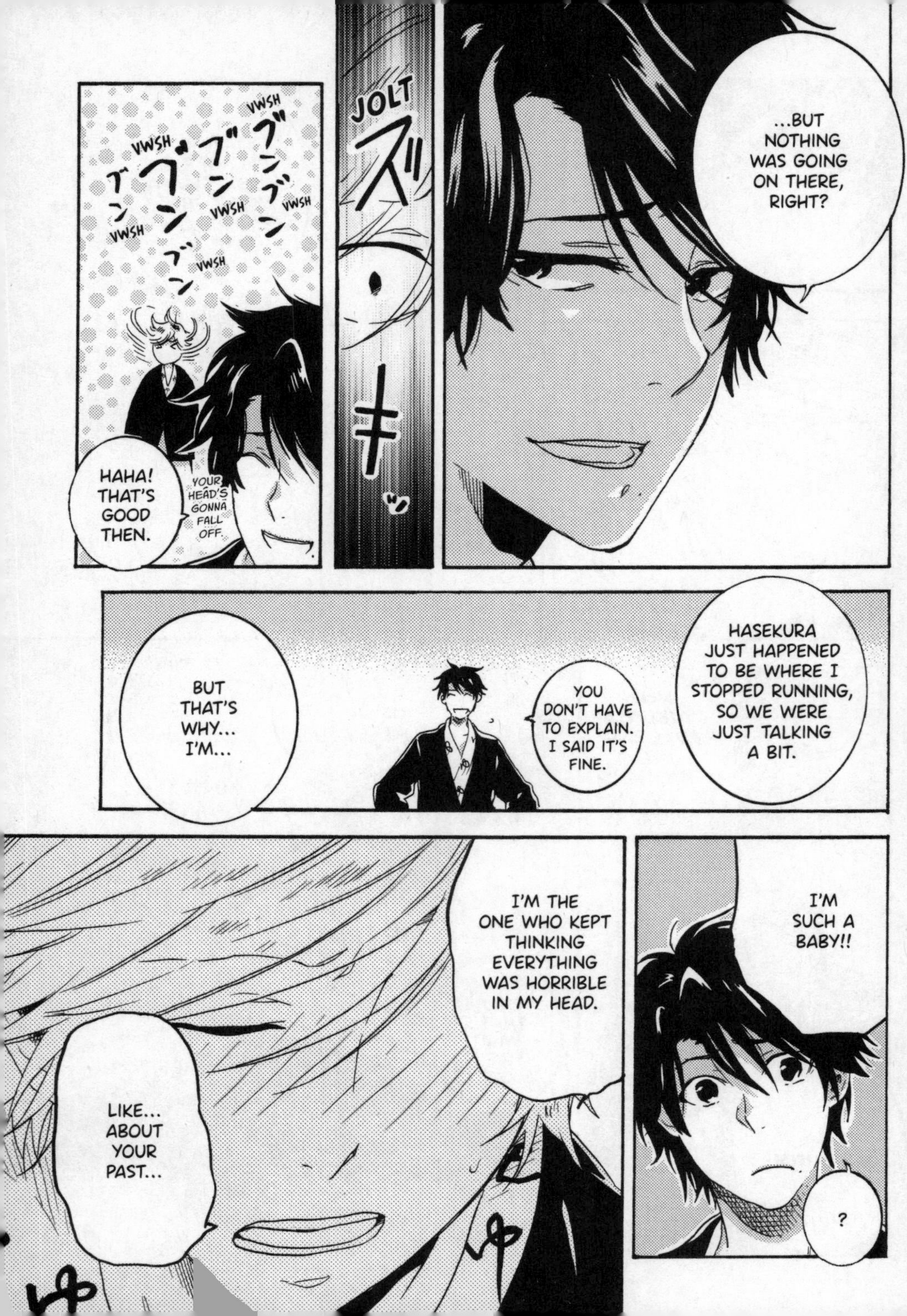
...BUT NOTHING WAS GOING ON THERE, RIGHT?
JOLT
ズキ
VWSH
VWSH
VWSH
VWSH
VWSH
ブンブン
ブンブン
ブンブン
ブンブン
YOUR HEAD'S GONNA FALL OFF.
HAHA! THAT'S GOOD THEN.
HASEKURA JUST HAPPENED TO BE WHERE I STOPPED RUNNING, SO WE WERE JUST TALKING A BIT.
YOU DON'T HAVE TO EXPLAIN. I SAID IT'S FINE.
BUT THAT'S WHY... I'M...
I'M SUCH A BABY!!
?
I'M THE ONE WHO KEPT THINKING EVERYTHING WAS HORRIBLE IN MY HEAD.
LIKE... ABOUT YOUR PAST...

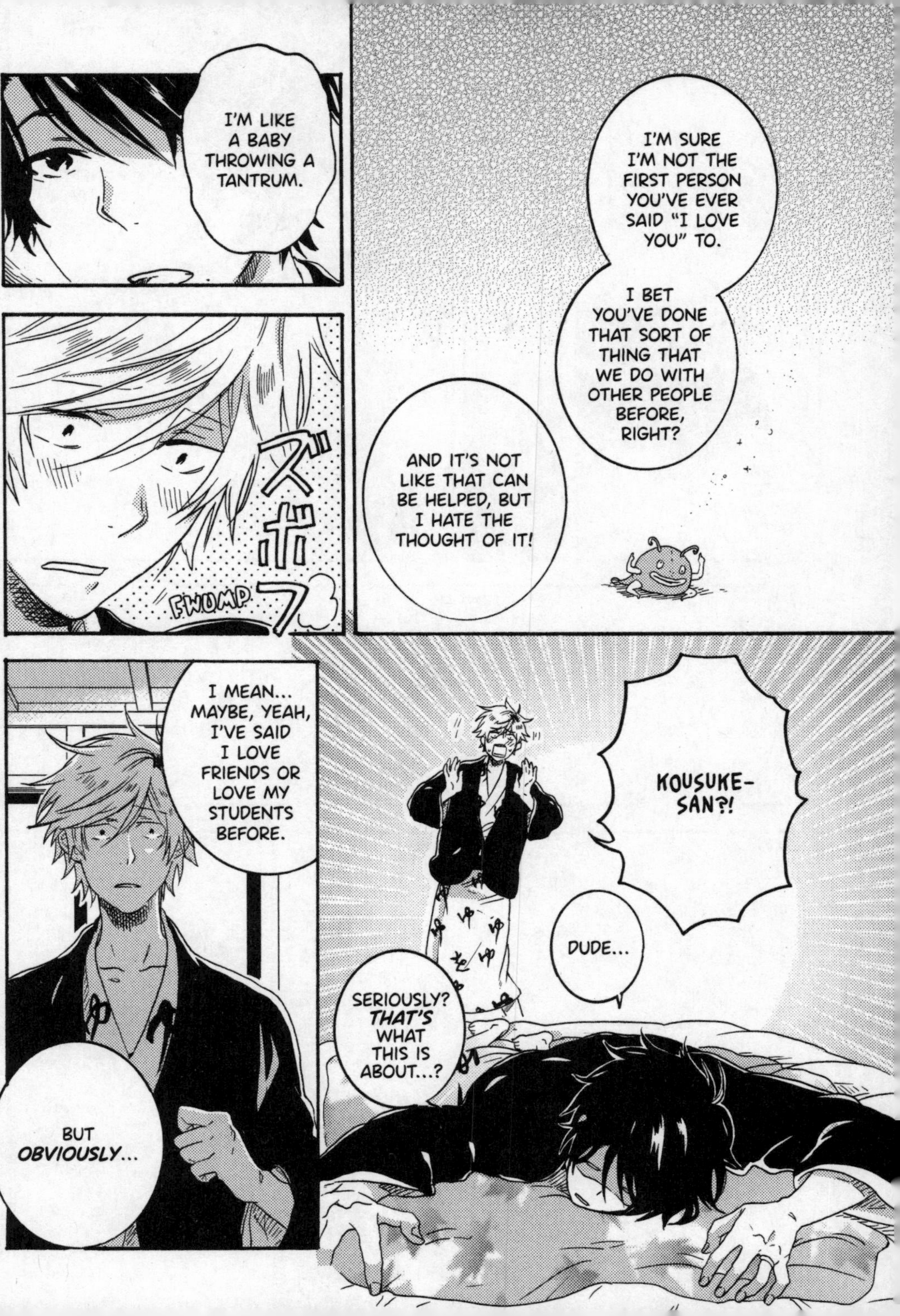
I'M SURE I'M NOT THE FIRST PERSON YOU'VE EVER SAID "I LOVE YOU" TO.
I BET YOU'VE DONE THAT SORT OF THING THAT WE DO WITH OTHER PEOPLE BEFORE, RIGHT?
AND IT'S NOT LIKE THAT CAN BE HELPED, BUT I HATE THE THOUGHT OF IT!
I'M LIKE A BABY THROWING A TANTRUM.
FWOMP
KOUSUKE-SAN?!
DUDE...
SERIOUSLY? *THAT'S* WHAT THIS IS ABOUT...?
I MEAN... MAYBE, YEAH, I'VE SAID I LOVE FRIENDS OR LOVE MY STUDENTS BEFORE.
BUT *OBVIOUSLY*...

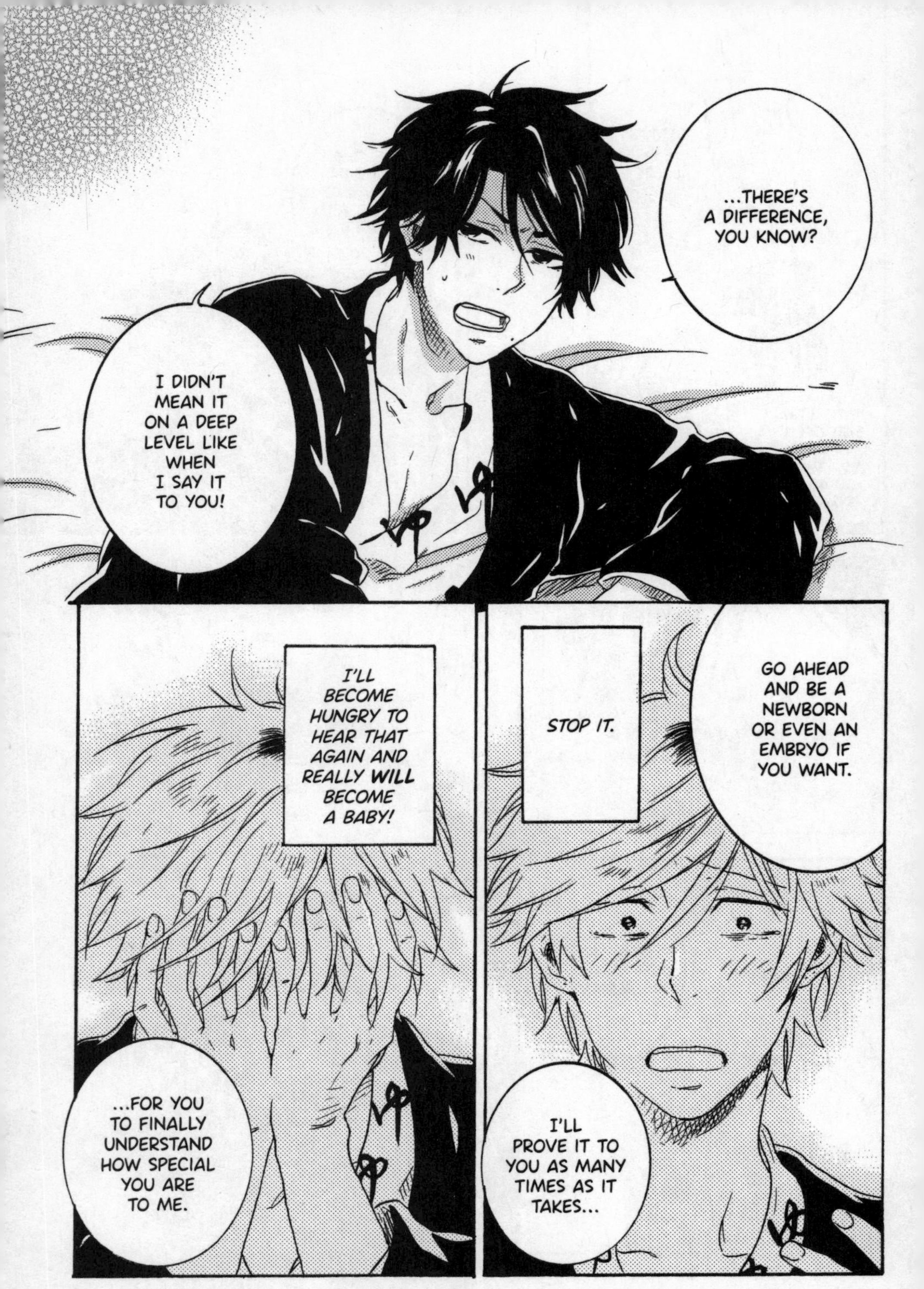
...THERE'S A DIFFERENCE, YOU KNOW?
I DIDN'T MEAN IT ON A DEEP LEVEL LIKE WHEN I SAY IT TO YOU!
GO AHEAD AND BE A NEWBORN OR EVEN AN EMBRYO IF YOU WANT.
STOP IT.
I'LL PROVE IT TO YOU AS MANY TIMES AS IT TAKES...
I'LL BECOME HUNGRY TO HEAR THAT AGAIN AND REALLY **WILL** BECOME A BABY!
...FOR YOU TO FINALLY UNDERSTAND HOW SPECIAL YOU ARE TO ME.

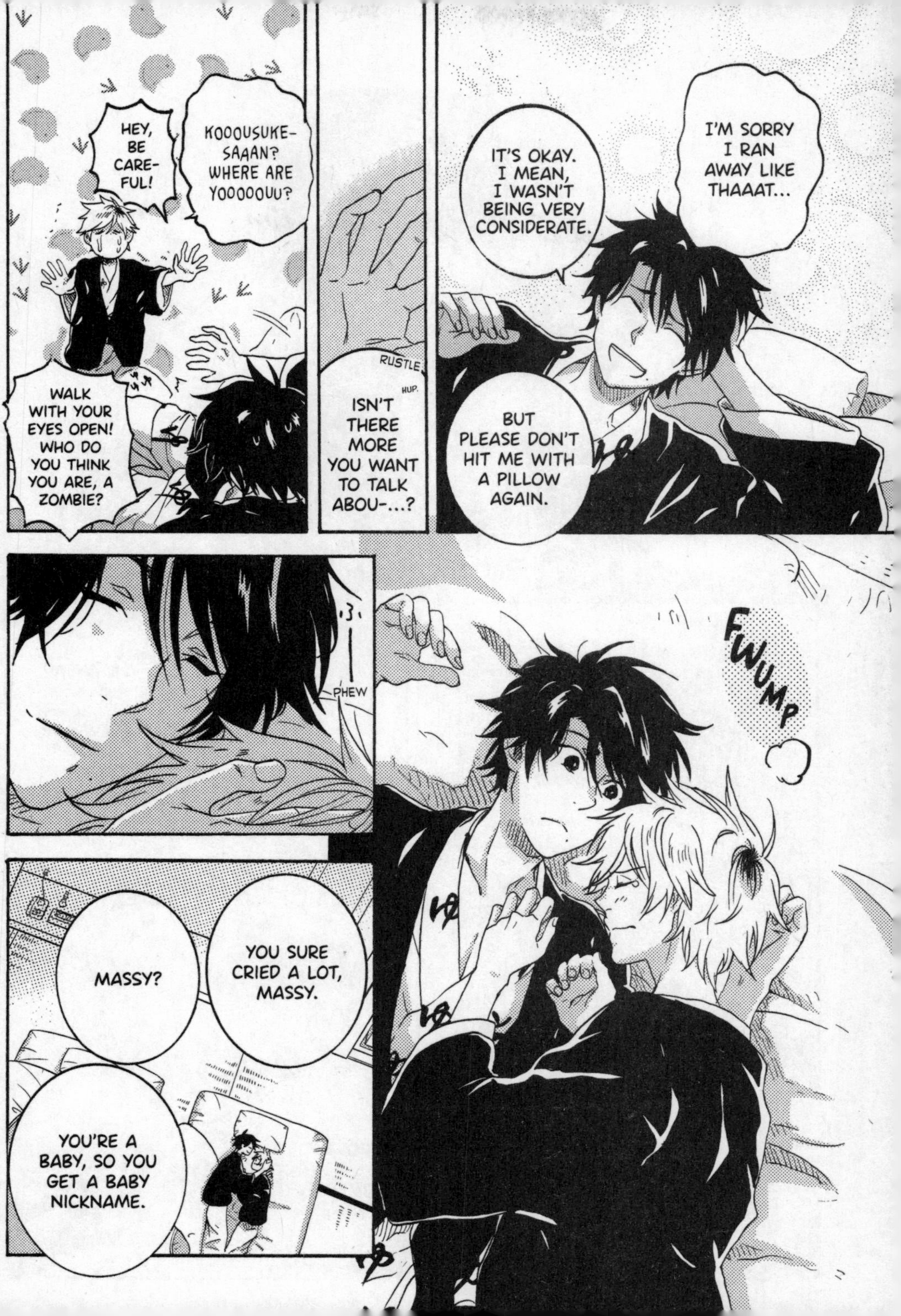
I'M SORRY I RAN AWAY LIKE THAAAT...
IT'S OKAY. I MEAN, I WASN'T BEING VERY CONSIDERATE.
BUT PLEASE DON'T HIT ME WITH A PILLOW AGAIN.
RUSTLE
HUP.
ISN'T THERE MORE YOU WANT TO TALK ABOU-...?
KOOOUSUKE-SAAAN? WHERE ARE YOOOOOUU?
HEY, BE CAREFUL!
WALK WITH YOUR EYES OPEN! WHO DO YOU THINK YOU ARE, A ZOMBIE?
FWUMP
PHEW
YOU SURE CRIED A LOT, MASSY.
MASSY?
YOU'RE A BABY, SO YOU GET A BABY NICKNAME.

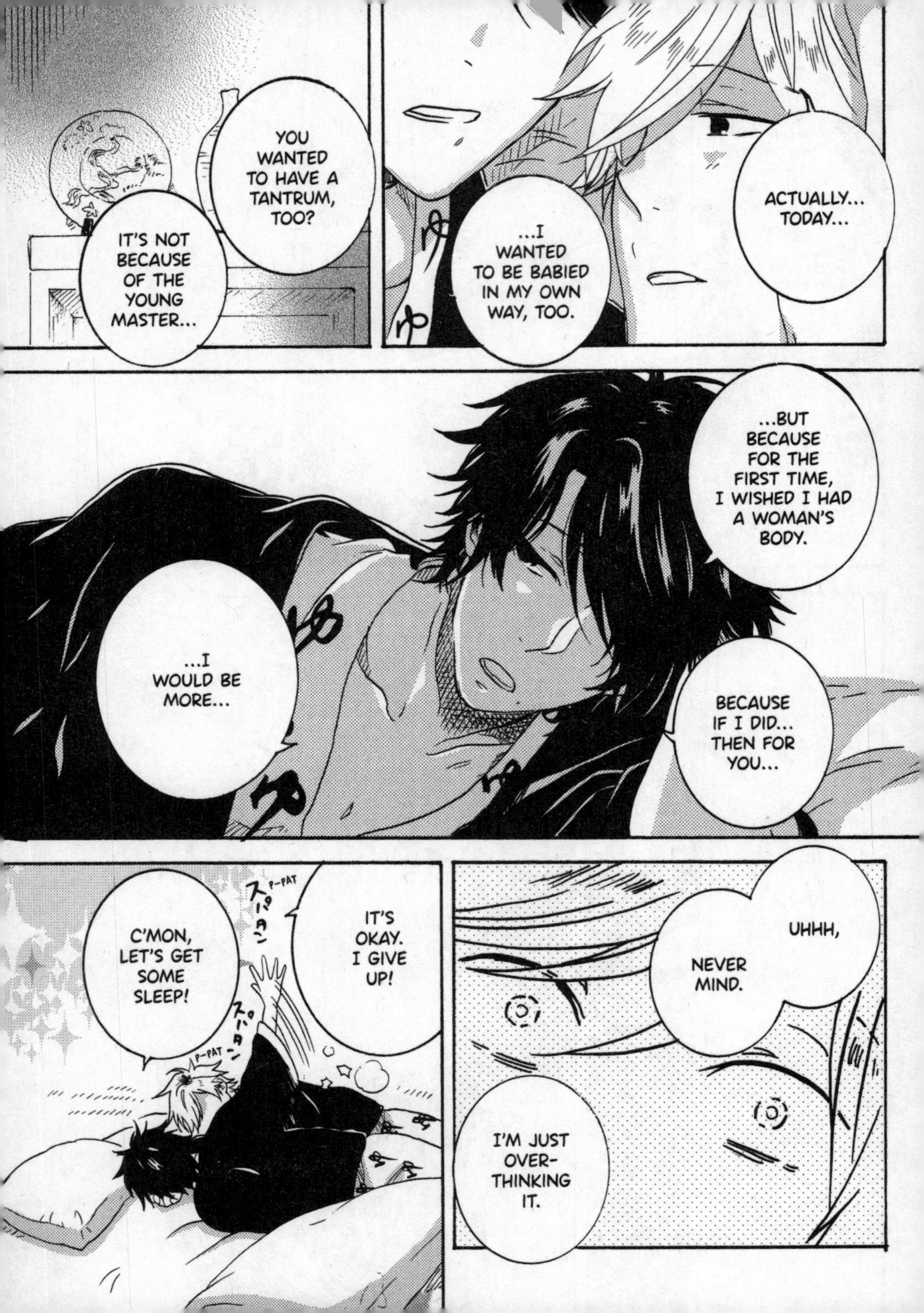
ACTUALLY... TODAY...
...I WANTED TO BE BABIED IN MY OWN WAY, TOO.
YOU WANTED TO HAVE A TANTRUM, TOO?
IT'S NOT BECAUSE OF THE YOUNG MASTER...
...BUT BECAUSE FOR THE FIRST TIME, I WISHED I HAD A WOMAN'S BODY.
BECAUSE IF I DID... THEN FOR YOU...
...I WOULD BE MORE...
UHHH,
NEVER MIND.
I'M JUST OVER-THINKING IT.
IT'S OKAY. I GIVE UP!
P-PAT
C'MON, LET'S GET SOME SLEEP!
P-PAT

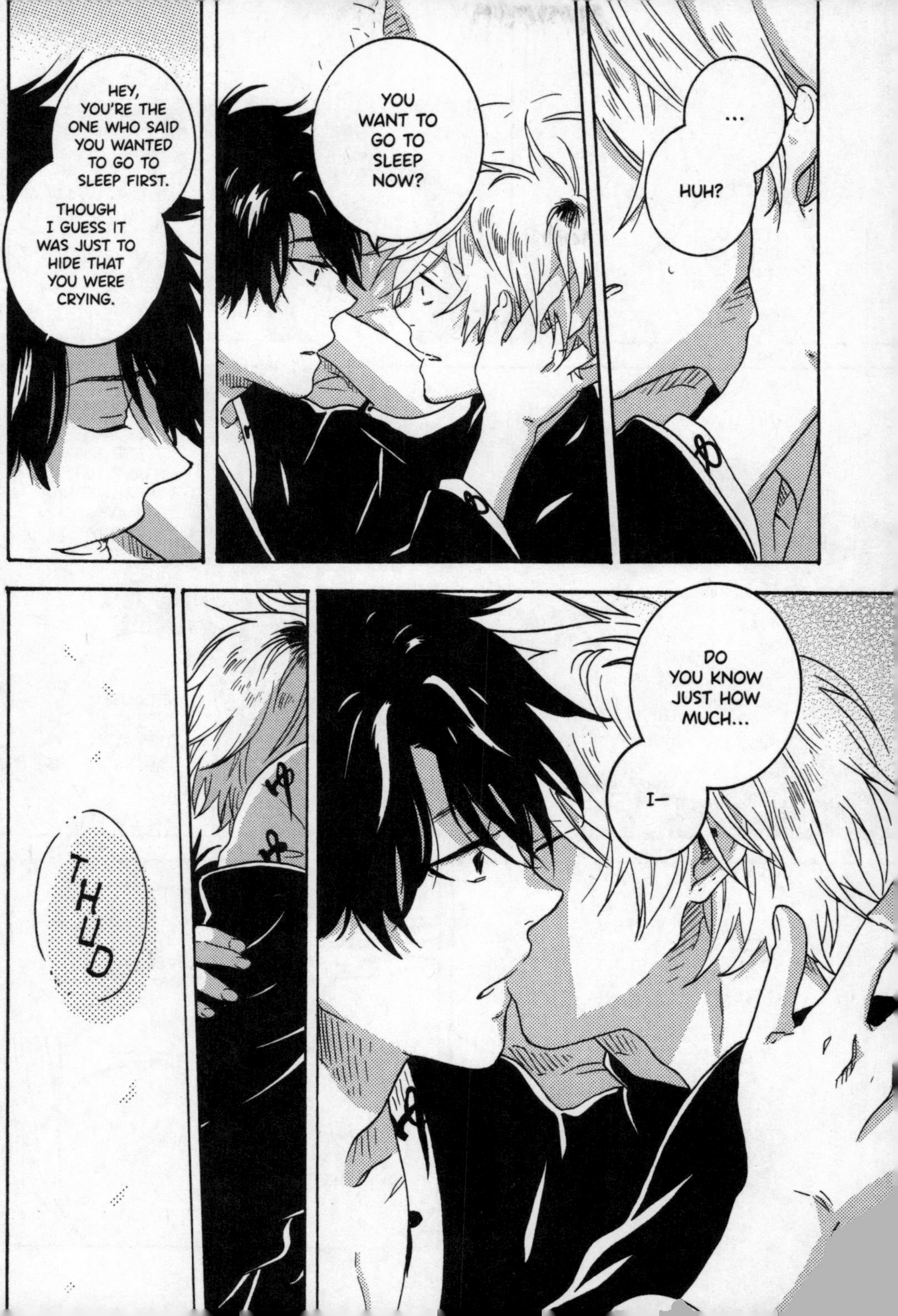
...
HUH?
YOU WANT TO GO TO SLEEP NOW?
HEY, YOU'RE THE ONE WHO SAID YOU WANTED TO GO TO SLEEP FIRST.
THOUGH I GUESS IT WAS JUST TO HIDE THAT YOU WERE CRYING.
DO YOU KNOW JUST HOW MUCH...
I—
THUD

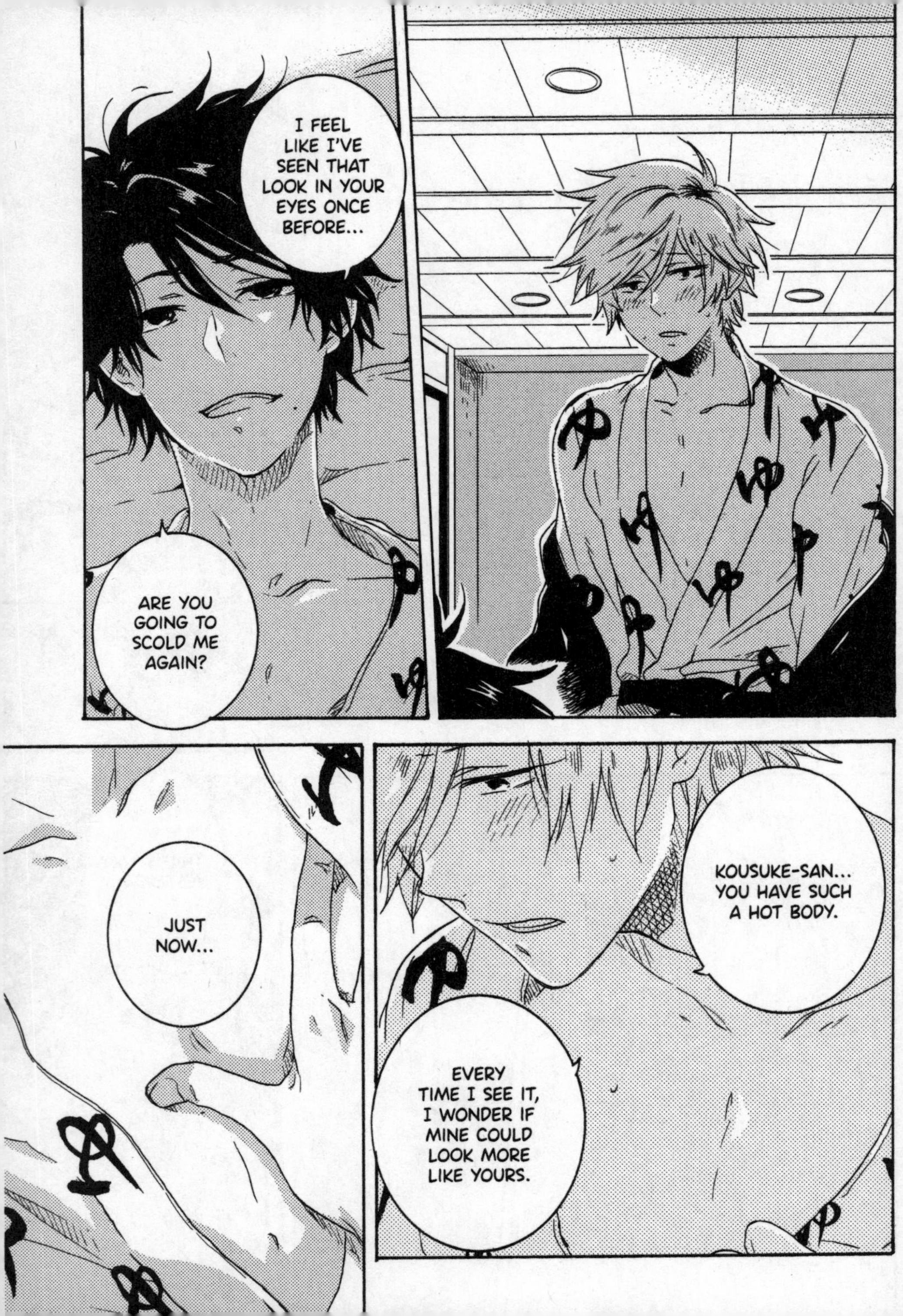
I FEEL LIKE I'VE SEEN THAT LOOK IN YOUR EYES ONCE BEFORE...
ARE YOU GOING TO SCOLD ME AGAIN?
KOUSUKE-SAN... YOU HAVE SUCH A HOT BODY.
EVERY TIME I SEE IT, I WONDER IF MINE COULD LOOK MORE LIKE YOURS.
JUST NOW...

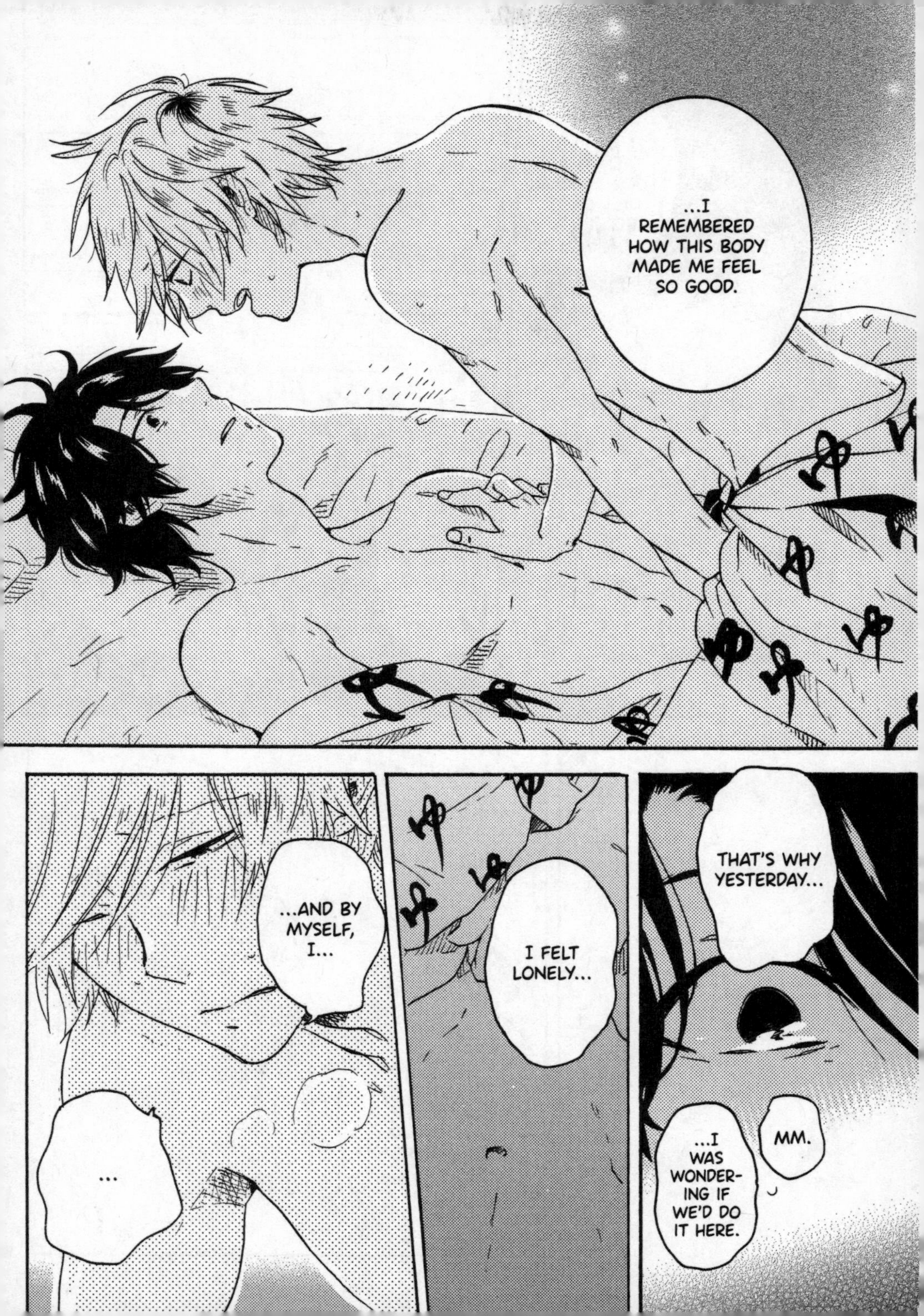
...I REMEMBERED HOW THIS BODY MADE ME FEEL SO GOOD.
THAT'S WHY YESTERDAY...
MM.
...I WAS WONDER-ING IF WE'D DO IT HERE.
I FELT LONELY...
...AND BY MYSELF, I...
...

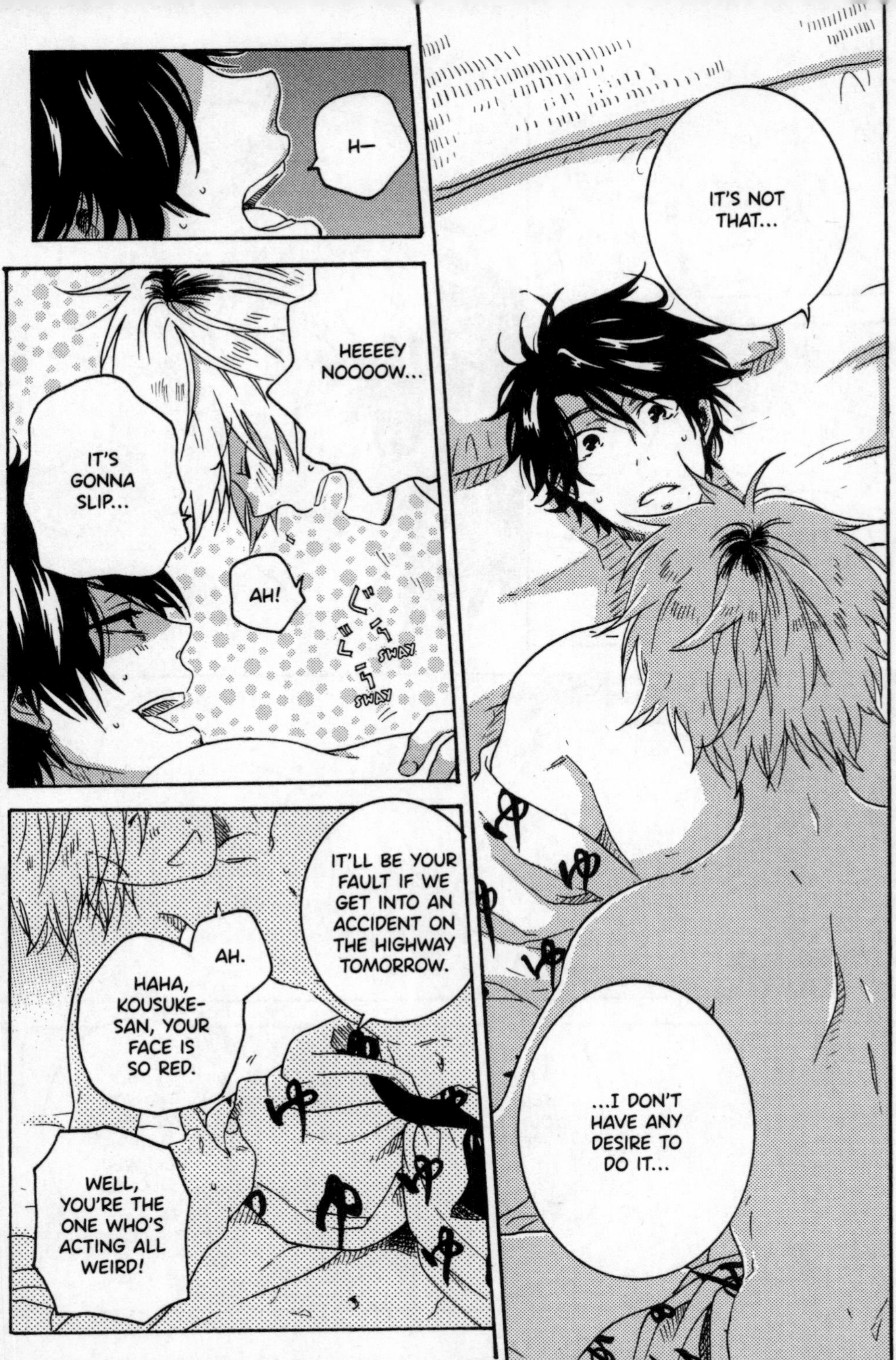
IT'S NOT THAT...
...I DON'T HAVE ANY DESIRE TO DO IT...
H—
HEEEEY NOOOOW...
IT'S GONNA SLIP...
AH!
SWAY
SWAY
IT'LL BE YOUR FAULT IF WE GET INTO AN ACCIDENT ON THE HIGHWAY TOMORROW.
AH.
HAHA, KOUSUKE-SAN, YOUR FACE IS SO RED.
WELL, YOU'RE THE ONE WHO'S ACTING ALL WEIRD!

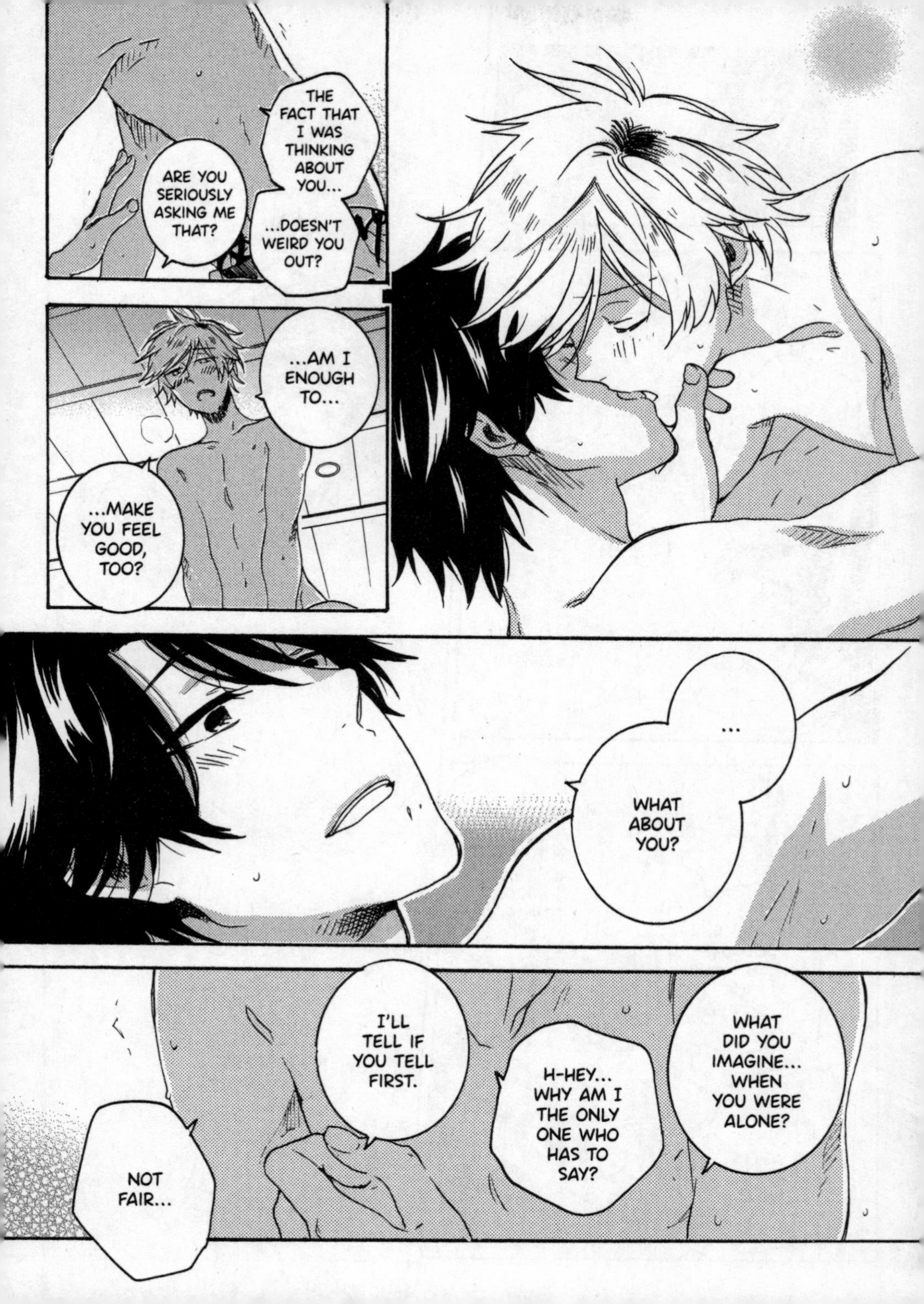
THE FACT THAT I WAS THINKING ABOUT YOU...
...DOESN'T WEIRD YOU OUT?
ARE YOU SERIOUSLY ASKING ME THAT?
...AM I ENOUGH TO...
...MAKE YOU FEEL GOOD, TOO?
... WHAT ABOUT YOU?
WHAT DID YOU IMAGINE... WHEN YOU WERE ALONE?
H-HEY... WHY AM I THE ONLY ONE WHO HAS TO SAY?
I'LL TELL IF YOU TELL FIRST.
NOT FAIR...

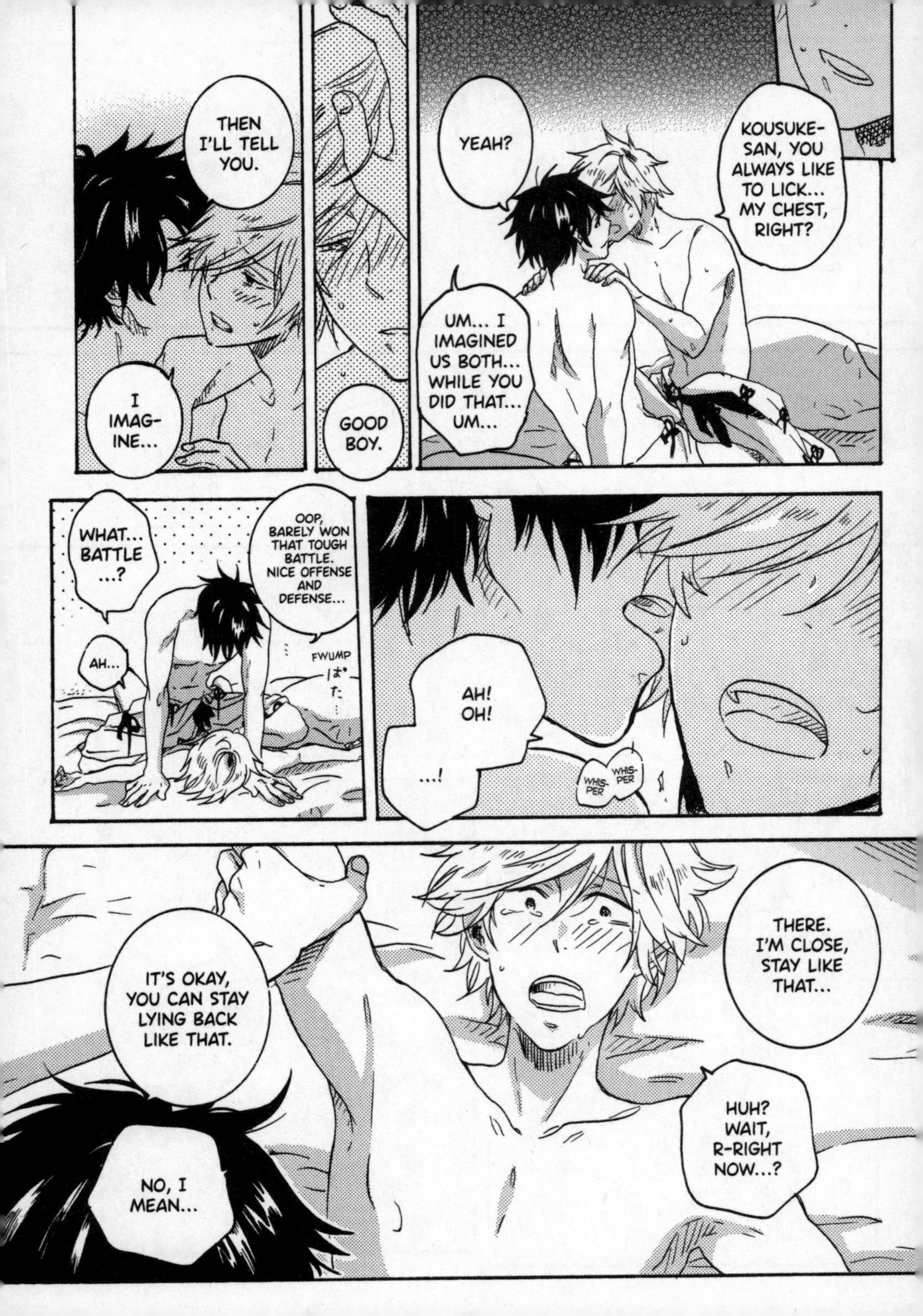

KOUSUKE-SAN, YOU ALWAYS LIKE TO LICK... MY CHEST, RIGHT?
YEAH?
UM... I IMAGINED US BOTH... WHILE YOU DID THAT... UM...
GOOD BOY.
THEN I'LL TELL YOU.
I IMAGINE...
AH! OH!
...!
WHISPER
WHISPER
OOP, BARELY WON THAT TOUGH BATTLE. NICE OFFENSE AND DEFENSE...
WHAT... BATTLE ...?
FWUMP
ぱた
AH...
THERE. I'M CLOSE, STAY LIKE THAT...
IT'S OKAY, YOU CAN STAY LYING BACK LIKE THAT.
HUH? WAIT, R-RIGHT NOW...?
NO, I MEAN...

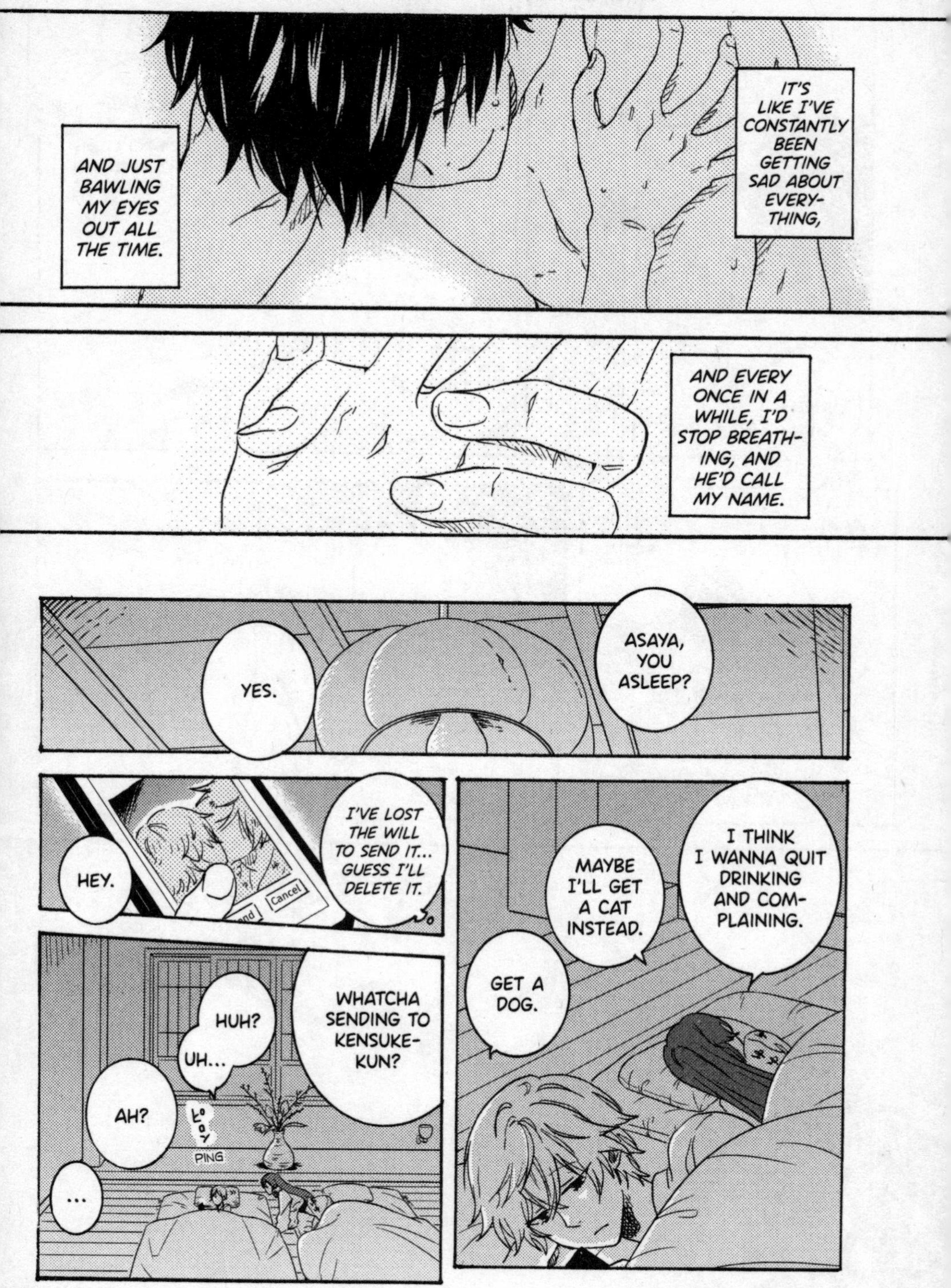
IT'S LIKE I'VE CONSTANTLY BEEN GETTING SAD ABOUT EVERY-THING,
AND JUST BAWLING MY EYES OUT ALL THE TIME.
AND EVERY ONCE IN A WHILE, I'D STOP BREATH-ING, AND HE'D CALL MY NAME.
ASAYA, YOU ASLEEP?
YES.
I THINK I WANNA QUIT DRINKING AND COM-PLAINING.
MAYBE I'LL GET A CAT INSTEAD.
GET A DOG.
I'VE LOST THE WILL TO SEND IT... GUESS I'LL DELETE IT.
Cancel
HEY.
WHATCHA SENDING TO KENSUKE-KUN?
HUH?
UH...
AH?
ピロン
PING
...

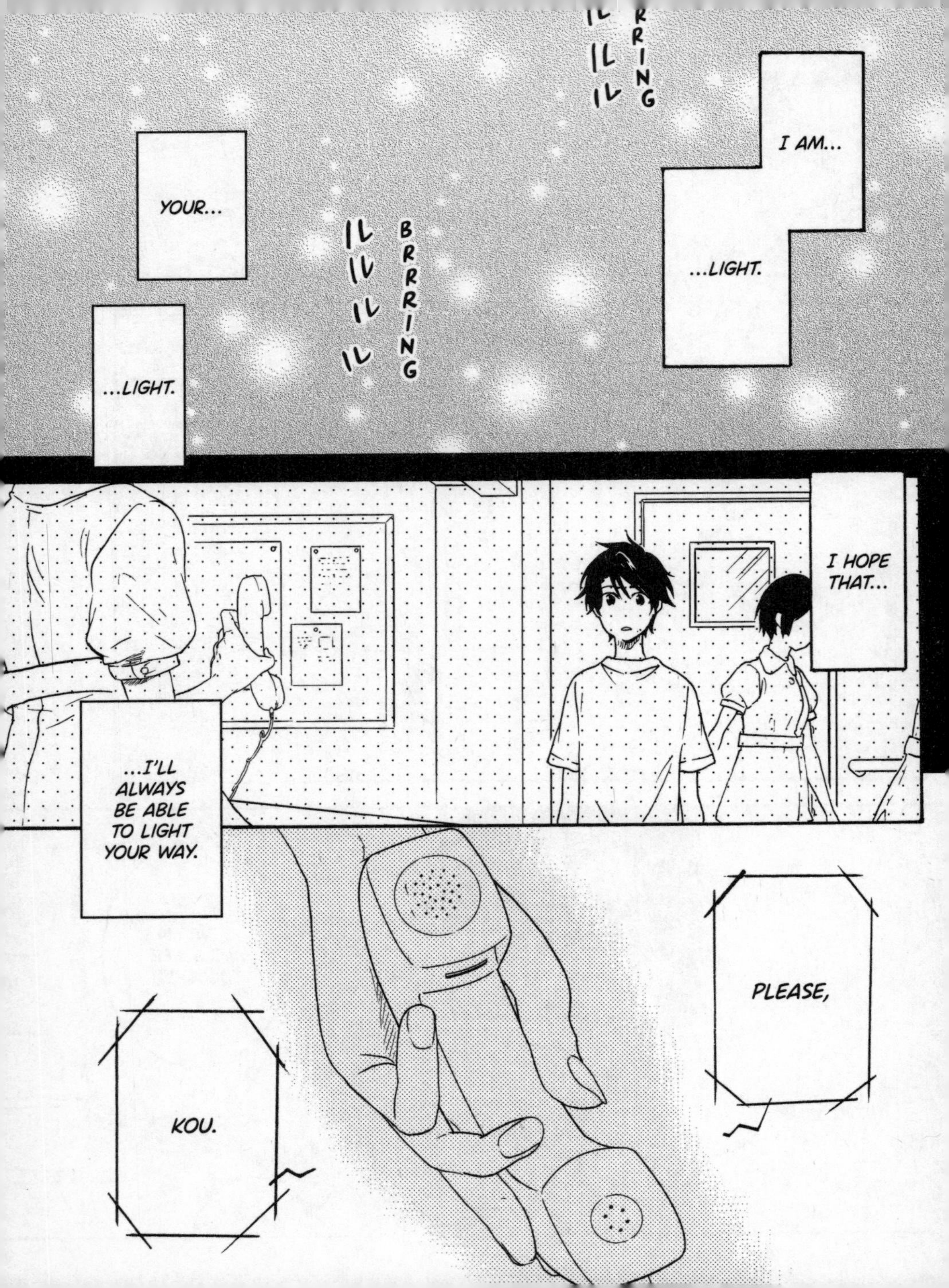
I AM...
...LIGHT.
ルルル RRING
ルルルル BRRRING
YOUR...
...LIGHT.
I HOPE THAT...
...I'LL ALWAYS BE ABLE TO LIGHT YOUR WAY.
PLEASE,
KOU.

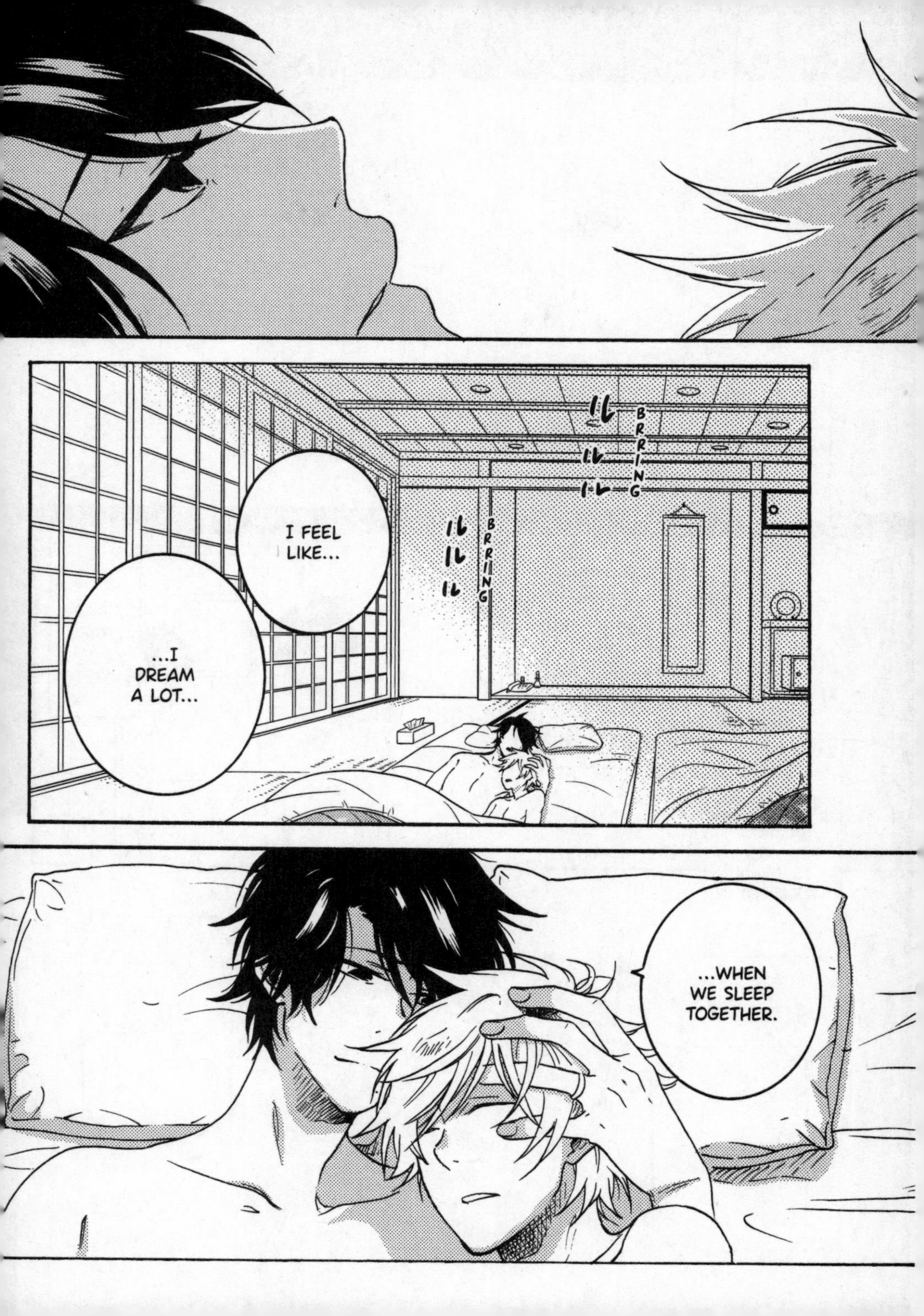
BRRING
BRRING
I FEEL LIKE...
...I DREAM A LOT...
...WHEN WE SLEEP TOGETHER.

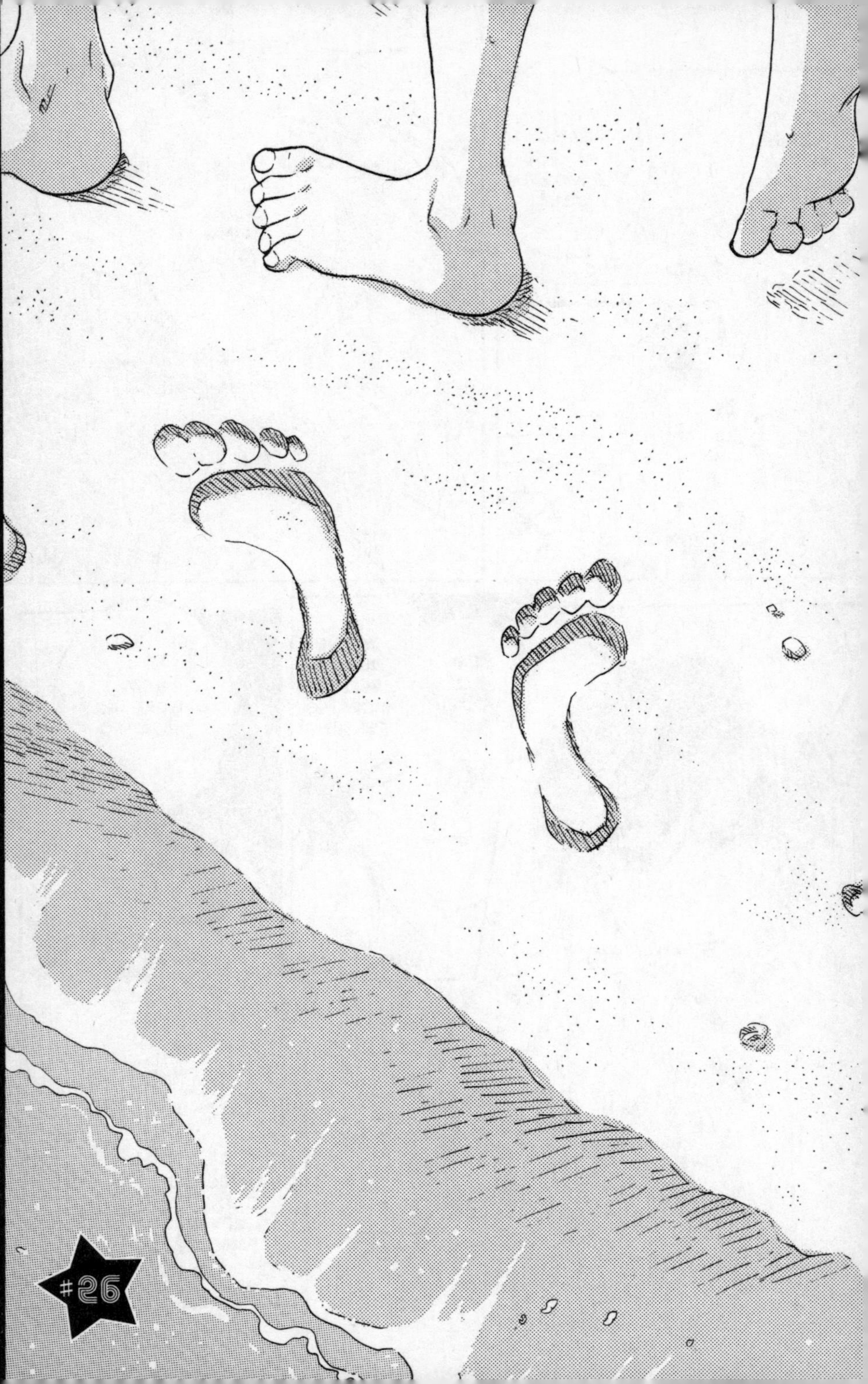
#26

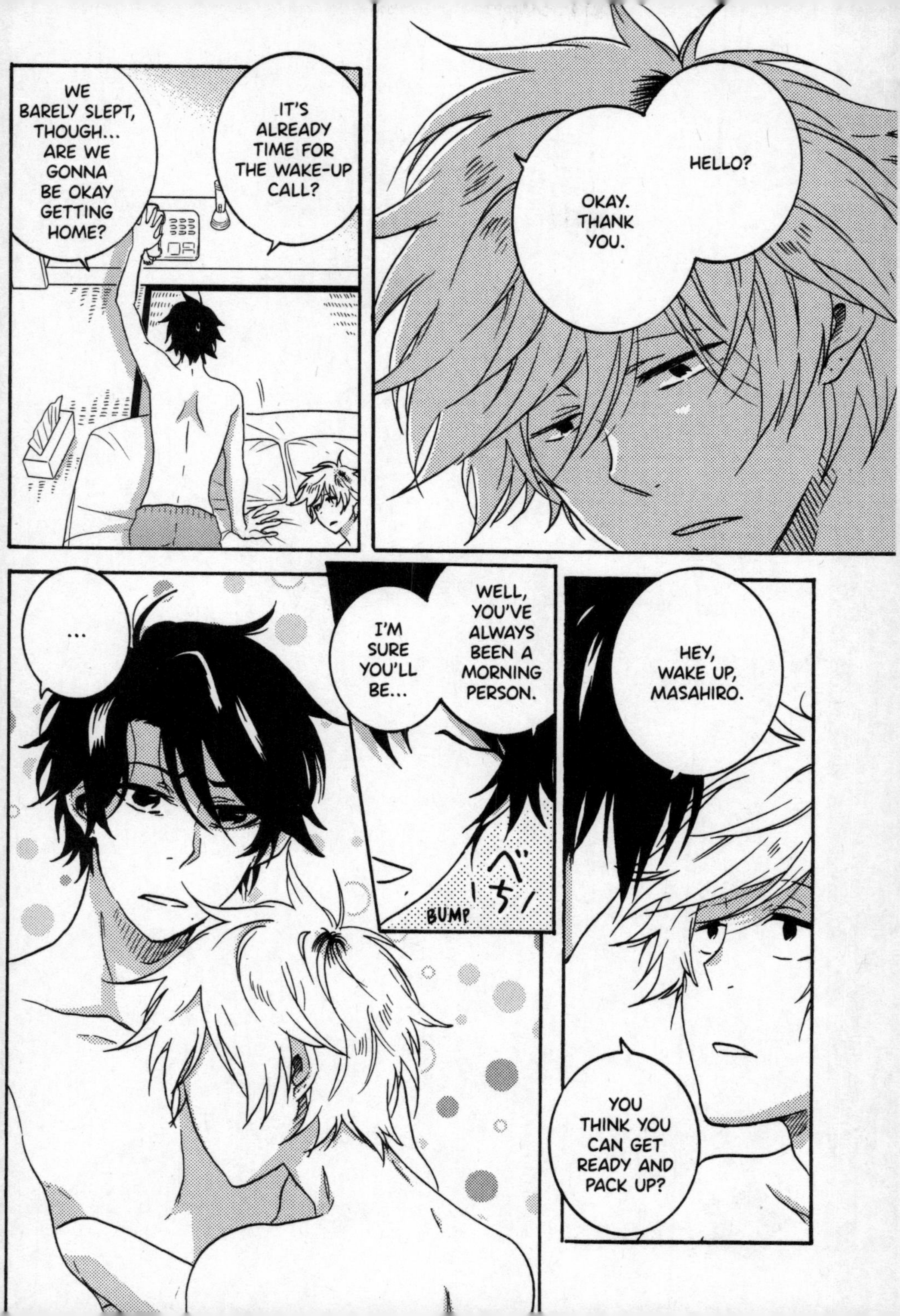
HELLO?
OKAY. THANK YOU.
IT'S ALREADY TIME FOR THE WAKE-UP CALL?
WE BARELY SLEPT, THOUGH... ARE WE GONNA BE OKAY GETTING HOME?
HEY, WAKE UP, MASAHIRO.
YOU THINK YOU CAN GET READY AND PACK UP?
WELL, YOU'VE ALWAYS BEEN A MORNING PERSON.
I'M SURE YOU'LL BE...
べち
BUMP
...

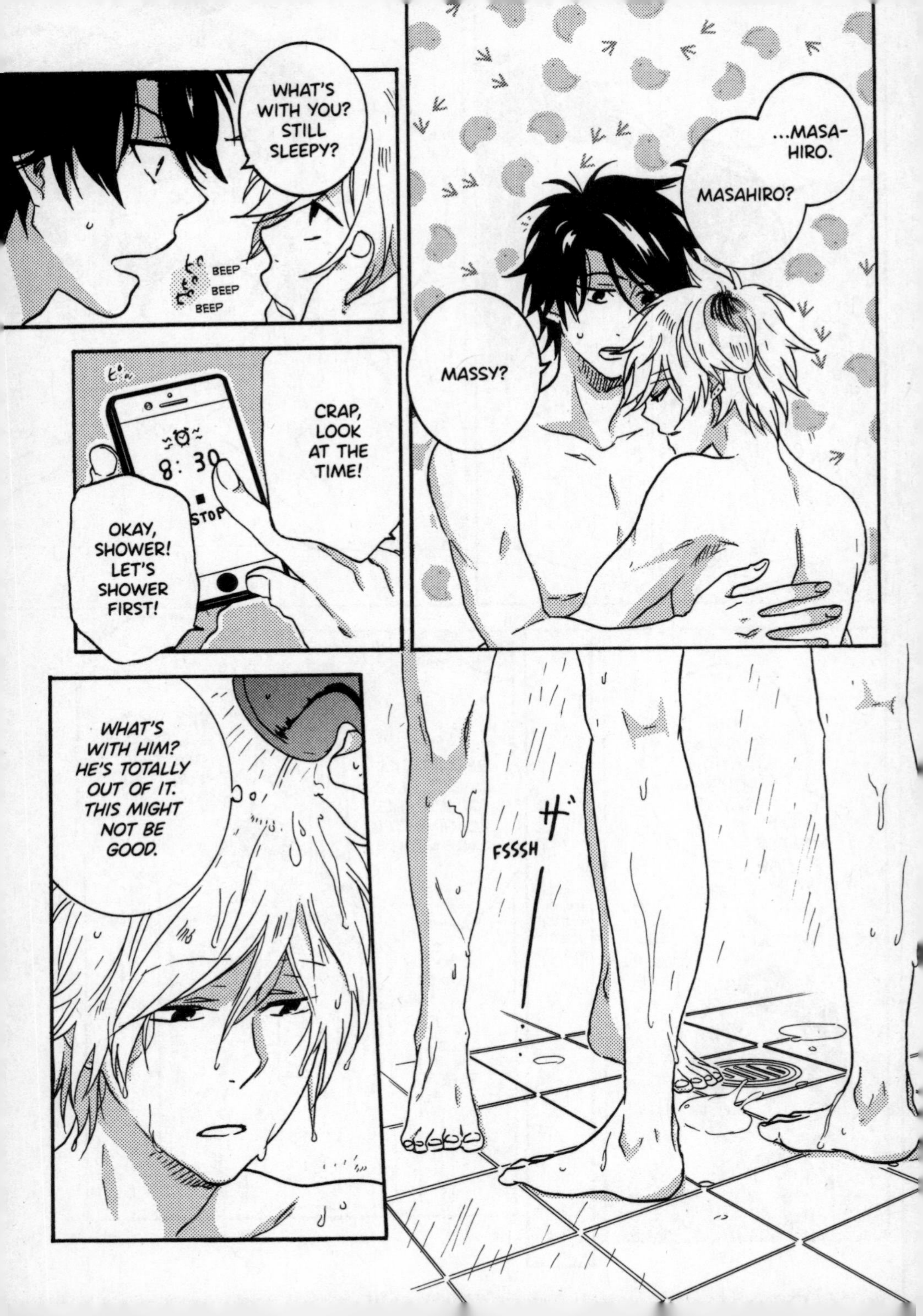
...MASA-HIRO.
MASAHIRO?
MASSY?
WHAT'S WITH YOU? STILL SLEEPY?
BEEP
BEEP
BEEP
8:30
STOP
CRAP, LOOK AT THE TIME!
OKAY, SHOWER! LET'S SHOWER FIRST!
FSSSH
WHAT'S WITH HIM? HE'S TOTALLY OUT OF IT. THIS MIGHT NOT BE GOOD.

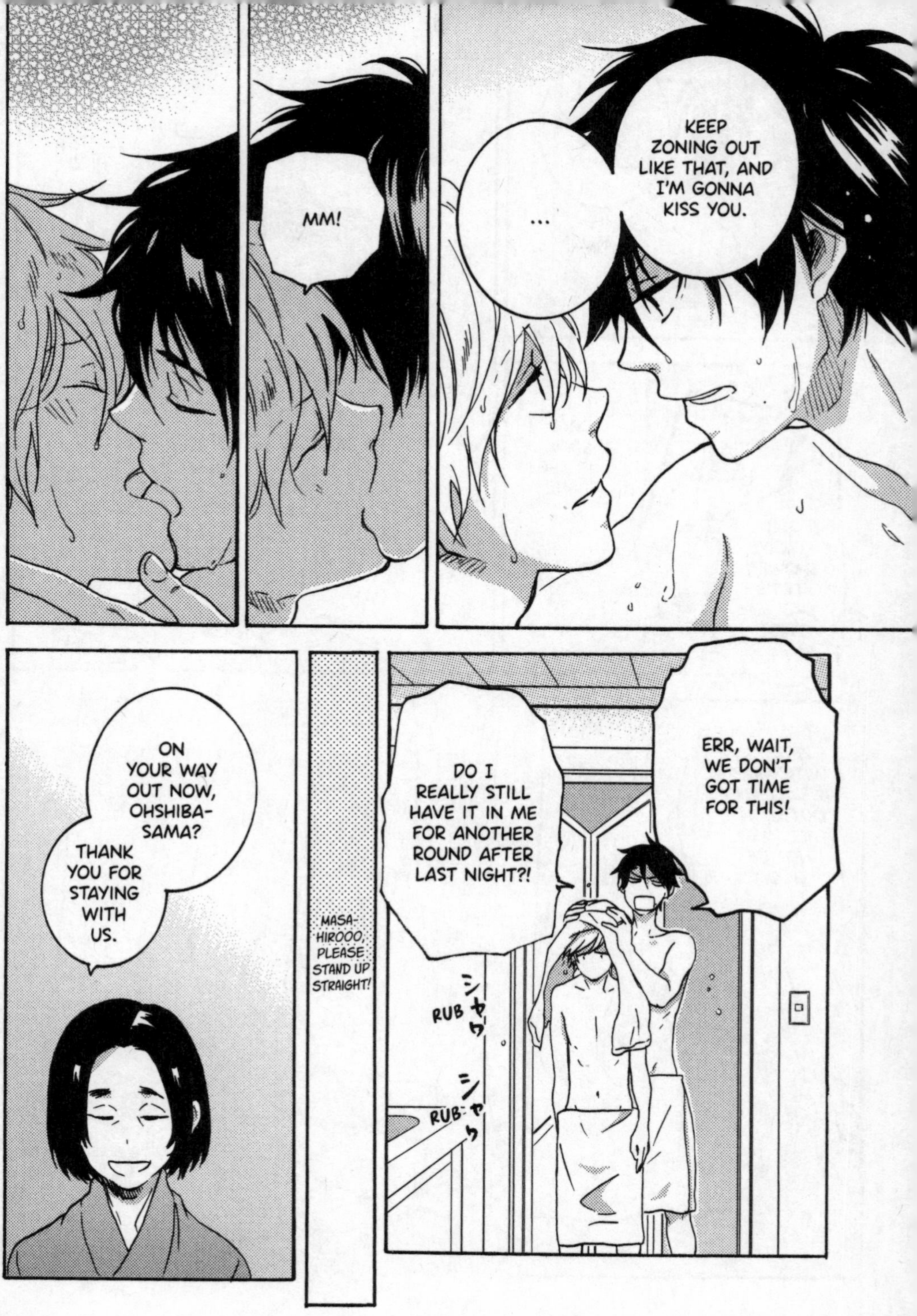

KEEP ZONING OUT LIKE THAT, AND I'M GONNA KISS YOU.
...
MM!
ERR, WAIT, WE DON'T GOT TIME FOR THIS!
DO I REALLY STILL HAVE IT IN ME FOR ANOTHER ROUND AFTER LAST NIGHT?!
RUB
RUB
MASA-HIROOO, PLEASE STAND UP STRAIGHT!
ON YOUR WAY OUT NOW, OHSHIBA-SAMA?
THANK YOU FOR STAYING WITH US.

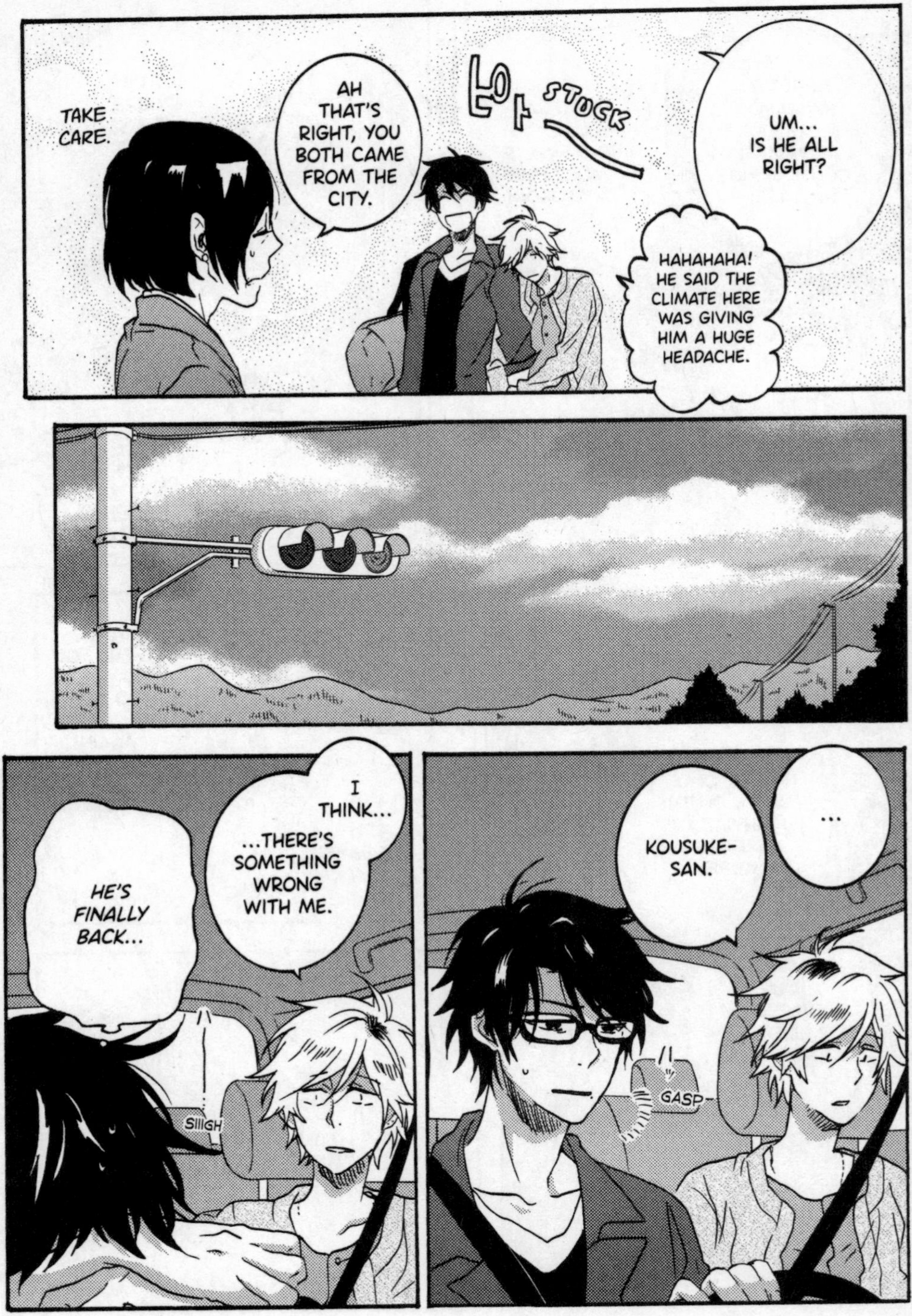
UM... IS HE ALL RIGHT?
STUCK
HAHAHAHA! HE SAID THE CLIMATE HERE WAS GIVING HIM A HUGE HEADACHE.
AH THAT'S RIGHT, YOU BOTH CAME FROM THE CITY.
TAKE CARE.
...
KOUSUKE-SAN.
GASP
I THINK...
...THERE'S SOMETHING WRONG WITH ME.
HE'S FINALLY BACK...
SIIIGH

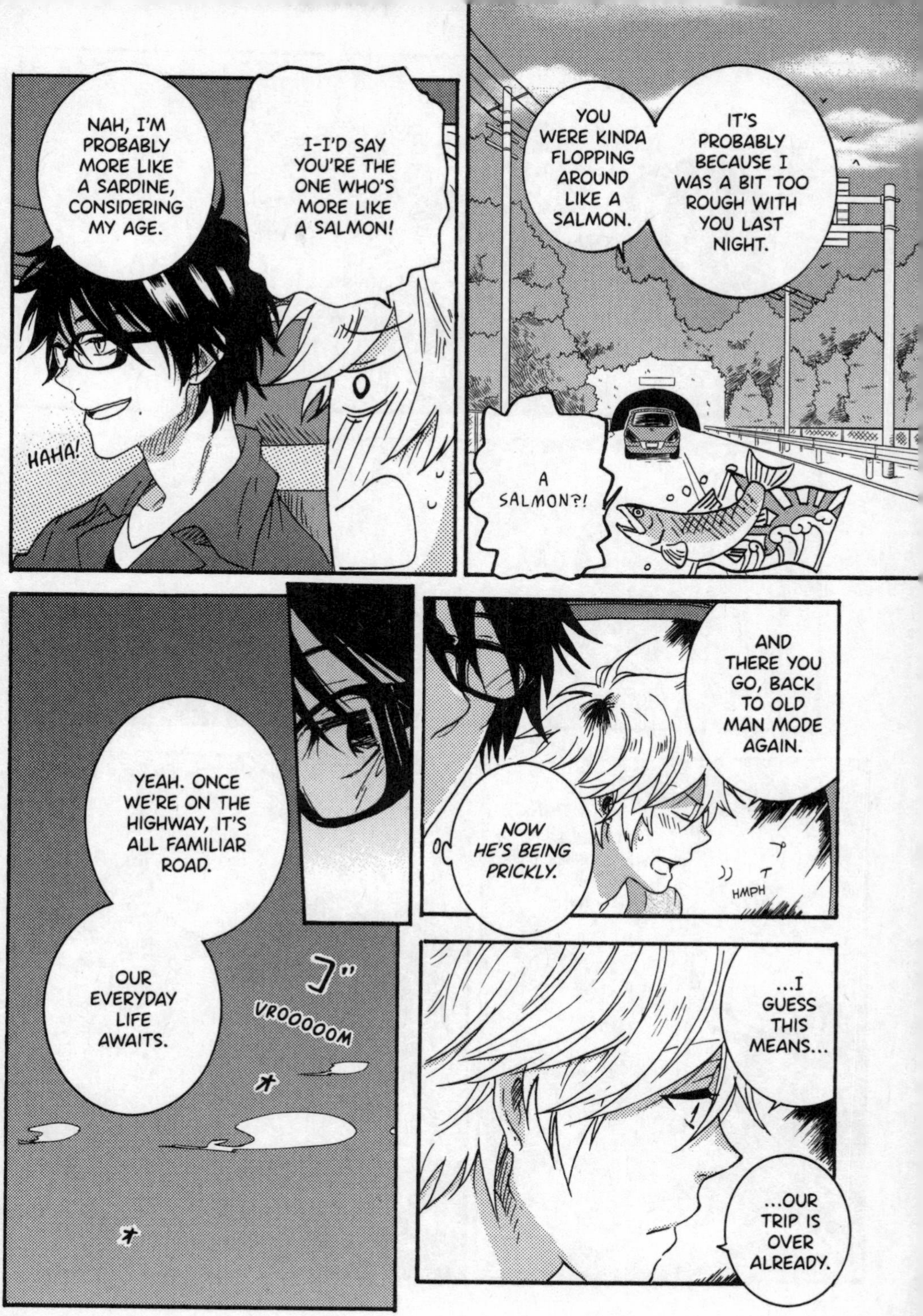
IT'S PROBABLY BECAUSE I WAS A BIT TOO ROUGH WITH YOU LAST NIGHT.
YOU WERE KINDA FLOPPING AROUND LIKE A SALMON.
A SALMON?!
I-I'D SAY YOU'RE THE ONE WHO'S MORE LIKE A SALMON!
NAH, I'M PROBABLY MORE LIKE A SARDINE, CONSIDERING MY AGE.
HAHA!
AND THERE YOU GO, BACK TO OLD MAN MODE AGAIN.
NOW HE'S BEING PRICKLY.
HMPH
...I GUESS THIS MEANS...
...OUR TRIP IS OVER ALREADY.
YEAH. ONCE WE'RE ON THE HIGHWAY, IT'S ALL FAMILIAR ROAD.
OUR EVERYDAY LIFE AWAITS.
VROOOOOM

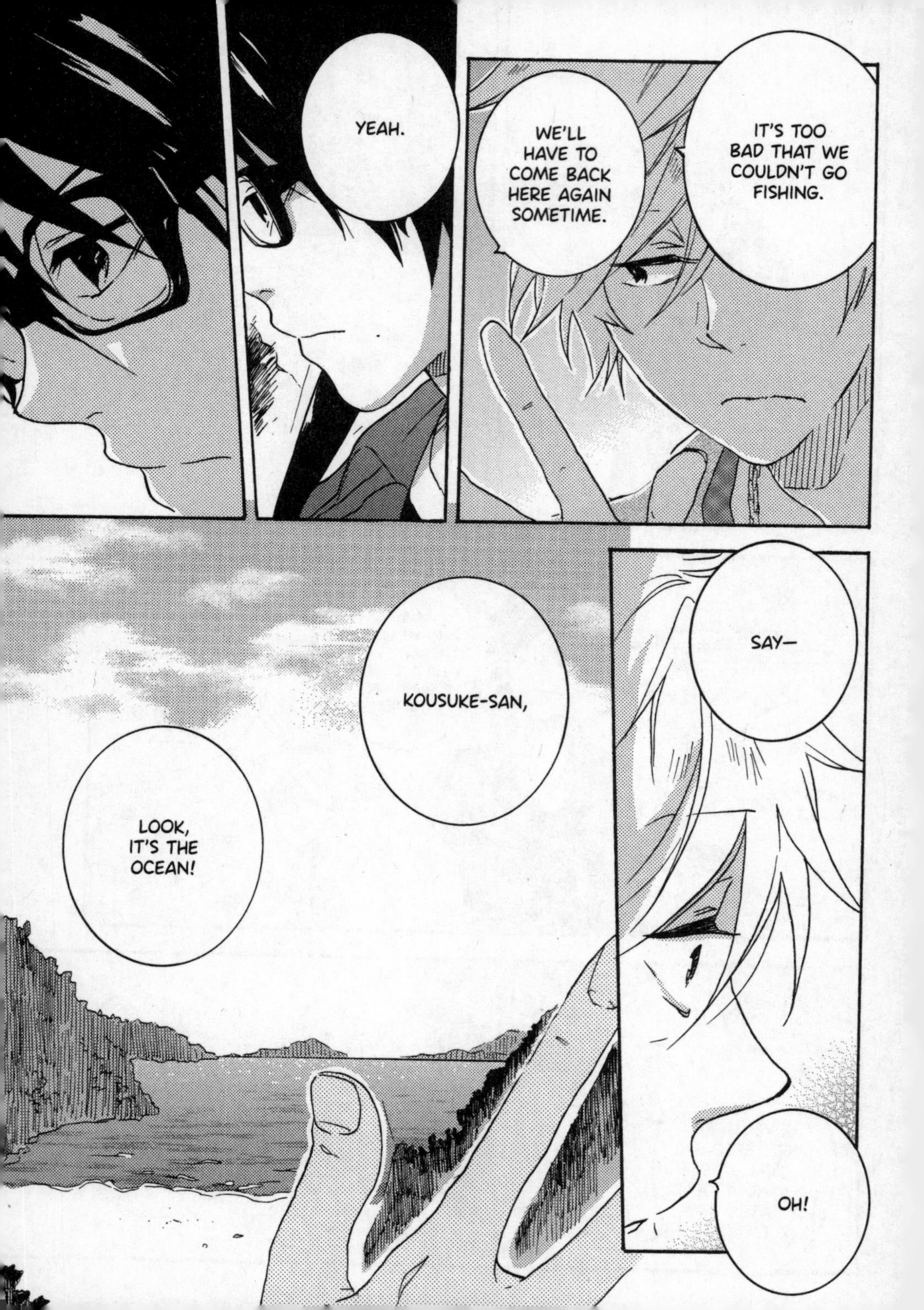
IT'S TOO BAD THAT WE COULDN'T GO FISHING.
WE'LL HAVE TO COME BACK HERE AGAIN SOMETIME.
YEAH.
SAY—
OH!
KOUSUKE-SAN,
LOOK, IT'S THE OCEAN!

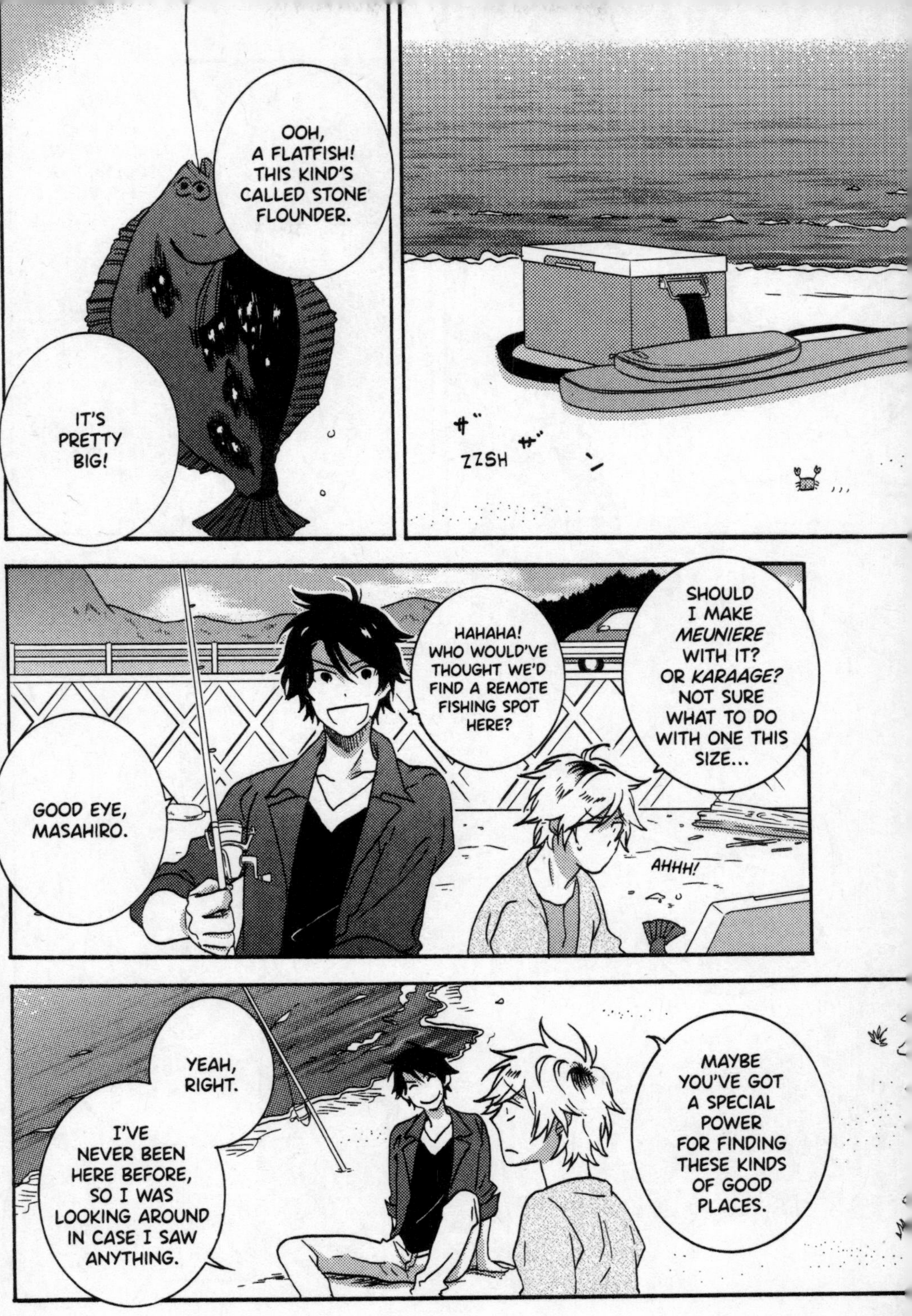
ザ ザ
ZZSH
OOH, A FLATFISH! THIS KIND'S CALLED STONE FLOUNDER.
IT'S PRETTY BIG!
SHOULD I MAKE *MEUNIERE* WITH IT? OR *KARAAGE?* NOT SURE WHAT TO DO WITH ONE THIS SIZE...
HAHAHA! WHO WOULD'VE THOUGHT WE'D FIND A REMOTE FISHING SPOT HERE?
AHHH!
GOOD EYE, MASAHIRO.
MAYBE YOU'VE GOT A SPECIAL POWER FOR FINDING THESE KINDS OF GOOD PLACES.
YEAH, RIGHT.
I'VE NEVER BEEN HERE BEFORE, SO I WAS LOOKING AROUND IN CASE I SAW ANYTHING.

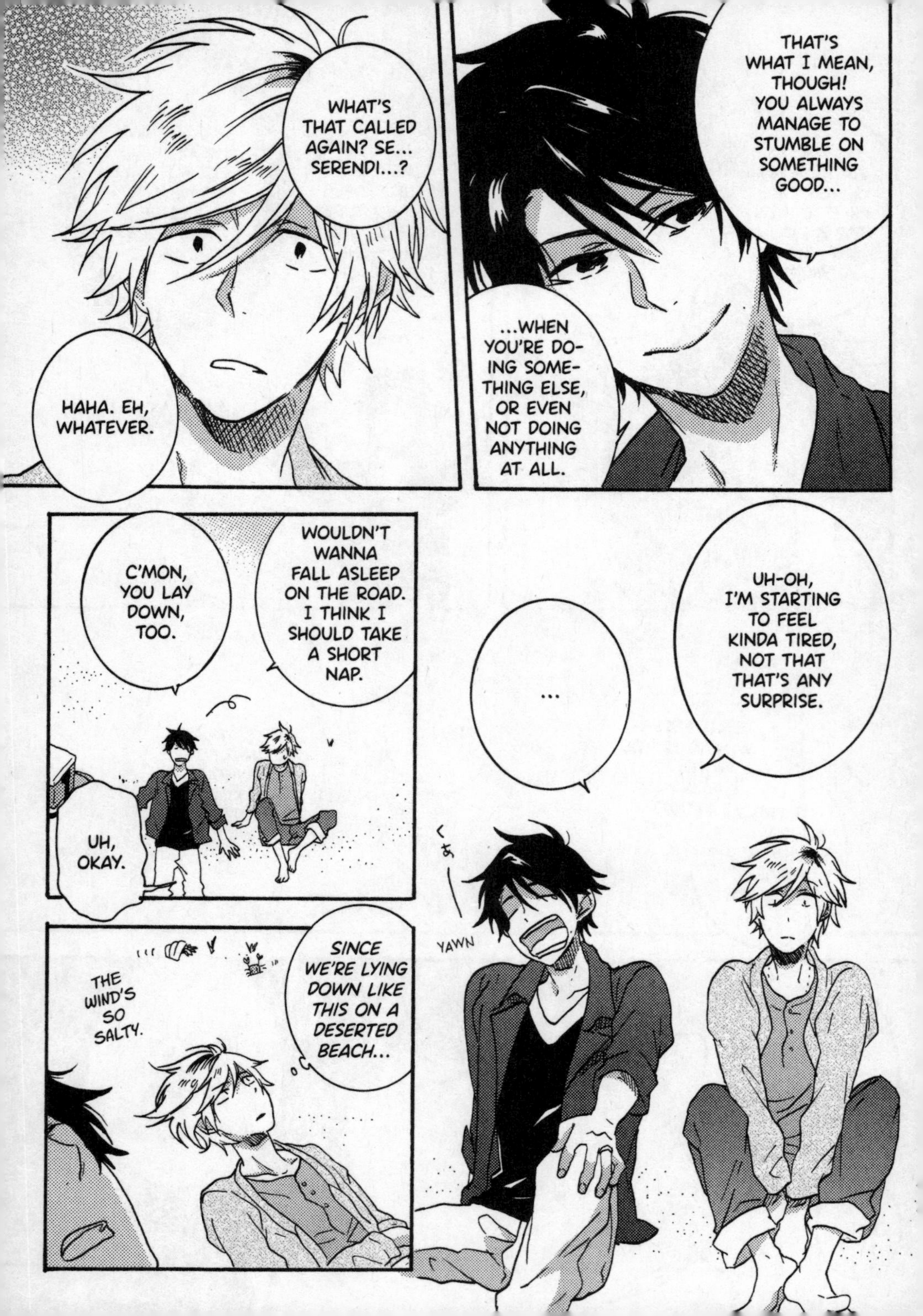
THAT'S WHAT I MEAN, THOUGH! YOU ALWAYS MANAGE TO STUMBLE ON SOMETHING GOOD...
...WHEN YOU'RE DOING SOMETHING ELSE, OR EVEN NOT DOING ANYTHING AT ALL.
WHAT'S THAT CALLED AGAIN? SE... SERENDI...?
HAHA. EH, WHATEVER.
UH-OH, I'M STARTING TO FEEL KINDA TIRED, NOT THAT THAT'S ANY SURPRISE.
...
くぁー
YAWN
WOULDN'T WANNA FALL ASLEEP ON THE ROAD. I THINK I SHOULD TAKE A SHORT NAP.
C'MON, YOU LAY DOWN, TOO.
UH, OKAY.
SINCE WE'RE LYING DOWN LIKE THIS ON A DESERTED BEACH...
THE WIND'S SO SALTY.

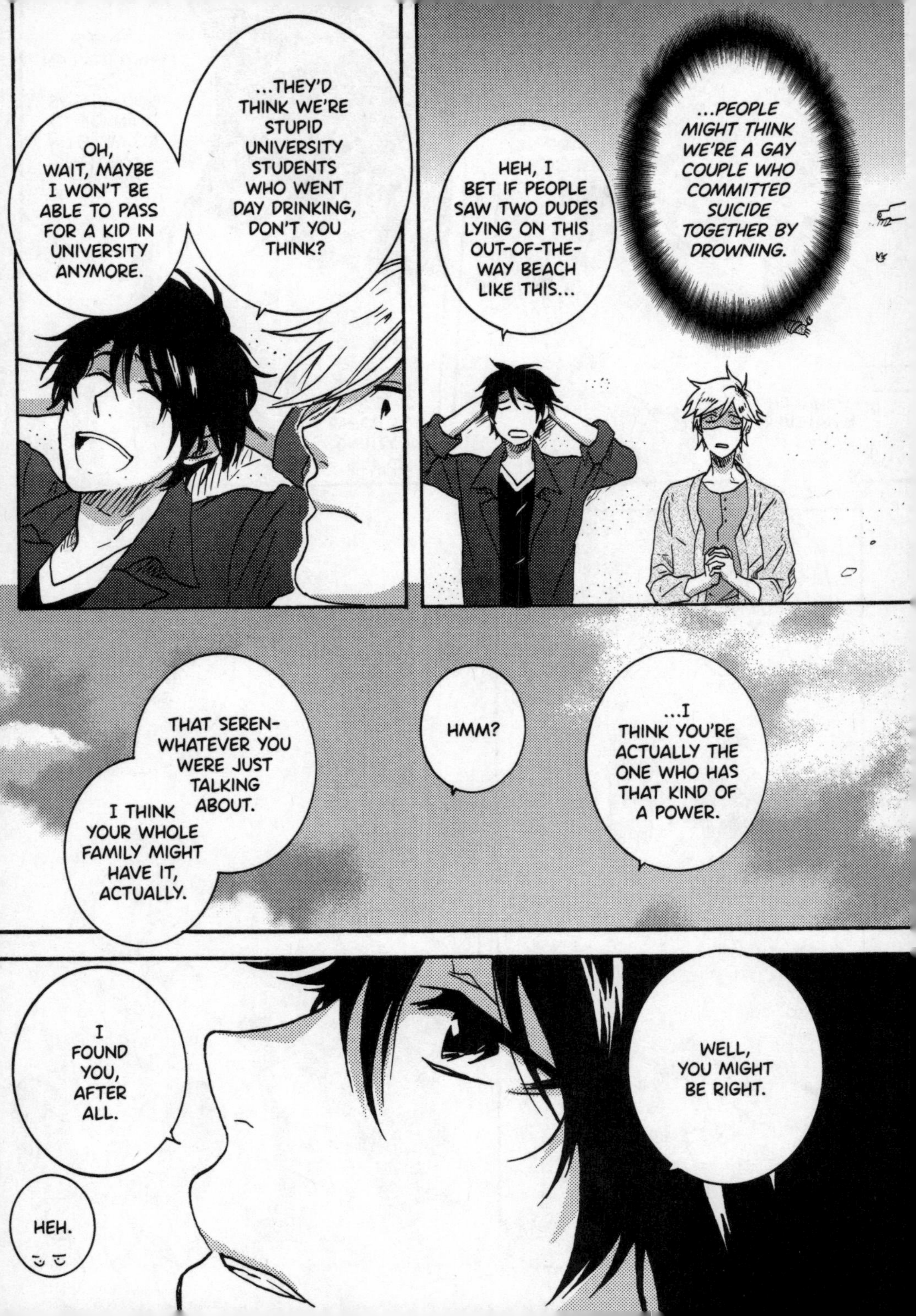
...PEOPLE MIGHT THINK WE'RE A GAY COUPLE WHO COMMITTED SUICIDE TOGETHER BY DROWNING.
HEH, I BET IF PEOPLE SAW TWO DUDES LYING ON THIS OUT-OF-THE-WAY BEACH LIKE THIS...
...THEY'D THINK WE'RE STUPID UNIVERSITY STUDENTS WHO WENT DAY DRINKING, DON'T YOU THINK?
OH, WAIT, MAYBE I WON'T BE ABLE TO PASS FOR A KID IN UNIVERSITY ANYMORE.
...I THINK YOU'RE ACTUALLY THE ONE WHO HAS THAT KIND OF A POWER.
HMM?
THAT SEREN-WHATEVER YOU WERE JUST TALKING ABOUT.
I THINK YOUR WHOLE FAMILY MIGHT HAVE IT, ACTUALLY.
WELL, YOU MIGHT BE RIGHT.
I FOUND YOU, AFTER ALL.
HEH.

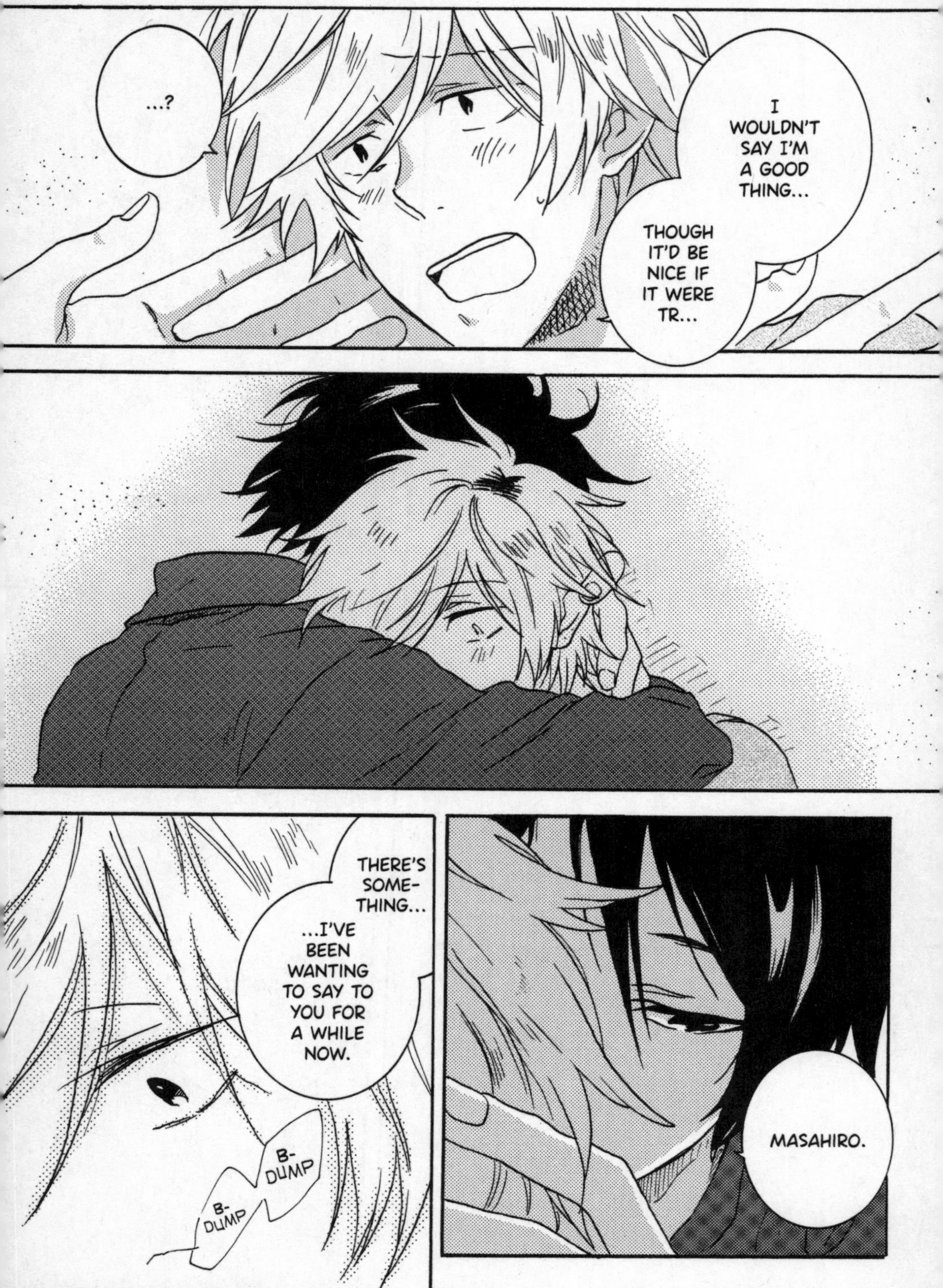
I WOULDN'T SAY I'M A GOOD THING...
THOUGH IT'D BE NICE IF IT WERE TR...
...?
MASAHIRO.
THERE'S SOME-THING...
...I'VE BEEN WANTING TO SAY TO YOU FOR A WHILE NOW.
B-DUMP
B-DUMP

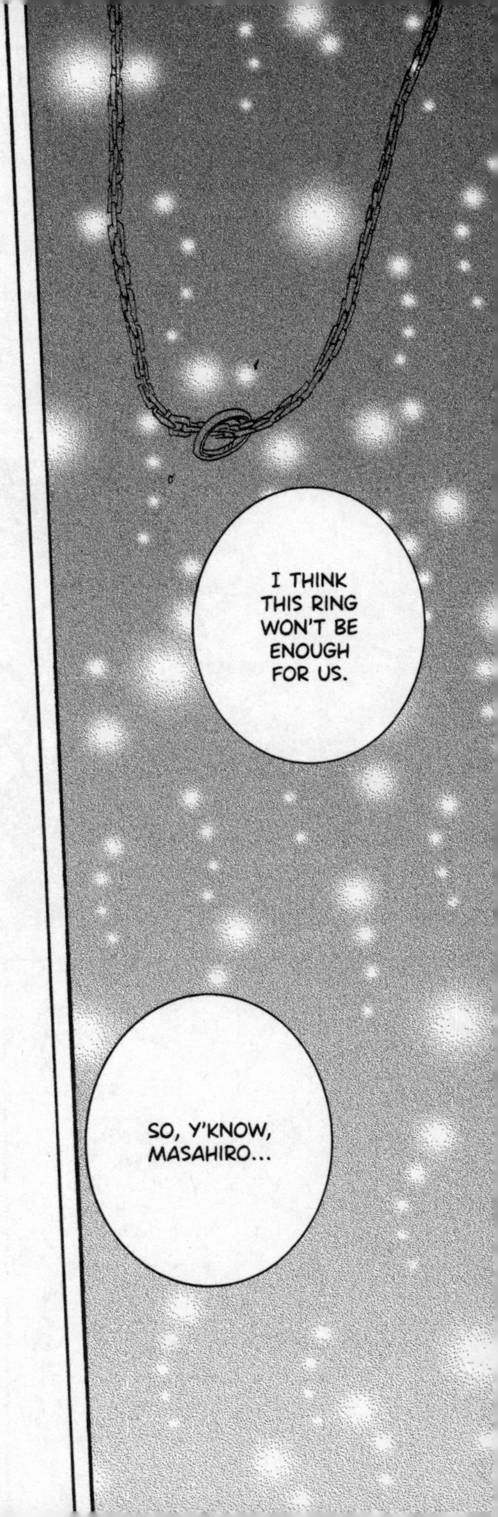
I THINK THIS RING WON'T BE ENOUGH FOR US.
SO, Y'KNOW, MASAHIRO...

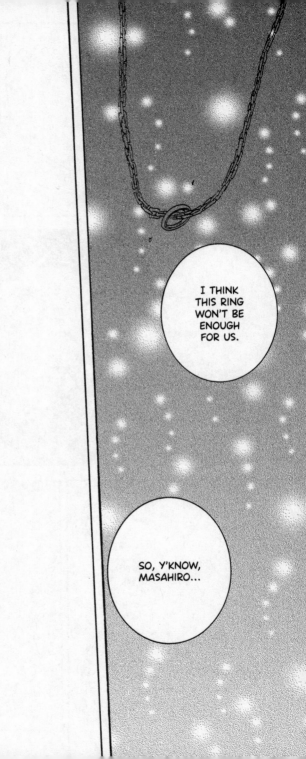

...LET'S GET
MARRIED.

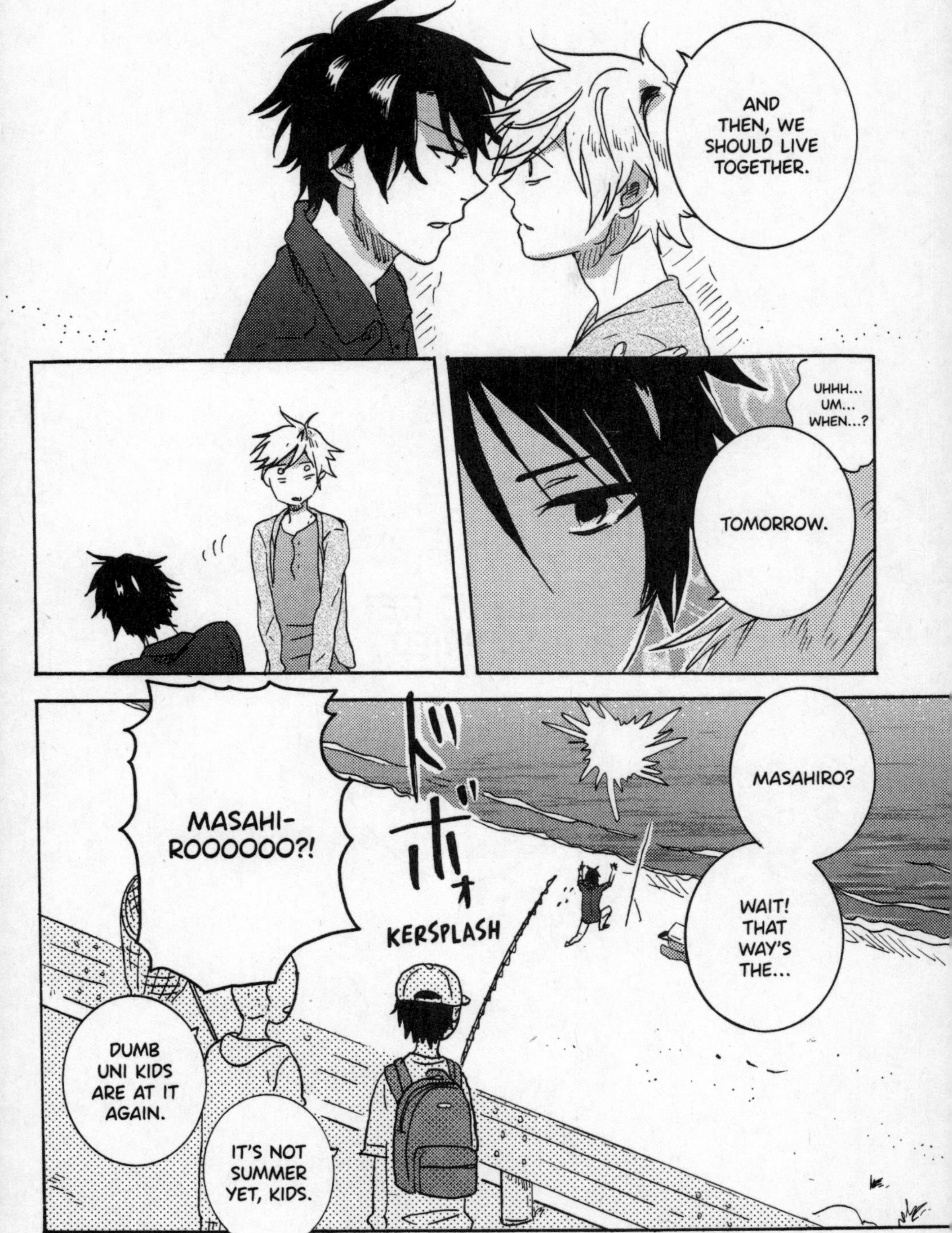
AND THEN, WE SHOULD LIVE TOGETHER.
UHHH... UM... WHEN...?
TOMORROW.
MASAHIRO?
WAIT! THAT WAY'S THE...
ドボォ
KERSPLASH
MASAHI-ROOOOOO?!
DUMB UNI KIDS ARE AT IT AGAIN.
IT'S NOT SUMMER YET, KIDS.

Hitorijime
My Hero

Flounder

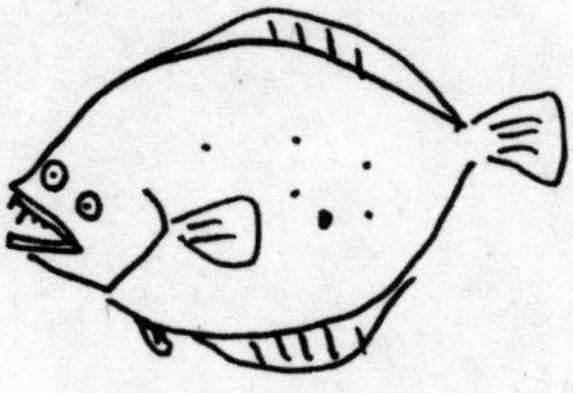

Flatfish

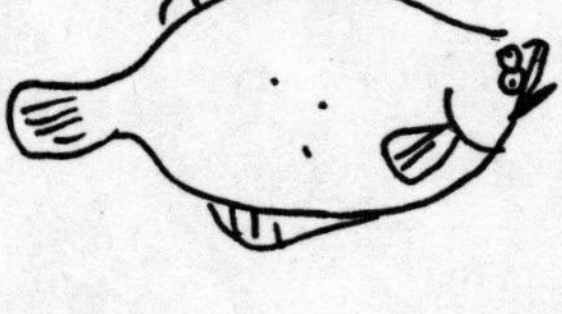

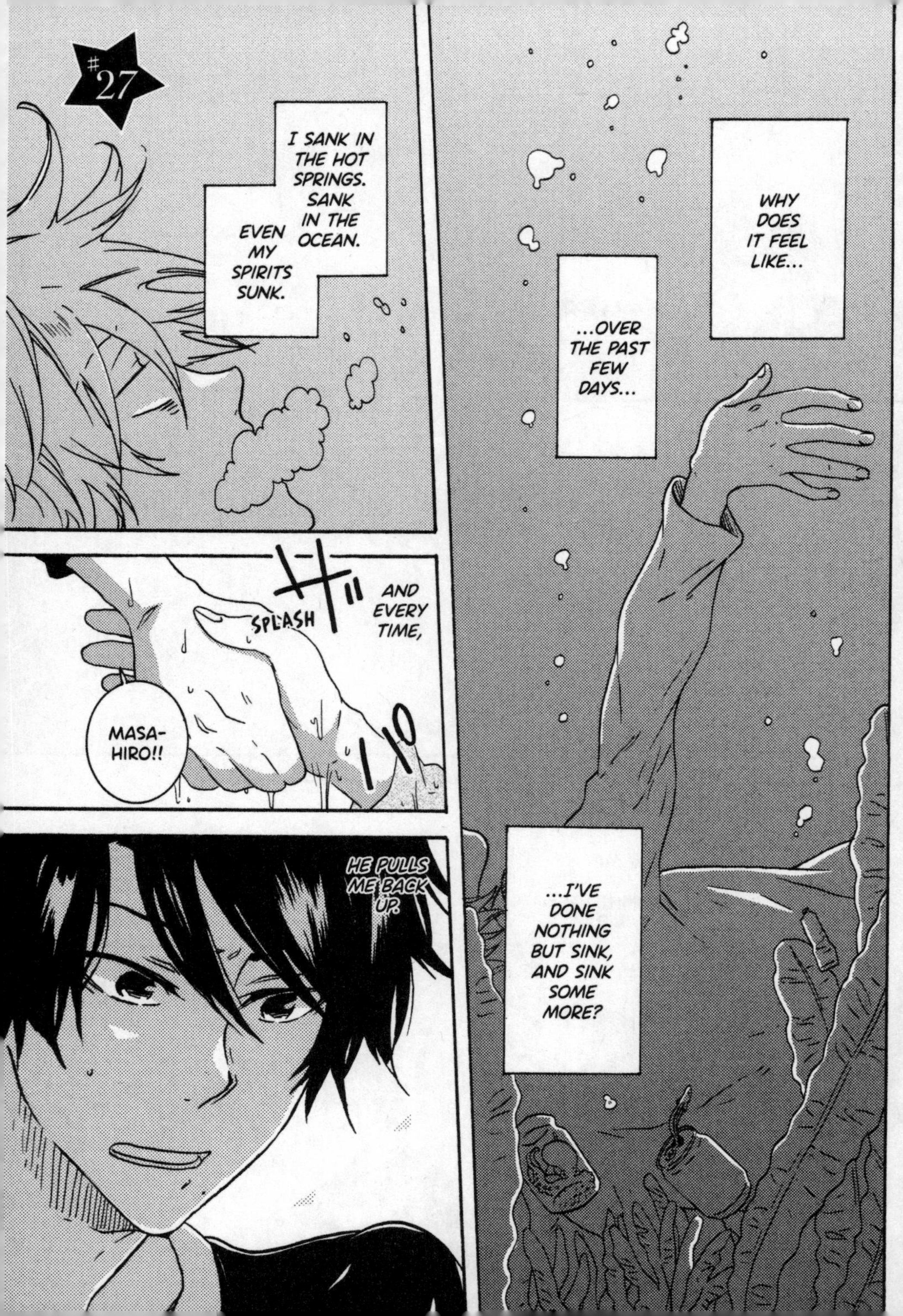
WHY DOES IT FEEL LIKE...
...OVER THE PAST FEW DAYS...
...I'VE DONE NOTHING BUT SINK, AND SINK SOME MORE?
#27
I SANK IN THE HOT SPRINGS. SANK IN THE OCEAN.
EVEN MY SPIRITS SUNK.
AND EVERY TIME,
SPLASH
MASA-HIRO!!
HE PULLS ME BACK UP.

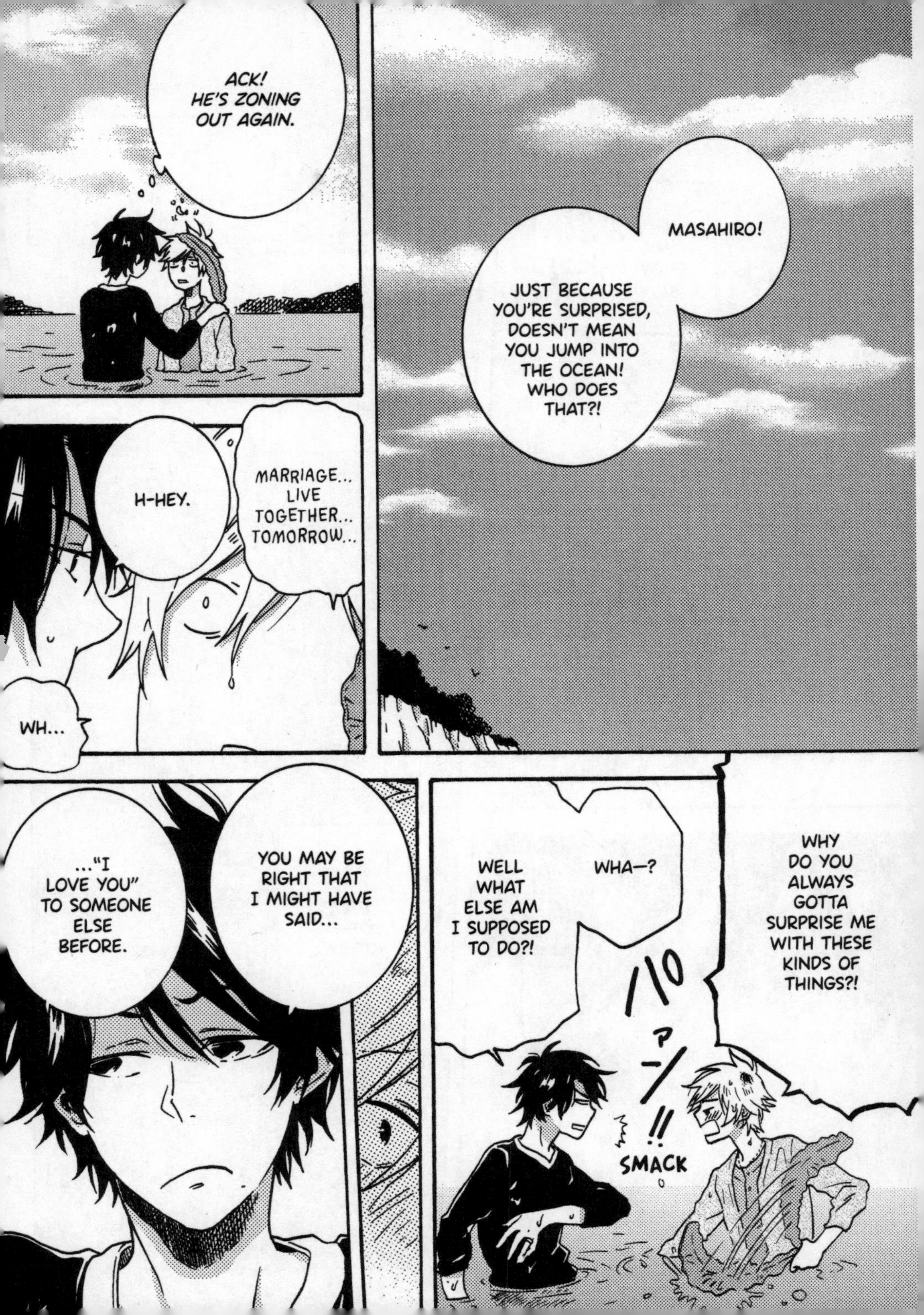
MASAHIRO!
JUST BECAUSE YOU'RE SURPRISED, DOESN'T MEAN YOU JUMP INTO THE OCEAN! WHO DOES THAT?!
ACK! HE'S ZONING OUT AGAIN.
MARRIAGE... LIVE TOGETHER... TOMORROW...
H-HEY.
WH...
WHY DO YOU ALWAYS GOTTA SURPRISE ME WITH THESE KINDS OF THINGS?!
WHA—?
WELL WHAT ELSE AM I SUPPOSED TO DO?!
!!
SMACK
YOU MAY BE RIGHT THAT I MIGHT HAVE SAID...
..."I LOVE YOU" TO SOMEONE ELSE BEFORE.

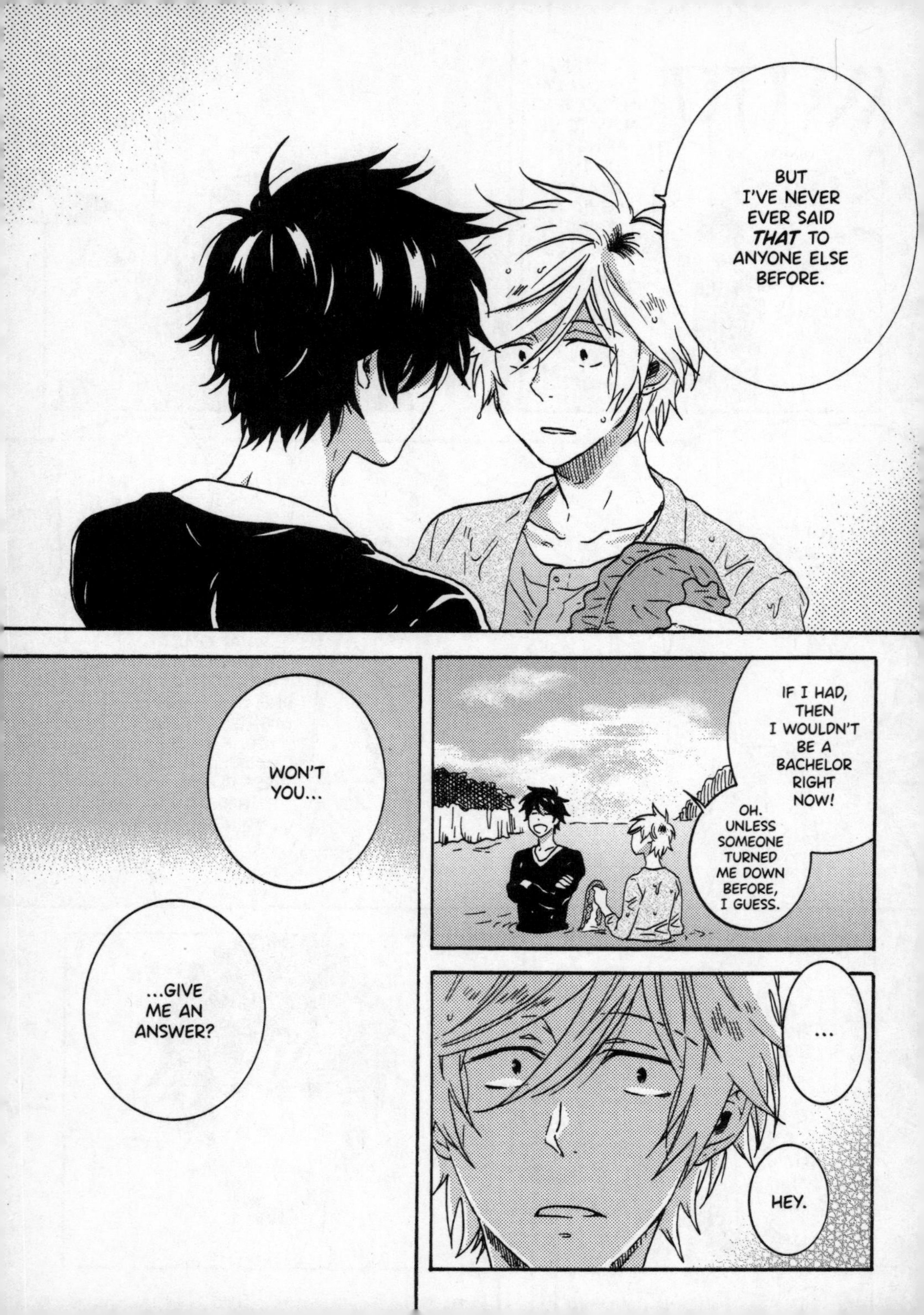
BUT I'VE NEVER EVER SAID ***THAT*** TO ANYONE ELSE BEFORE.
IF I HAD, THEN I WOULDN'T BE A BACHELOR RIGHT NOW!
OH. UNLESS SOMEONE TURNED ME DOWN BEFORE, I GUESS.
...
HEY.
WON'T YOU...
...GIVE ME AN ANSWER?

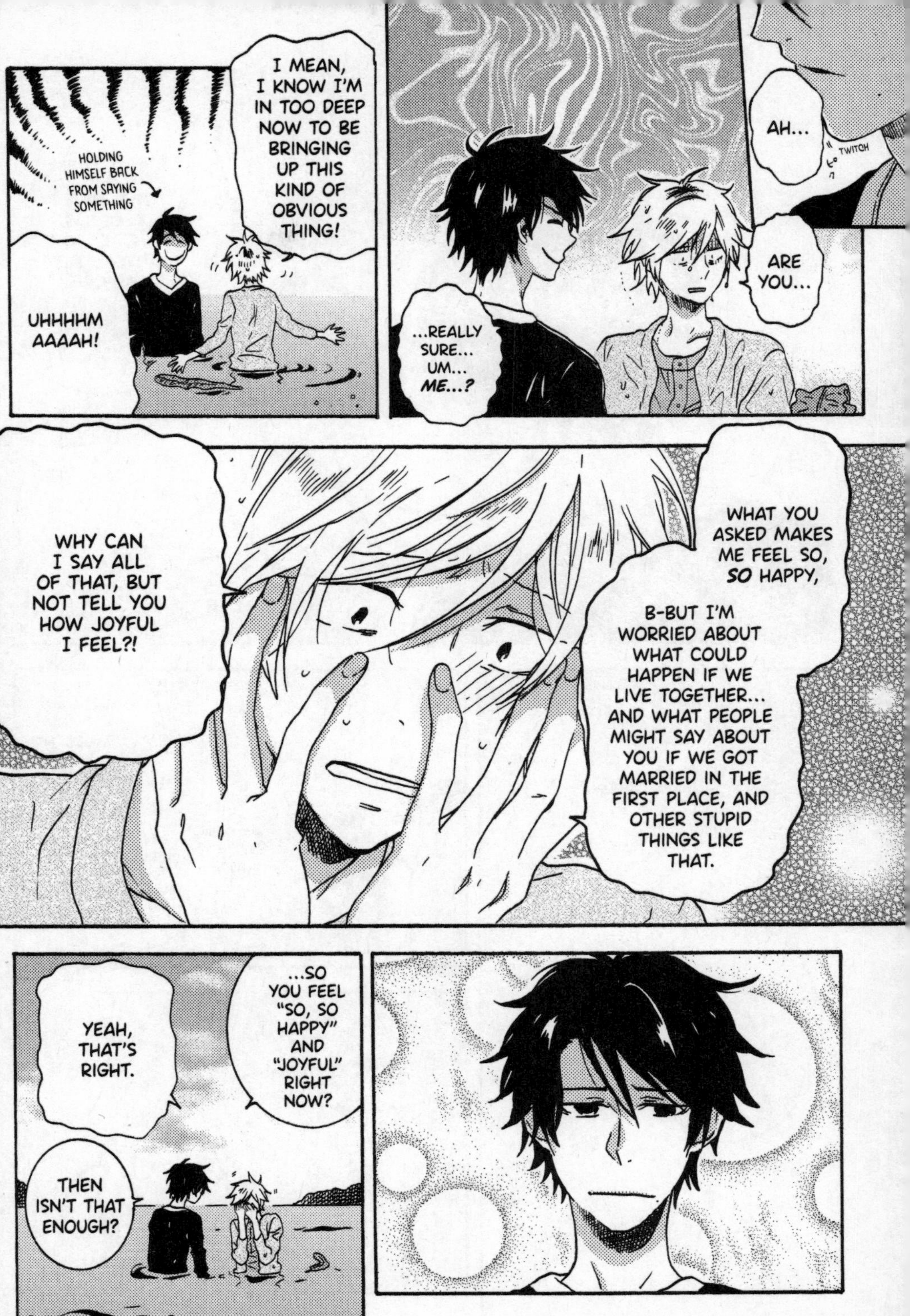
AH...
TWITCH
ARE YOU...
...REALLY SURE... UM... *ME...?*
I MEAN, I KNOW I'M IN TOO DEEP NOW TO BE BRINGING UP THIS KIND OF OBVIOUS THING!
HOLDING HIMSELF BACK FROM SAYING SOMETHING
UHHHHM AAAAH!
WHAT YOU ASKED MAKES ME FEEL SO, *SO* HAPPY,
B-BUT I'M WORRIED ABOUT WHAT COULD HAPPEN IF WE LIVE TOGETHER... AND WHAT PEOPLE MIGHT SAY ABOUT YOU IF WE GOT MARRIED IN THE FIRST PLACE, AND OTHER STUPID THINGS LIKE THAT.
WHY CAN I SAY ALL OF THAT, BUT NOT TELL YOU HOW JOYFUL I FEEL?!
...SO YOU FEEL "SO, SO HAPPY" AND "JOYFUL" RIGHT NOW?
YEAH, THAT'S RIGHT.
THEN ISN'T THAT ENOUGH?

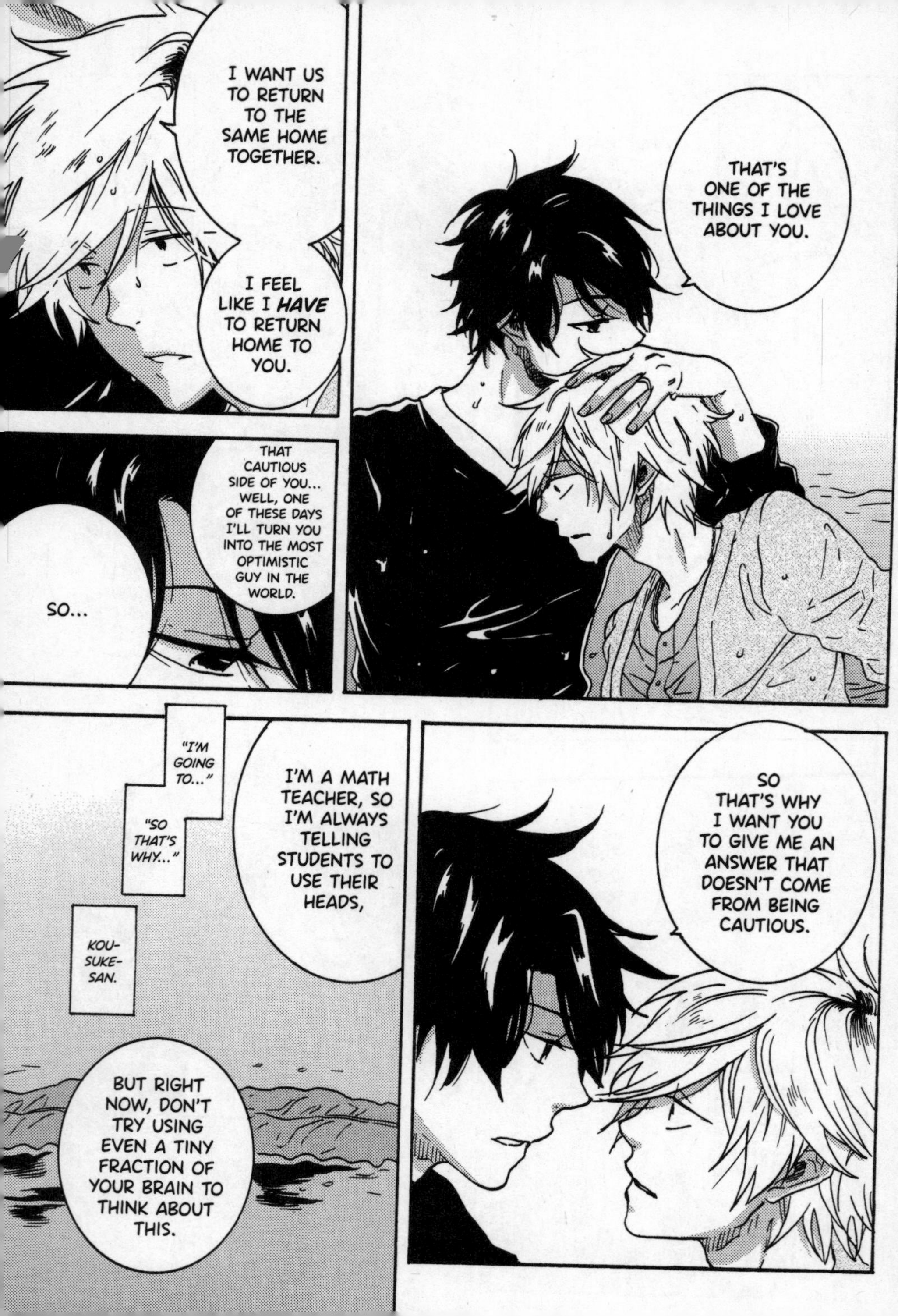
THAT'S ONE OF THE THINGS I LOVE ABOUT YOU.
I WANT US TO RETURN TO THE SAME HOME TOGETHER.
I FEEL LIKE I *HAVE* TO RETURN HOME TO YOU.
THAT CAUTIOUS SIDE OF YOU... WELL, ONE OF THESE DAYS I'LL TURN YOU INTO THE MOST OPTIMISTIC GUY IN THE WORLD.
SO...
SO THAT'S WHY I WANT YOU TO GIVE ME AN ANSWER THAT DOESN'T COME FROM BEING CAUTIOUS.
I'M A MATH TEACHER, SO I'M ALWAYS TELLING STUDENTS TO USE THEIR HEADS,
"I'M GOING TO..."
"SO THAT'S WHY..."
KOU-SUKE-SAN.
BUT RIGHT NOW, DON'T TRY USING EVEN A TINY FRACTION OF YOUR BRAIN TO THINK ABOUT THIS.

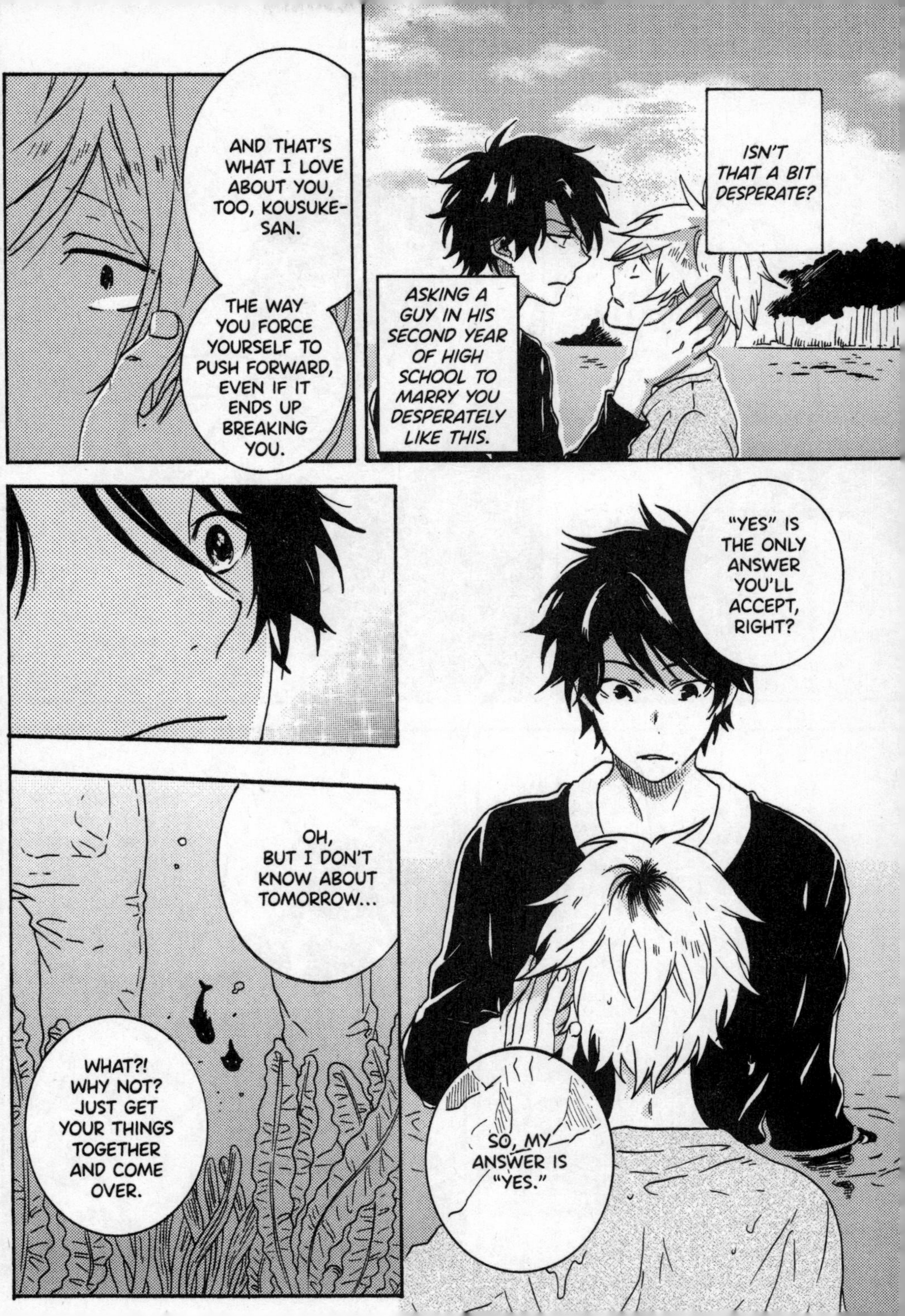
ISN'T THAT A BIT DESPERATE?
ASKING A GUY IN HIS SECOND YEAR OF HIGH SCHOOL TO MARRY YOU DESPERATELY LIKE THIS.
AND THAT'S WHAT I LOVE ABOUT YOU, TOO, KOUSUKE-SAN.
THE WAY YOU FORCE YOURSELF TO PUSH FORWARD, EVEN IF IT ENDS UP BREAKING YOU.
"YES" IS THE ONLY ANSWER YOU'LL ACCEPT, RIGHT?
SO, MY ANSWER IS "YES."
OH, BUT I DON'T KNOW ABOUT TOMORROW...
WHAT?! WHY NOT? JUST GET YOUR THINGS TOGETHER AND COME OVER.

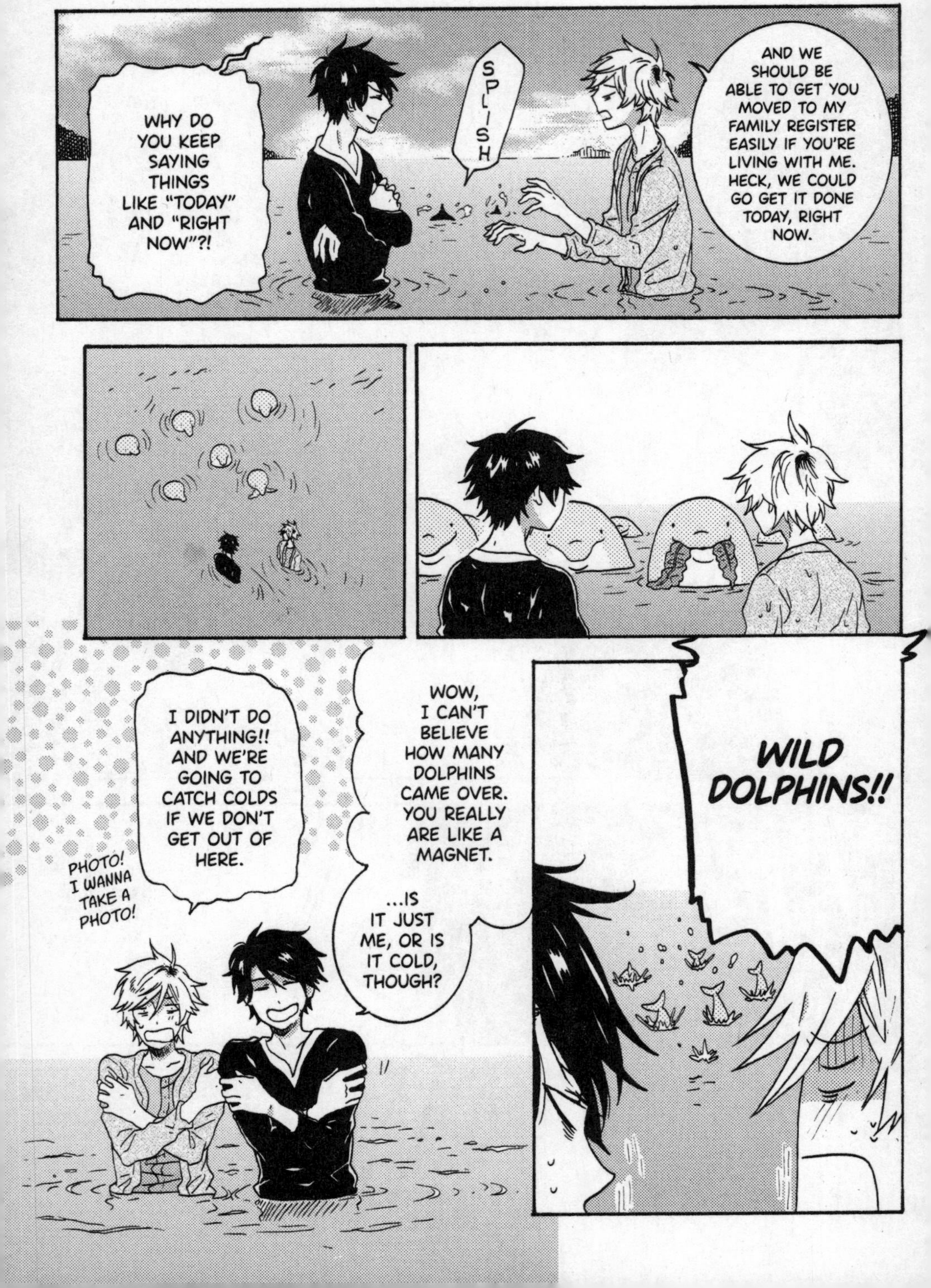
AND WE SHOULD BE ABLE TO GET YOU MOVED TO MY FAMILY REGISTER EASILY IF YOU'RE LIVING WITH ME. HECK, WE COULD GO GET IT DONE TODAY, RIGHT NOW.
SPLISH
WHY DO YOU KEEP SAYING THINGS LIKE "TODAY" AND "RIGHT NOW"?!
WILD DOLPHINS!!
WOW, I CAN'T BELIEVE HOW MANY DOLPHINS CAME OVER. YOU REALLY ARE LIKE A MAGNET.
I DIDN'T DO ANYTHING!! AND WE'RE GOING TO CATCH COLDS IF WE DON'T GET OUT OF HERE.
...IS IT JUST ME, OR IS IT COLD, THOUGH?
PHOTO! I WANNA TAKE A PHOTO!

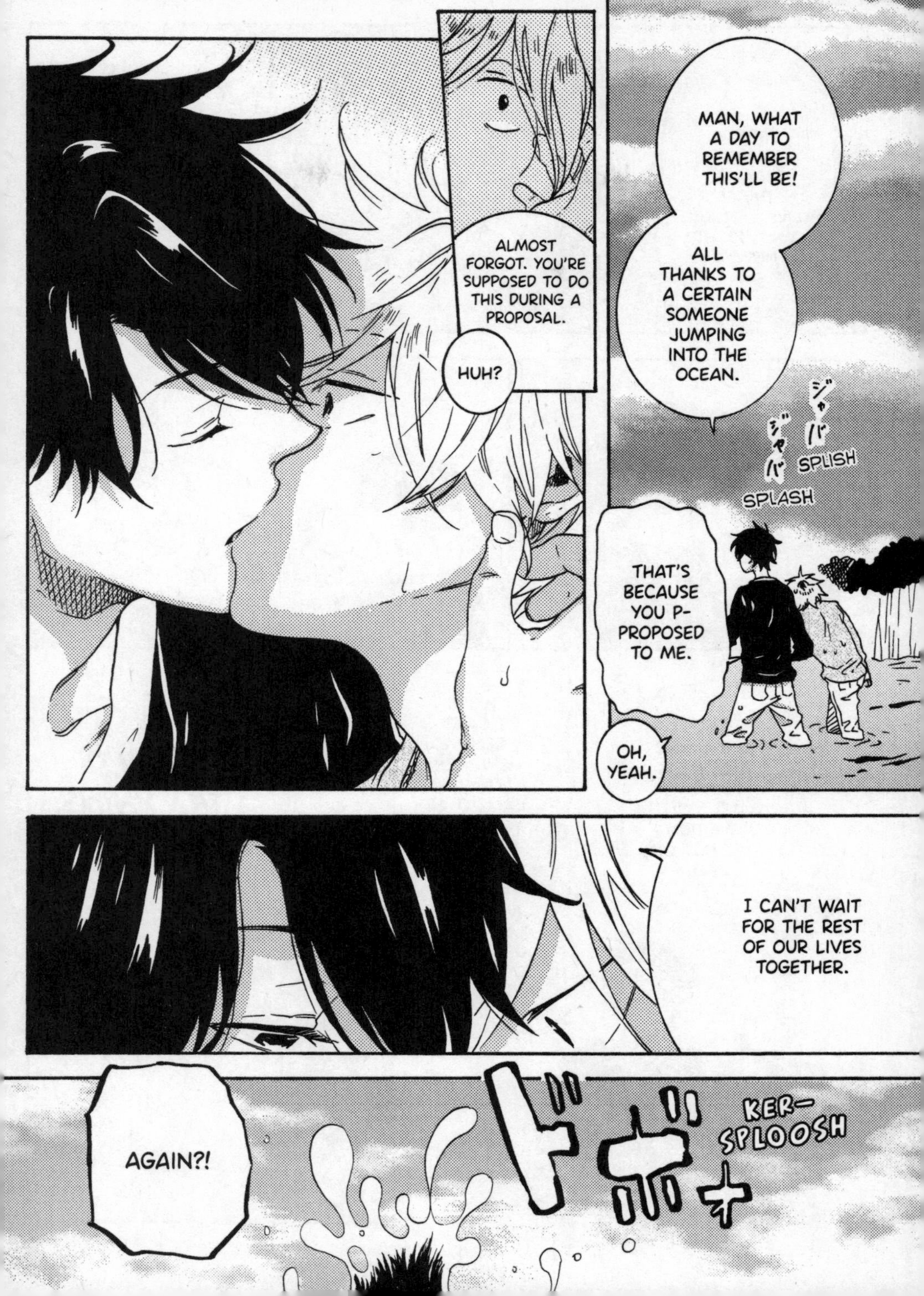
MAN, WHAT A DAY TO REMEMBER THIS'LL BE!
ALL THANKS TO A CERTAIN SOMEONE JUMPING INTO THE OCEAN.
ジャバ
ジャバ
SPLISH
SPLASH
THAT'S BECAUSE YOU P-PROPOSED TO ME.
OH, YEAH.
ALMOST FORGOT. YOU'RE SUPPOSED TO DO THIS DURING A PROPOSAL.
HUH?
I CAN'T WAIT FOR THE REST OF OUR LIVES TOGETHER.
KER-SPLOOSH
AGAIN?!

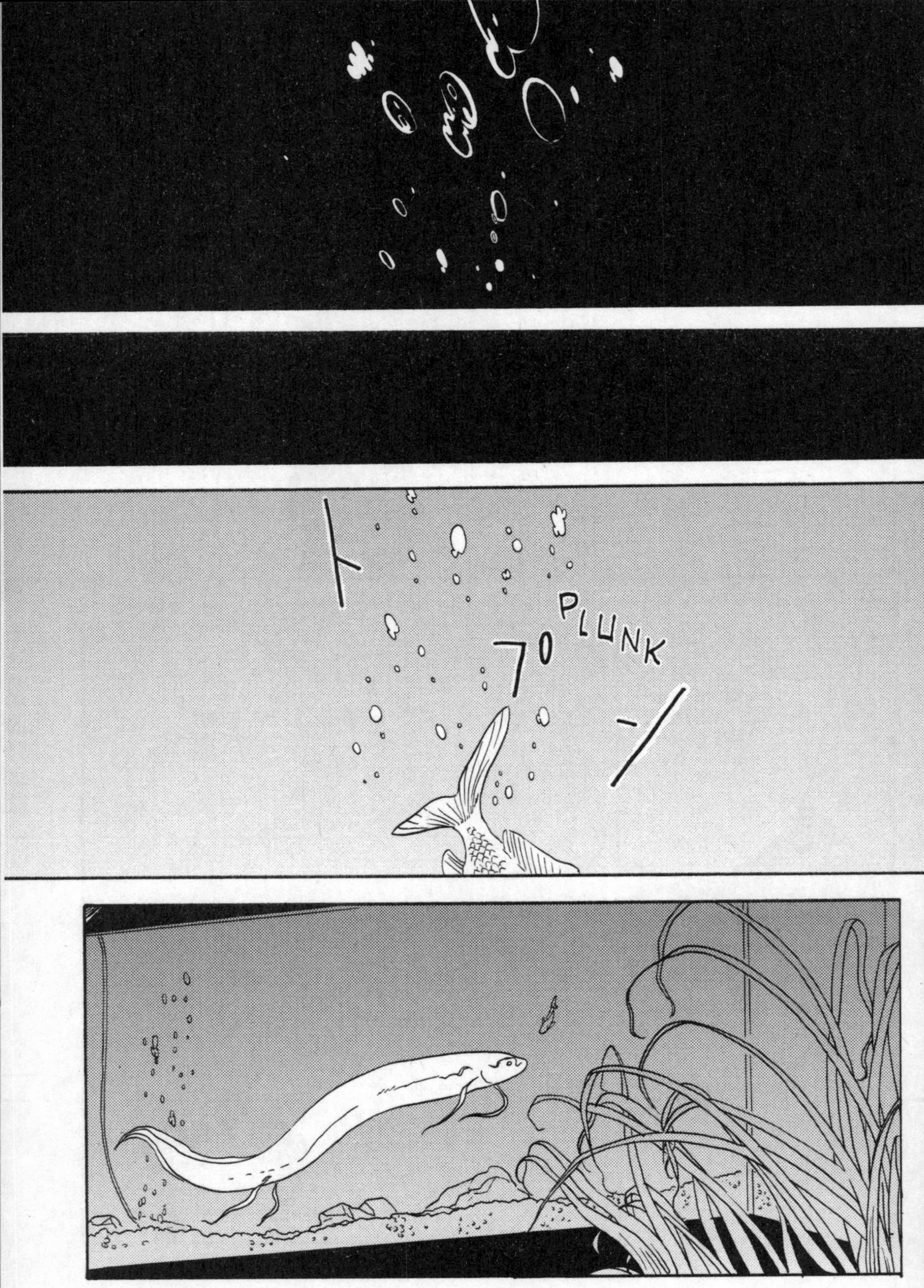
PLUNK

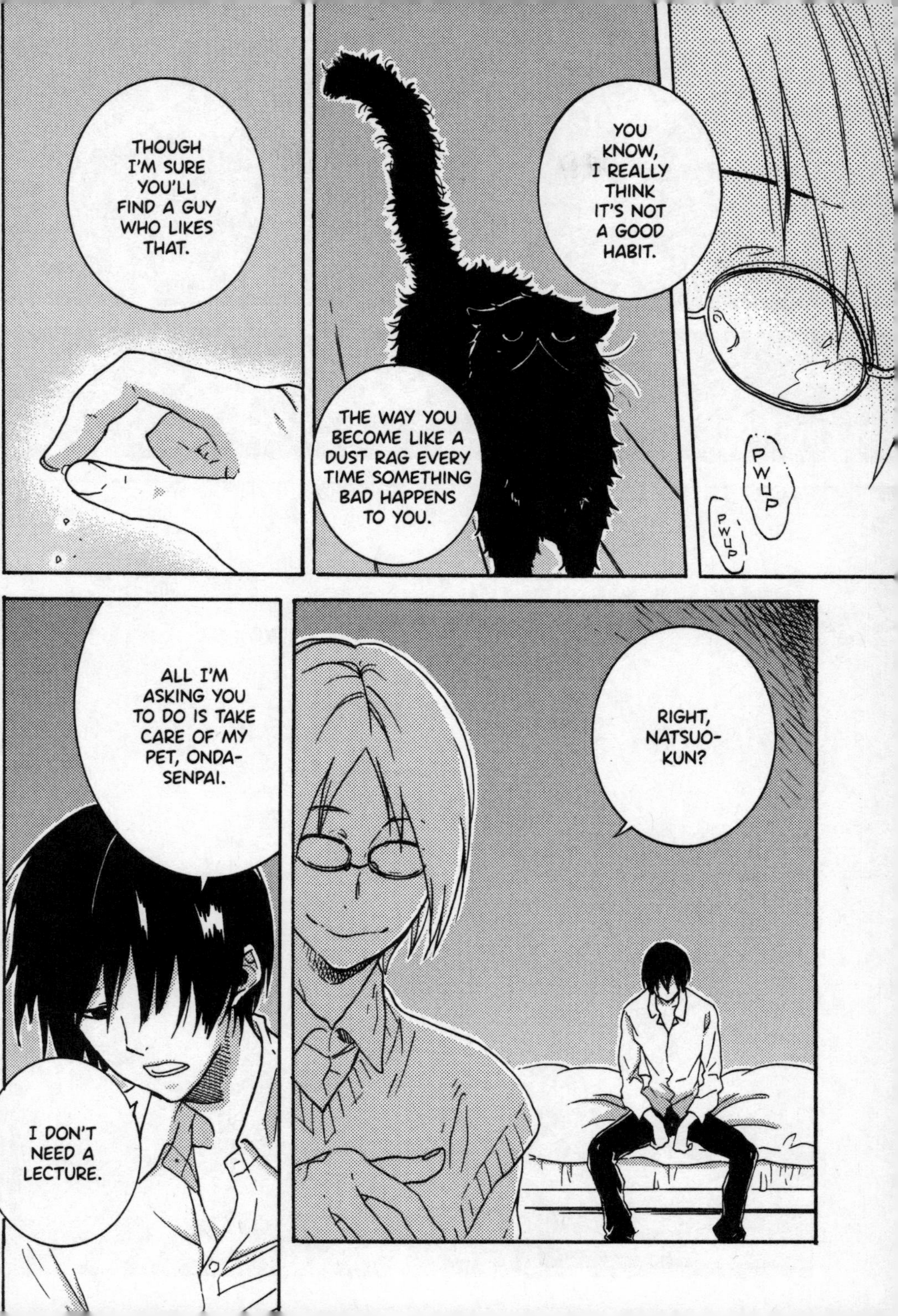
YOU KNOW, I REALLY THINK IT'S NOT A GOOD HABIT.
PWUP
PWUP
THE WAY YOU BECOME LIKE A DUST RAG EVERY TIME SOMETHING BAD HAPPENS TO YOU.
THOUGH I'M SURE YOU'LL FIND A GUY WHO LIKES THAT.
RIGHT, NATSUO-KUN?
ALL I'M ASKING YOU TO DO IS TAKE CARE OF MY PET, ONDA-SENPAI.
I DON'T NEED A LECTURE.

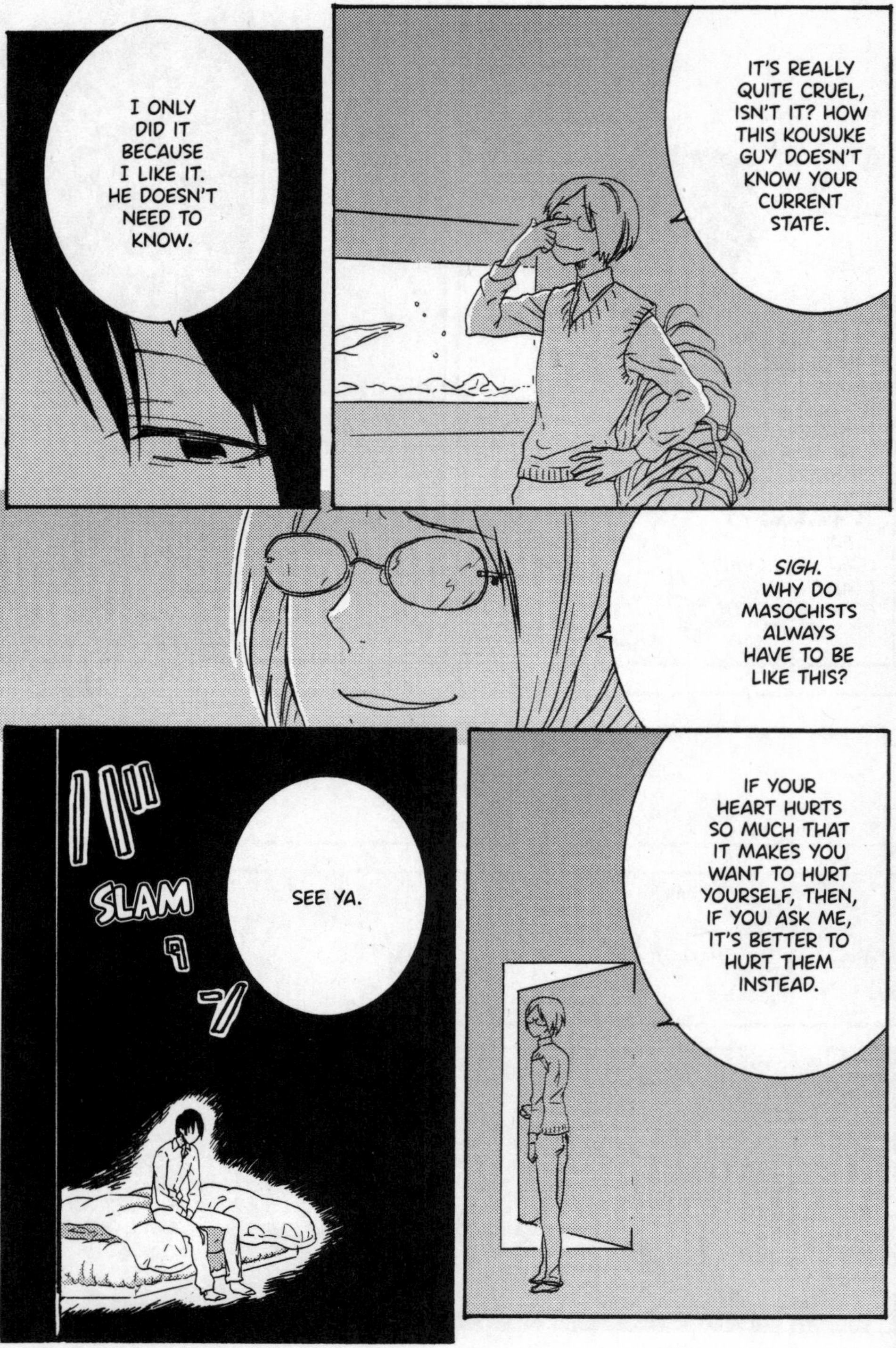
IT'S REALLY QUITE CRUEL, ISN'T IT? HOW THIS KOUSUKE GUY DOESN'T KNOW YOUR CURRENT STATE.
I ONLY DID IT BECAUSE I LIKE IT. HE DOESN'T NEED TO KNOW.
SIGH. WHY DO MASOCHISTS ALWAYS HAVE TO BE LIKE THIS?
IF YOUR HEART HURTS SO MUCH THAT IT MAKES YOU WANT TO HURT YOURSELF, THEN, IF YOU ASK ME, IT'S BETTER TO HURT THEM INSTEAD.
SEE YA.
SLAM

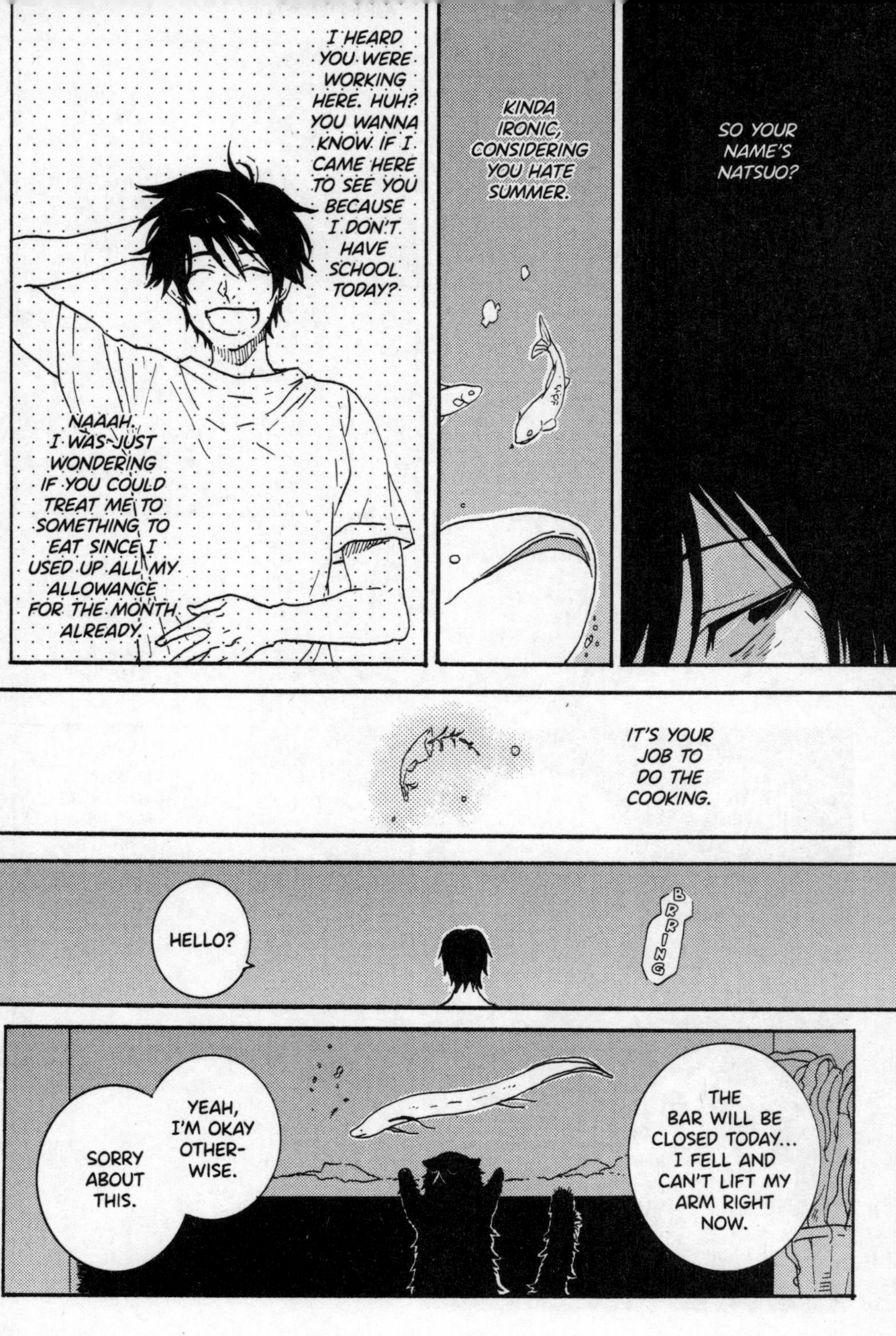

SO YOUR NAME'S NATSUO?
KINDA IRONIC, CONSIDERING YOU HATE SUMMER.
I HEARD YOU WERE WORKING HERE. HUH? YOU WANNA KNOW IF I CAME HERE TO SEE YOU BECAUSE I DON'T HAVE SCHOOL TODAY?
NAAAH. I WAS JUST WONDERING IF YOU COULD TREAT ME TO SOMETHING TO EAT SINCE I USED UP ALL MY ALLOWANCE FOR THE MONTH ALREADY.
IT'S YOUR JOB TO DO THE COOKING.
BRRING
HELLO?
THE BAR WILL BE CLOSED TODAY... I FELL AND CAN'T LIFT MY ARM RIGHT NOW.
YEAH, I'M OKAY OTHER-WISE.
SORRY ABOUT THIS.

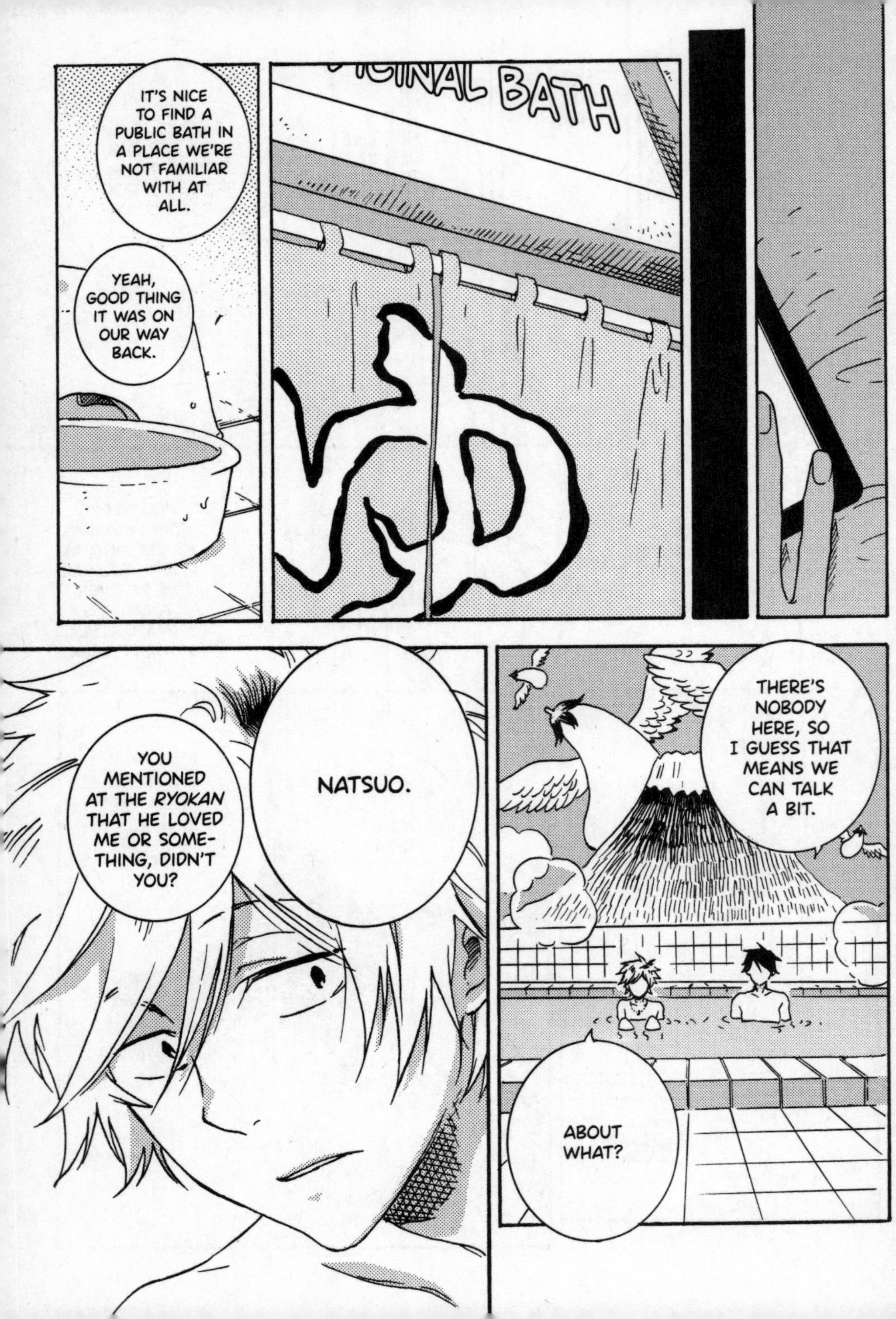
ICINAL BATH
IT'S NICE TO FIND A PUBLIC BATH IN A PLACE WE'RE NOT FAMILIAR WITH AT ALL.
YEAH, GOOD THING IT WAS ON OUR WAY BACK.
THERE'S NOBODY HERE, SO I GUESS THAT MEANS WE CAN TALK A BIT.
ABOUT WHAT?
NATSUO.
YOU MENTIONED AT THE *RYOKAN* THAT HE LOVED ME OR SOME-THING, DIDN'T YOU?

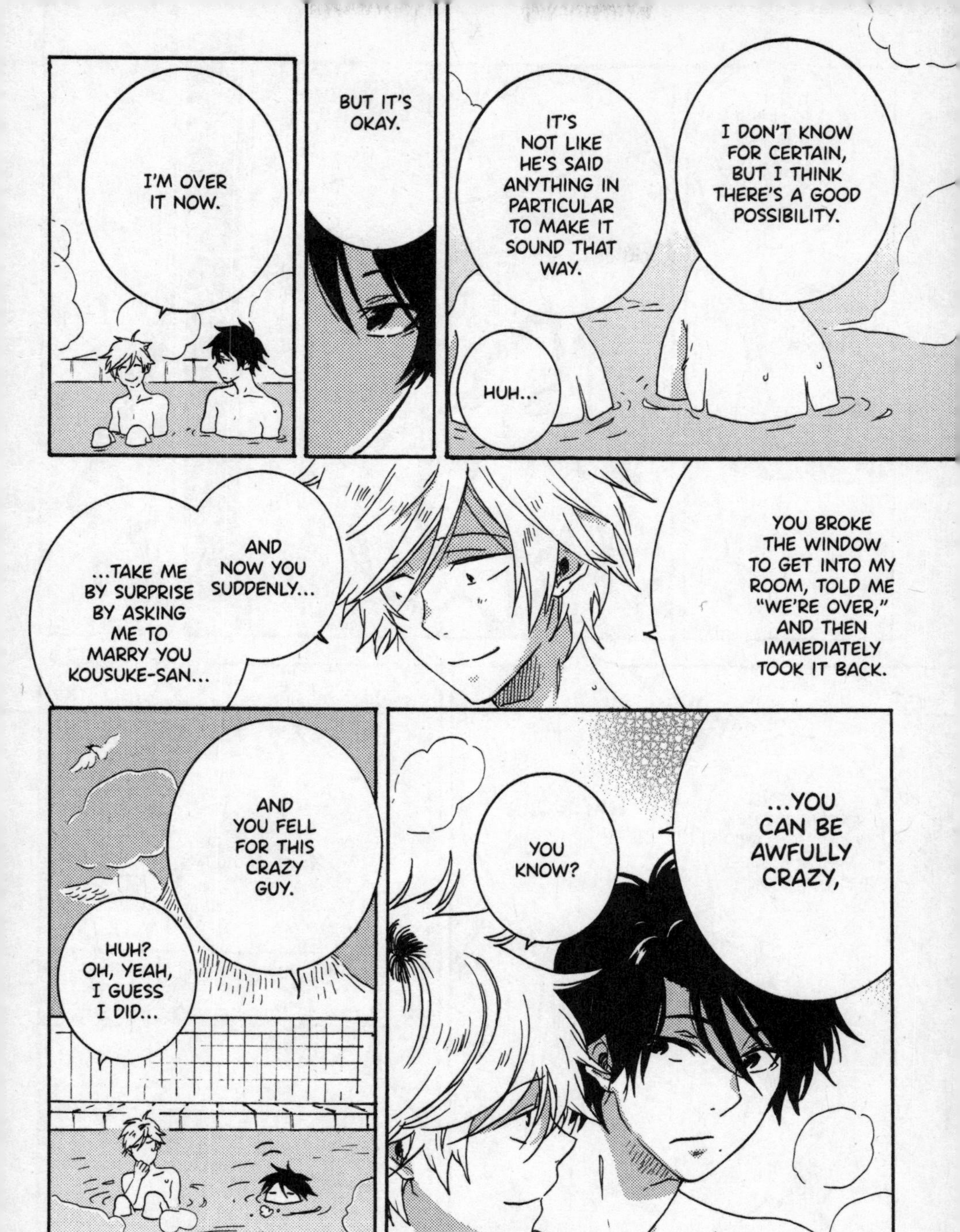
I DON'T KNOW FOR CERTAIN, BUT I THINK THERE'S A GOOD POSSIBILITY.
IT'S NOT LIKE HE'S SAID ANYTHING IN PARTICULAR TO MAKE IT SOUND THAT WAY.
HUH...
BUT IT'S OKAY.
I'M OVER IT NOW.
YOU BROKE THE WINDOW TO GET INTO MY ROOM, TOLD ME "WE'RE OVER," AND THEN IMMEDIATELY TOOK IT BACK.
AND NOW YOU SUDDENLY...
...TAKE ME BY SURPRISE BY ASKING ME TO MARRY YOU KOUSUKE-SAN...
...YOU CAN BE AWFULLY CRAZY,
YOU KNOW?
AND YOU FELL FOR THIS CRAZY GUY.
HUH? OH, YEAH, I GUESS I DID...

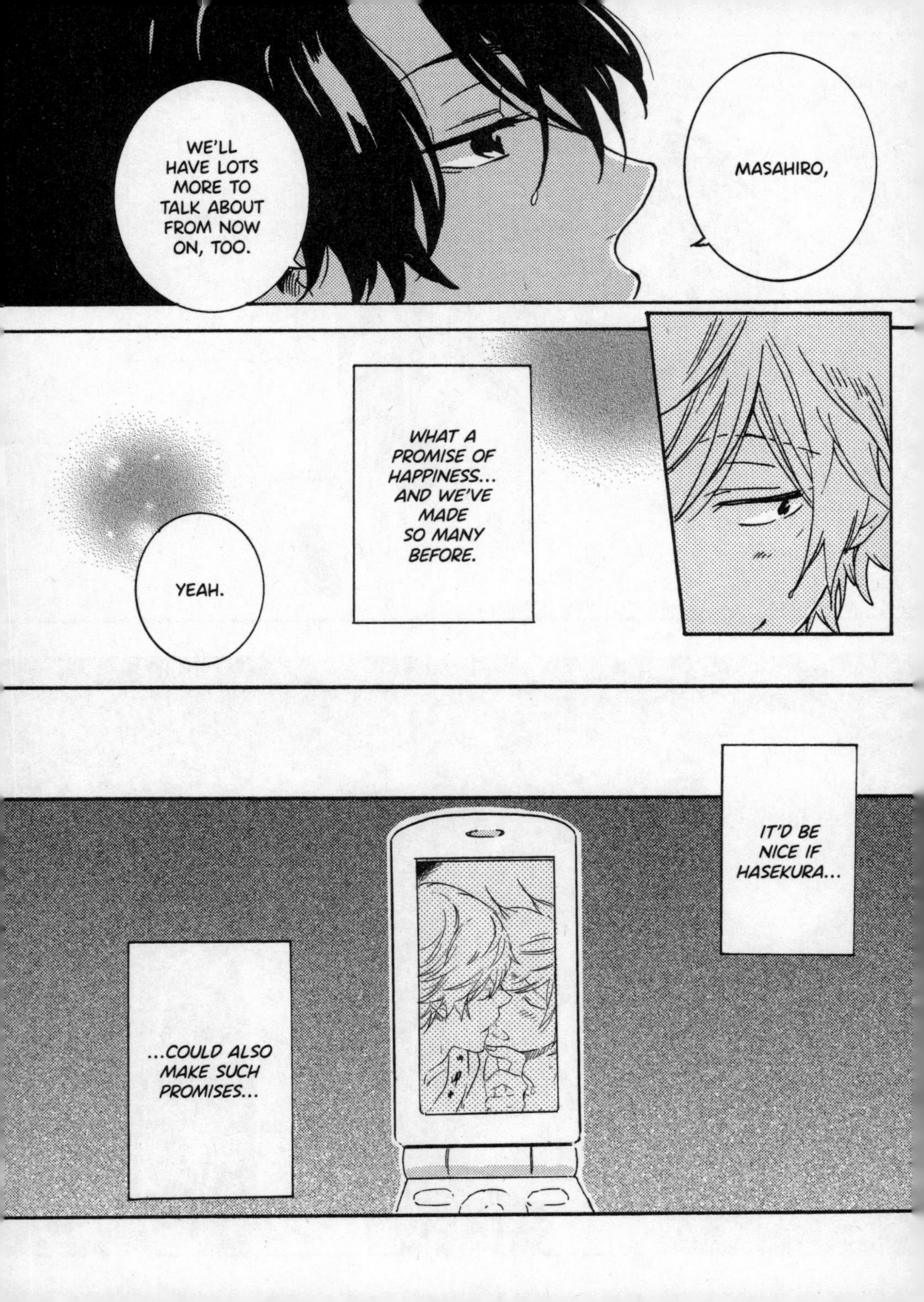
MASAHIRO,
WE'LL HAVE LOTS MORE TO TALK ABOUT FROM NOW ON, TOO.
WHAT A PROMISE OF HAPPINESS... AND WE'VE MADE SO MANY BEFORE.
YEAH.
IT'D BE NICE IF HASEKURA...
...COULD ALSO MAKE SUCH PROMISES...

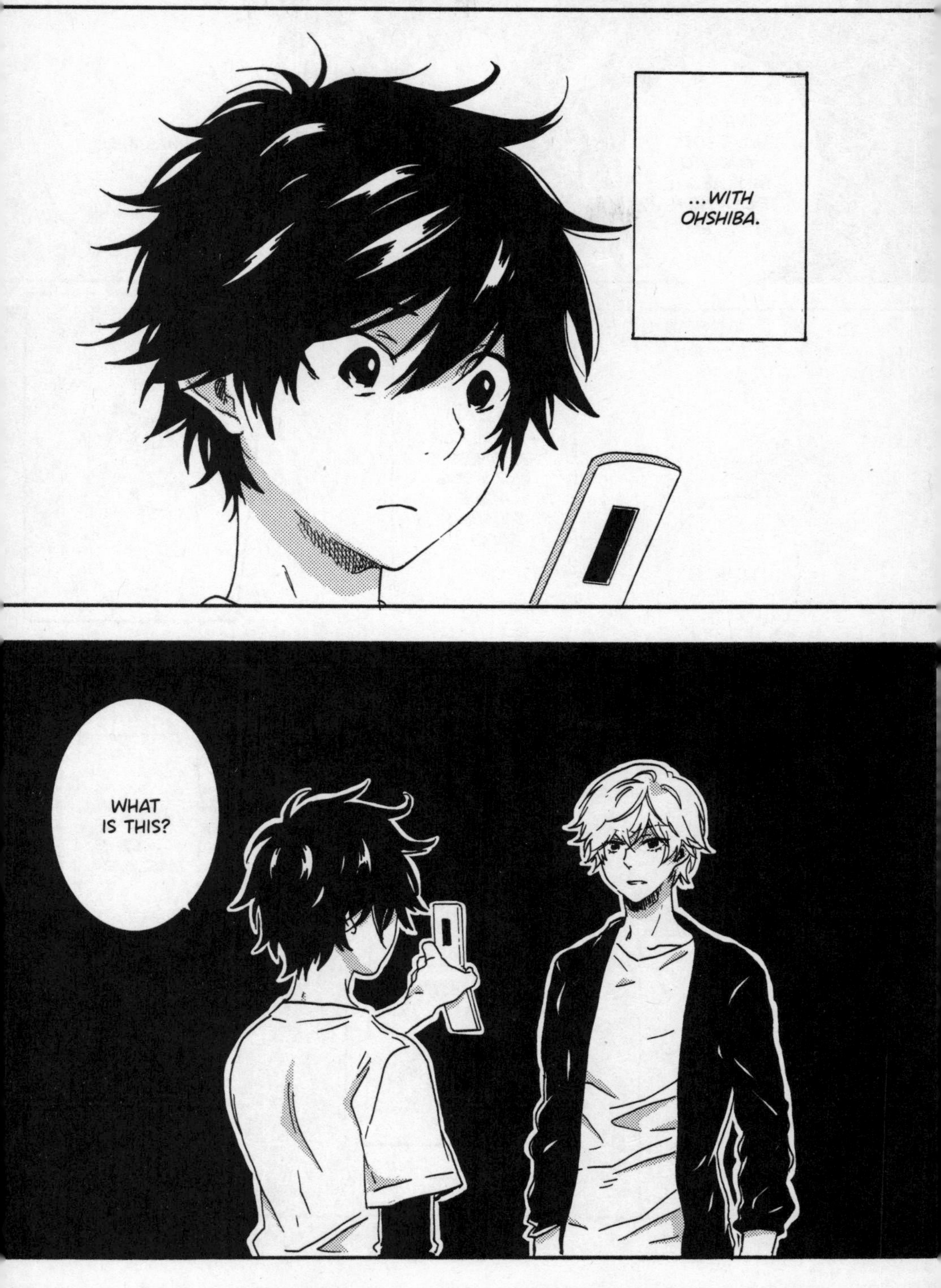
...WITH OHSHIBA.
WHAT IS THIS?

Hitorijime
My Hero

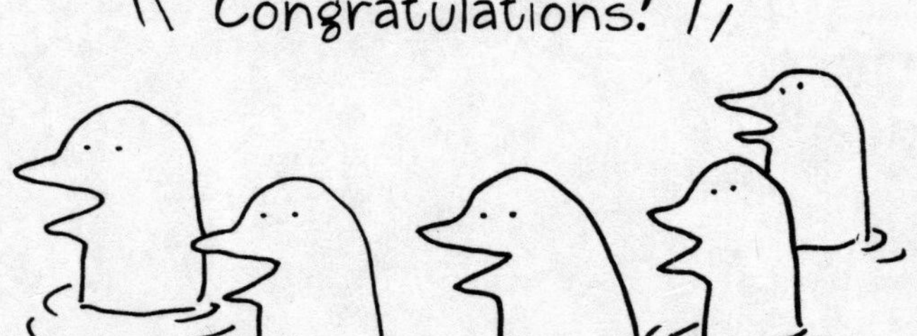
\\ Congratulations! //

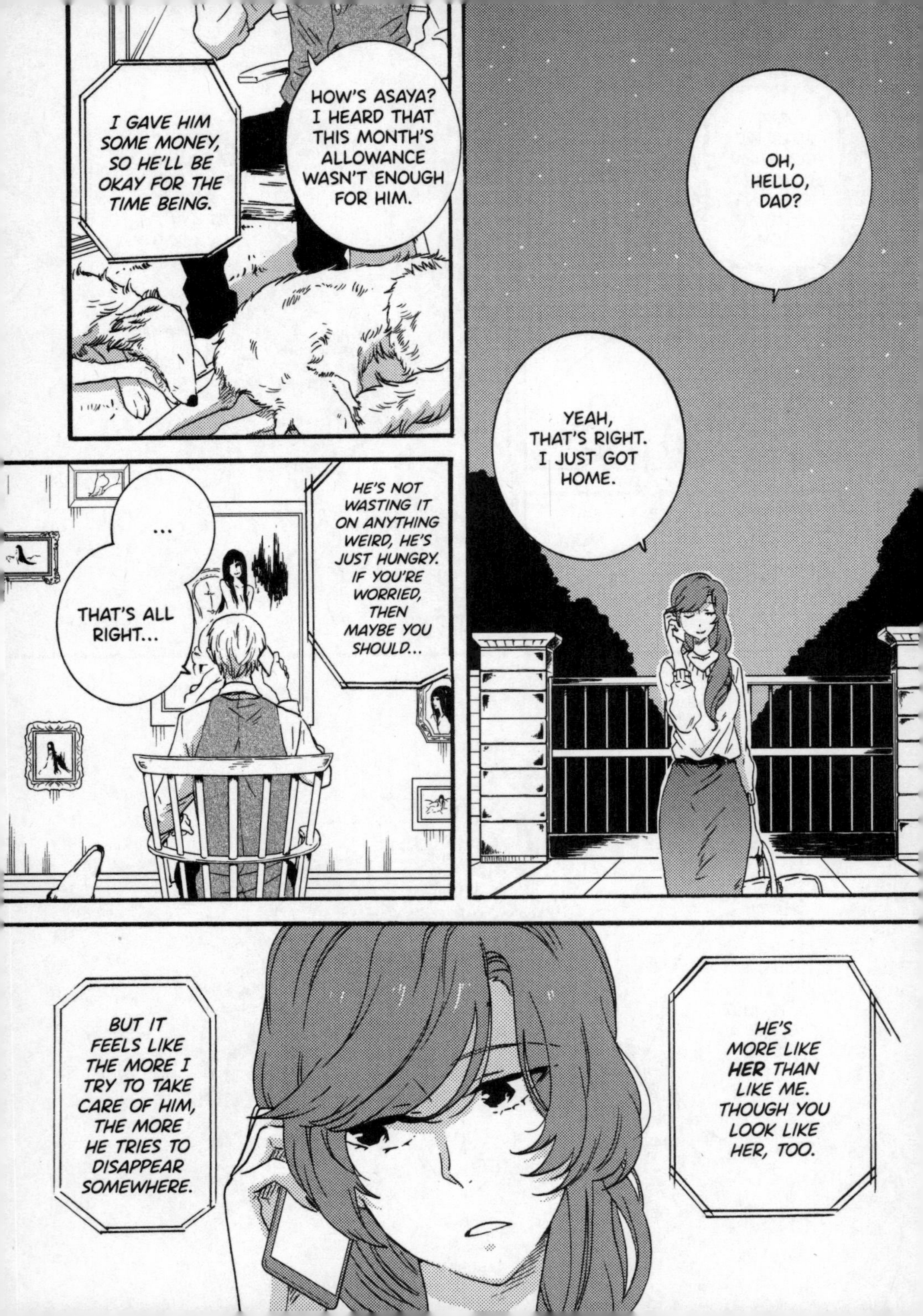
OH, HELLO, DAD?
YEAH, THAT'S RIGHT. I JUST GOT HOME.
HOW'S ASAYA? I HEARD THAT THIS MONTH'S ALLOWANCE WASN'T ENOUGH FOR HIM.
I GAVE HIM SOME MONEY, SO HE'LL BE OKAY FOR THE TIME BEING.
HE'S NOT WASTING IT ON ANYTHING WEIRD, HE'S JUST HUNGRY. IF YOU'RE WORRIED, THEN MAYBE YOU SHOULD...
...
THAT'S ALL RIGHT...
HE'S MORE LIKE **HER** THAN LIKE ME. THOUGH YOU LOOK LIKE HER, TOO.
BUT IT FEELS LIKE THE MORE I TRY TO TAKE CARE OF HIM, THE MORE HE TRIES TO DISAPPEAR SOMEWHERE.

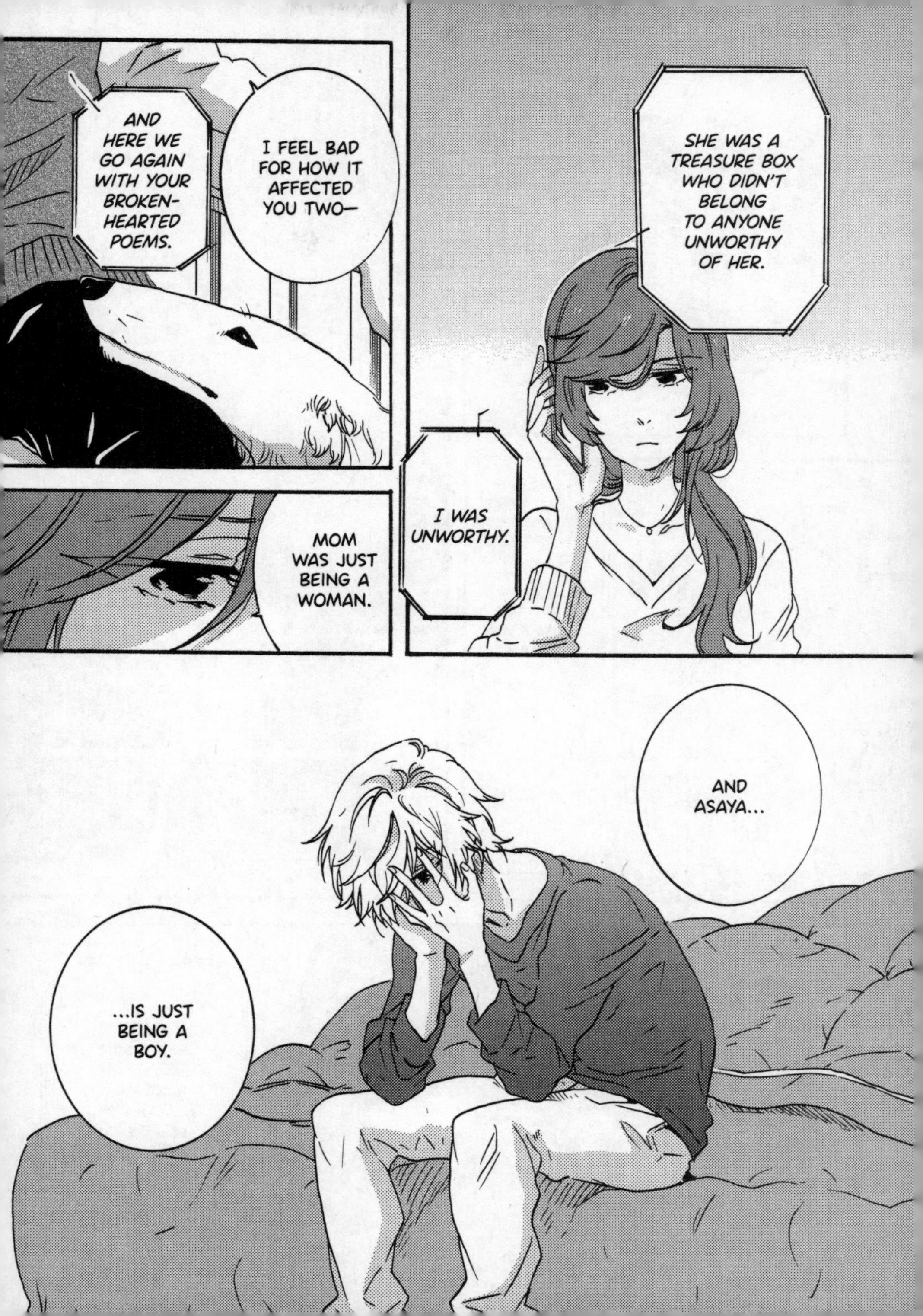
SHE WAS A TREASURE BOX WHO DIDN'T BELONG TO ANYONE UNWORTHY OF HER.
I WAS UNWORTHY.
I FEEL BAD FOR HOW IT AFFECTED YOU TWO—
AND HERE WE GO AGAIN WITH YOUR BROKEN-HEARTED POEMS.
MOM WAS JUST BEING A WOMAN.
AND ASAYA...
...IS JUST BEING A BOY.

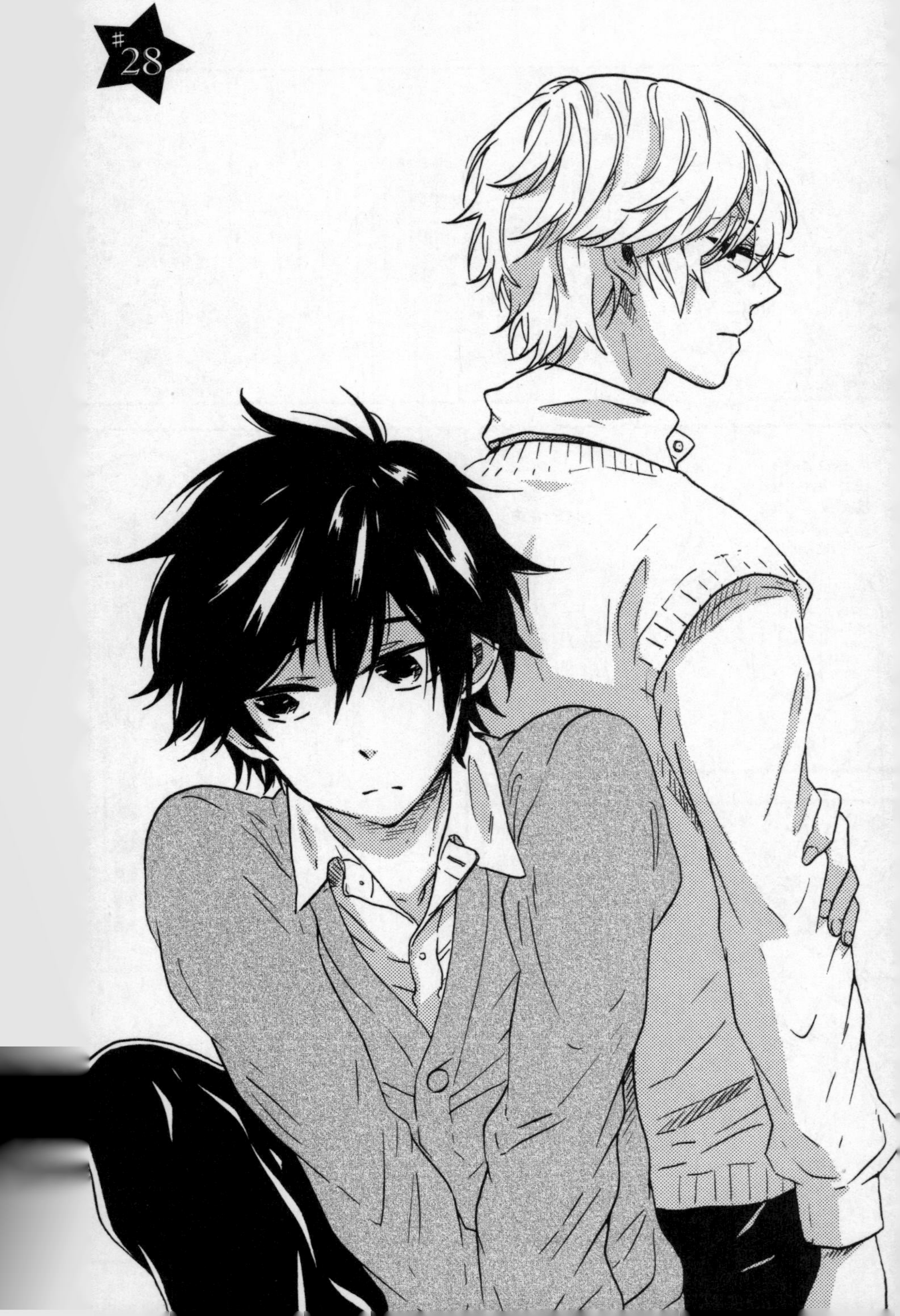
#28

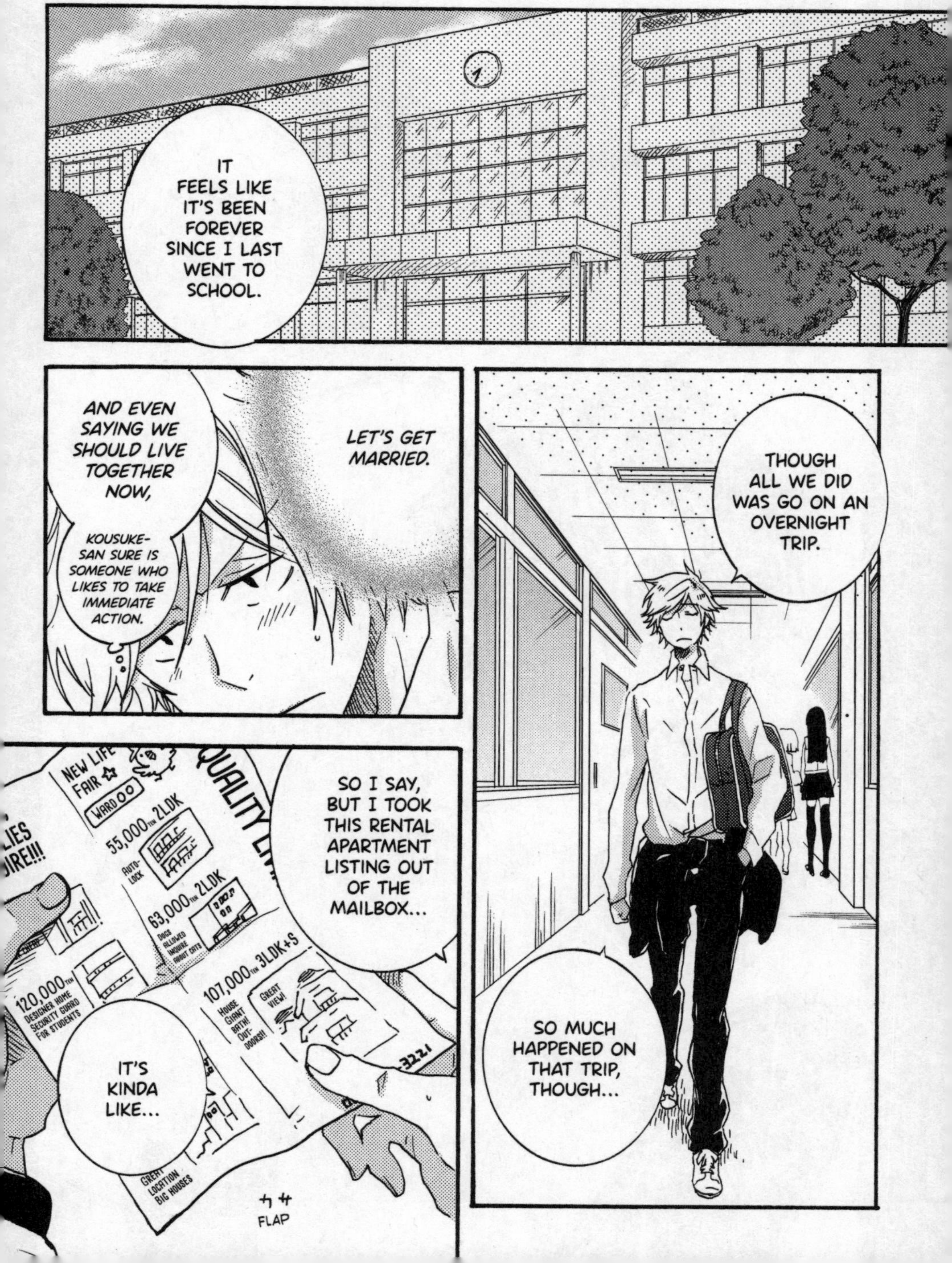
IT FEELS LIKE IT'S BEEN FOREVER SINCE I LAST WENT TO SCHOOL.
THOUGH ALL WE DID WAS GO ON AN OVERNIGHT TRIP.
SO MUCH HAPPENED ON THAT TRIP, THOUGH...
LET'S GET MARRIED.
AND EVEN SAYING WE SHOULD LIVE TOGETHER NOW,
KOUSUKE-SAN SURE IS SOMEONE WHO LIKES TO TAKE IMMEDIATE ACTION.
SO I SAY, BUT I TOOK THIS RENTAL APARTMENT LISTING OUT OF THE MAILBOX...
IT'S KINDA LIKE...
NEW LIFE FAIR
FLAP

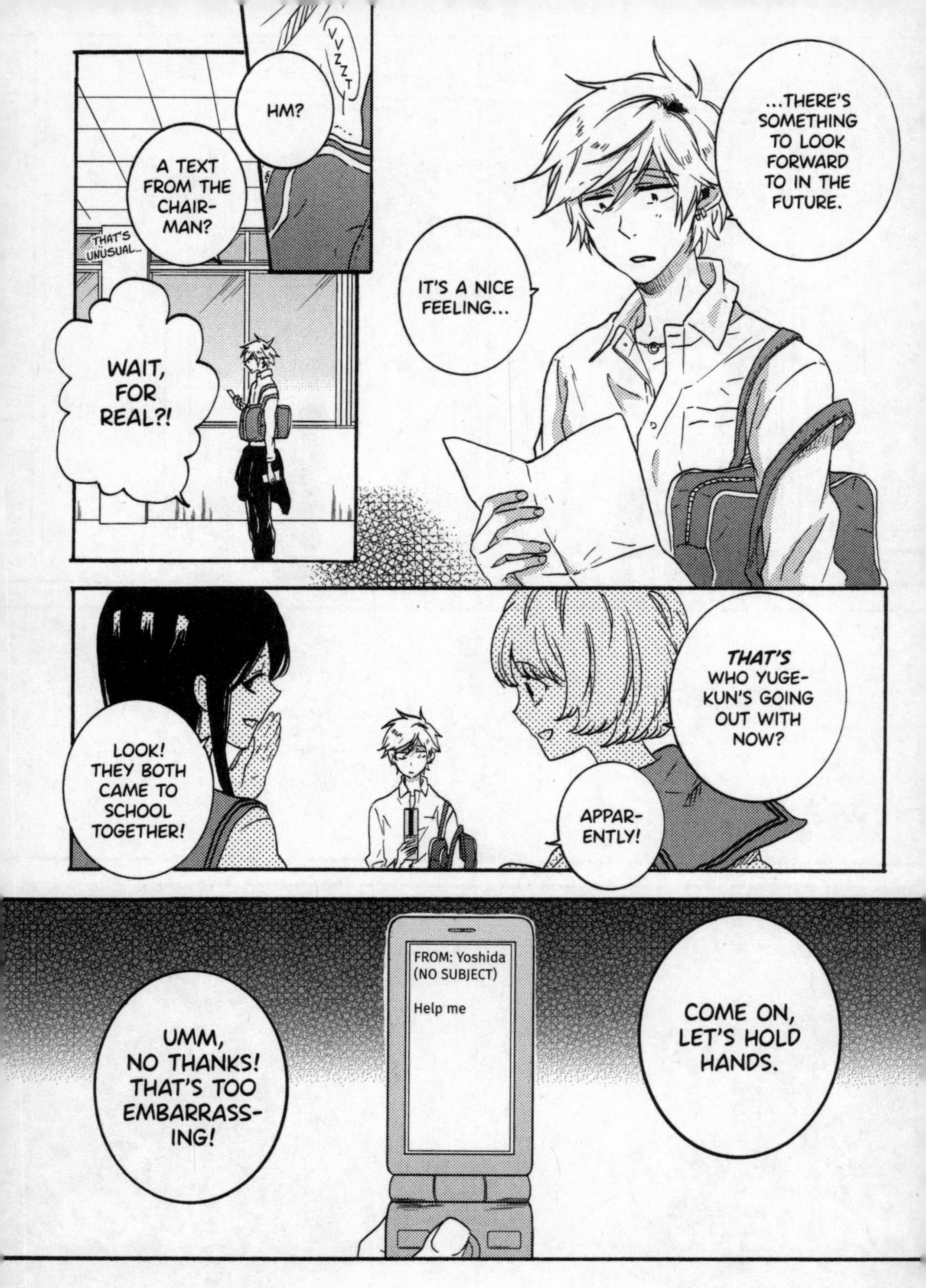
...THERE'S SOMETHING TO LOOK FORWARD TO IN THE FUTURE.
IT'S A NICE FEELING...
VVZZZT
HM?
A TEXT FROM THE CHAIRMAN?
THAT'S UNUSUAL...
WAIT, FOR REAL?!
THAT'S WHO YUGE-KUN'S GOING OUT WITH NOW?
APPARENTLY!
LOOK! THEY BOTH CAME TO SCHOOL TOGETHER!
COME ON, LET'S HOLD HANDS.
FROM: Yoshida
(NO SUBJECT)
Help me
UMM, NO THANKS! THAT'S TOO EMBARRASSING!

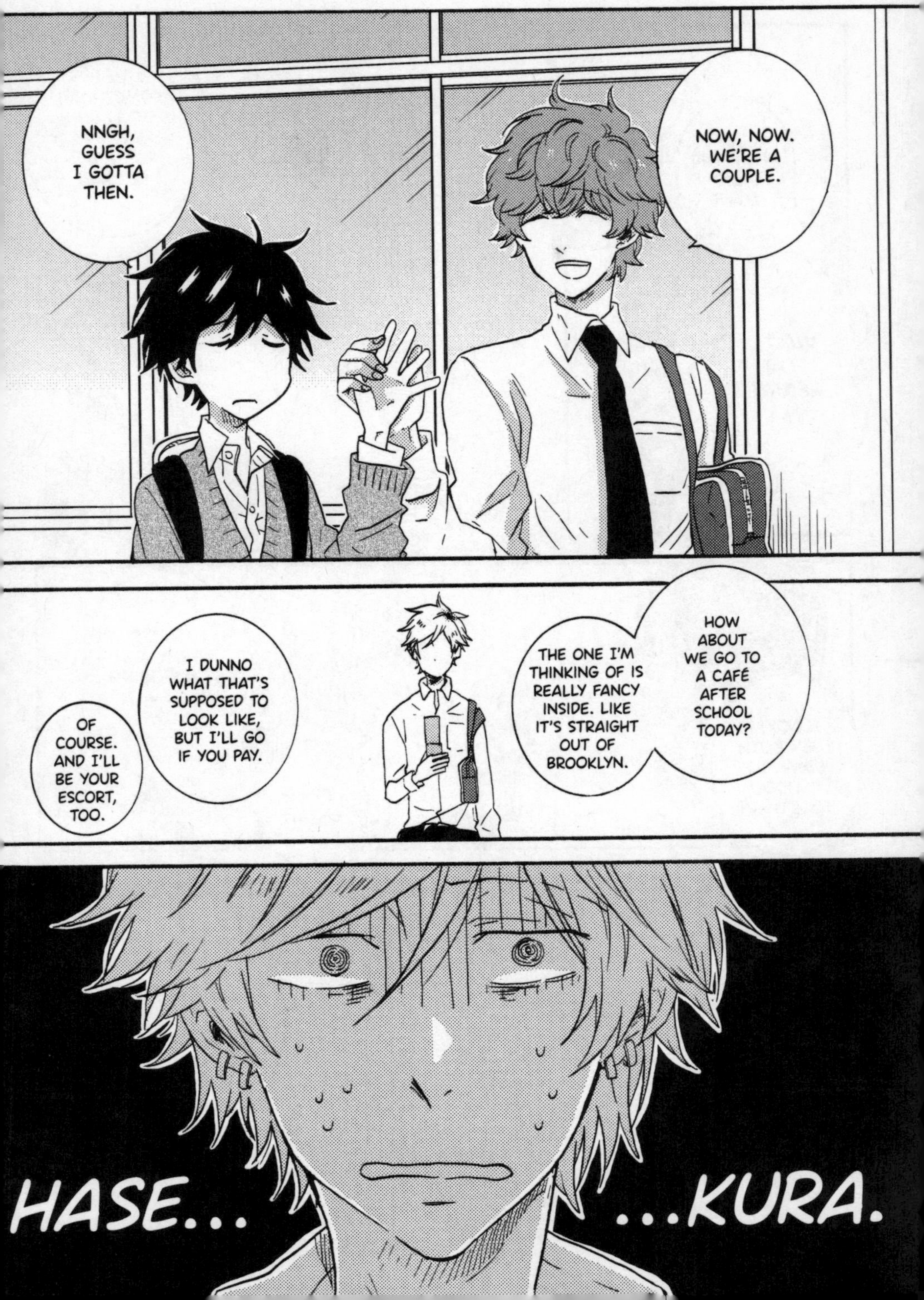
NOW, NOW. WE'RE A COUPLE.
NNGH, GUESS I GOTTA THEN.
HOW ABOUT WE GO TO A CAFÉ AFTER SCHOOL TODAY?
THE ONE I'M THINKING OF IS REALLY FANCY INSIDE. LIKE IT'S STRAIGHT OUT OF BROOKLYN.
I DUNNO WHAT THAT'S SUPPOSED TO LOOK LIKE, BUT I'LL GO IF YOU PAY.
OF COURSE. AND I'LL BE YOUR ESCORT, TOO.
HASE...
...KURA.

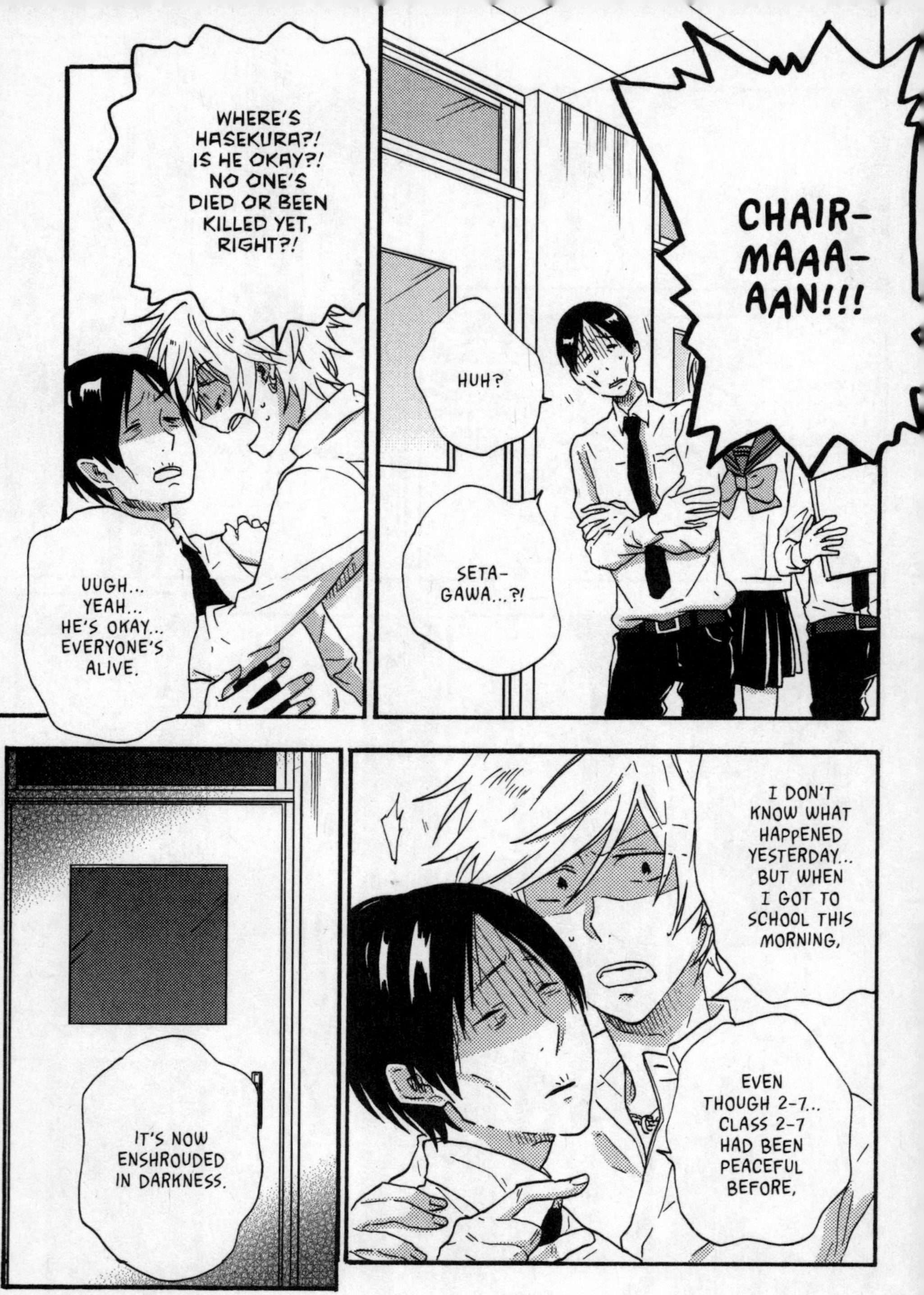
CHAIR-MAAAA-AAN!!!
HUH?
SETA-GAWA...?!
WHERE'S HASEKURA?! IS HE OKAY?! NO ONE'S DIED OR BEEN KILLED YET, RIGHT?!
UUGH... YEAH... HE'S OKAY... EVERYONE'S ALIVE.
I DON'T KNOW WHAT HAPPENED YESTERDAY... BUT WHEN I GOT TO SCHOOL THIS MORNING,
EVEN THOUGH 2-7... CLASS 2-7 HAD BEEN PEACEFUL BEFORE,
IT'S NOW ENSHROUDED IN DARKNESS.

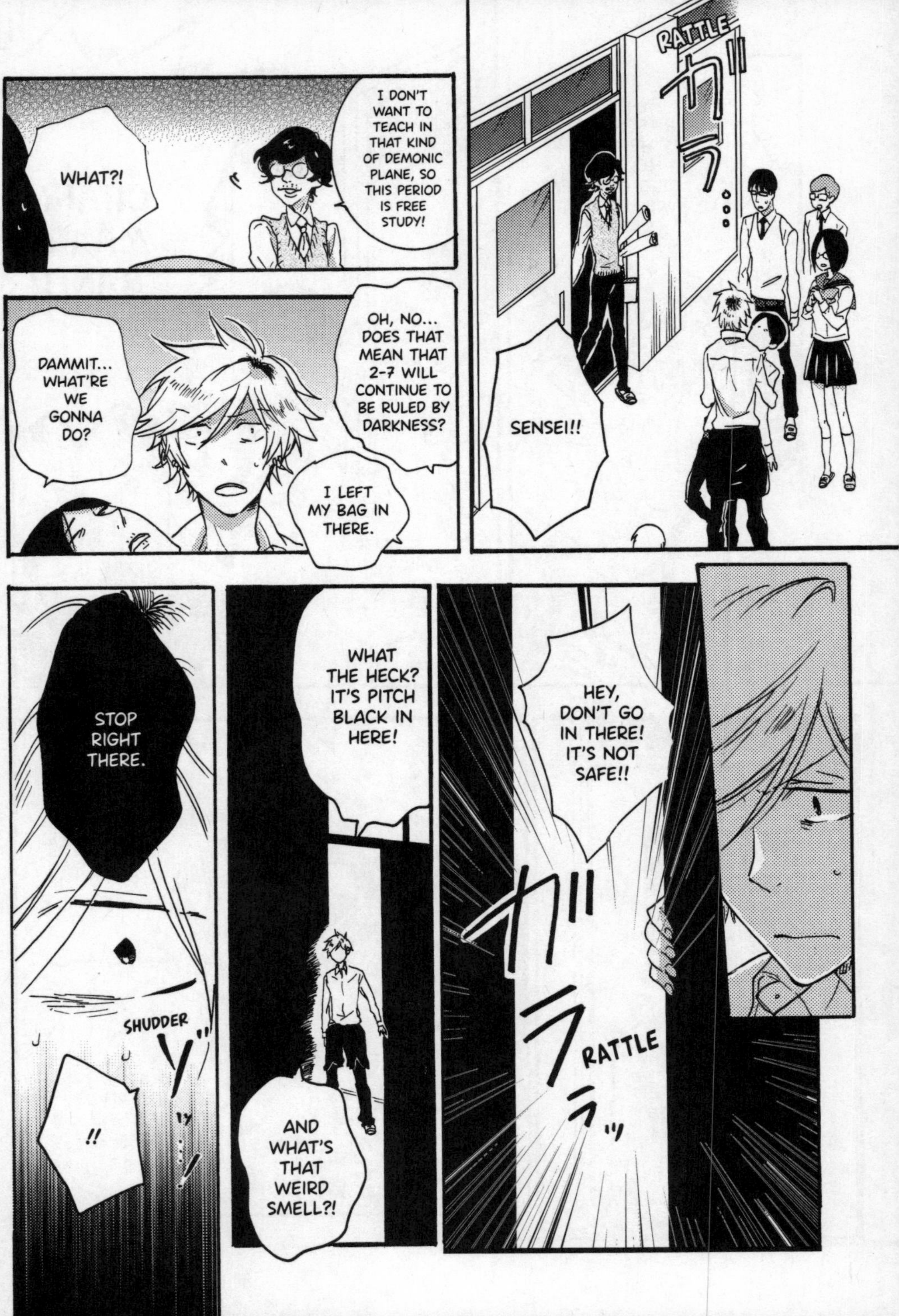
RATTLE
カラ
SENSEI!!
I DON'T WANT TO TEACH IN THAT KIND OF DEMONIC PLANE, SO THIS PERIOD IS FREE STUDY!
WHAT?!
OH, NO... DOES THAT MEAN THAT 2-7 WILL CONTINUE TO BE RULED BY DARKNESS?
DAMMIT... WHAT'RE WE GONNA DO?
I LEFT MY BAG IN THERE.
HEY, DON'T GO IN THERE! IT'S NOT SAFE!!
ガラ
ラッ
RATTLE
WHAT THE HECK? IT'S PITCH BLACK IN HERE!
AND WHAT'S THAT WEIRD SMELL?!
STOP RIGHT THERE.
SHUDDER
!!

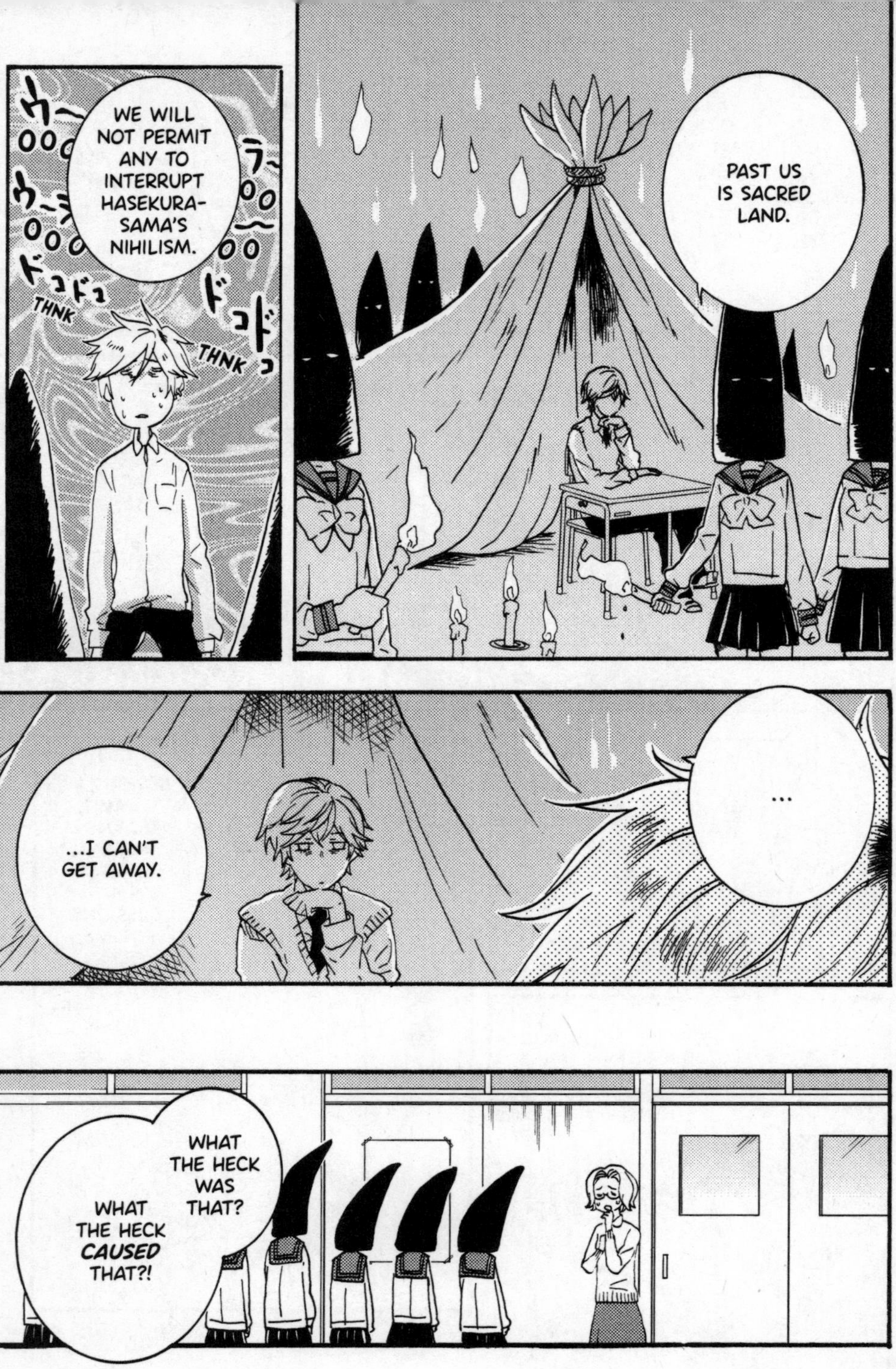
PAST US IS SACRED LAND.
WE WILL NOT PERMIT ANY TO INTERRUPT HASEKURA-SAMA'S NIHILISM.
THNK
THNK
...
...I CAN'T GET AWAY.
WHAT THE HECK WAS THAT?
WHAT THE HECK *CAUSED* THAT?!

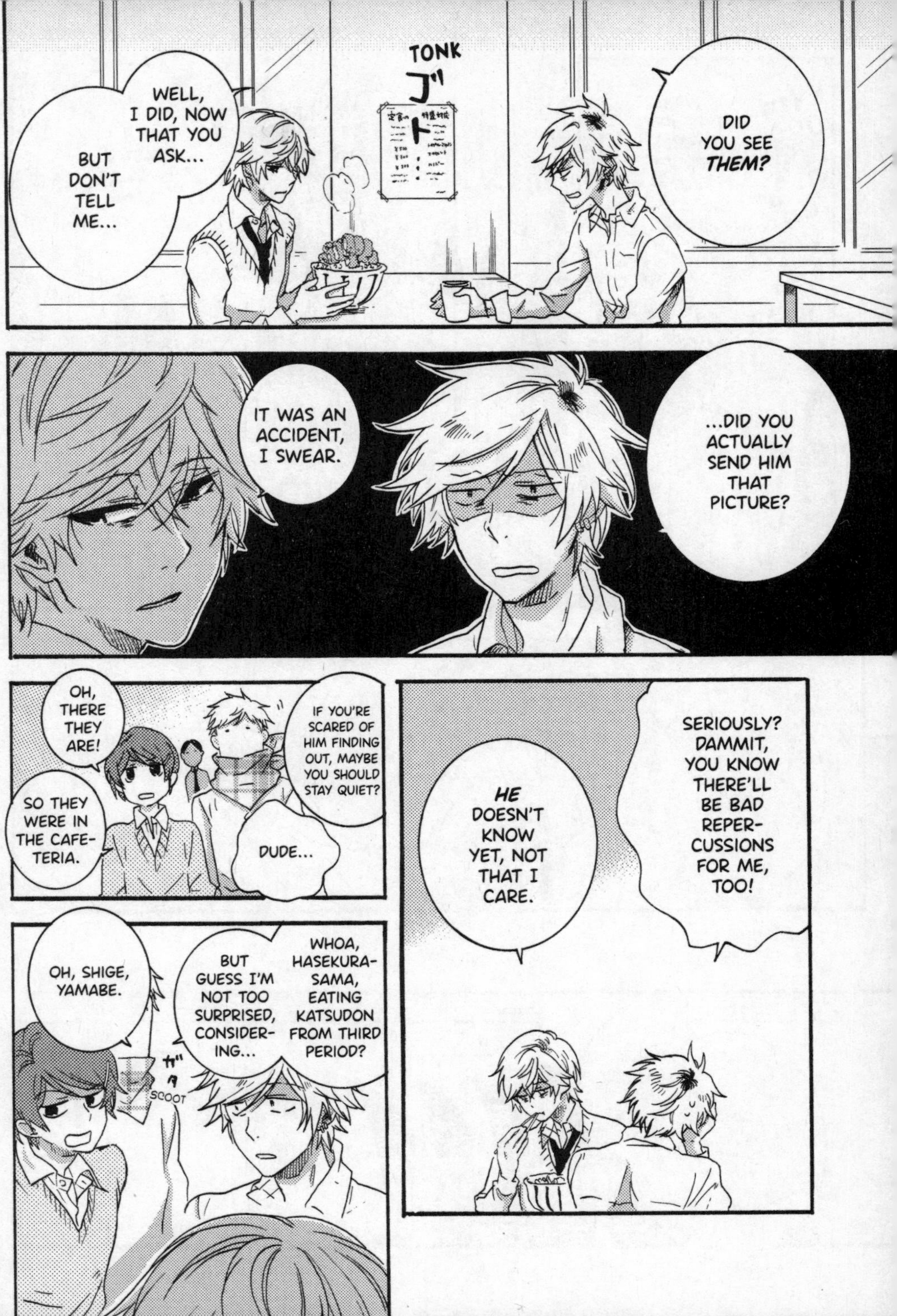
DID YOU SEE *THEM?*
TONK
ゴト
WELL, I DID, NOW THAT YOU ASK...
BUT DON'T TELL ME...
...DID YOU ACTUALLY SEND HIM THAT PICTURE?
IT WAS AN ACCIDENT, I SWEAR.
SERIOUSLY? DAMMIT, YOU KNOW THERE'LL BE BAD REPERCUSSIONS FOR ME, TOO!
HE DOESN'T KNOW YET, NOT THAT I CARE.
IF YOU'RE SCARED OF HIM FINDING OUT, MAYBE YOU SHOULD STAY QUIET?
OH, THERE THEY ARE!
DUDE...
SO THEY WERE IN THE CAFETERIA.
WHOA, HASEKURA-SAMA, EATING KATSUDON FROM THIRD PERIOD?
BUT GUESS I'M NOT TOO SURPRISED, CONSIDERING...
ガタ
SCOOT
OH, SHIGE, YAMABE.

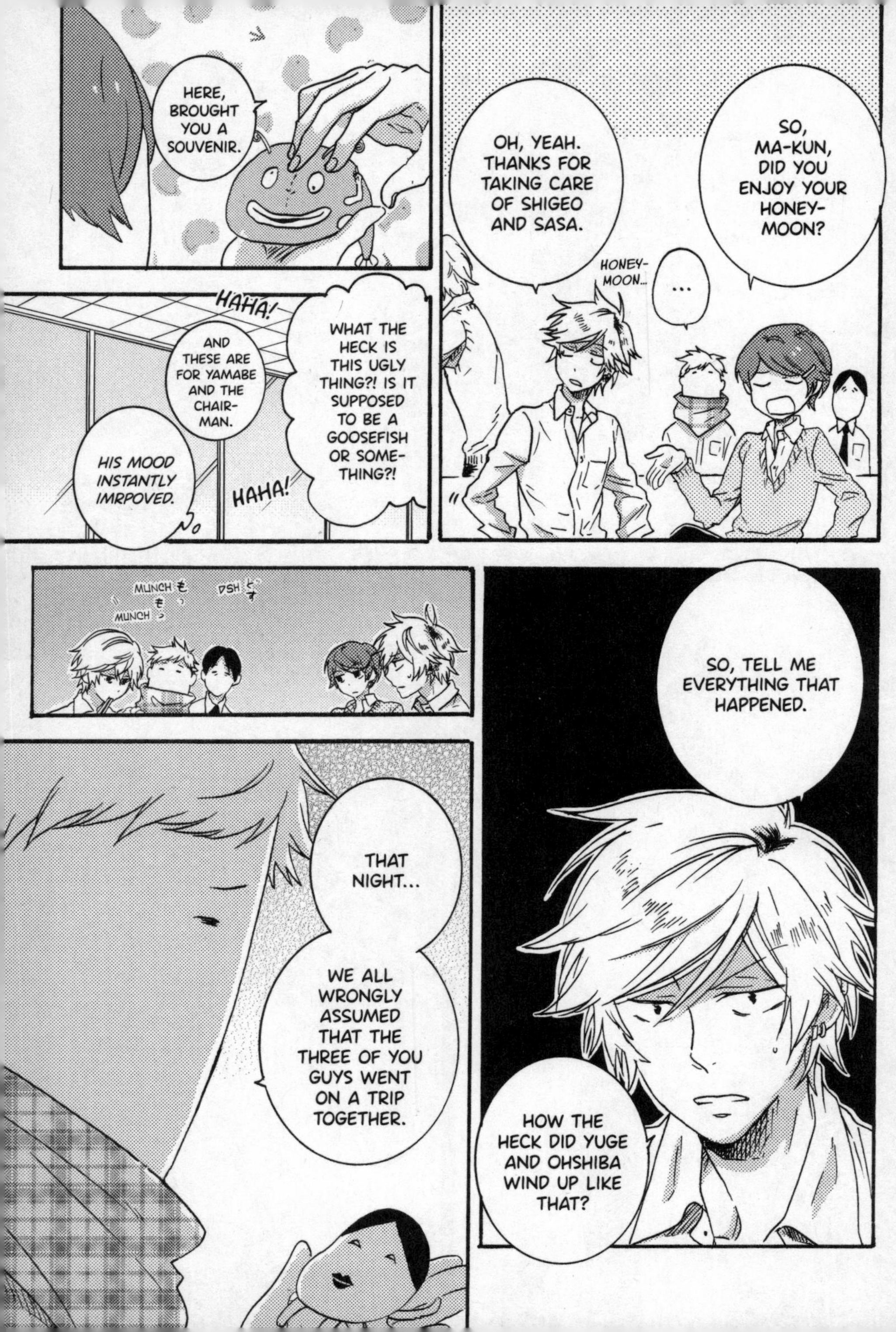
SO, MA-KUN, DID YOU ENJOY YOUR HONEY-MOON?
...
HONEY-MOON...
OH, YEAH. THANKS FOR TAKING CARE OF SHIGEO AND SASA.
HERE, BROUGHT YOU A SOUVENIR.
WHAT THE HECK IS THIS UGLY THING?! IS IT SUPPOSED TO BE A GOOSEFISH OR SOME-THING?!
HAHA!
AND THESE ARE FOR YAMABE AND THE CHAIR-MAN.
HAHA!
HIS MOOD INSTANTLY IMRPOVED.
SO, TELL ME EVERYTHING THAT HAPPENED.
HOW THE HECK DID YUGE AND OHSHIBA WIND UP LIKE THAT?
DSH
MUNCH
MUNCH
THAT NIGHT...
WE ALL WRONGLY ASSUMED THAT THE THREE OF YOU GUYS WENT ON A TRIP TOGETHER.

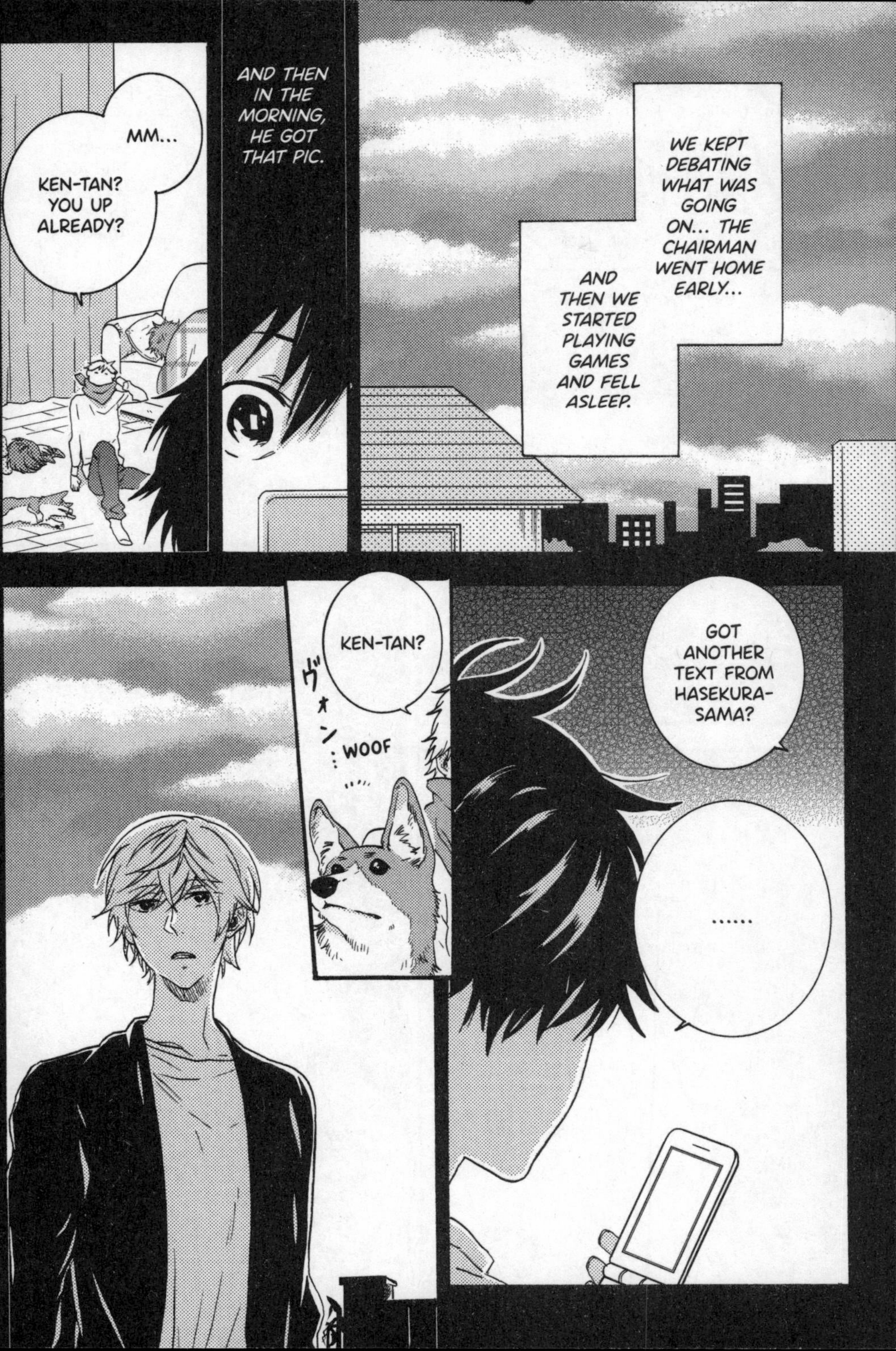
WE KEPT DEBATING WHAT WAS GOING ON... THE CHAIRMAN WENT HOME EARLY...
AND THEN WE STARTED PLAYING GAMES AND FELL ASLEEP.
AND THEN IN THE MORNING, HE GOT THAT PIC.
MM...
KEN-TAN? YOU UP ALREADY?
GOT ANOTHER TEXT FROM HASEKURA-SAMA?
......
KEN-TAN?
ヴォン…
WOOF

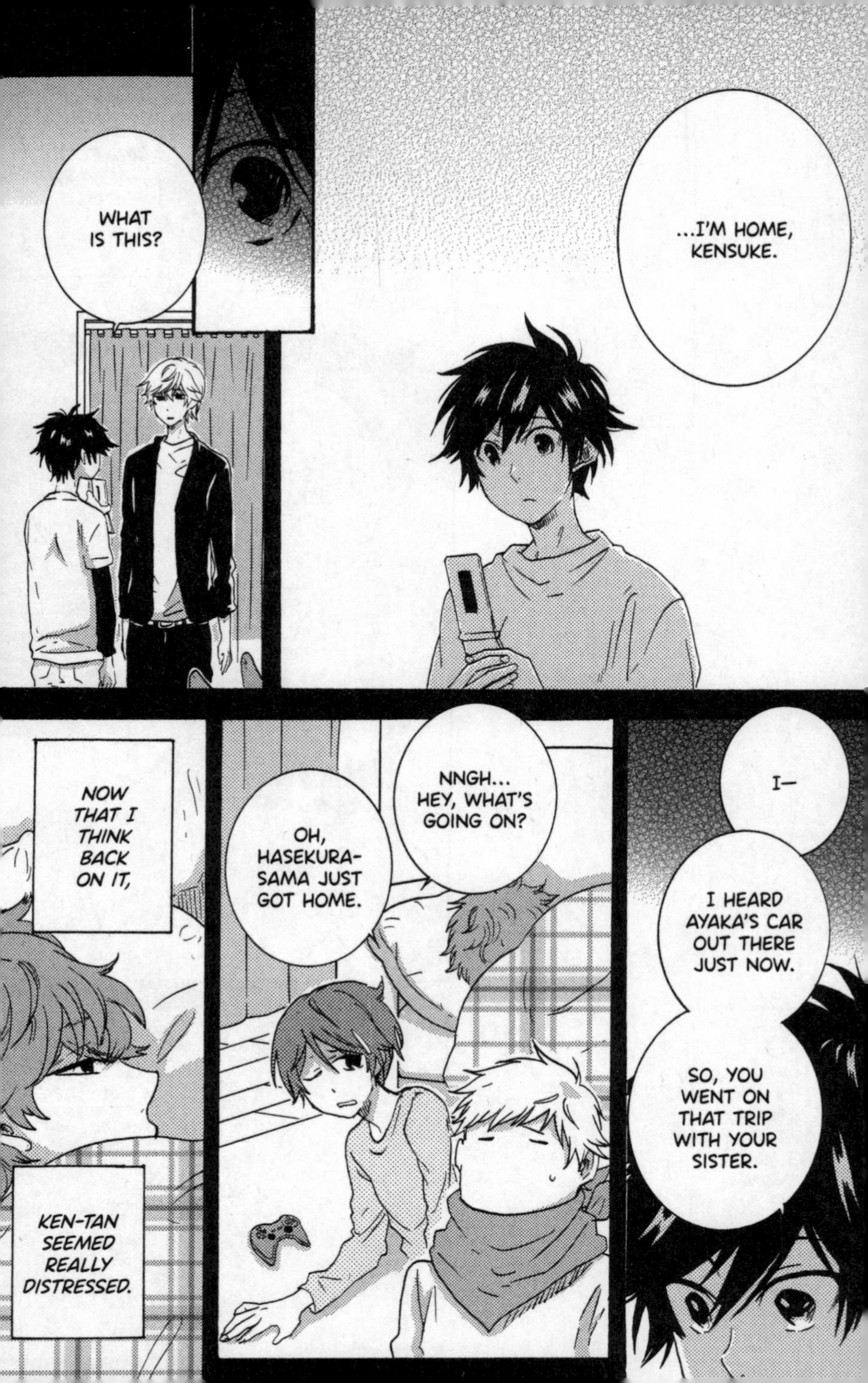
...I'M HOME, KENSUKE.
WHAT IS THIS?
I—
I HEARD AYAKA'S CAR OUT THERE JUST NOW.
SO, YOU WENT ON THAT TRIP WITH YOUR SISTER.
NNGH... HEY, WHAT'S GOING ON?
OH, HASEKURA-SAMA JUST GOT HOME.
NOW THAT I THINK BACK ON IT,
KEN-TAN SEEMED REALLY DISTRESSED.

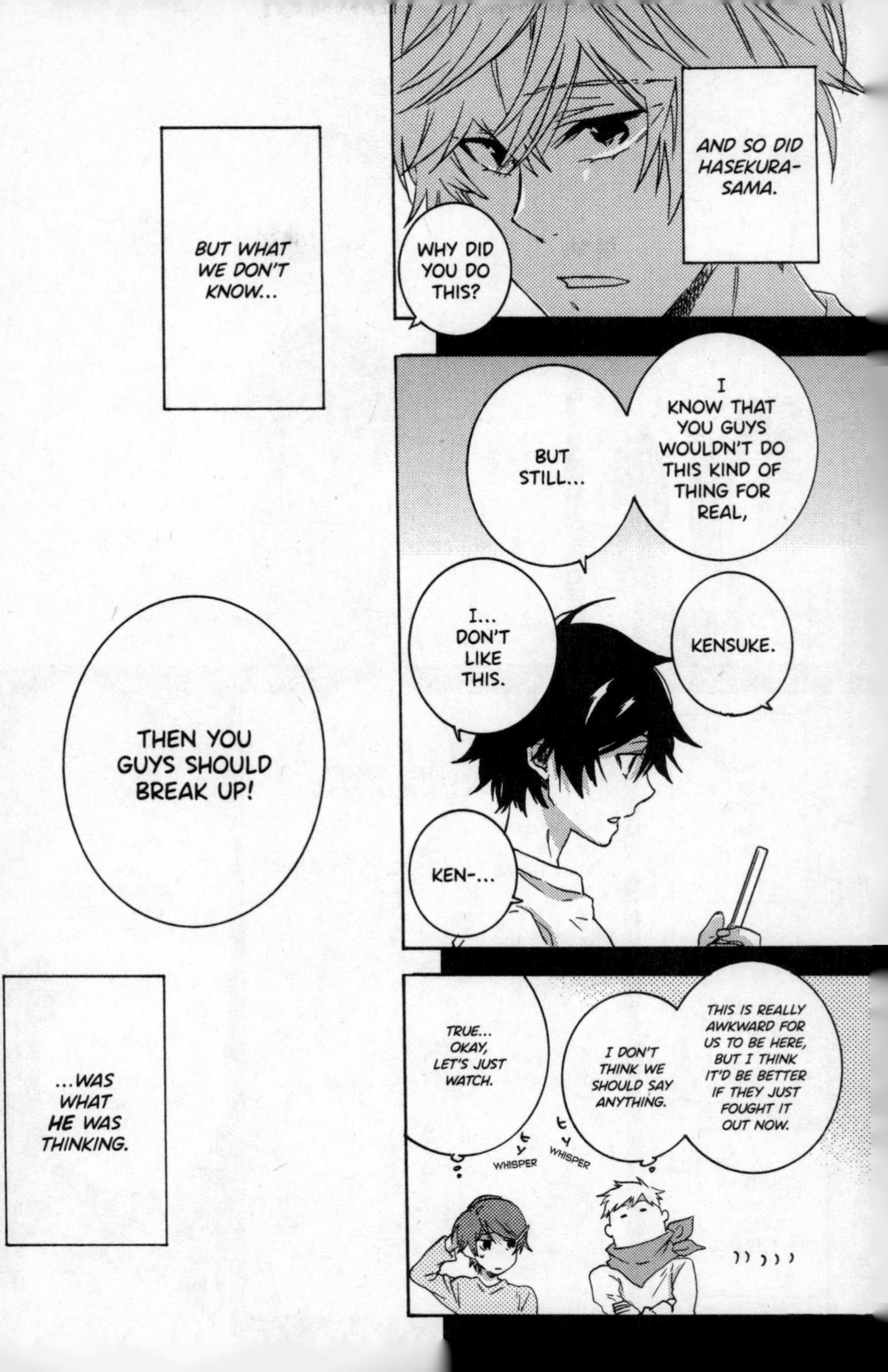
AND SO DID HASEKURA-SAMA.
WHY DID YOU DO THIS?
I KNOW THAT YOU GUYS WOULDN'T DO THIS KIND OF THING FOR REAL,
BUT STILL...
KENSUKE.
I... DON'T LIKE THIS.
KEN-...
THIS IS REALLY AWKWARD FOR US TO BE HERE, BUT I THINK IT'D BE BETTER IF THEY JUST FOUGHT IT OUT NOW.
I DON'T THINK WE SHOULD SAY ANYTHING.
WHISPER
TRUE... OKAY, LET'S JUST WATCH.
WHISPER
BUT WHAT WE DON'T KNOW...
THEN YOU GUYS SHOULD BREAK UP!
...WAS WHAT HE WAS THINKING.

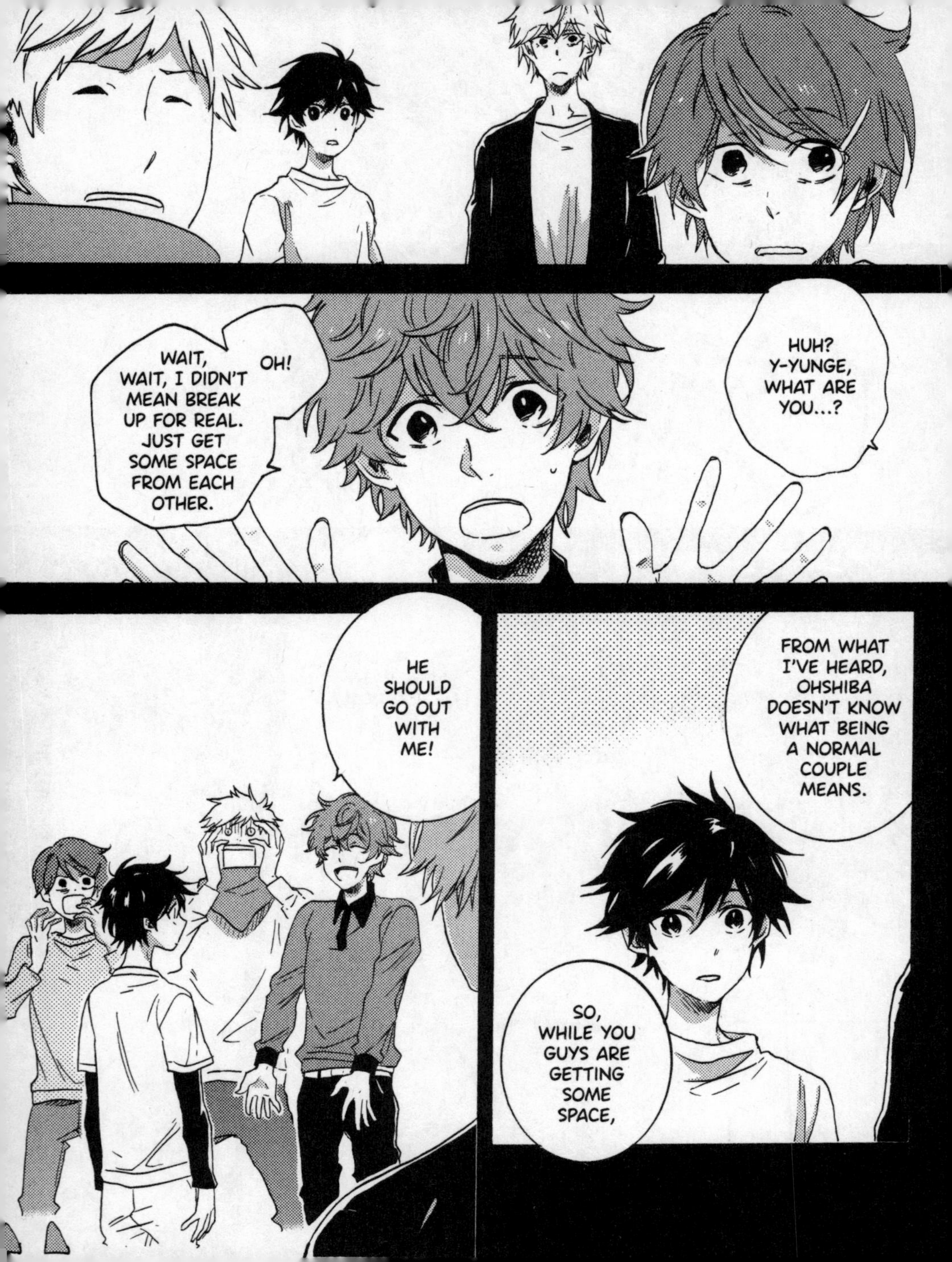
HUH? Y-YUNGE, WHAT ARE YOU...?
OH!
WAIT, WAIT, I DIDN'T MEAN BREAK UP FOR REAL. JUST GET SOME SPACE FROM EACH OTHER.
FROM WHAT I'VE HEARD, OHSHIBA DOESN'T KNOW WHAT BEING A NORMAL COUPLE MEANS.
SO, WHILE YOU GUYS ARE GETTING SOME SPACE,
HE SHOULD GO OUT WITH ME!

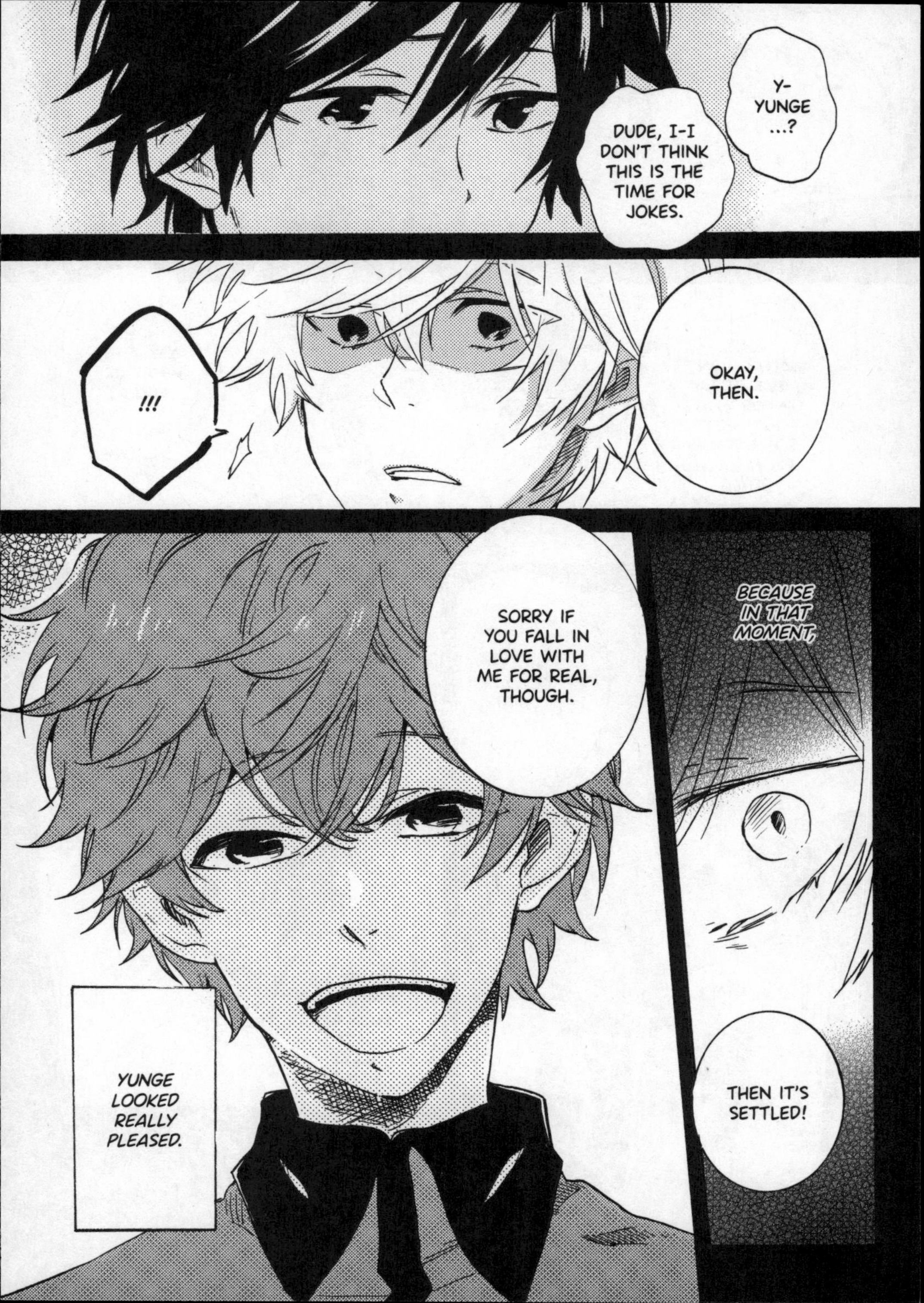
Y- YUNGE ...?
DUDE, I-I DON'T THINK THIS IS THE TIME FOR JOKES.
OKAY, THEN.
!!!
BECAUSE IN THAT MOMENT,
THEN IT'S SETTLED!
SORRY IF YOU FALL IN LOVE WITH ME FOR REAL, THOUGH.
YUNGE LOOKED REALLY PLEASED.

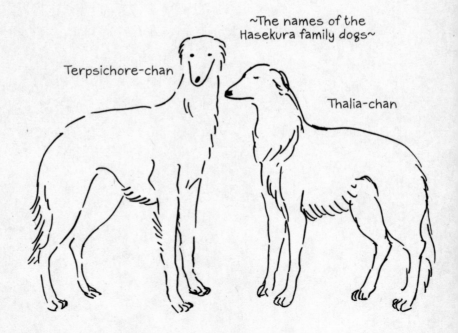

~The names of the
Hasekura family dogs~

Terpsichore-chan

Thalia-chan

Hitorijime
My Hero

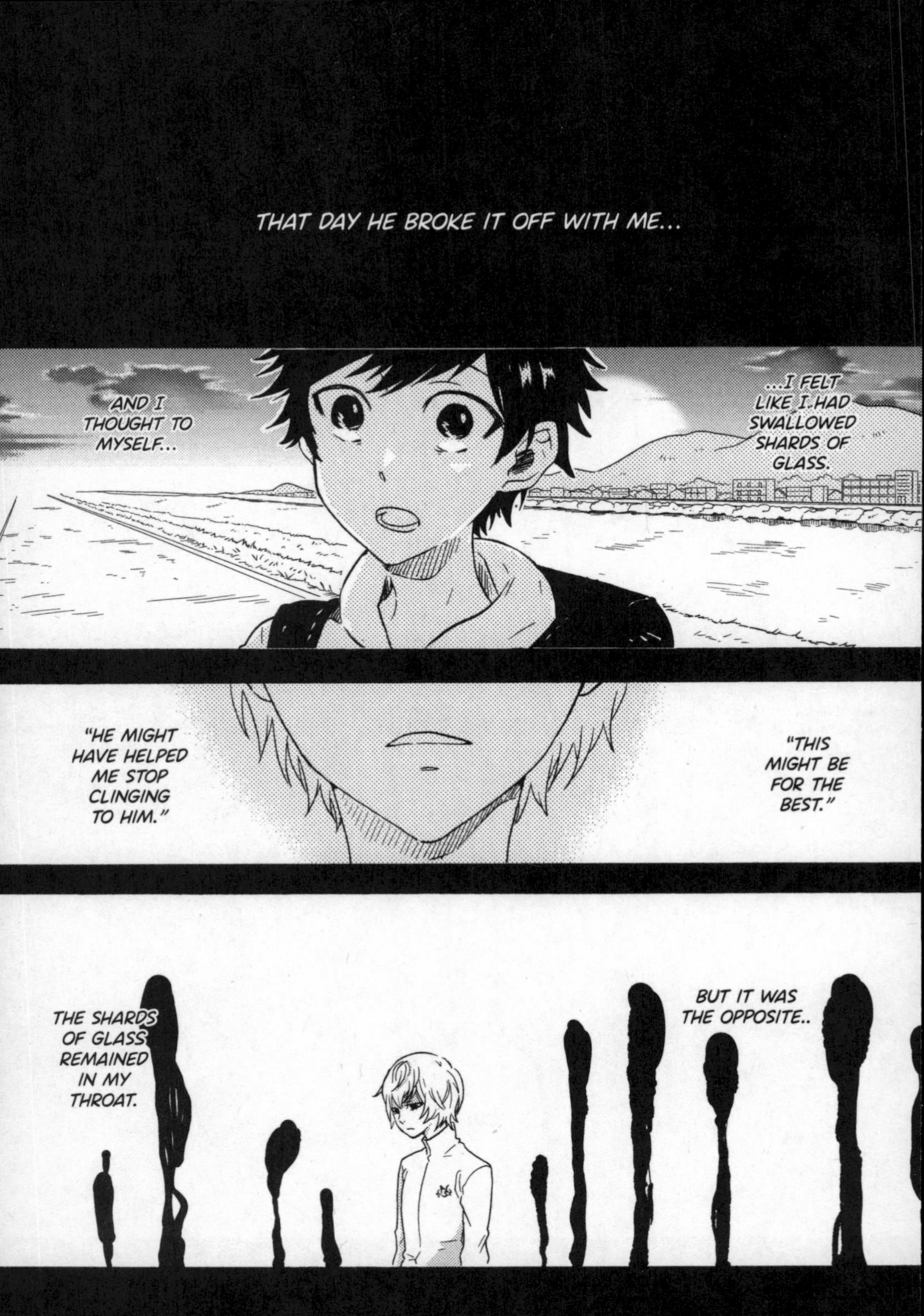
THAT DAY HE BROKE IT OFF WITH ME...
...I FELT LIKE I HAD SWALLOWED SHARDS OF GLASS.
AND I THOUGHT TO MYSELF...
"THIS MIGHT BE FOR THE BEST."
"HE MIGHT HAVE HELPED ME STOP CLINGING TO HIM."
BUT IT WAS THE OPPOSITE..
THE SHARDS OF GLASS REMAINED IN MY THROAT.

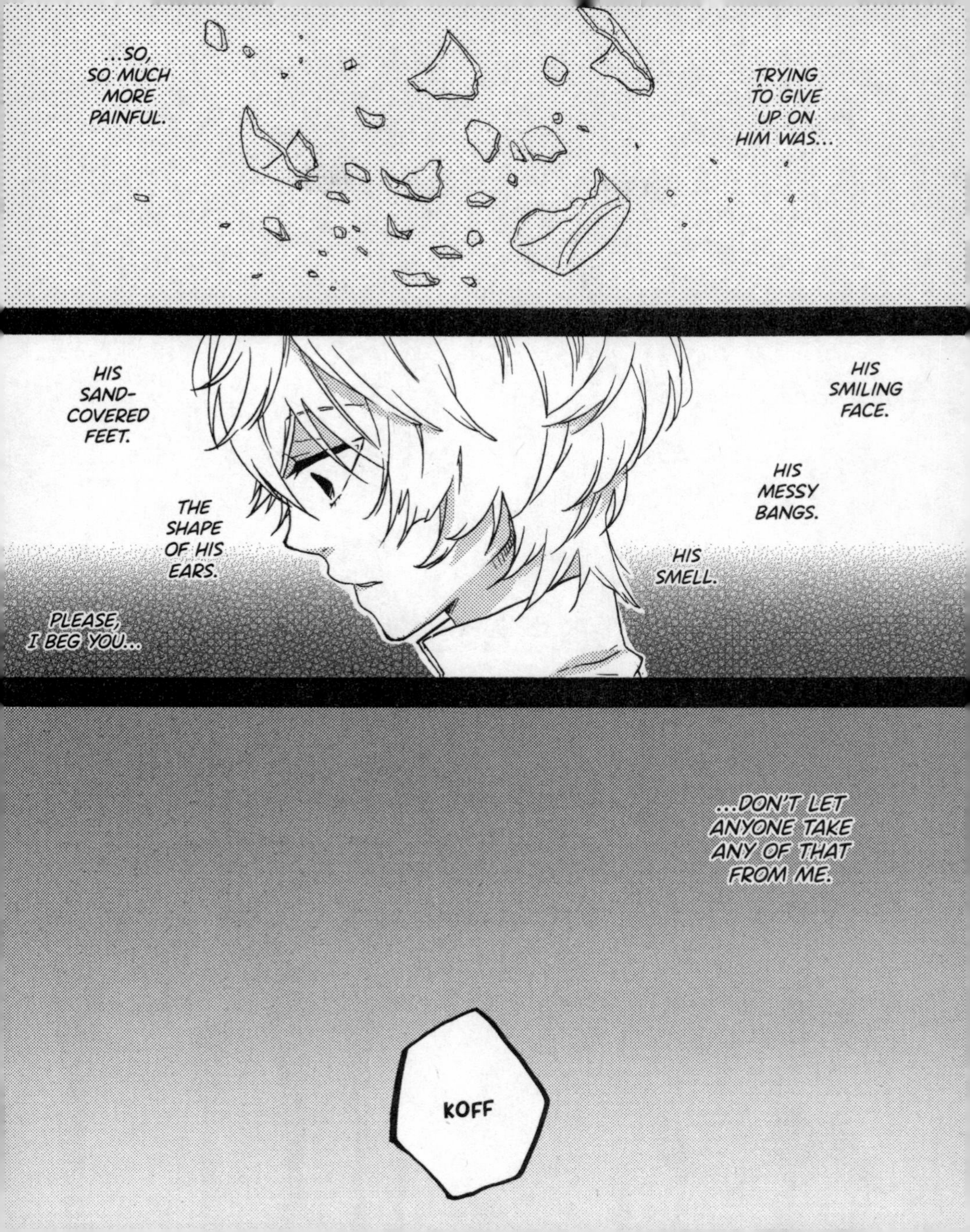
TRYING TO GIVE UP ON HIM WAS...
...SO, SO MUCH MORE PAINFUL.
HIS SMILING FACE.
HIS MESSY BANGS.
HIS SMELL.
HIS SAND-COVERED FEET.
THE SHAPE OF HIS EARS.
PLEASE, I BEG YOU...
...DON'T LET ANYONE TAKE ANY OF THAT FROM ME.
KOFF

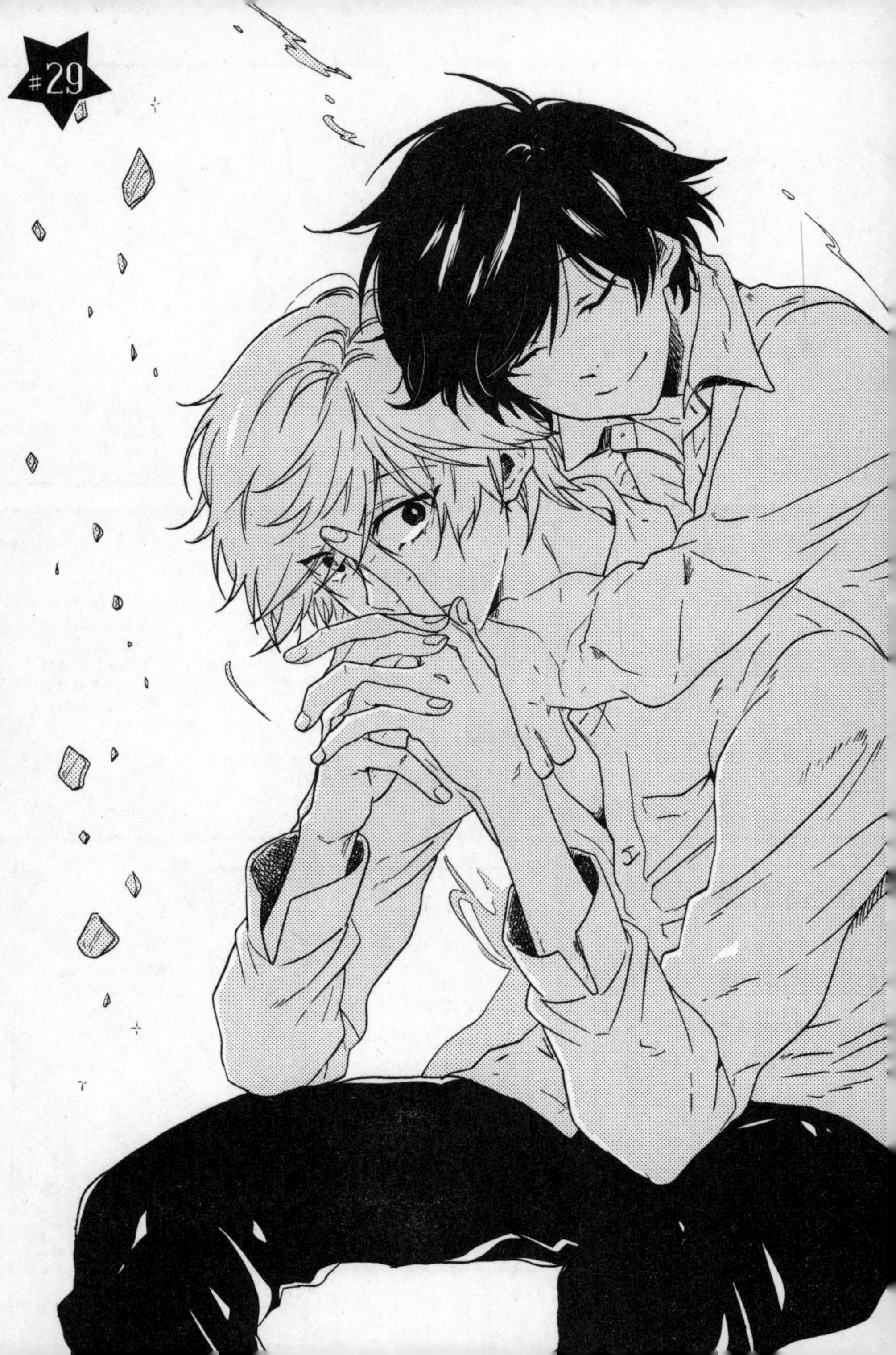
#29

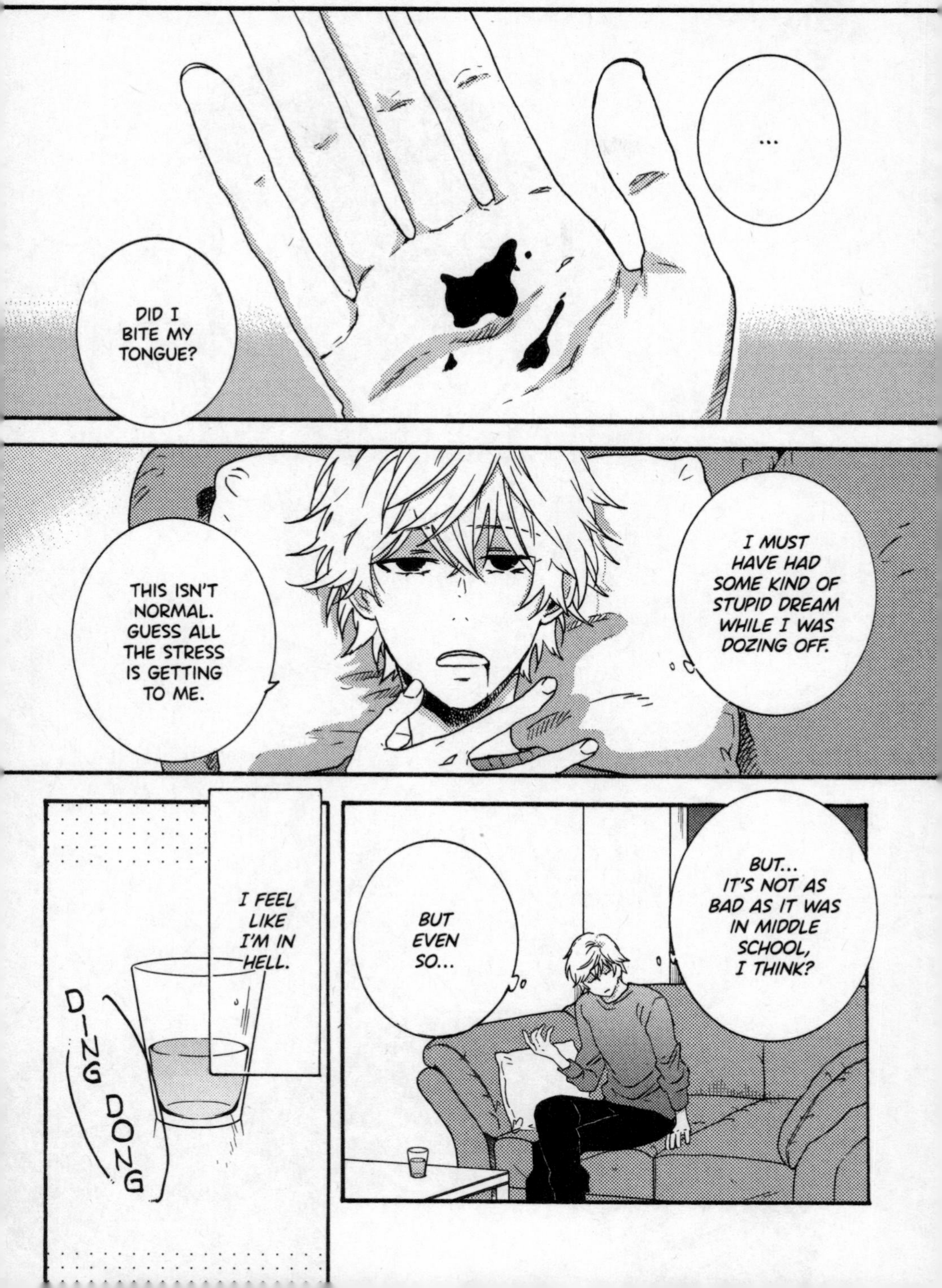
...
DID I BITE MY TONGUE?
I MUST HAVE HAD SOME KIND OF STUPID DREAM WHILE I WAS DOZING OFF.
THIS ISN'T NORMAL. GUESS ALL THE STRESS IS GETTING TO ME.
BUT... IT'S NOT AS BAD AS IT WAS IN MIDDLE SCHOOL, I THINK?
BUT EVEN SO...
I FEEL LIKE I'M IN HELL.
DING DONG

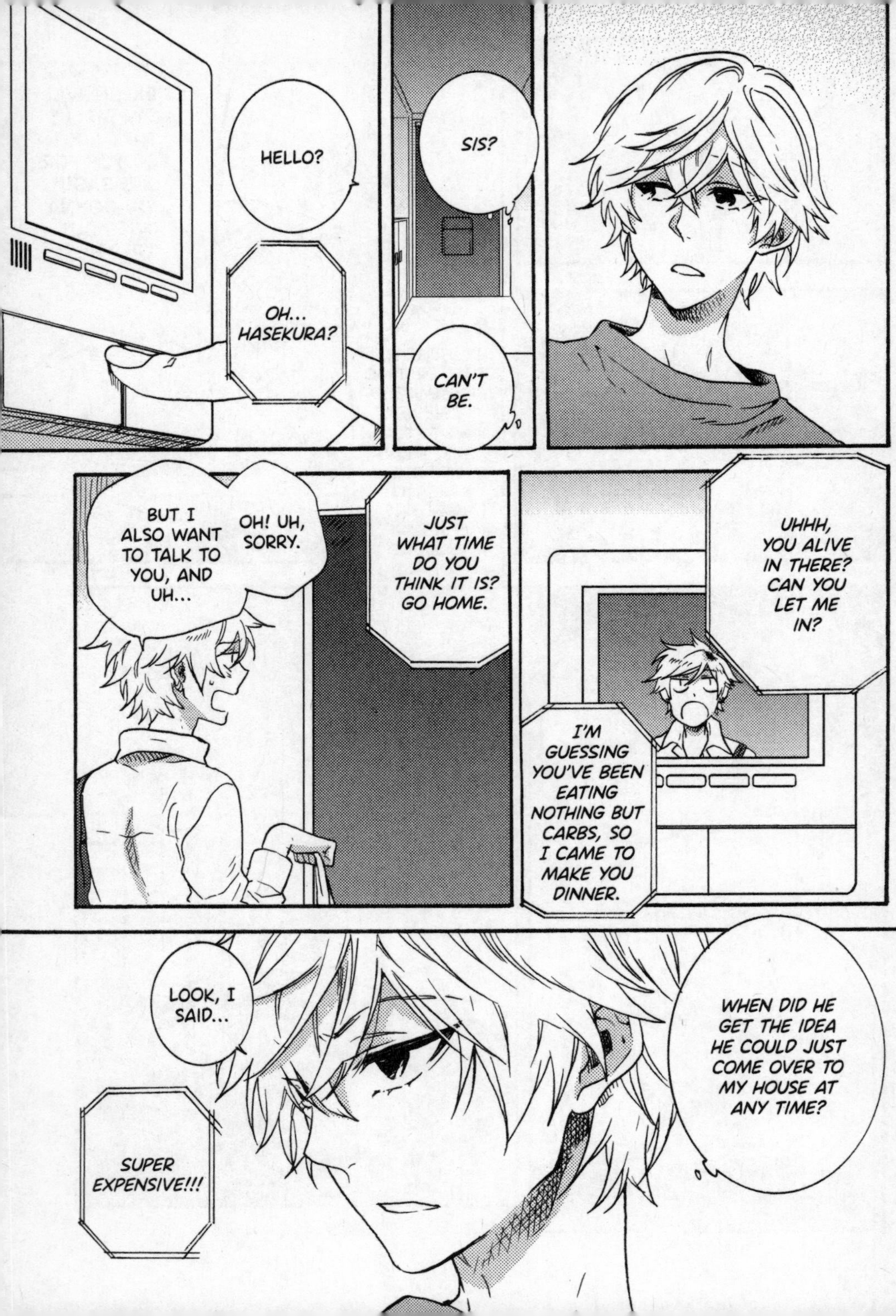
SIS?
CAN'T BE.
HELLO?
OH... HASEKURA?
UHHH, YOU ALIVE IN THERE? CAN YOU LET ME IN?
I'M GUESSING YOU'VE BEEN EATING NOTHING BUT CARBS, SO I CAME TO MAKE YOU DINNER.
JUST WHAT TIME DO YOU THINK IT IS? GO HOME.
OH! UH, SORRY.
BUT I ALSO WANT TO TALK TO YOU, AND UH...
WHEN DID HE GET THE IDEA HE COULD JUST COME OVER TO MY HOUSE AT ANY TIME?
LOOK, I SAID...
SUPER EXPENSIVE!!!

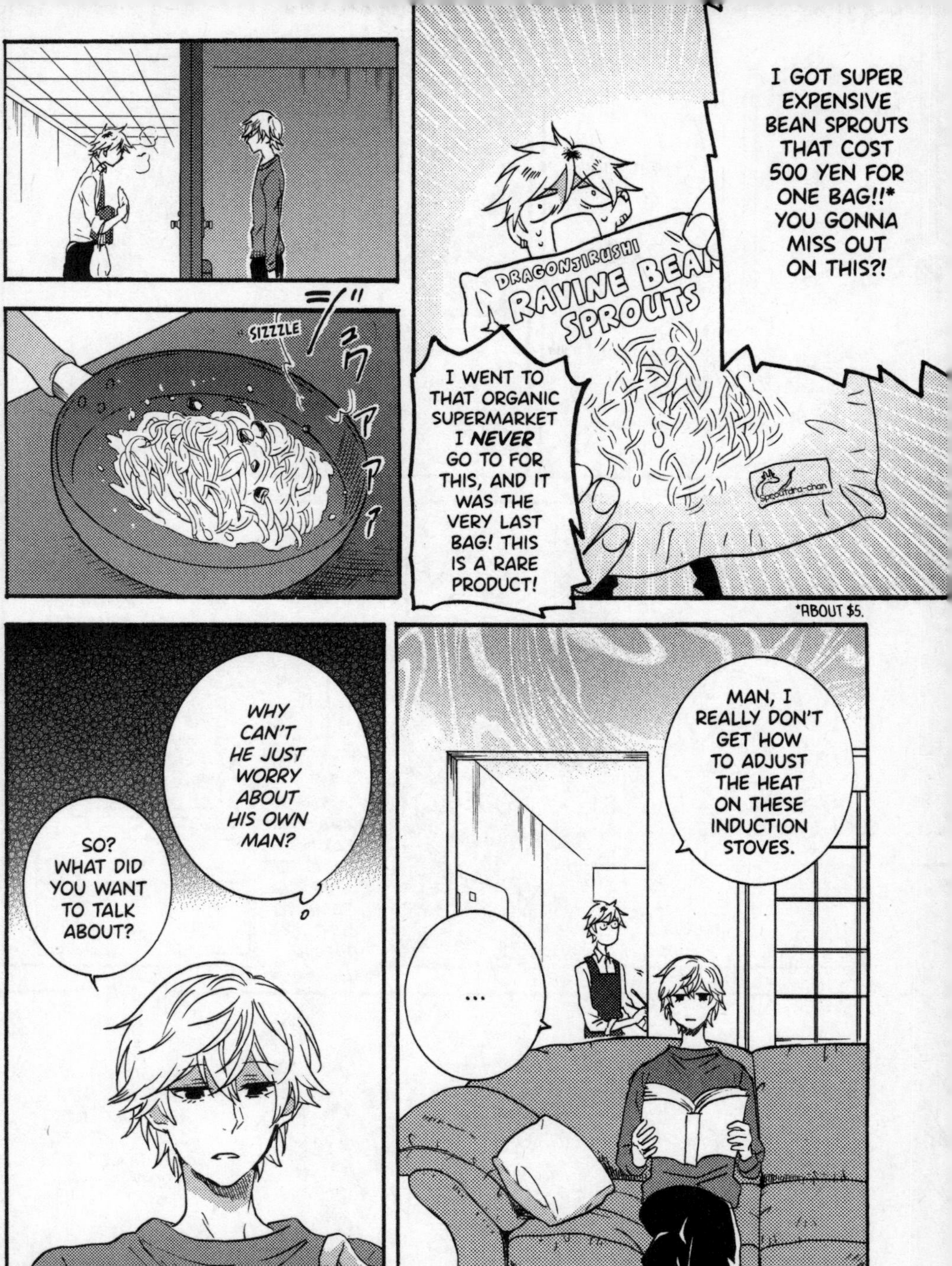
I GOT SUPER EXPENSIVE BEAN SPROUTS THAT COST 500 YEN FOR ONE BAG!!* YOU GONNA MISS OUT ON THIS?!
DRAGONJIRUSHI
RAVINE BEAN SPROUTS
Sproutdra-chan
I WENT TO THAT ORGANIC SUPERMARKET I NEVER GO TO FOR THIS, AND IT WAS THE VERY LAST BAG! THIS IS A RARE PRODUCT!
*ABOUT $5.
SIZZZLE
MAN, I REALLY DON'T GET HOW TO ADJUST THE HEAT ON THESE INDUCTION STOVES.
...
WHY CAN'T HE JUST WORRY ABOUT HIS OWN MAN?
SO? WHAT DID YOU WANT TO TALK ABOUT?

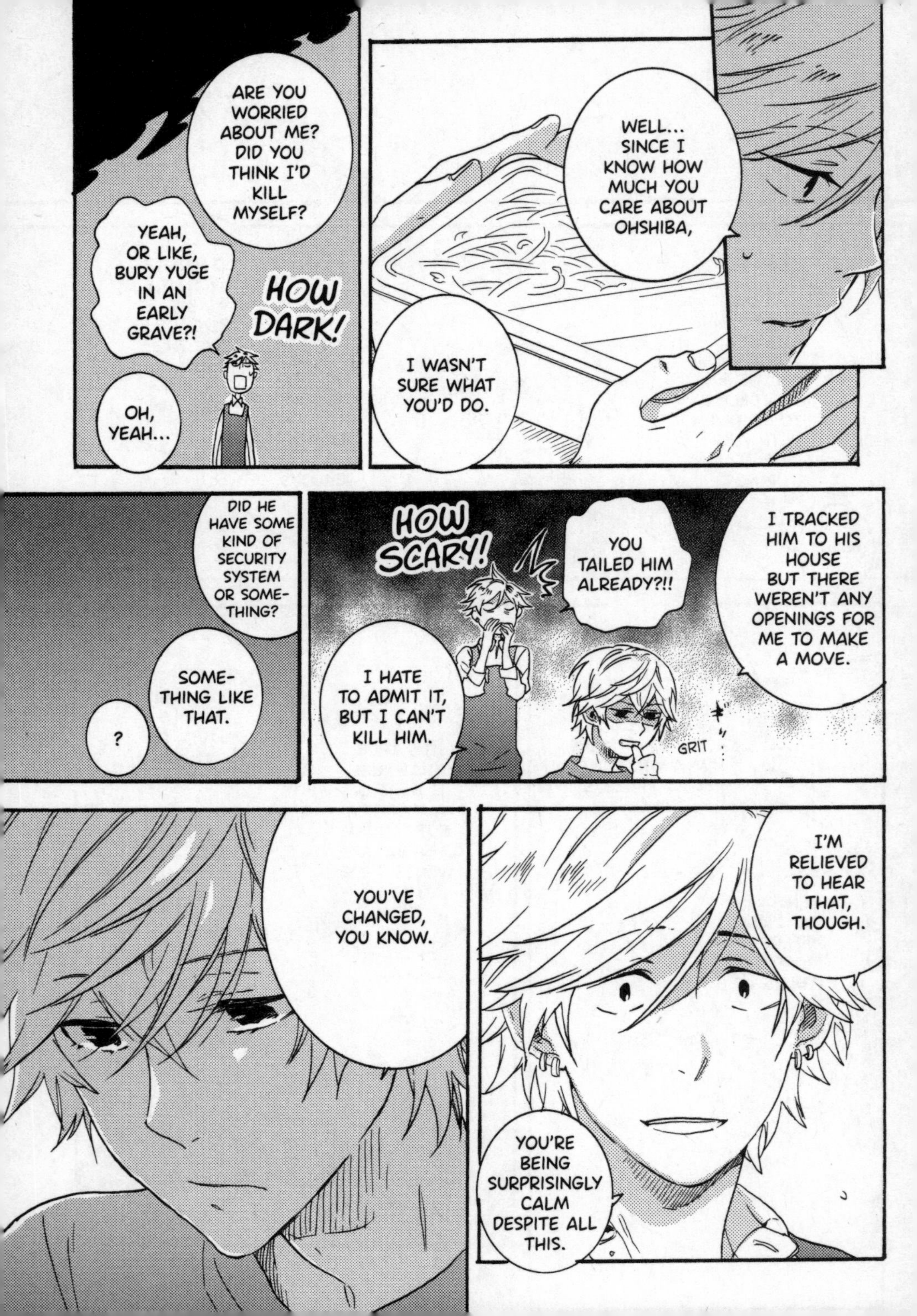
WELL... SINCE I KNOW HOW MUCH YOU CARE ABOUT OHSHIBA,
I WASN'T SURE WHAT YOU'D DO.
ARE YOU WORRIED ABOUT ME? DID YOU THINK I'D KILL MYSELF?
YEAH, OR LIKE, BURY YUGE IN AN EARLY GRAVE?!
HOW DARK!
OH, YEAH...
I TRACKED HIM TO HIS HOUSE BUT THERE WEREN'T ANY OPENINGS FOR ME TO MAKE A MOVE.
YOU TAILED HIM ALREADY?!!
HOW SCARY!
GRIT
I HATE TO ADMIT IT, BUT I CAN'T KILL HIM.
DID HE HAVE SOME KIND OF SECURITY SYSTEM OR SOME-THING?
SOME-THING LIKE THAT.
?
I'M RELIEVED TO HEAR THAT, THOUGH.
YOU'RE BEING SURPRISINGLY CALM DESPITE ALL THIS.
YOU'VE CHANGED, YOU KNOW.

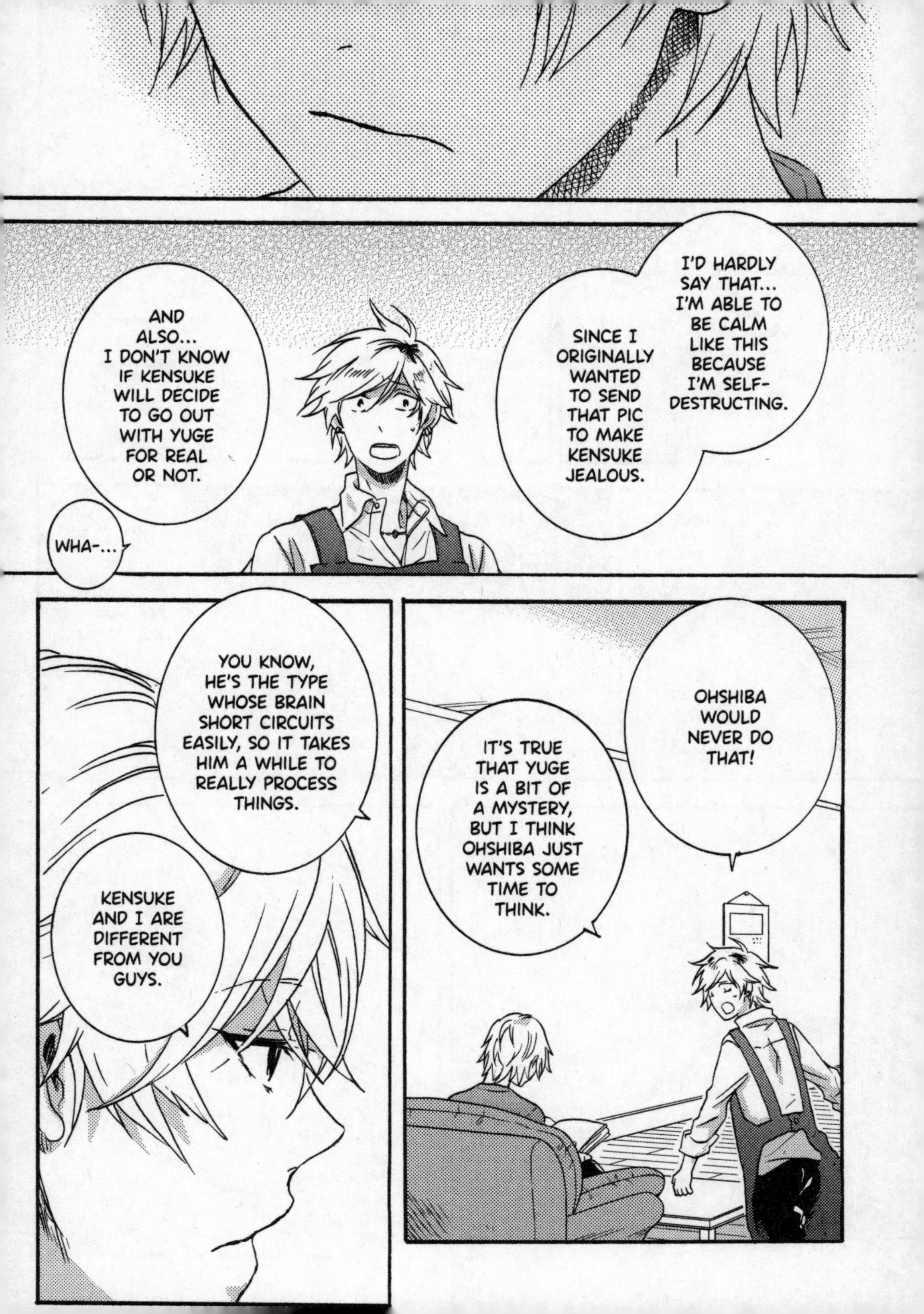
I'D HARDLY SAY THAT... I'M ABLE TO BE CALM LIKE THIS BECAUSE I'M SELF-DESTRUCTING.
SINCE I ORIGINALLY WANTED TO SEND THAT PIC TO MAKE KENSUKE JEALOUS.
AND ALSO... I DON'T KNOW IF KENSUKE WILL DECIDE TO GO OUT WITH YUGE FOR REAL OR NOT.
WHA-...
OHSHIBA WOULD NEVER DO THAT!
IT'S TRUE THAT YUGE IS A BIT OF A MYSTERY, BUT I THINK OHSHIBA JUST WANTS SOME TIME TO THINK.
YOU KNOW, HE'S THE TYPE WHOSE BRAIN SHORT CIRCUITS EASILY, SO IT TAKES HIM A WHILE TO REALLY PROCESS THINGS.
KENSUKE AND I ARE DIFFERENT FROM YOU GUYS.

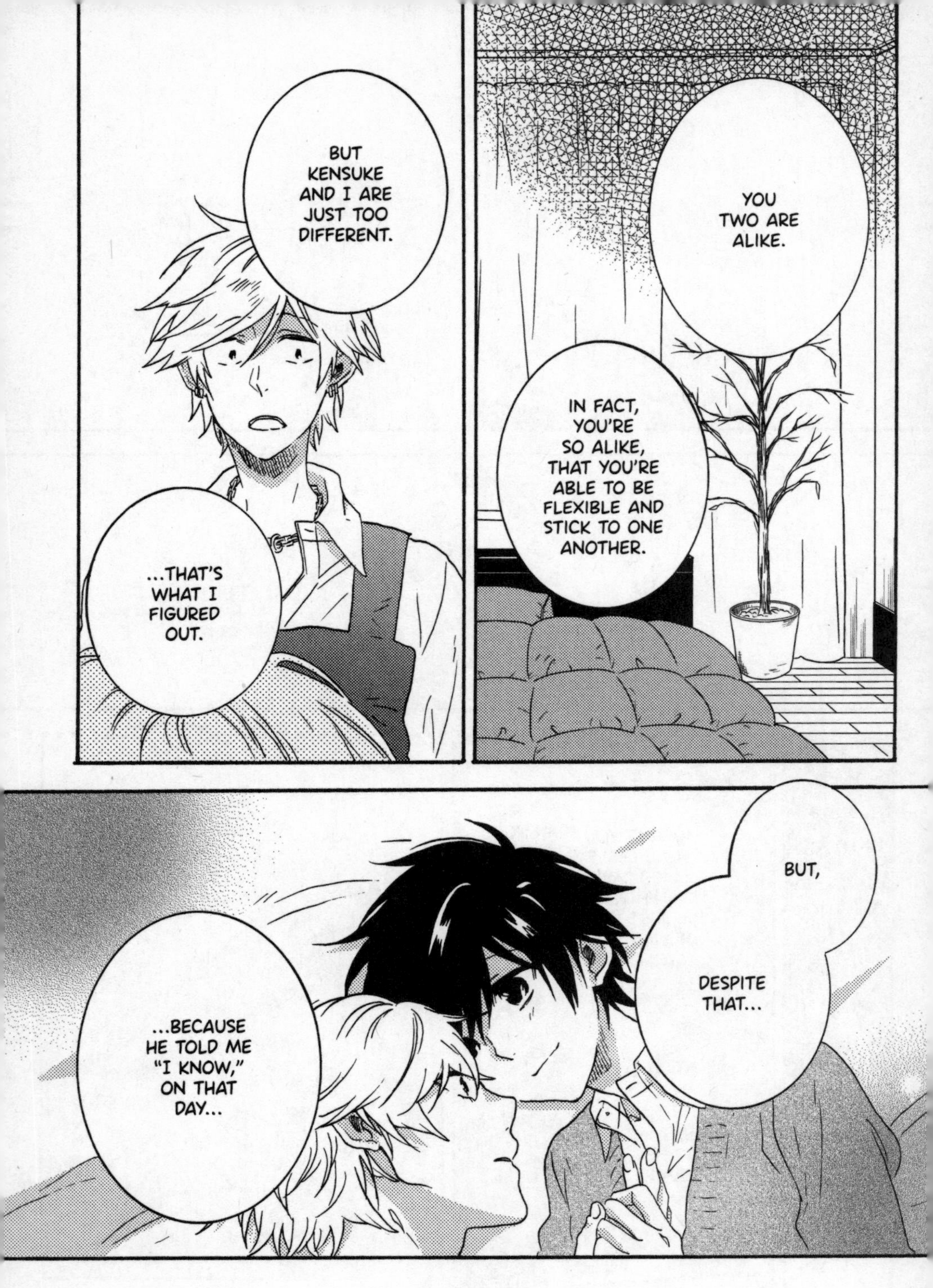
YOU TWO ARE ALIKE.
IN FACT, YOU'RE SO ALIKE, THAT YOU'RE ABLE TO BE FLEXIBLE AND STICK TO ONE ANOTHER.
BUT KENSUKE AND I ARE JUST TOO DIFFERENT.
...THAT'S WHAT I FIGURED OUT.
BUT,
DESPITE THAT...
...BECAUSE HE TOLD ME "I KNOW," ON THAT DAY...

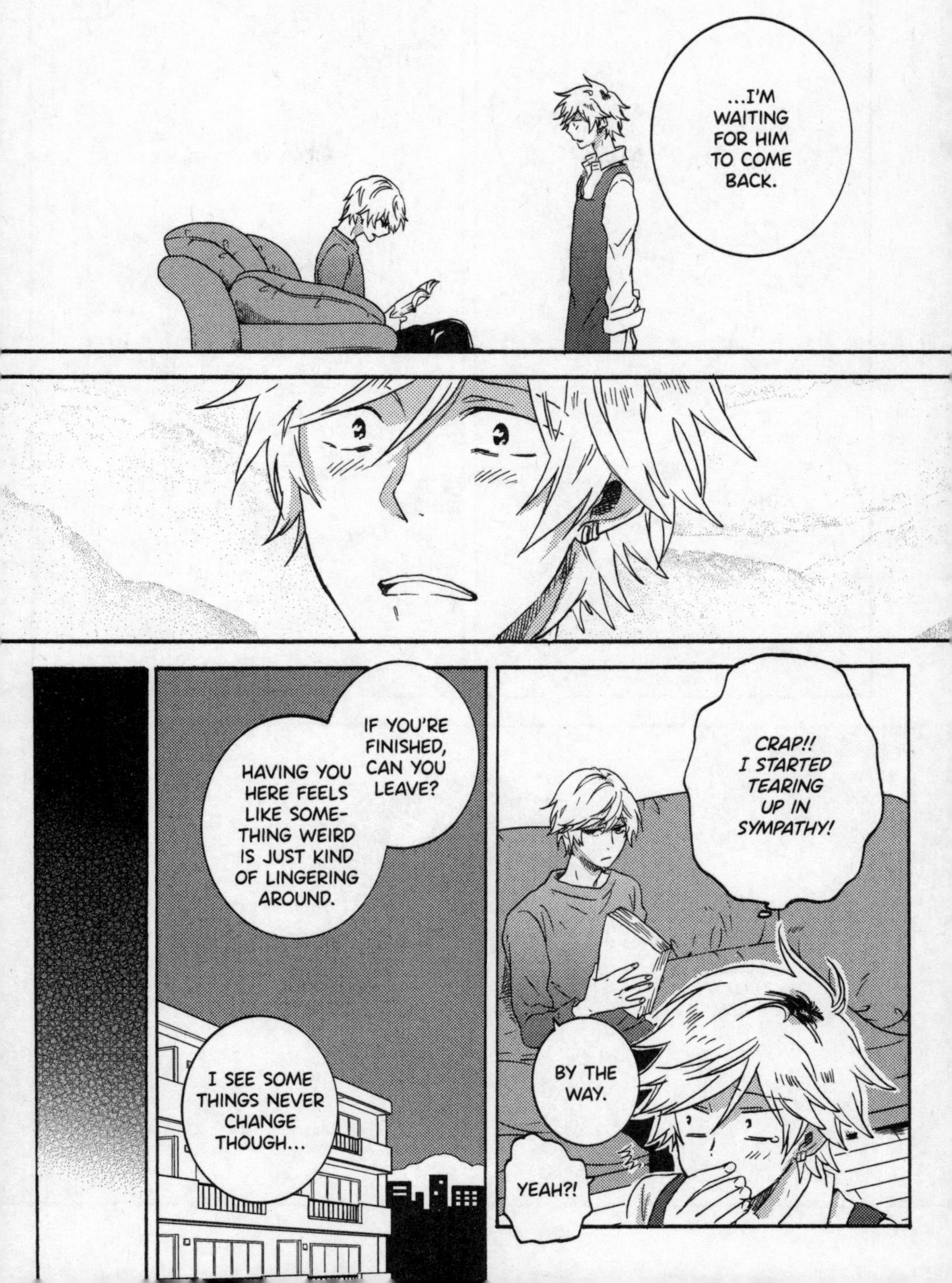
...I'M WAITING FOR HIM TO COME BACK.
CRAP!! I STARTED TEARING UP IN SYMPATHY!
BY THE WAY.
YEAH?!
IF YOU'RE FINISHED, CAN YOU LEAVE?
HAVING YOU HERE FEELS LIKE SOME-THING WEIRD IS JUST KIND OF LINGERING AROUND.
I SEE SOME THINGS NEVER CHANGE THOUGH...

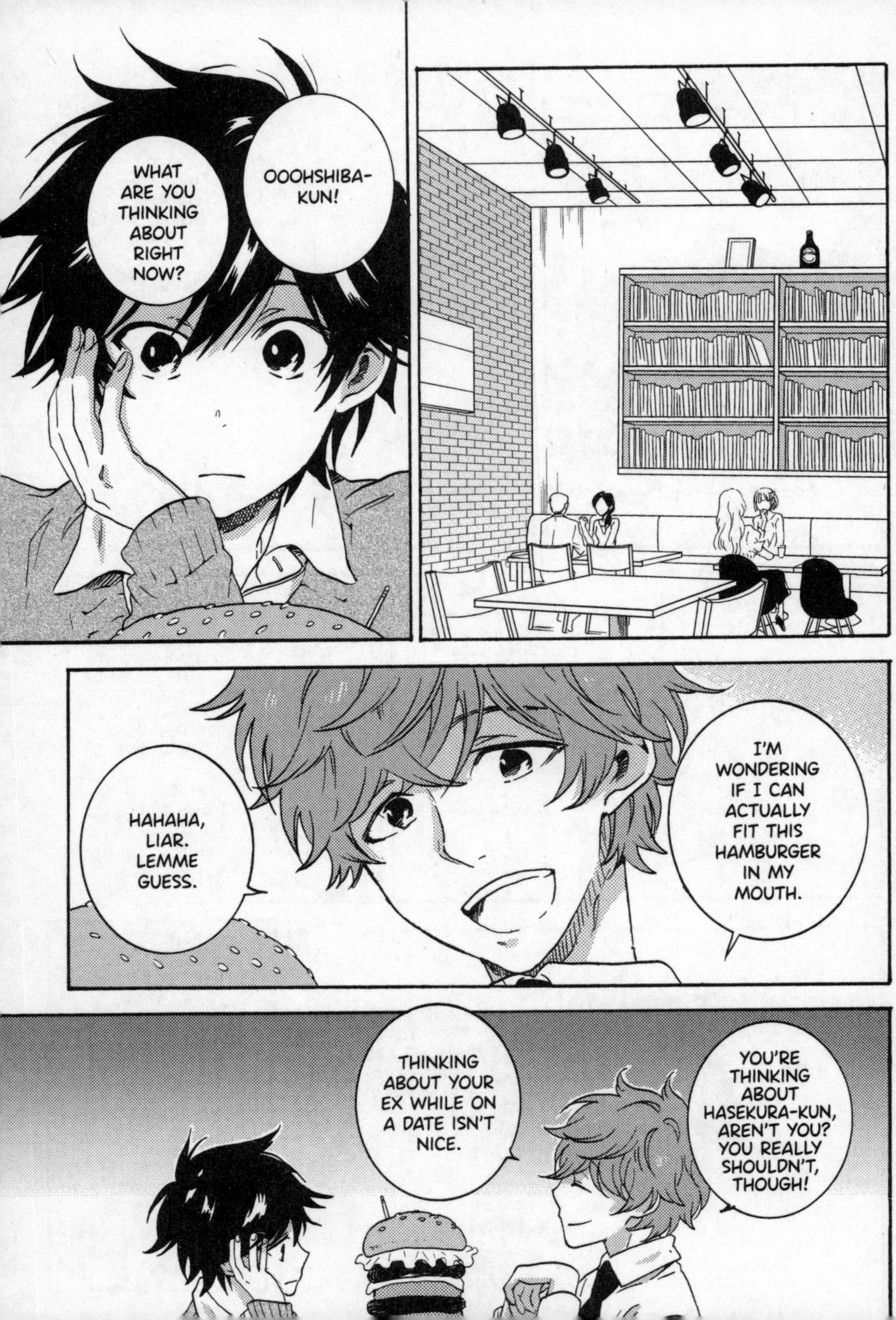
OOOHSHIBA-KUN!
WHAT ARE YOU THINKING ABOUT RIGHT NOW?
I'M WONDERING IF I CAN ACTUALLY FIT THIS HAMBURGER IN MY MOUTH.
HAHAHA, LIAR. LEMME GUESS.
YOU'RE THINKING ABOUT HASEKURA-KUN, AREN'T YOU? YOU REALLY SHOULDN'T, THOUGH!
THINKING ABOUT YOUR EX WHILE ON A DATE ISN'T NICE.

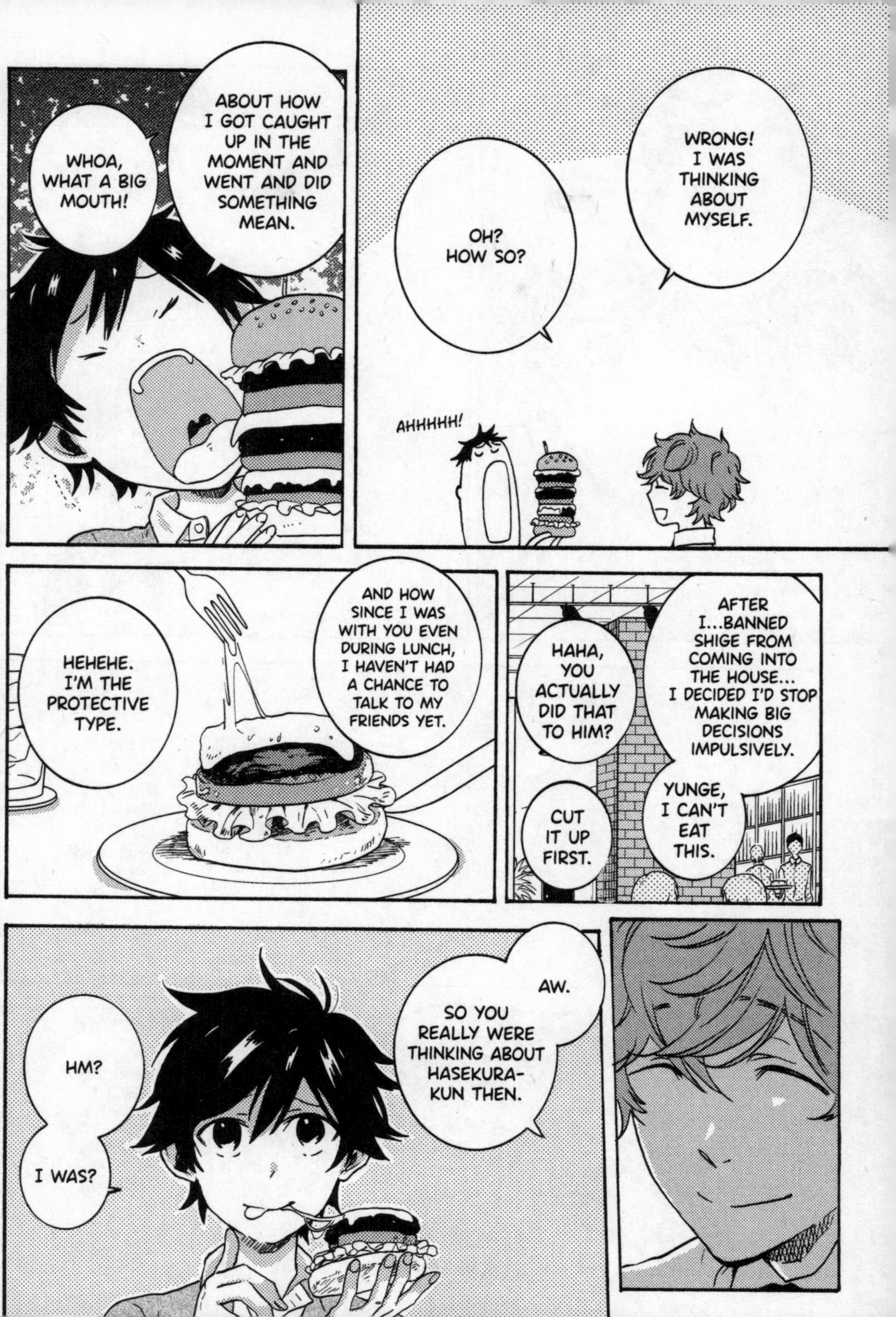
WRONG! I WAS THINKING ABOUT MYSELF.
OH? HOW SO?
AHHHHH!
ABOUT HOW I GOT CAUGHT UP IN THE MOMENT AND WENT AND DID SOMETHING MEAN.
WHOA, WHAT A BIG MOUTH!
AFTER I...BANNED SHIGE FROM COMING INTO THE HOUSE... I DECIDED I'D STOP MAKING BIG DECISIONS IMPULSIVELY.
HAHA, YOU ACTUALLY DID THAT TO HIM?
YUNGE, I CAN'T EAT THIS.
CUT IT UP FIRST.
AND HOW SINCE I WAS WITH YOU EVEN DURING LUNCH, I HAVEN'T HAD A CHANCE TO TALK TO MY FRIENDS YET.
HEHEHE. I'M THE PROTECTIVE TYPE.
AW.
SO YOU REALLY WERE THINKING ABOUT HASEKURA-KUN THEN.
HM?
I WAS?

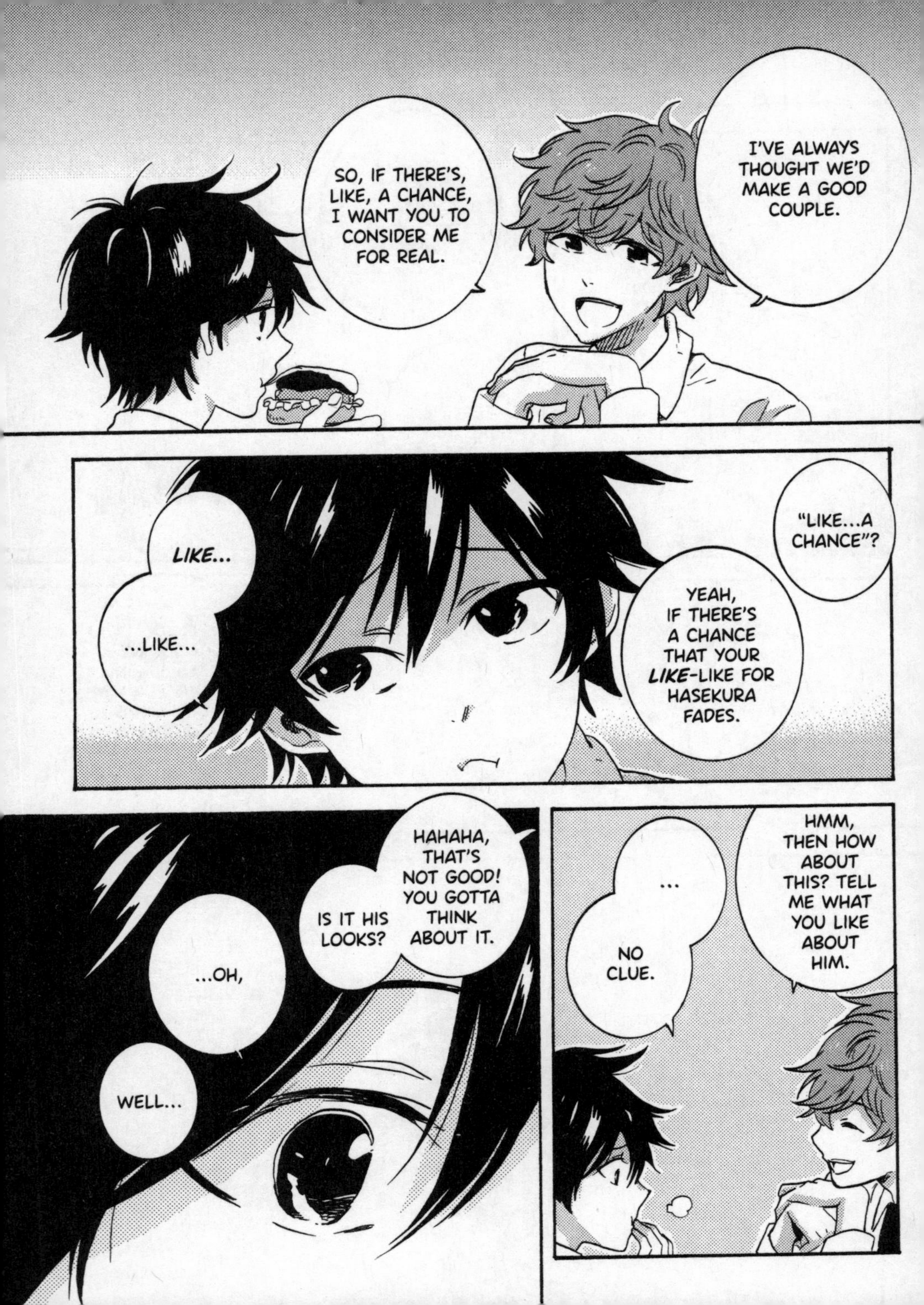
I'VE ALWAYS THOUGHT WE'D MAKE A GOOD COUPLE.
SO, IF THERE'S, LIKE, A CHANCE, I WANT YOU TO CONSIDER ME FOR REAL.
"LIKE...A CHANCE"?
YEAH, IF THERE'S A CHANCE THAT YOUR *LIKE*-LIKE FOR HASEKURA FADES.
LIKE...
...LIKE...
HMM, THEN HOW ABOUT THIS? TELL ME WHAT YOU LIKE ABOUT HIM.
...
NO CLUE.
HAHAHA, THAT'S NOT GOOD! YOU GOTTA THINK ABOUT IT.
IS IT HIS LOOKS?
...OH,
WELL...

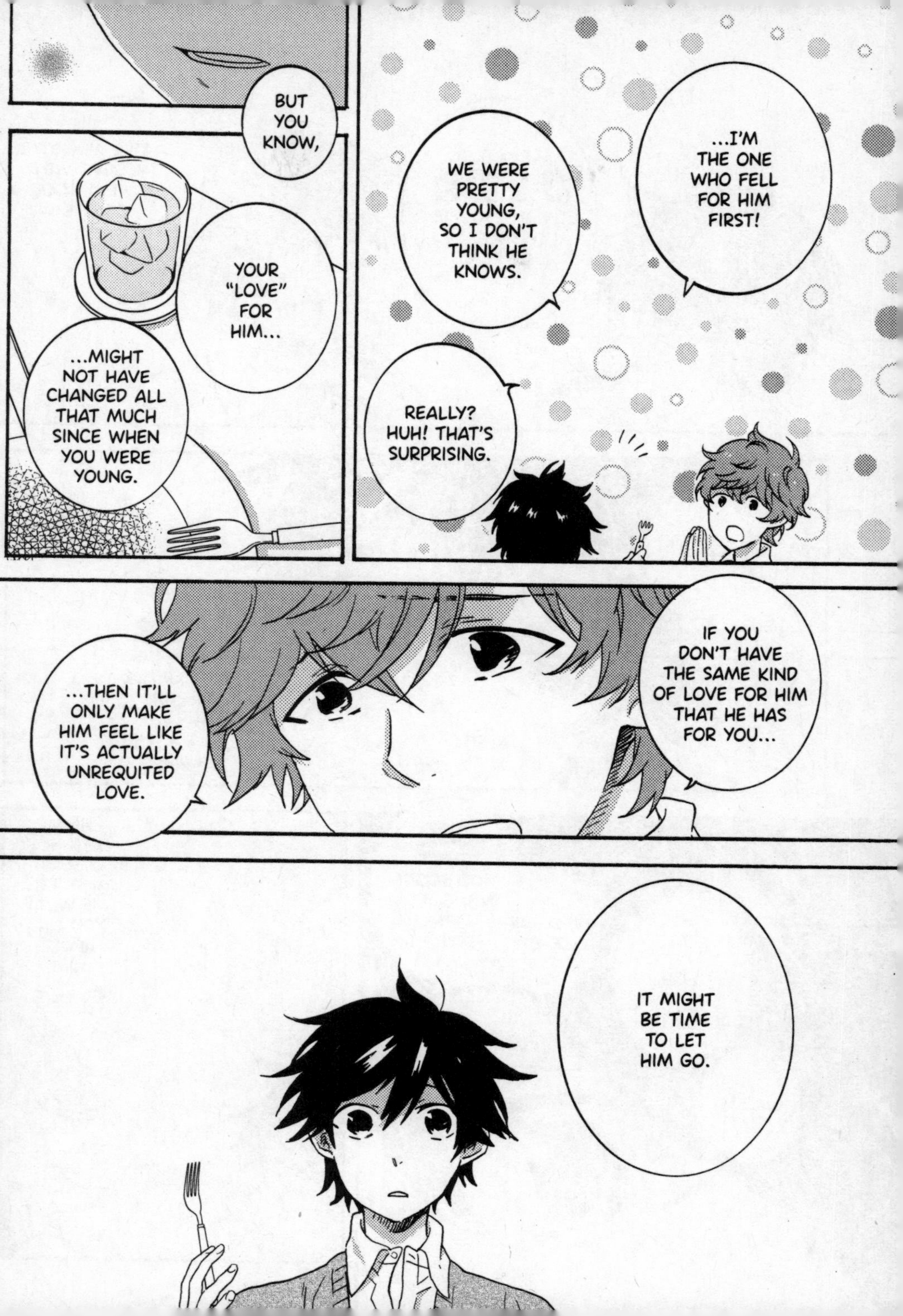
...I'M THE ONE WHO FELL FOR HIM FIRST!
WE WERE PRETTY YOUNG, SO I DON'T THINK HE KNOWS.
REALLY? HUH! THAT'S SURPRISING.
BUT YOU KNOW,
YOUR "LOVE" FOR HIM...
...MIGHT NOT HAVE CHANGED ALL THAT MUCH SINCE WHEN YOU WERE YOUNG.
IF YOU DON'T HAVE THE SAME KIND OF LOVE FOR HIM THAT HE HAS FOR YOU...
...THEN IT'LL ONLY MAKE HIM FEEL LIKE IT'S ACTUALLY UNREQUITED LOVE.
IT MIGHT BE TIME TO LET HIM GO.

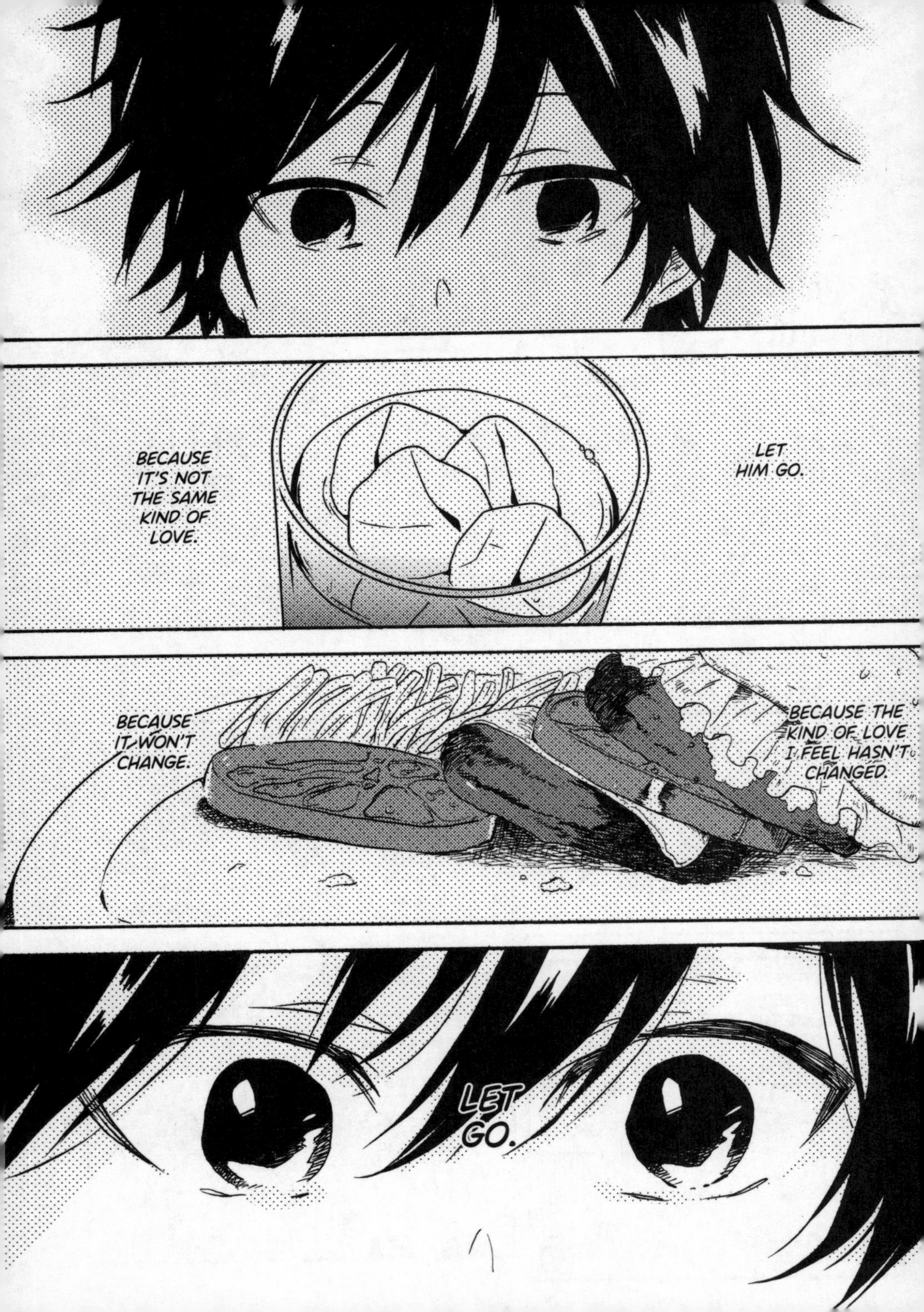
LET HIM GO.
BECAUSE IT'S NOT THE SAME KIND OF LOVE.
BECAUSE THE KIND OF LOVE I FEEL HASN'T CHANGED.
BECAUSE IT WON'T CHANGE.
LET GO.

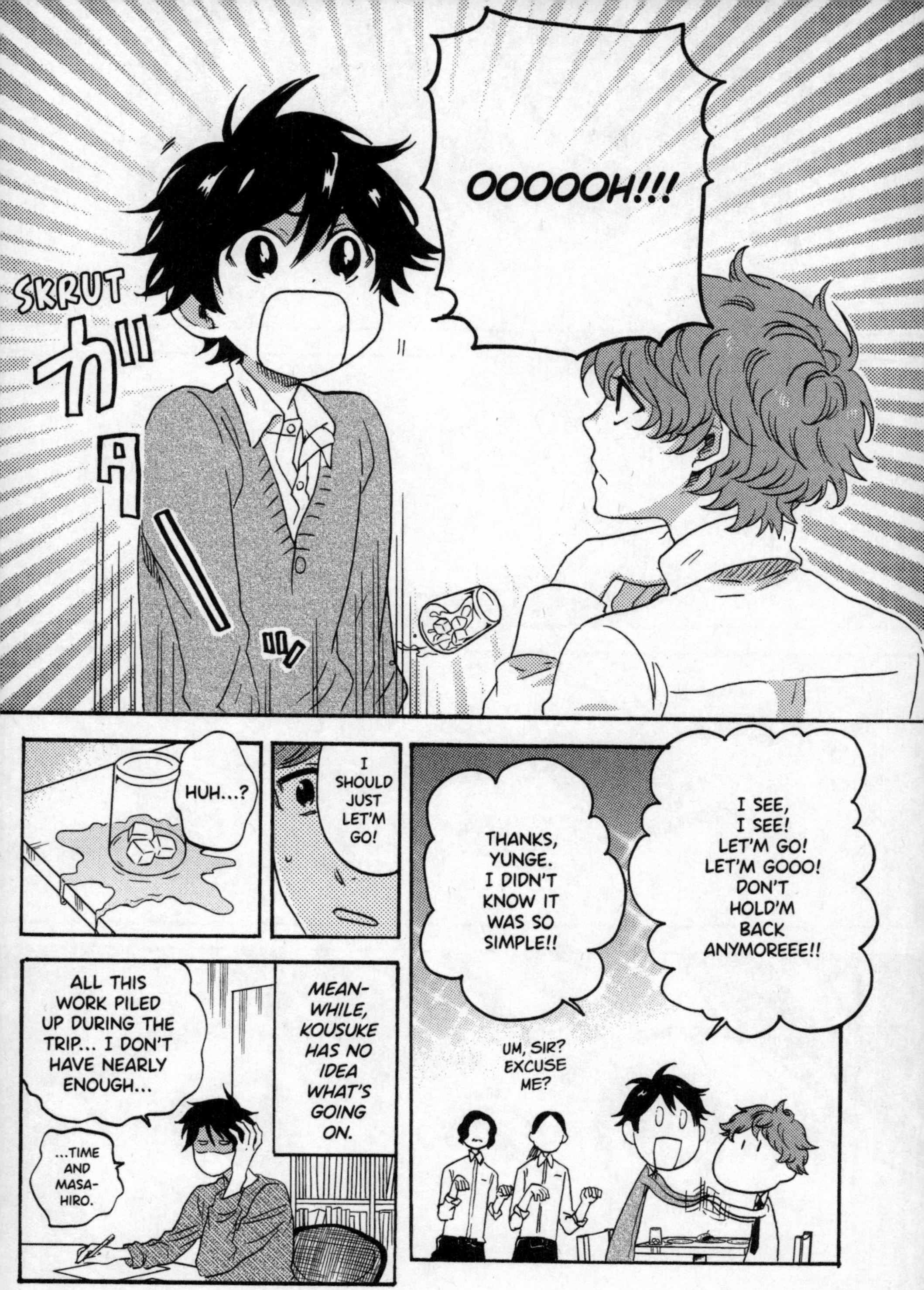
OOOOOH!!!
SKRUT
カッ
タ
I SEE, I SEE! LET'M GO! LET'M GOOO! DON'T HOLD'M BACK ANYMOREEE!!
THANKS, YUNGE. I DIDN'T KNOW IT WAS SO SIMPLE!!
UM, SIR? EXCUSE ME?
I SHOULD JUST LET'M GO!
HUH...?
MEAN-WHILE, KOUSUKE HAS NO IDEA WHAT'S GOING ON.
ALL THIS WORK PILED UP DURING THE TRIP... I DON'T HAVE NEARLY ENOUGH...
...TIME AND MASA-HIRO.

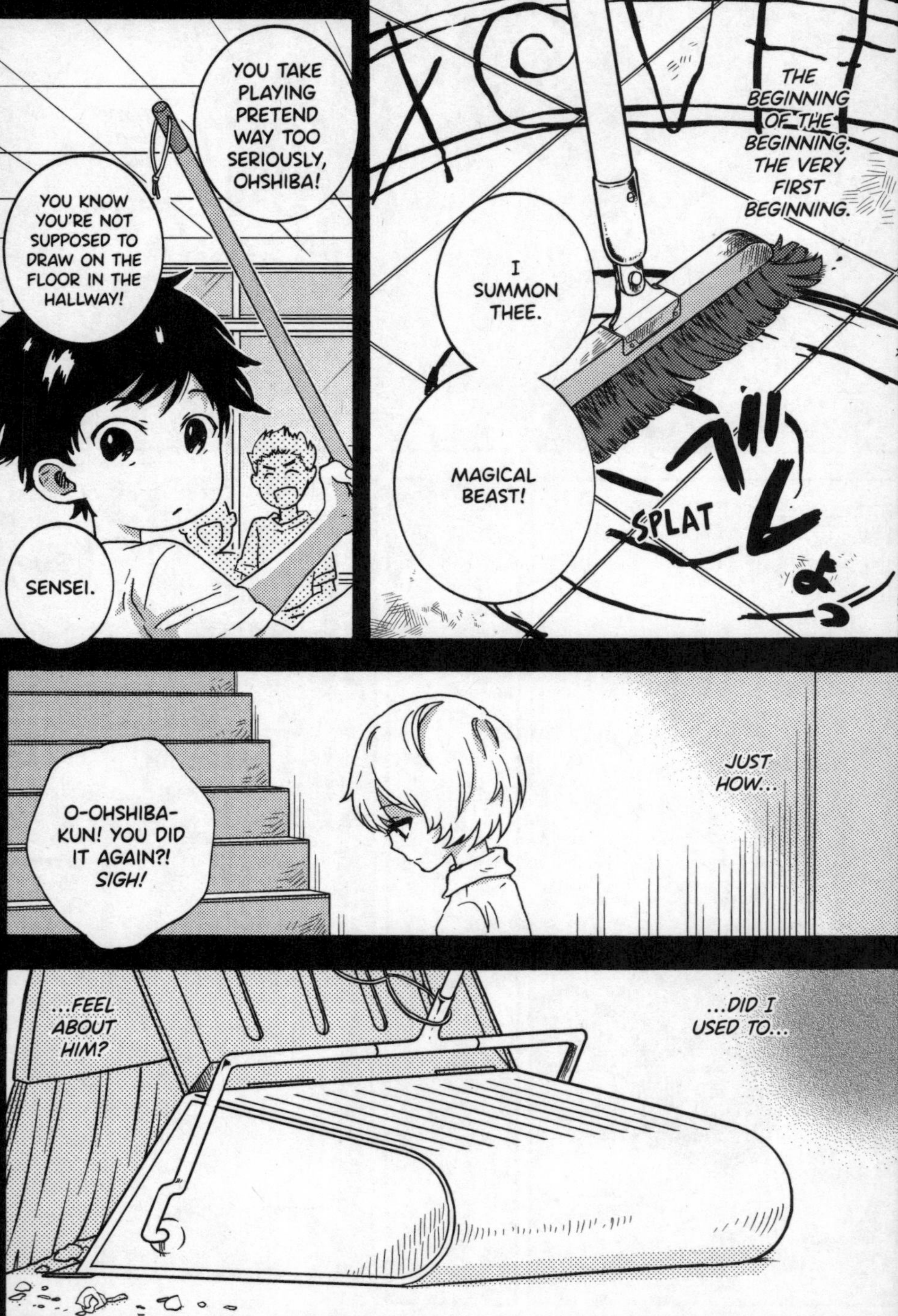
THE BEGINNING OF THE BEGINNING. THE VERY FIRST BEGINNING.
I SUMMON THEE.
MAGICAL BEAST!
SPLAT
YOU TAKE PLAYING PRETEND WAY TOO SERIOUSLY, OHSHIBA!
YOU KNOW YOU'RE NOT SUPPOSED TO DRAW ON THE FLOOR IN THE HALLWAY!
SENSEI.
JUST HOW...
O-OHSHIBA-KUN! YOU DID IT AGAIN?! SIGH!
...DID I USED TO...
...FEEL ABOUT HIM?

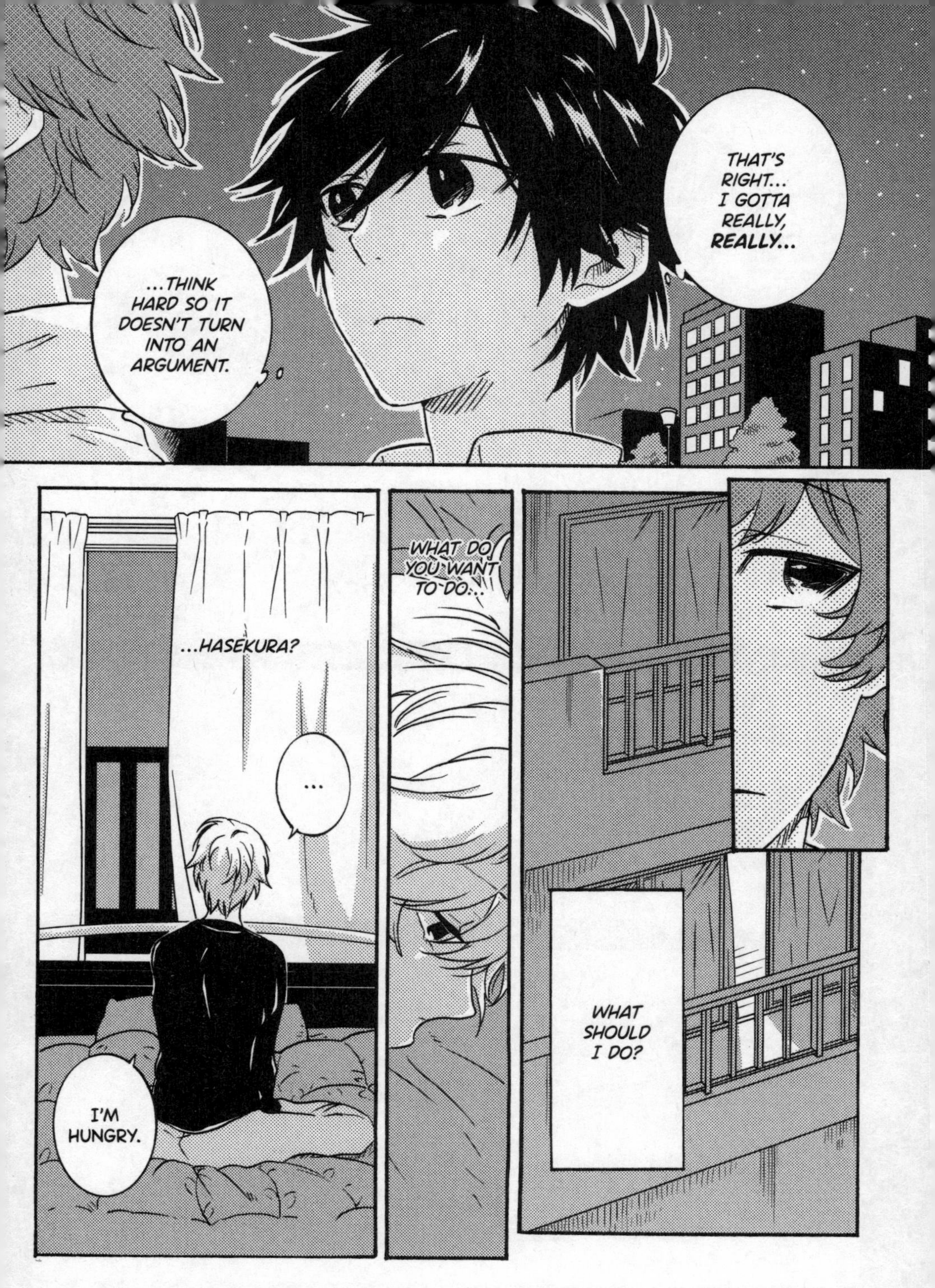
THAT'S RIGHT... I GOTTA REALLY, **REALLY...**
...THINK HARD SO IT DOESN'T TURN INTO AN ARGUMENT.
WHAT SHOULD I DO?
WHAT DO YOU WANT TO DO...
...HASEKURA?
...
I'M HUNGRY.

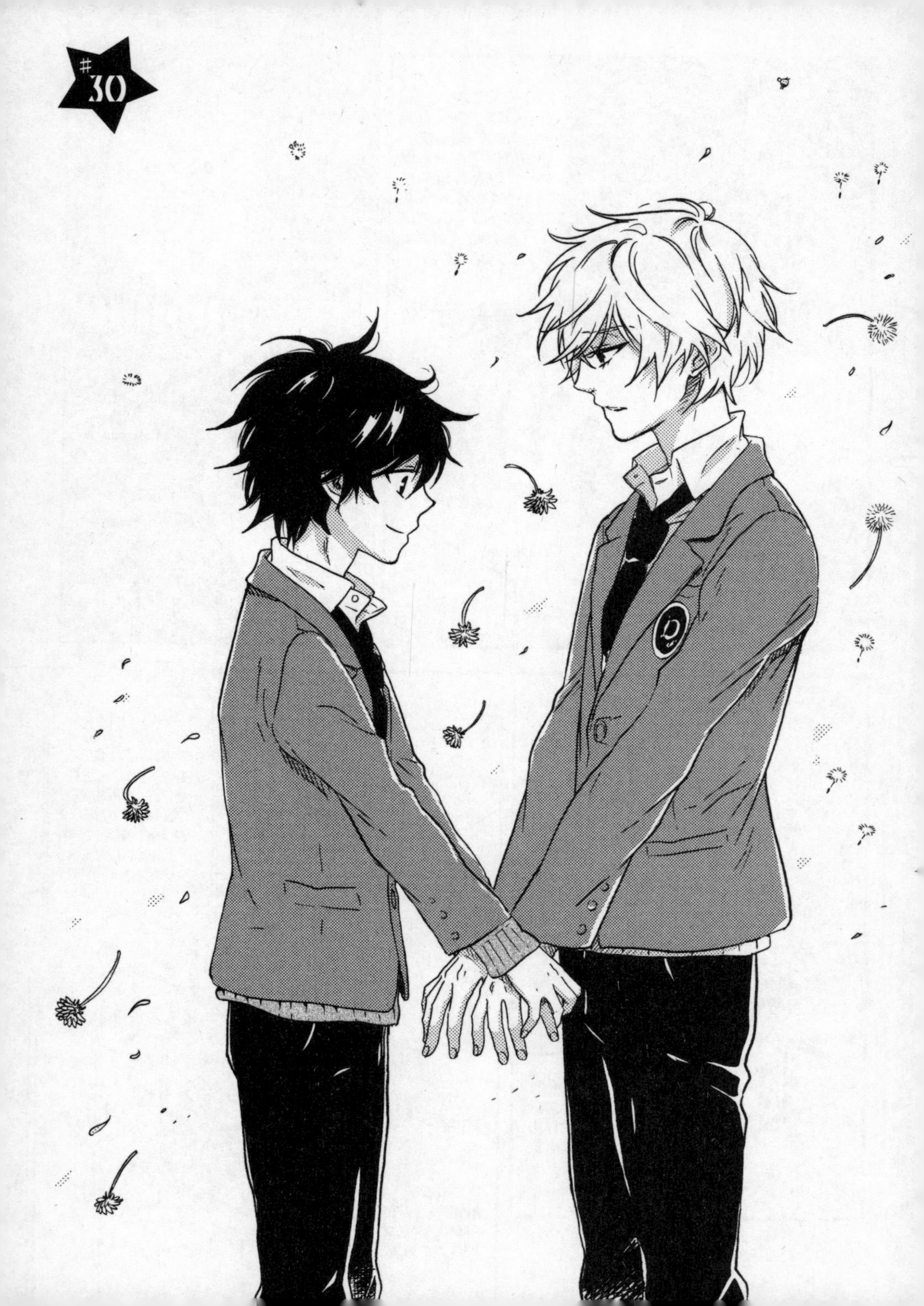
#30

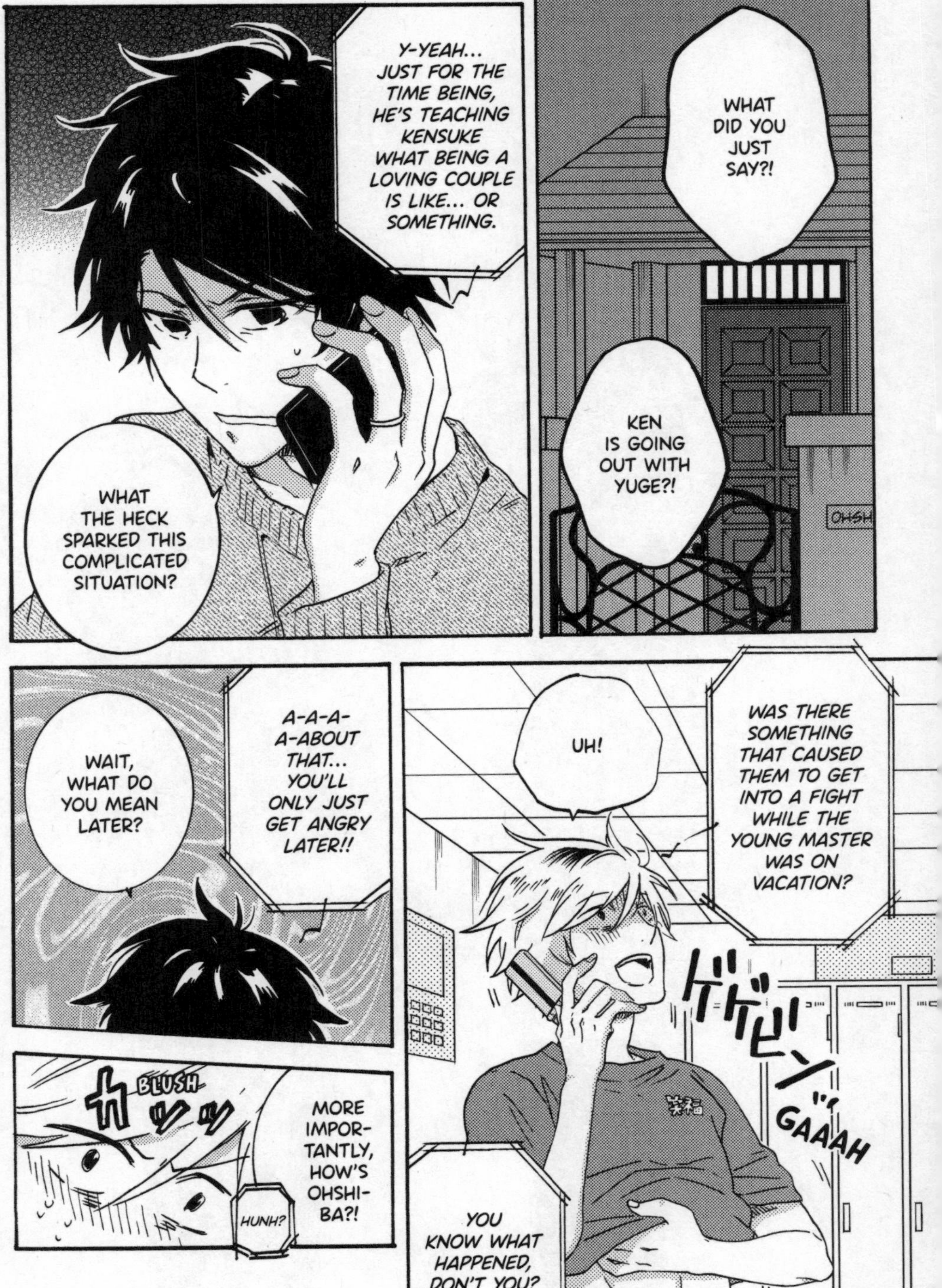
WHAT DID YOU JUST SAY?!
KEN IS GOING OUT WITH YUGE?!
OHSH
Y-YEAH... JUST FOR THE TIME BEING, HE'S TEACHING KENSUKE WHAT BEING A LOVING COUPLE IS LIKE... OR SOMETHING.
WHAT THE HECK SPARKED THIS COMPLICATED SITUATION?
WAS THERE SOMETHING THAT CAUSED THEM TO GET INTO A FIGHT WHILE THE YOUNG MASTER WAS ON VACATION?
UH!
GAAAH
YOU KNOW WHAT HAPPENED, DON'T YOU?
A-A-A-A-ABOUT THAT... YOU'LL ONLY JUST GET ANGRY LATER!!
WAIT, WHAT DO YOU MEAN LATER?
BLUSH
MORE IMPOR-TANTLY, HOW'S OHSHI-BA?!
HUNH?

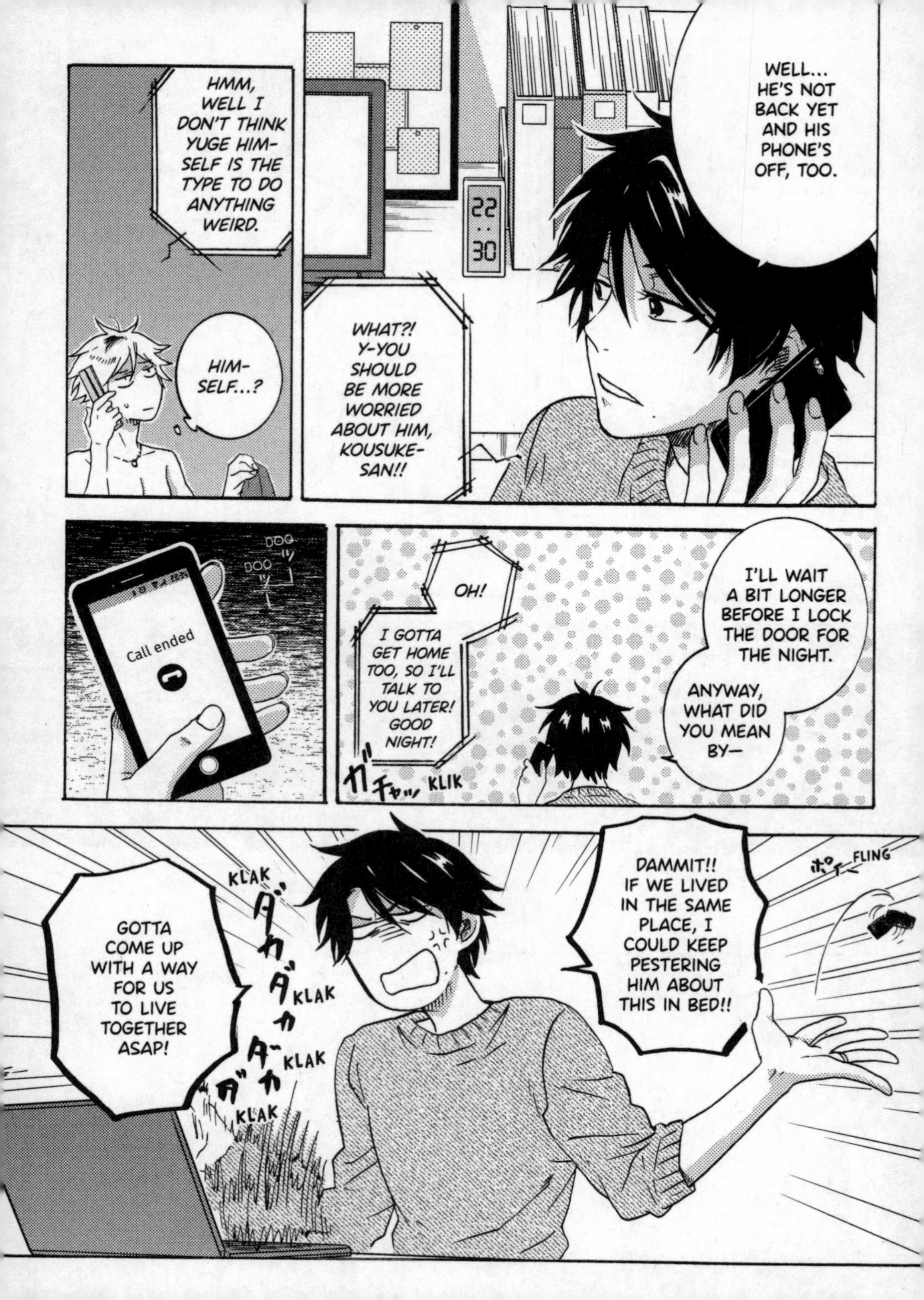

22:30
WELL... HE'S NOT BACK YET AND HIS PHONE'S OFF, TOO.
WHAT?! Y-YOU SHOULD BE MORE WORRIED ABOUT HIM, KOUSUKE-SAN!!
HMM, WELL I DON'T THINK YUGE HIM-SELF IS THE TYPE TO DO ANYTHING WEIRD.
HIM-SELF...?
I'LL WAIT A BIT LONGER BEFORE I LOCK THE DOOR FOR THE NIGHT.
ANYWAY, WHAT DID YOU MEAN BY—
OH!
I GOTTA GET HOME TOO, SO I'LL TALK TO YOU LATER! GOOD NIGHT!
KLIK
DOO
DOO
Call ended
FLING
DAMMIT!! IF WE LIVED IN THE SAME PLACE, I COULD KEEP PESTERING HIM ABOUT THIS IN BED!!
KLAK
KLAK
KLAK
KLAK
GOTTA COME UP WITH A WAY FOR US TO LIVE TOGETHER ASAP!

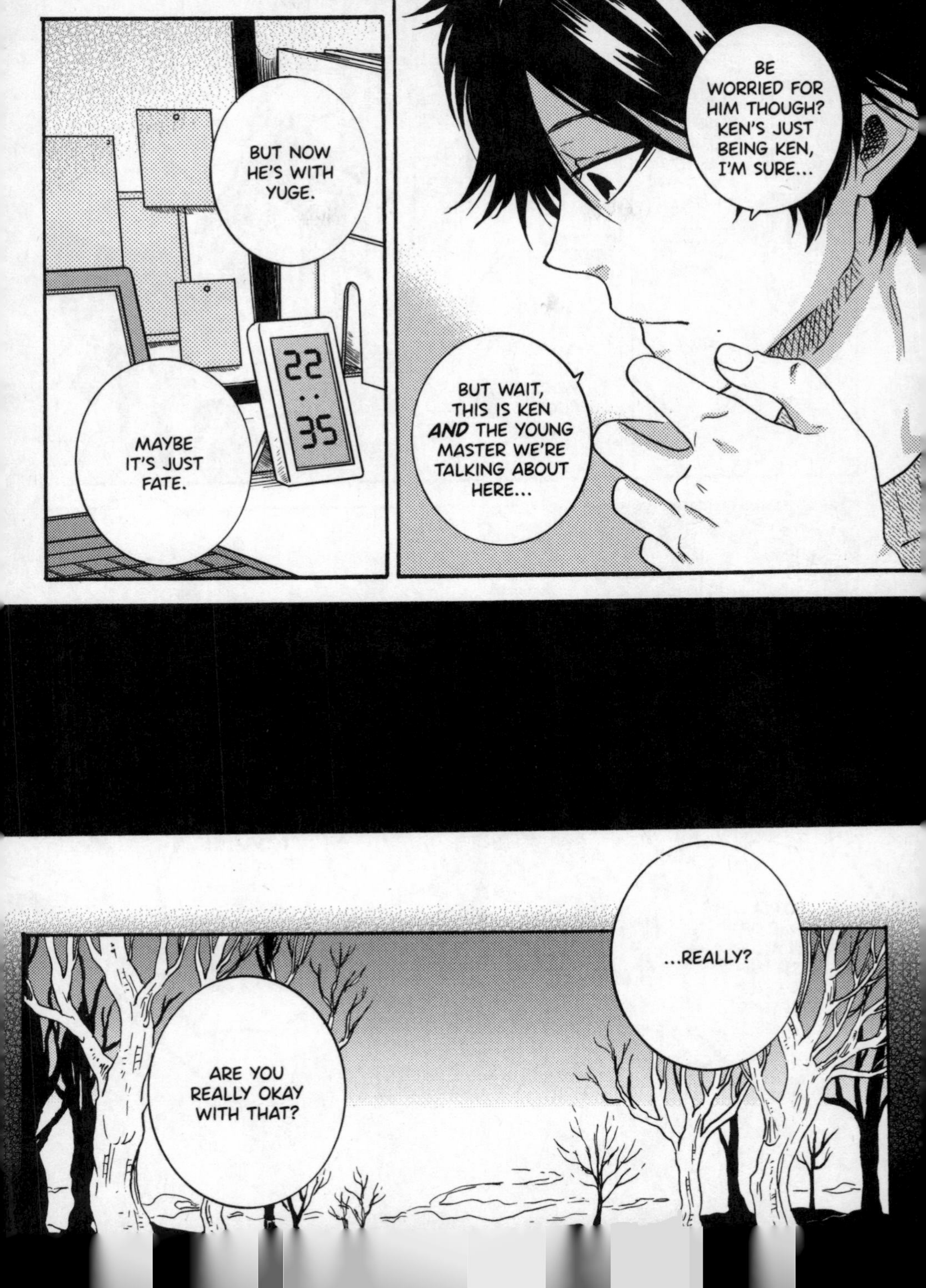
BE WORRIED FOR HIM THOUGH? KEN'S JUST BEING KEN, I'M SURE...
BUT WAIT, THIS IS KEN **AND** THE YOUNG MASTER WE'RE TALKING ABOUT HERE...
BUT NOW HE'S WITH YUGE.
22:35
MAYBE IT'S JUST FATE.
...REALLY?
ARE YOU REALLY OKAY WITH THAT?

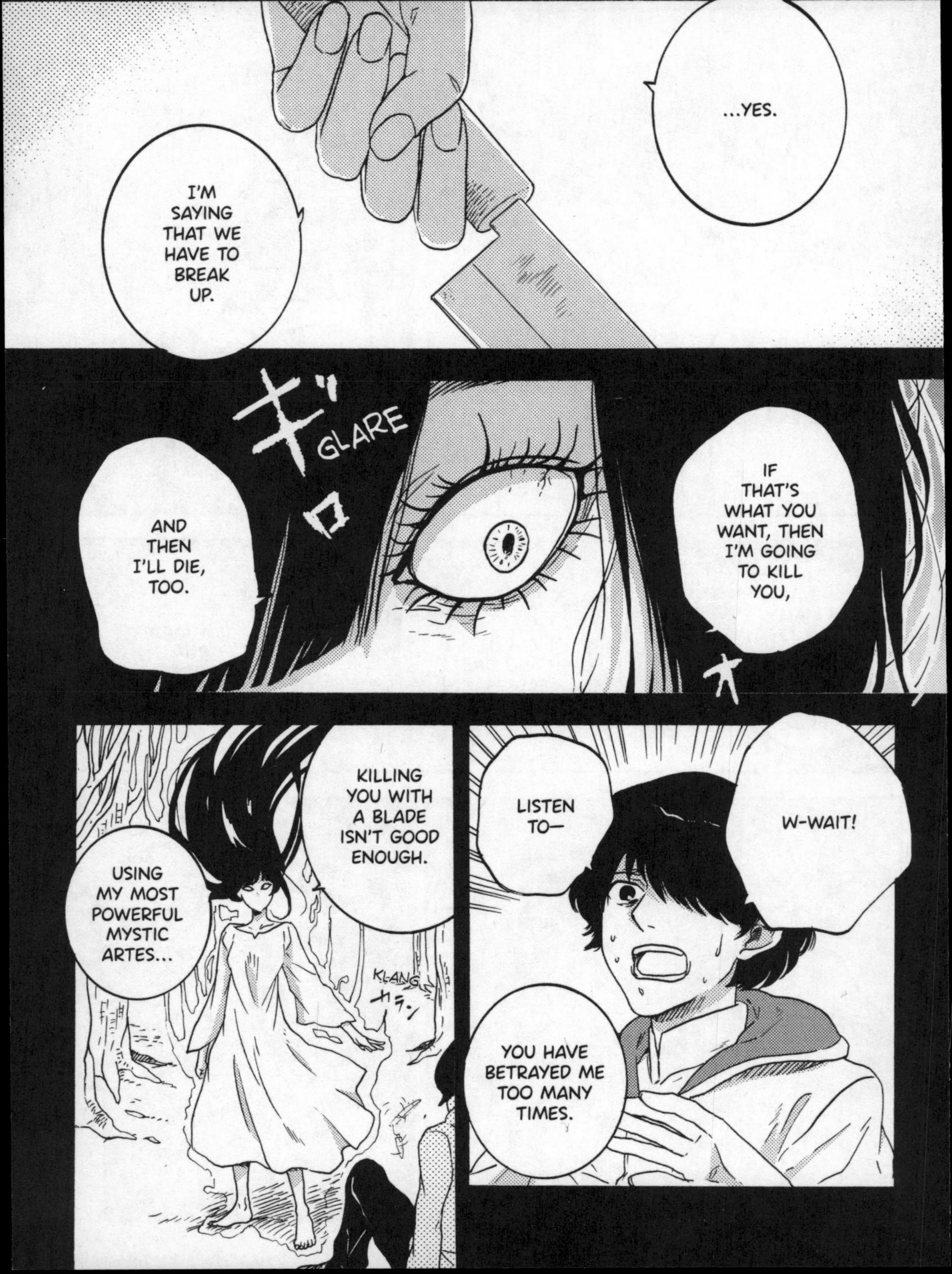
...YES.
I'M SAYING THAT WE HAVE TO BREAK UP.
IF THAT'S WHAT YOU WANT, THEN I'M GOING TO KILL YOU,
ギロ GLARE
AND THEN I'LL DIE, TOO.
W-WAIT!
LISTEN TO—
YOU HAVE BETRAYED ME TOO MANY TIMES.
KILLING YOU WITH A BLADE ISN'T GOOD ENOUGH.
USING MY MOST POWERFUL MYSTIC ARTES...
KLANG カラン

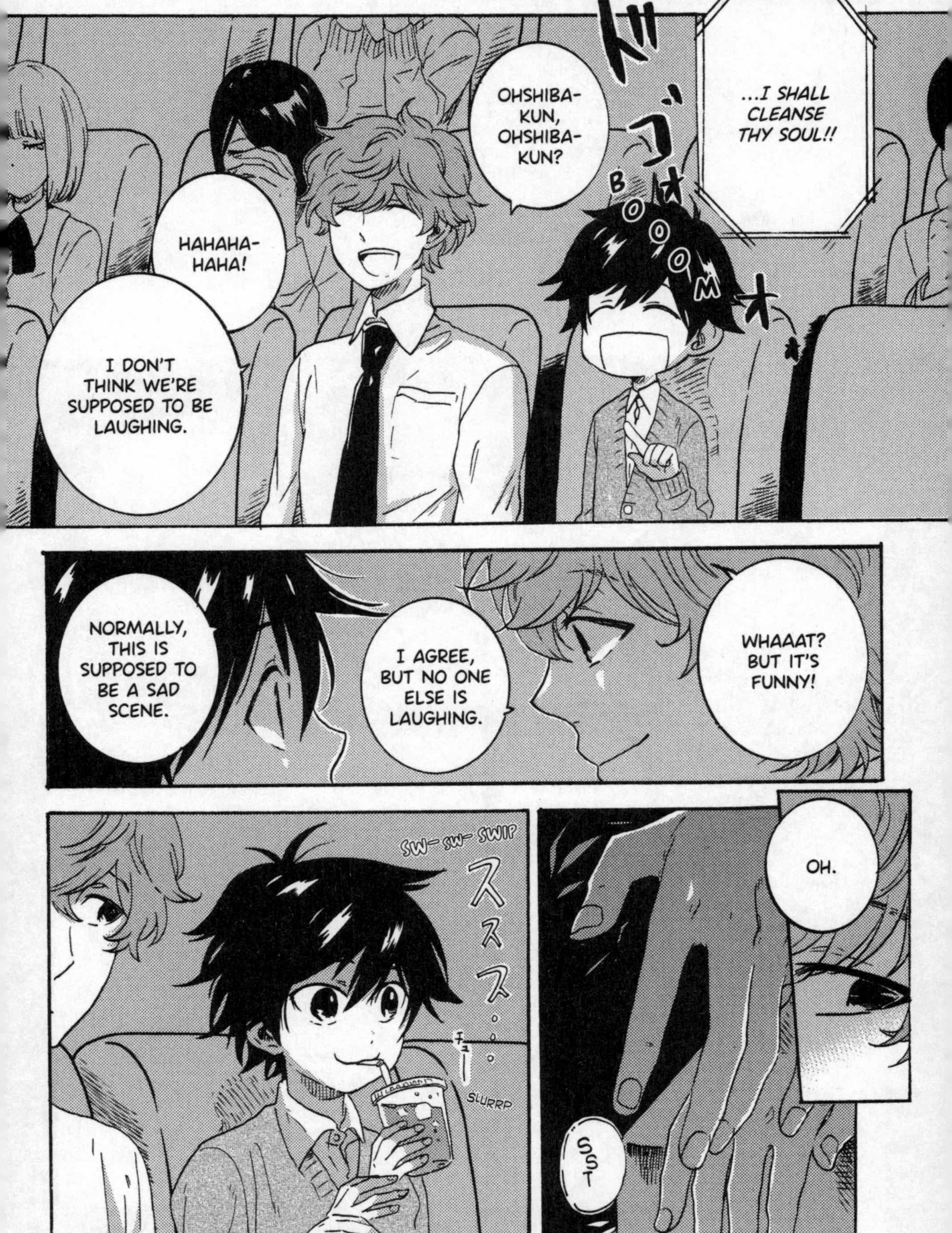
...I SHALL CLEANSE THY SOUL!!
BOOOOM
OHSHIBA-KUN, OHSHIBA-KUN?
HAHAHA-HAHA!
I DON'T THINK WE'RE SUPPOSED TO BE LAUGHING.
WHAAAT? BUT IT'S FUNNY!
I AGREE, BUT NO ONE ELSE IS LAUGHING.
NORMALLY, THIS IS SUPPOSED TO BE A SAD SCENE.
OH.
SST
SW-SW-SWIP
SLURRP

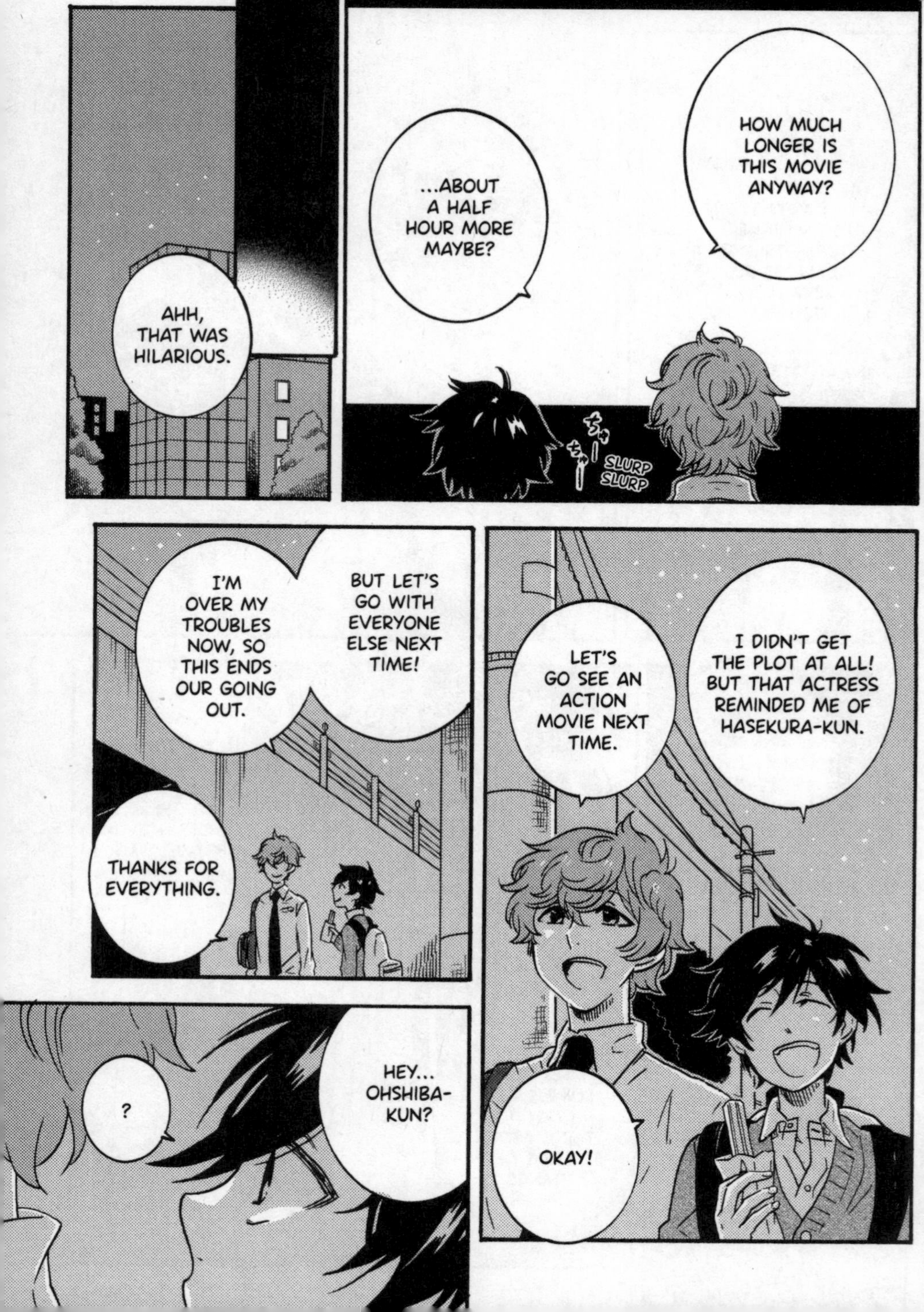
HOW MUCH LONGER IS THIS MOVIE ANYWAY?
...ABOUT A HALF HOUR MORE MAYBE?
ちゅー ちゅー
SLURP SLURP
AHH, THAT WAS HILARIOUS.
I DIDN'T GET THE PLOT AT ALL! BUT THAT ACTRESS REMINDED ME OF HASEKURA-KUN.
LET'S GO SEE AN ACTION MOVIE NEXT TIME.
OKAY!
I'M OVER MY TROUBLES NOW, SO THIS ENDS OUR GOING OUT.
BUT LET'S GO WITH EVERYONE ELSE NEXT TIME!
THANKS FOR EVERYTHING.
HEY... OHSHIBA-KUN?
?

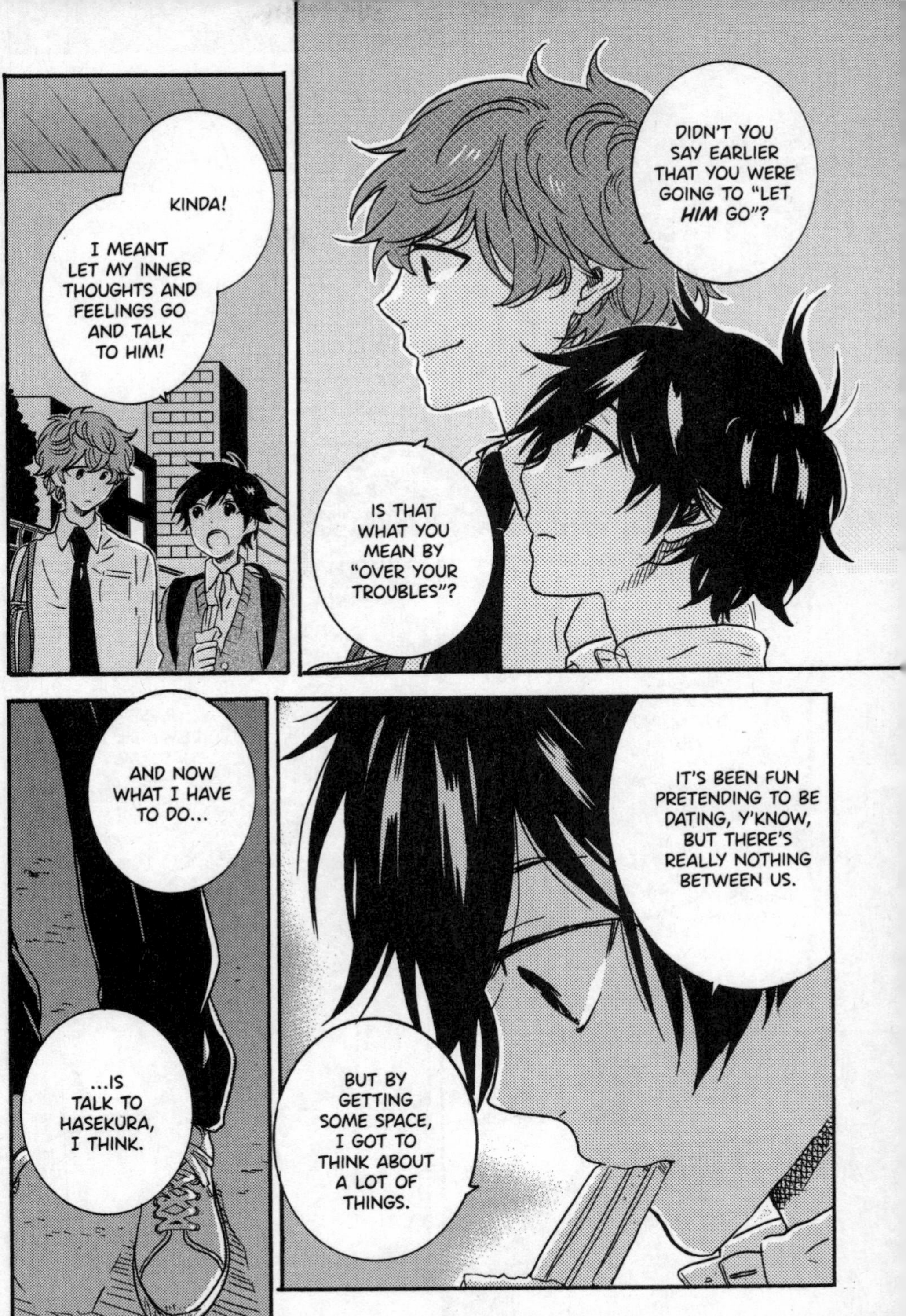
DIDN'T YOU SAY EARLIER THAT YOU WERE GOING TO "LET *HIM* GO"?
IS THAT WHAT YOU MEAN BY "OVER YOUR TROUBLES"?
KINDA!
I MEANT LET MY INNER THOUGHTS AND FEELINGS GO AND TALK TO HIM!
IT'S BEEN FUN PRETENDING TO BE DATING, Y'KNOW, BUT THERE'S REALLY NOTHING BETWEEN US.
BUT BY GETTING SOME SPACE, I GOT TO THINK ABOUT A LOT OF THINGS.
AND NOW WHAT I HAVE TO DO...
...IS TALK TO HASEKURA, I THINK.

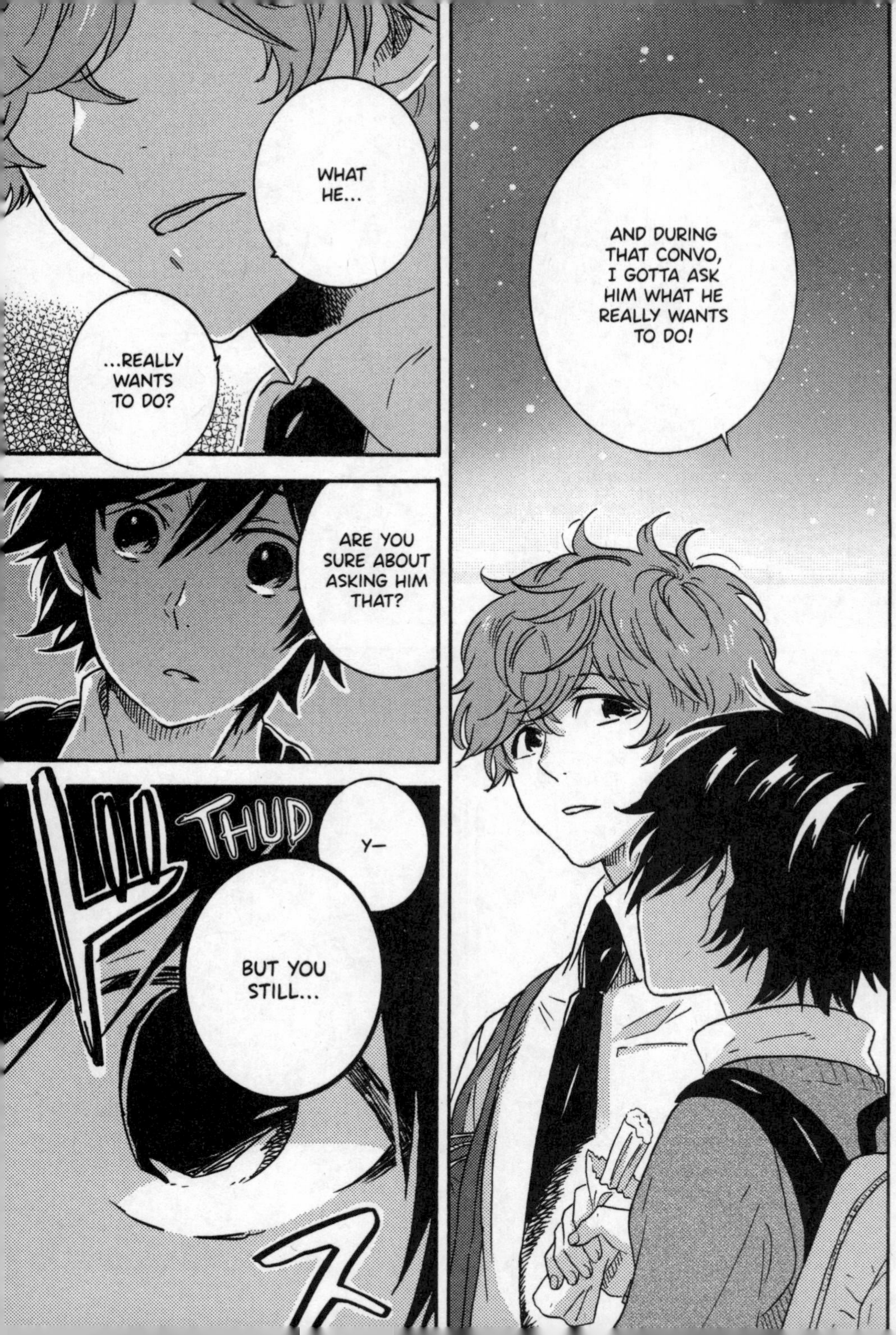
AND DURING THAT CONVO, I GOTTA ASK HIM WHAT HE REALLY WANTS TO DO!
WHAT HE...
...REALLY WANTS TO DO?
ARE YOU SURE ABOUT ASKING HIM THAT?
Y—
THUD
BUT YOU STILL...

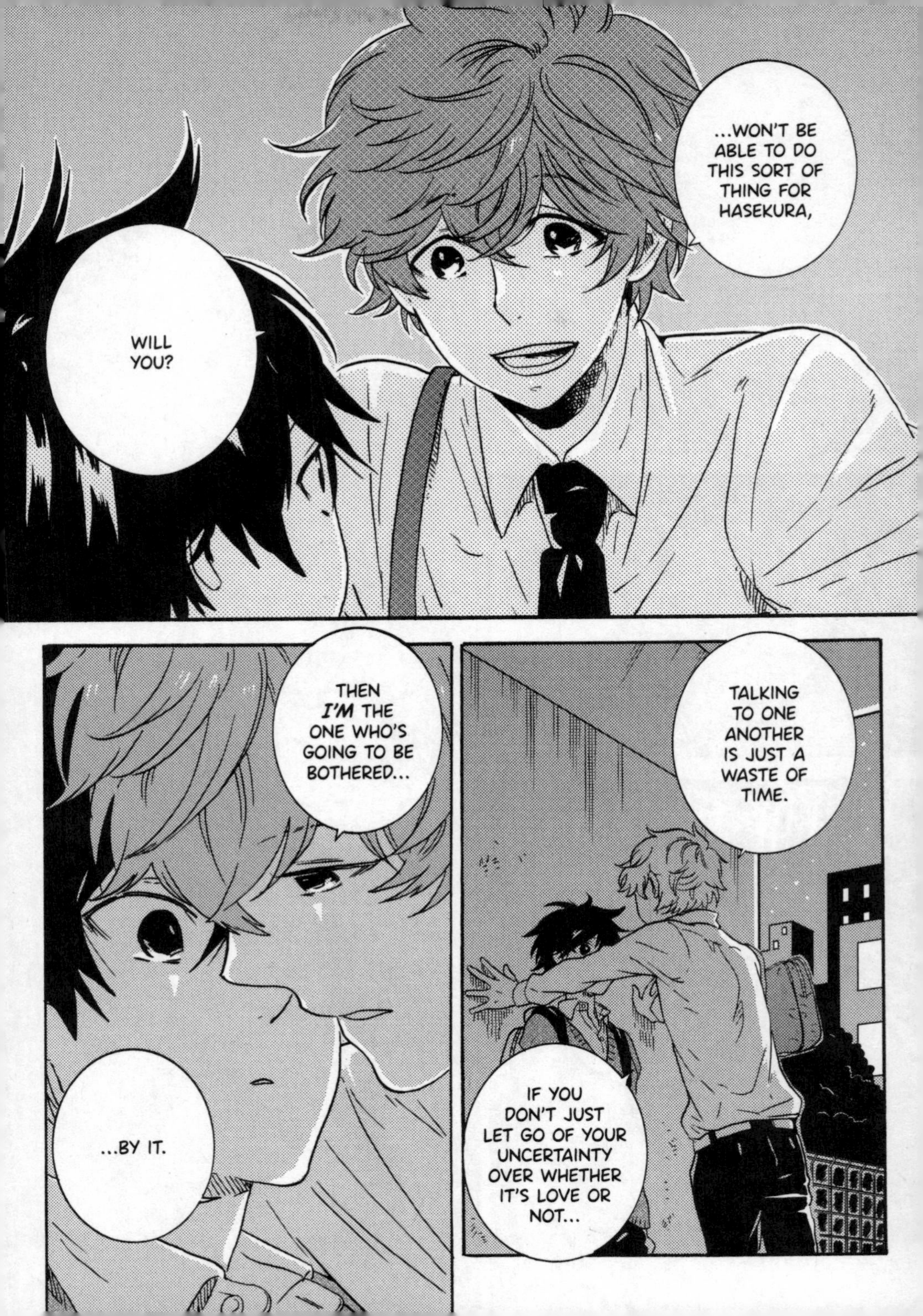
...WON'T BE ABLE TO DO THIS SORT OF THING FOR HASEKURA,
WILL YOU?
TALKING TO ONE ANOTHER IS JUST A WASTE OF TIME.
IF YOU DON'T JUST LET GO OF YOUR UNCERTAINTY OVER WHETHER IT'S LOVE OR NOT...
THEN *I'M* THE ONE WHO'S GOING TO BE BOTHERED...
...BY IT.

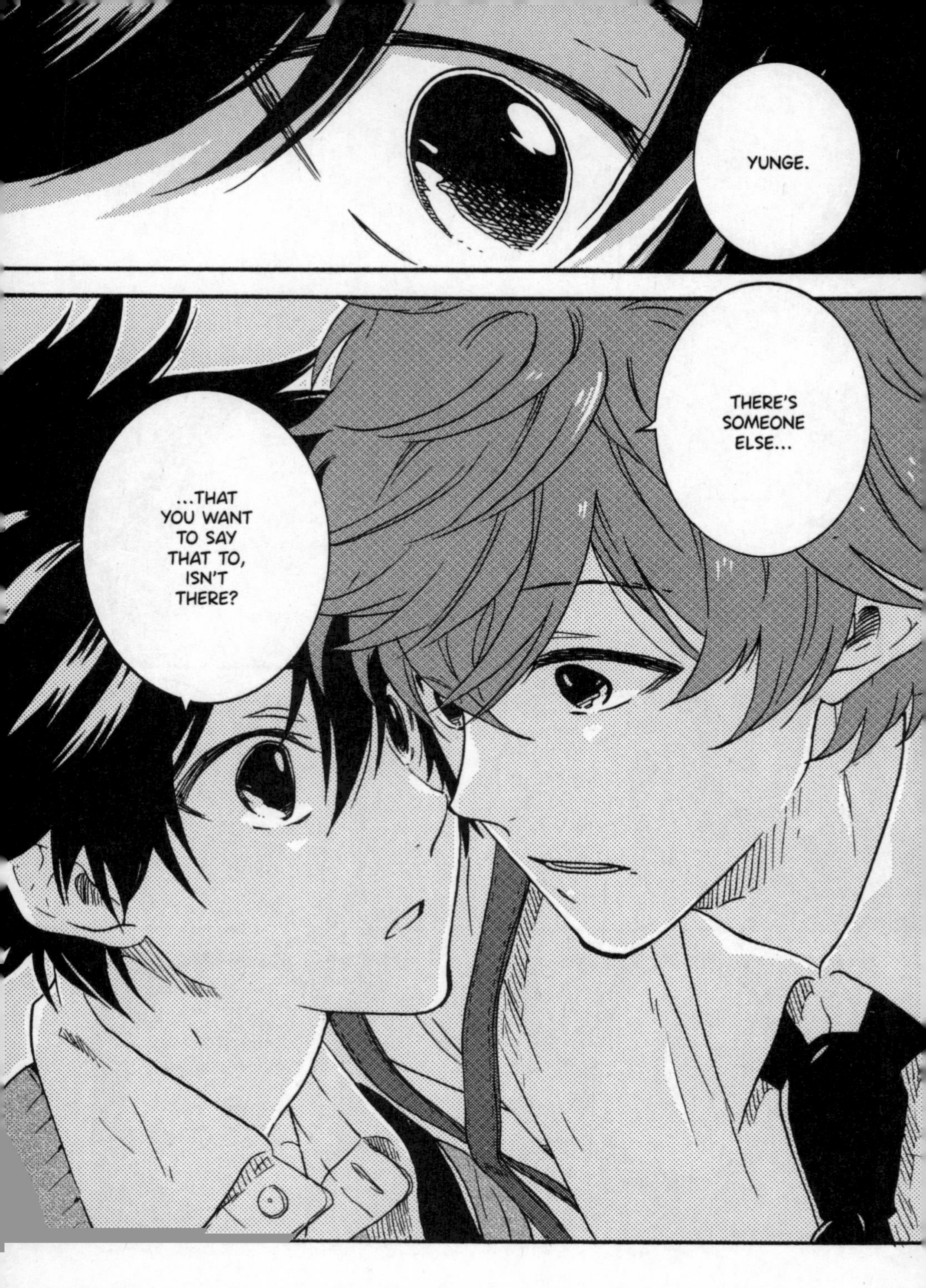
YUNGE.
THERE'S SOMEONE ELSE...
...THAT YOU WANT TO SAY THAT TO, ISN'T THERE?

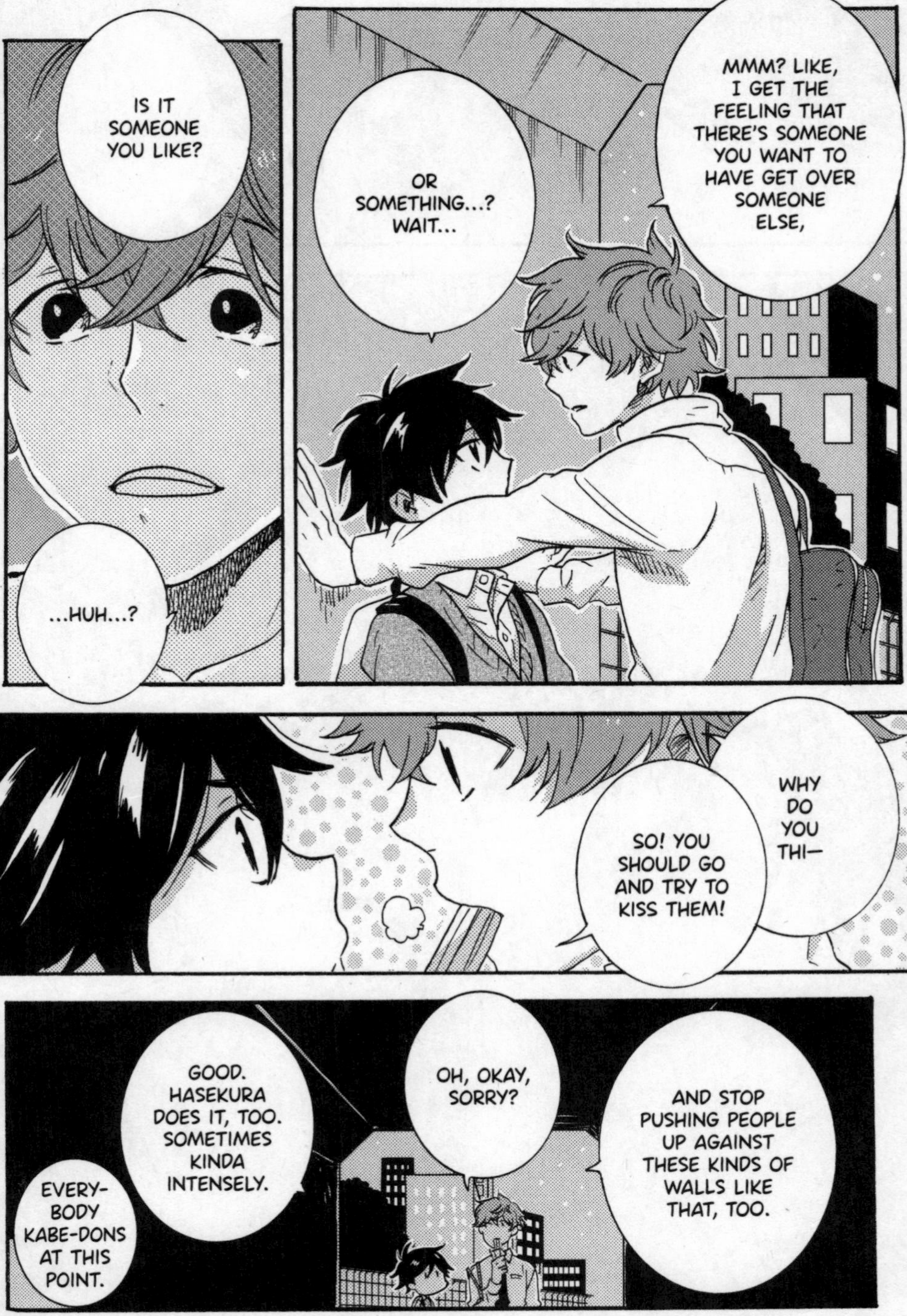
MMM? LIKE, I GET THE FEELING THAT THERE'S SOMEONE YOU WANT TO HAVE GET OVER SOMEONE ELSE,
OR SOMETHING...? WAIT...
IS IT SOMEONE YOU LIKE?
...HUH...?
WHY DO YOU THI—
SO! YOU SHOULD GO AND TRY TO KISS THEM!
AND STOP PUSHING PEOPLE UP AGAINST THESE KINDS OF WALLS LIKE THAT, TOO.
OH, OKAY, SORRY?
GOOD. HASEKURA DOES IT, TOO. SOMETIMES KINDA INTENSELY.
EVERY-BODY KABE-DONS AT THIS POINT.

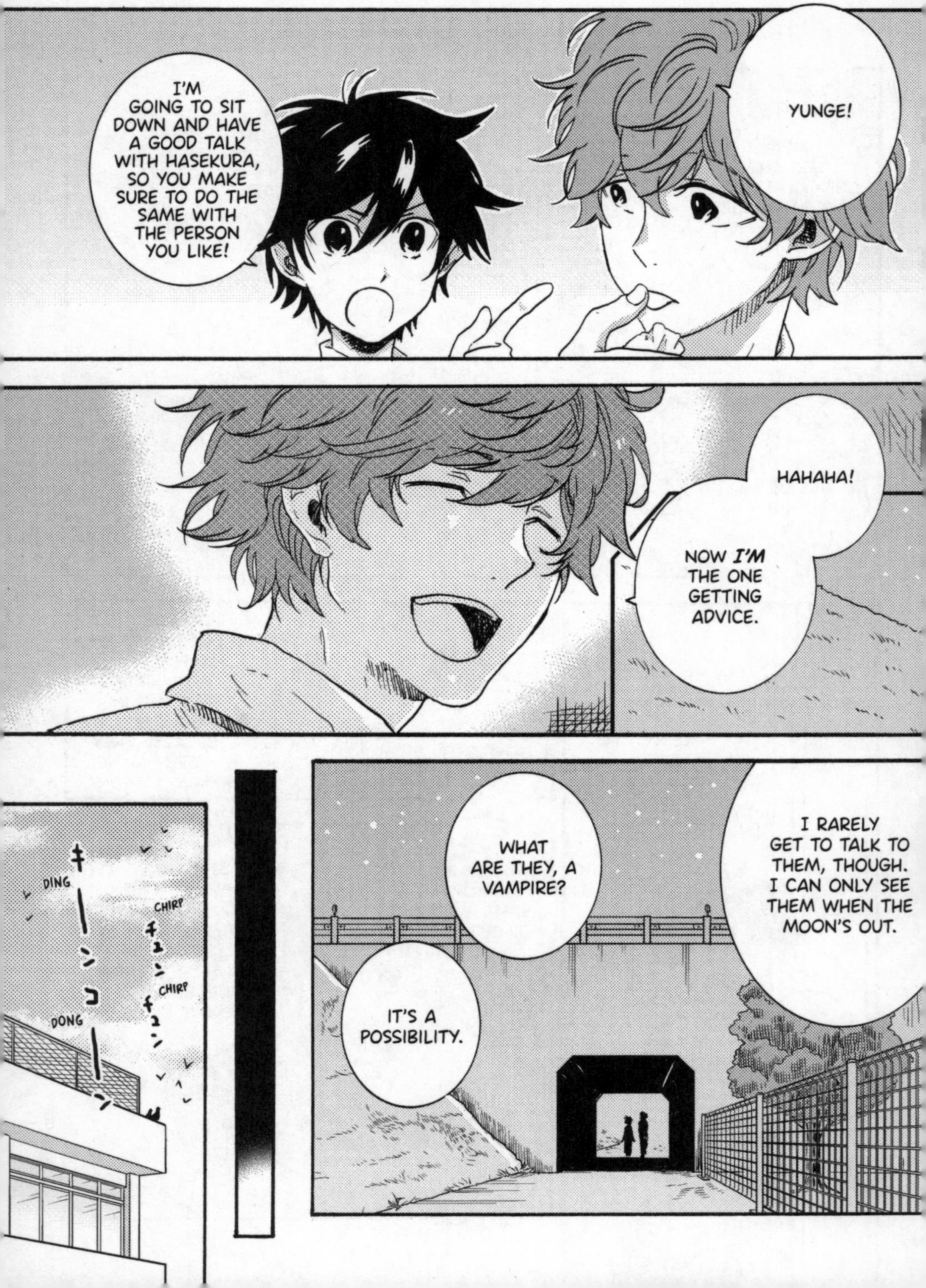
YUNGE!
I'M GOING TO SIT DOWN AND HAVE A GOOD TALK WITH HASEKURA, SO YOU MAKE SURE TO DO THE SAME WITH THE PERSON YOU LIKE!
HAHAHA!
NOW *I'M* THE ONE GETTING ADVICE.
I RARELY GET TO TALK TO THEM, THOUGH. I CAN ONLY SEE THEM WHEN THE MOON'S OUT.
WHAT ARE THEY, A VAMPIRE?
IT'S A POSSIBILITY.
チュンチュン
CHIRP
CHIRP
キーンコーン
DING
DONG

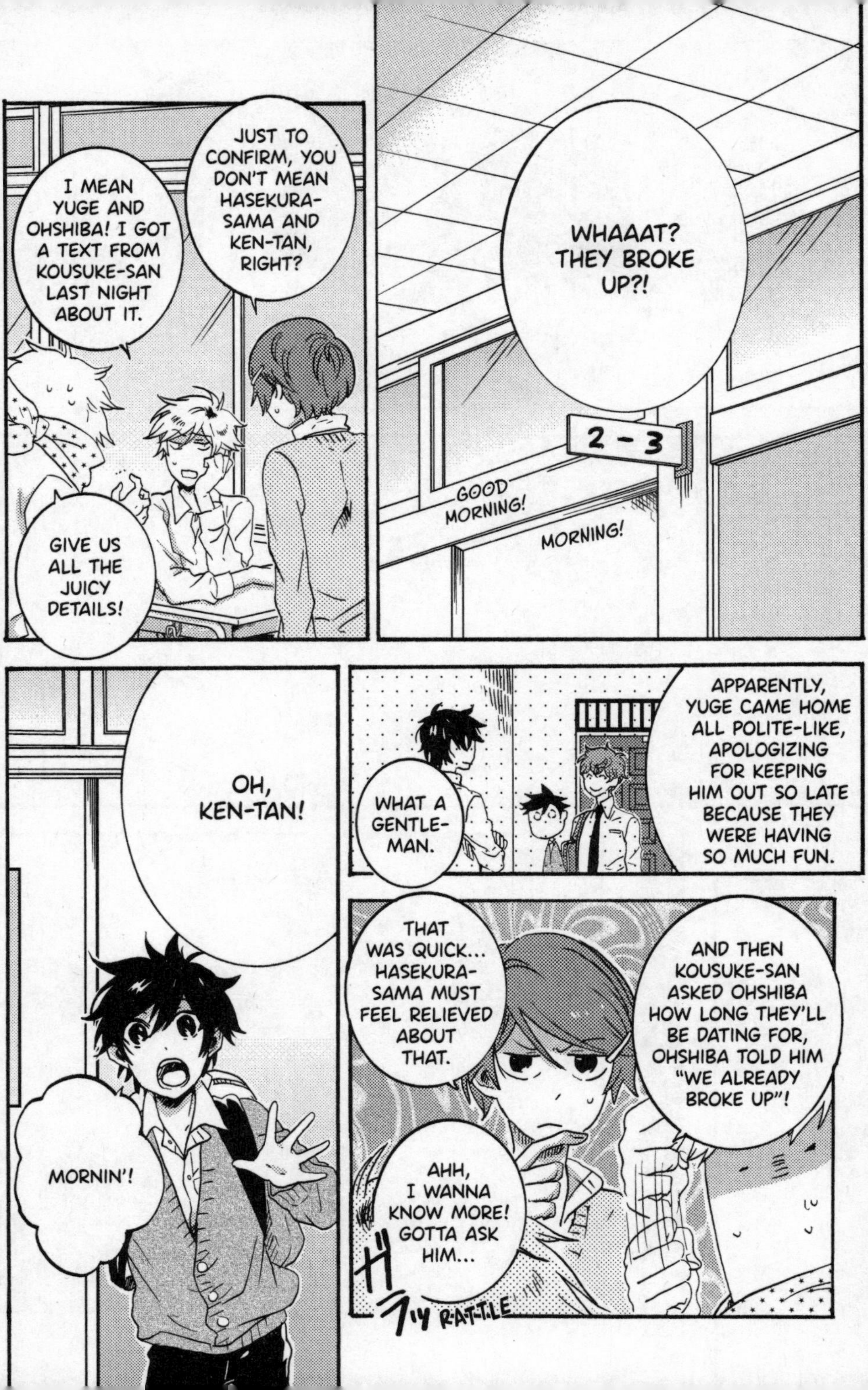
WHAAAT? THEY BROKE UP?!
2 - 3
GOOD MORNING!
MORNING!
JUST TO CONFIRM, YOU DON'T MEAN HASEKURA-SAMA AND KEN-TAN, RIGHT?
I MEAN YUGE AND OHSHIBA! I GOT A TEXT FROM KOUSUKE-SAN LAST NIGHT ABOUT IT.
GIVE US ALL THE JUICY DETAILS!
APPARENTLY, YUGE CAME HOME ALL POLITE-LIKE, APOLOGIZING FOR KEEPING HIM OUT SO LATE BECAUSE THEY WERE HAVING SO MUCH FUN.
WHAT A GENTLE-MAN.
AND THEN KOUSUKE-SAN ASKED OHSHIBA HOW LONG THEY'LL BE DATING FOR, OHSHIBA TOLD HIM "WE ALREADY BROKE UP"!
THAT WAS QUICK... HASEKURA-SAMA MUST FEEL RELIEVED ABOUT THAT.
AHH, I WANNA KNOW MORE! GOTTA ASK HIM...
RATTLE
OH, KEN-TAN!
MORNIN'!

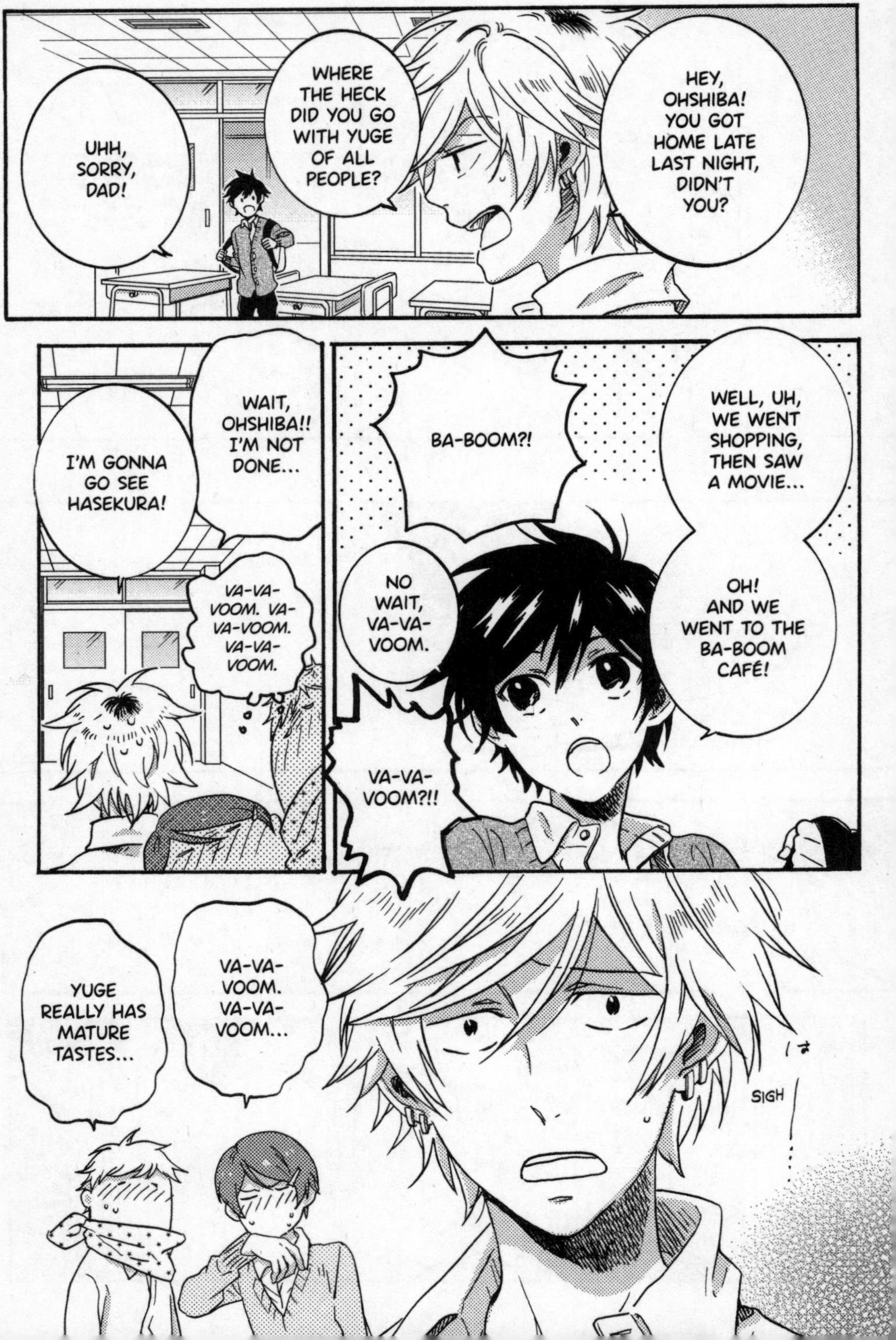
HEY, OHSHIBA! YOU GOT HOME LATE LAST NIGHT, DIDN'T YOU?
WHERE THE HECK DID YOU GO WITH YUGE OF ALL PEOPLE?
UHH, SORRY, DAD!
WELL, UH, WE WENT SHOPPING, THEN SAW A MOVIE...
OH! AND WE WENT TO THE BA-BOOM CAFÉ!
BA-BOOM?!
NO WAIT, VA-VA-VOOM.
VA-VA-VOOM?!!
WAIT, OHSHIBA!! I'M NOT DONE...
I'M GONNA GO SEE HASEKURA!
VA-VA-VOOM. VA-VA-VOOM. VA-VA-VOOM.
SIGH
VA-VA-VOOM. VA-VA-VOOM...
YUGE REALLY HAS MATURE TASTES...

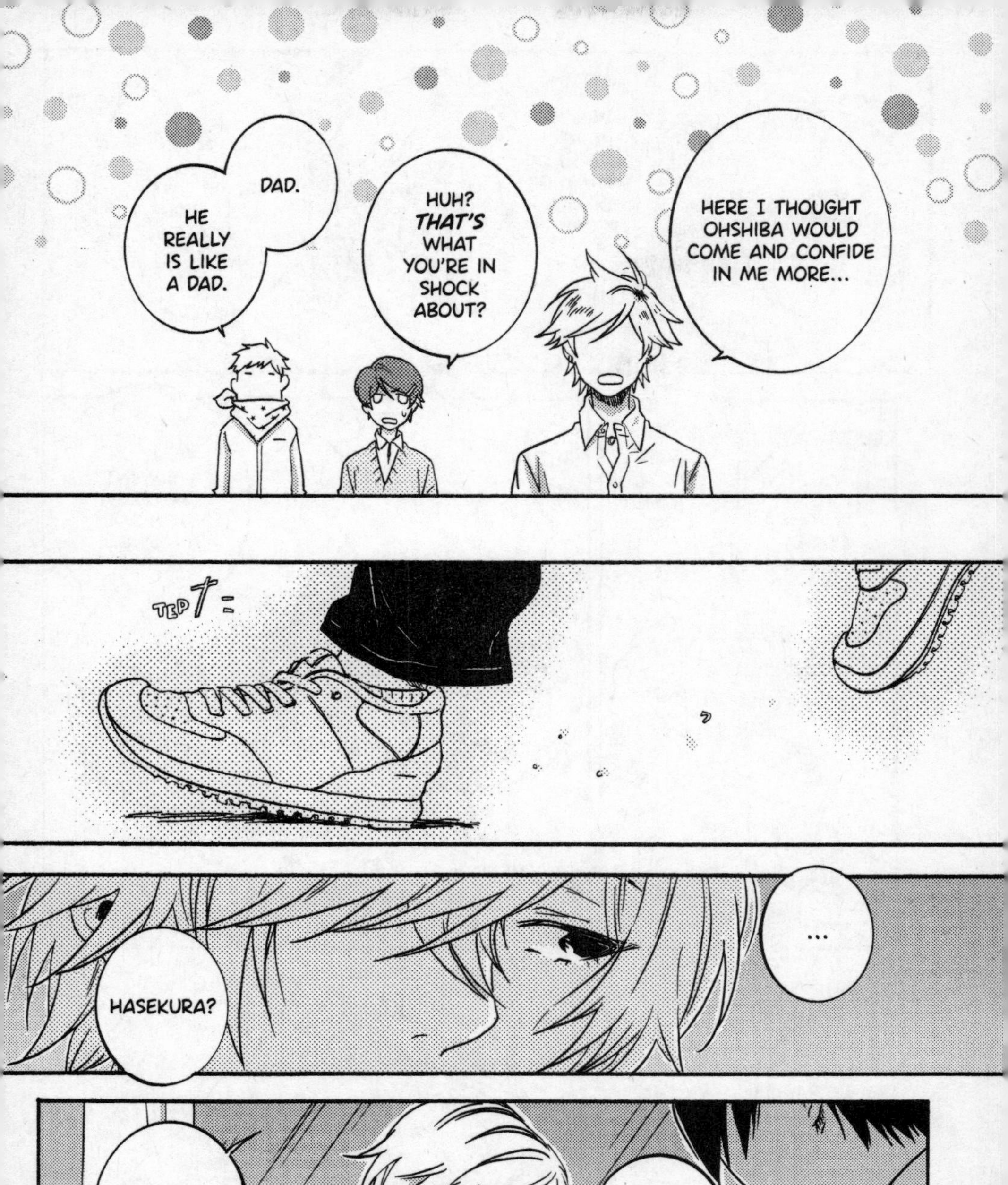
HERE I THOUGHT OHSHIBA WOULD COME AND CONFIDE IN ME MORE...
HUH? *THAT'S* WHAT YOU'RE IN SHOCK ABOUT?
DAD.
HE REALLY IS LIKE A DAD.
TEP
...
HASEKURA?
UM, SO I NEED YOU TO...
...FILL OUT THIS SHEET.
UHHH...

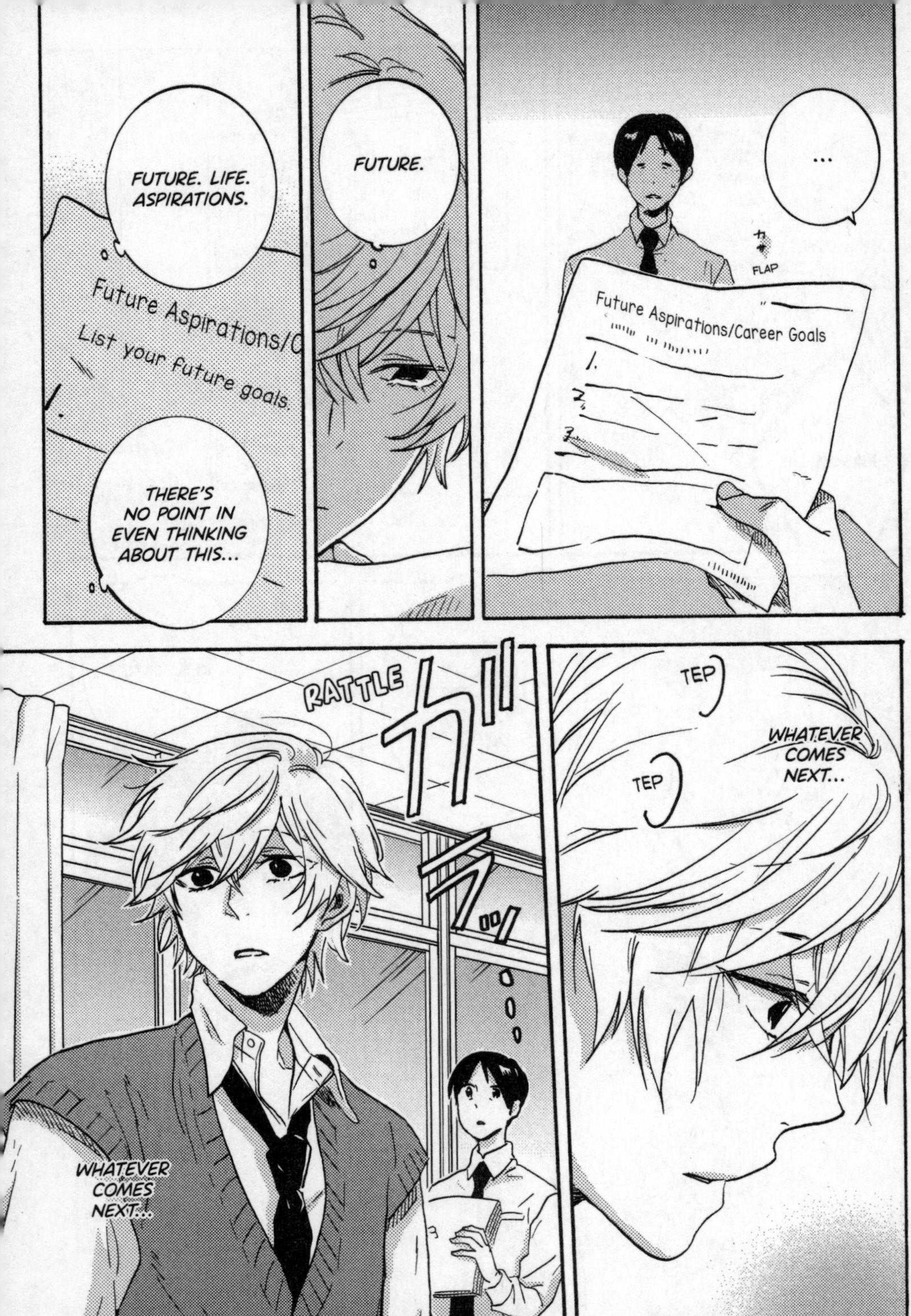
...
FLAP
Future Aspirations/Career Goals
1.
2.
3.
FUTURE.
FUTURE. LIFE. ASPIRATIONS.
Future Aspirations/C
List your future goals.
1.
THERE'S NO POINT IN EVEN THINKING ABOUT THIS...
TEP
TEP
WHATEVER COMES NEXT...
RATTLE
WHATEVER COMES NEXT...

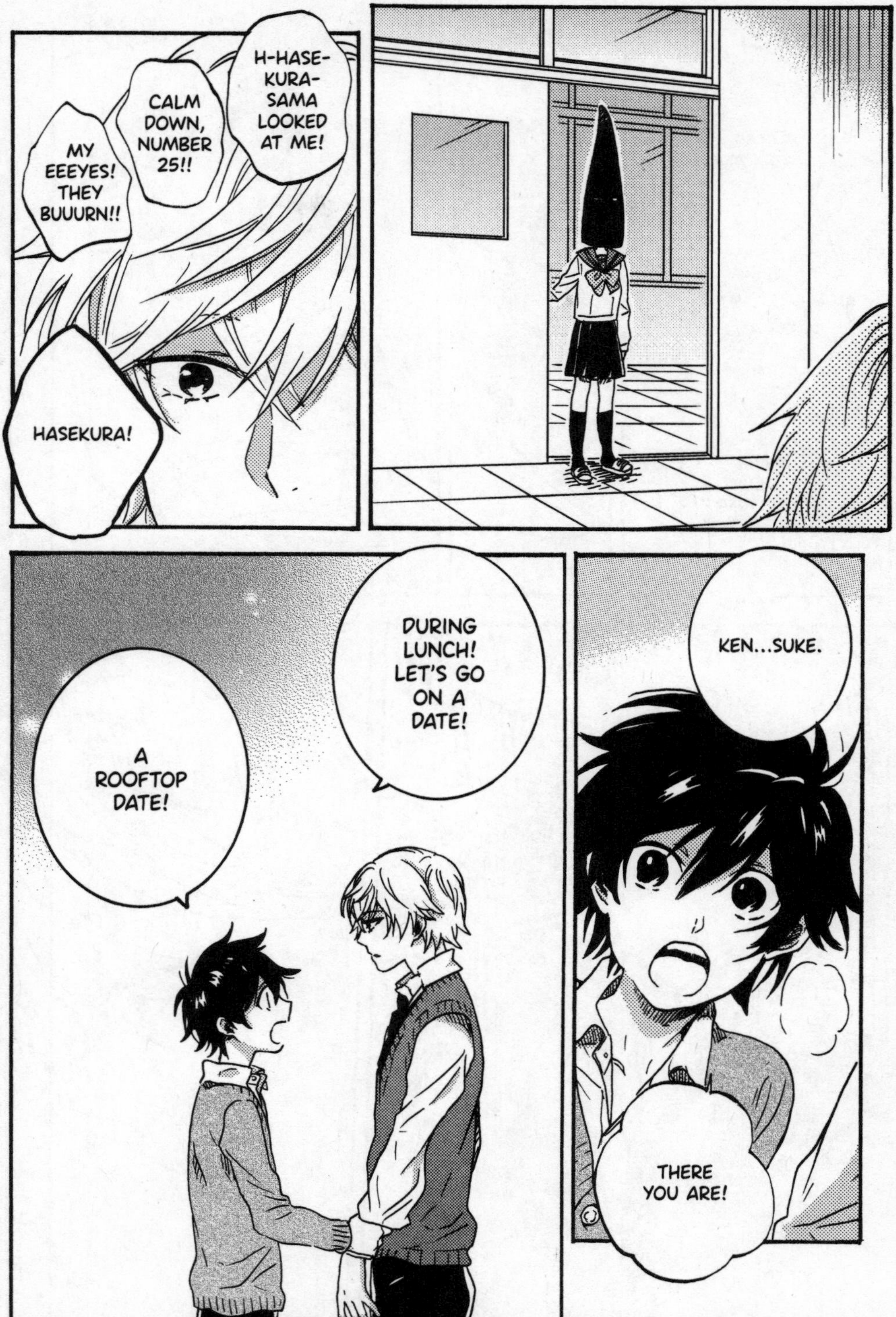
H-HASE-KURA-SAMA LOOKED AT ME!
CALM DOWN, NUMBER 25!!
MY EEEYES! THEY BUUURN!!
HASEKURA!
KEN...SUKE.
THERE YOU ARE!
DURING LUNCH! LET'S GO ON A DATE!
A ROOFTOP DATE!

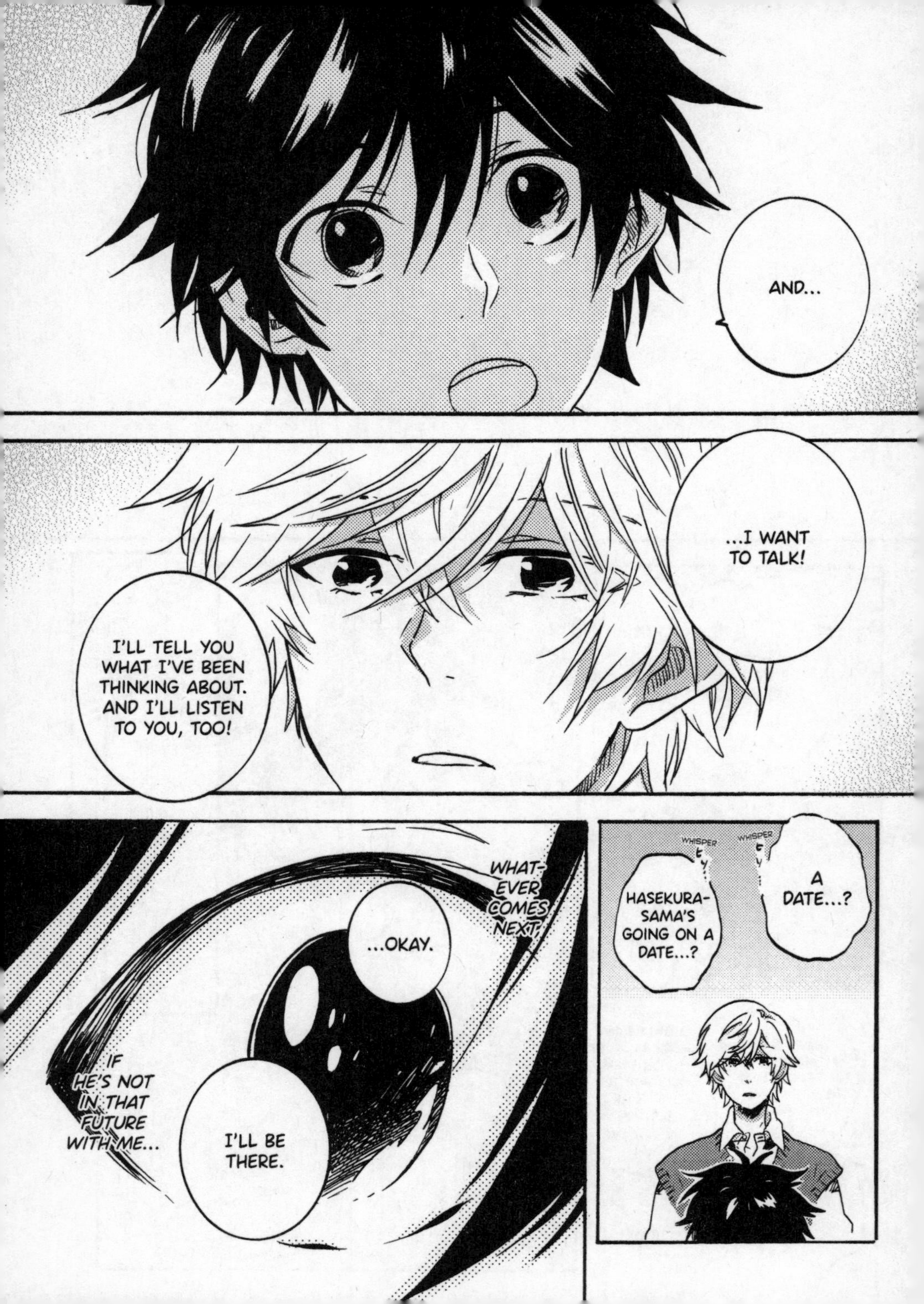
AND...
...I WANT TO TALK!
I'LL TELL YOU WHAT I'VE BEEN THINKING ABOUT. AND I'LL LISTEN TO YOU, TOO!
WHISPER
WHISPER
A DATE...?
HASEKURA-SAMA'S GOING ON A DATE...?
WHAT-EVER COMES NEXT,
...OKAY.
IF HE'S NOT IN THAT FUTURE WITH ME...
I'LL BE THERE.

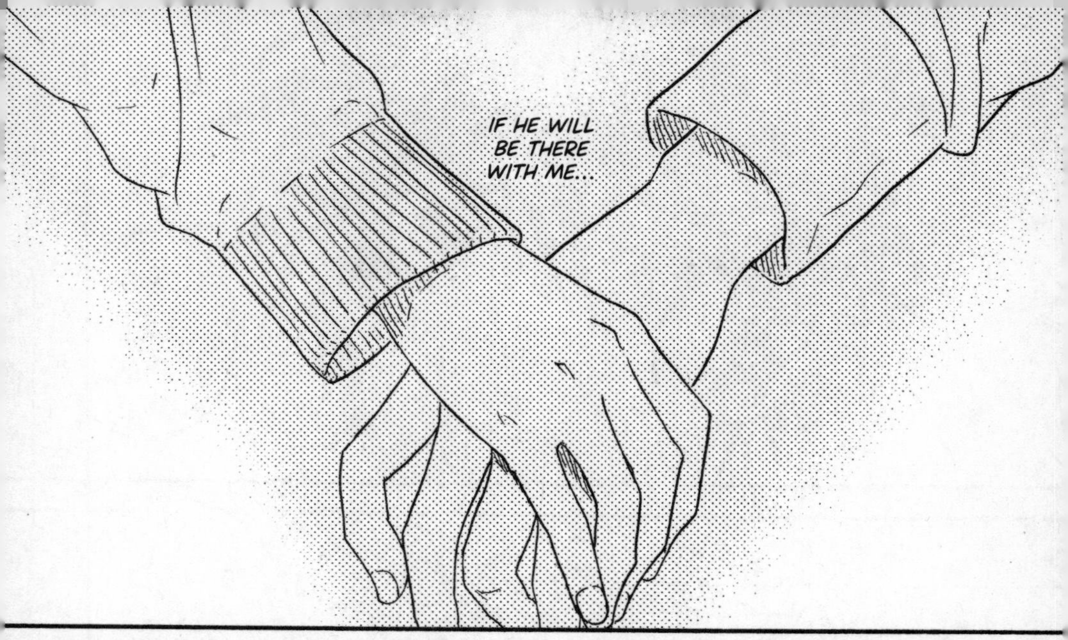
IF HE WILL BE THERE WITH ME...

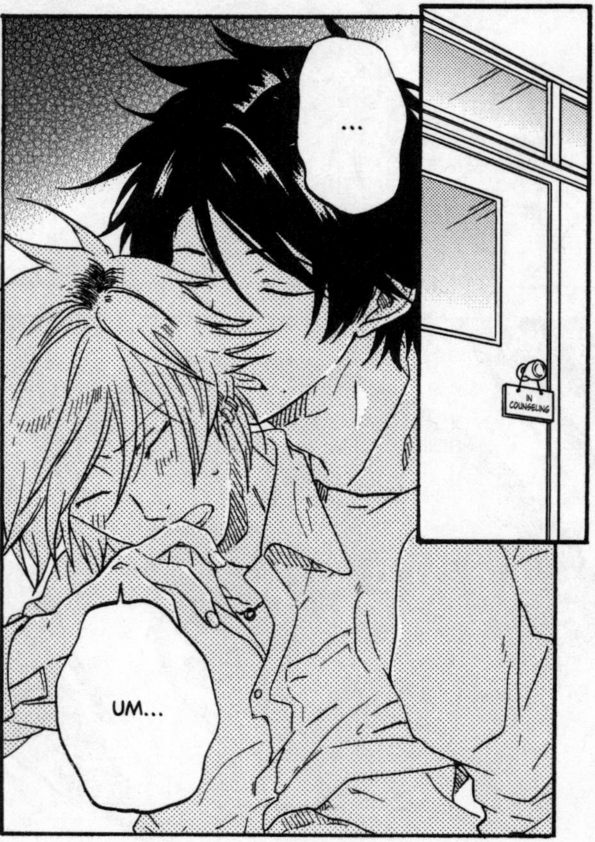
...
IN COUNSELING
UM...

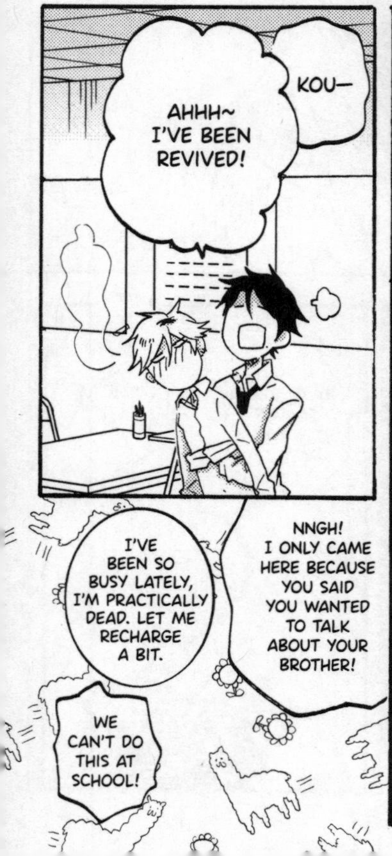
KOU—
AHHH~ I'VE BEEN REVIVED!
NNGH! I ONLY CAME HERE BECAUSE YOU SAID YOU WANTED TO TALK ABOUT YOUR BROTHER!
I'VE BEEN SO BUSY LATELY, I'M PRACTICALLY DEAD. LET ME RECHARGE A BIT.
WE CAN'T DO THIS AT SCHOOL!

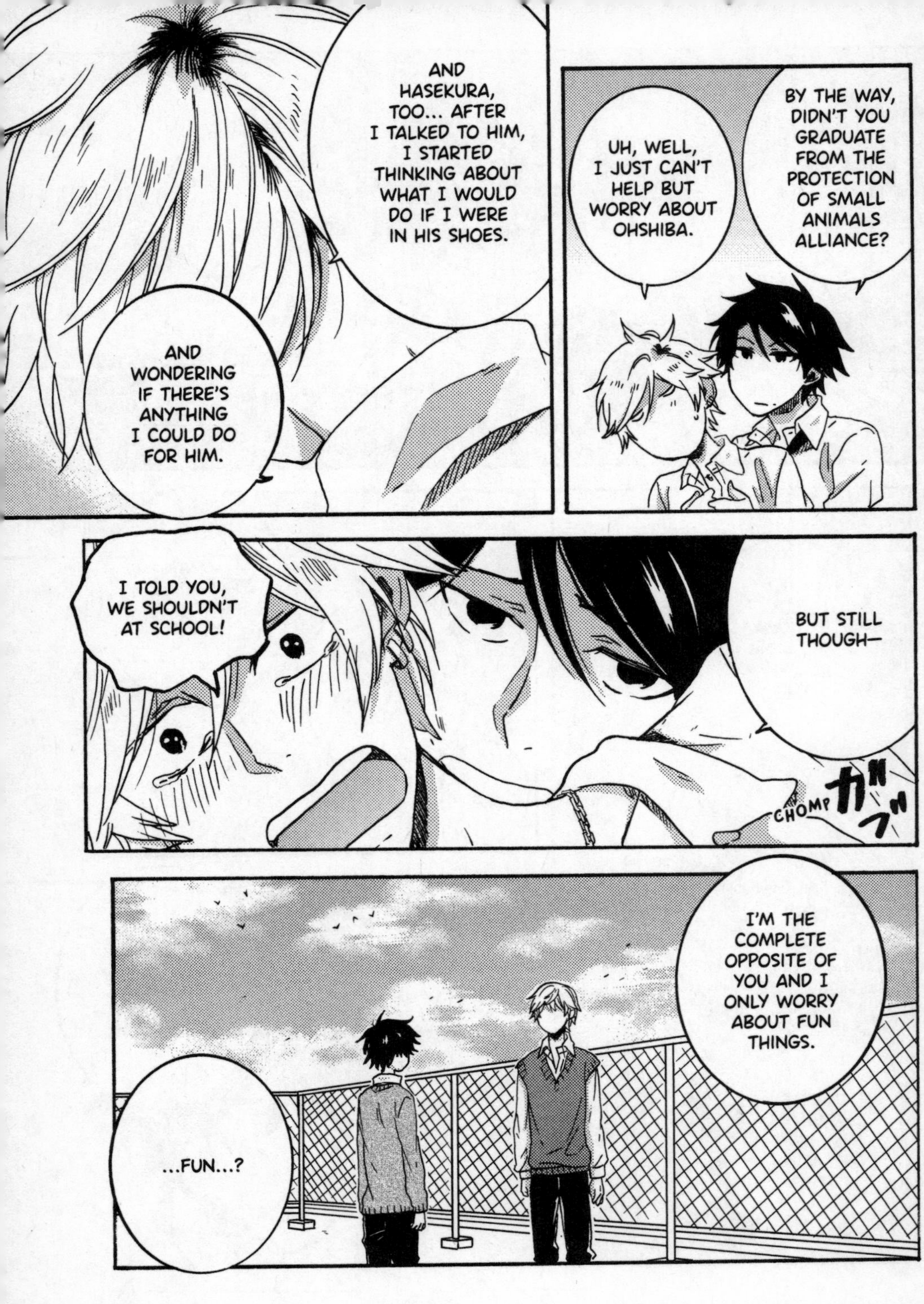
BY THE WAY, DIDN'T YOU GRADUATE FROM THE PROTECTION OF SMALL ANIMALS ALLIANCE?
UH, WELL, I JUST CAN'T HELP BUT WORRY ABOUT OHSHIBA.
AND HASEKURA, TOO... AFTER I TALKED TO HIM, I STARTED THINKING ABOUT WHAT I WOULD DO IF I WERE IN HIS SHOES.
AND WONDERING IF THERE'S ANYTHING I COULD DO FOR HIM.
BUT STILL THOUGH—
CHOMP
I TOLD YOU, WE SHOULDN'T AT SCHOOL!
I'M THE COMPLETE OPPOSITE OF YOU AND I ONLY WORRY ABOUT FUN THINGS.
...FUN...?

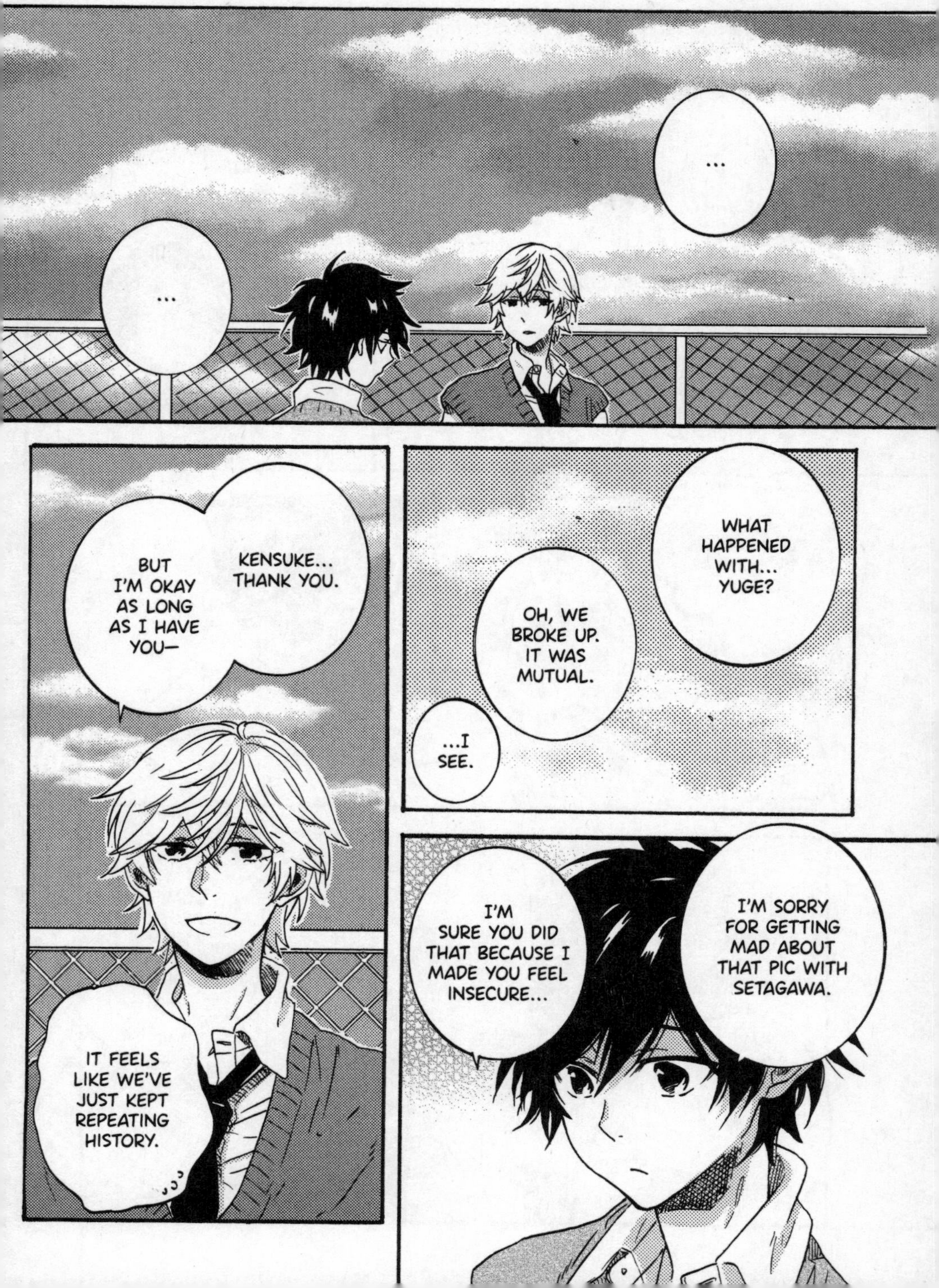
...
...
WHAT HAPPENED WITH... YUGE?
OH, WE BROKE UP. IT WAS MUTUAL.
...I SEE.
I'M SORRY FOR GETTING MAD ABOUT THAT PIC WITH SETAGAWA.
I'M SURE YOU DID THAT BECAUSE I MADE YOU FEEL INSECURE...
KENSUKE... THANK YOU.
BUT I'M OKAY AS LONG AS I HAVE YOU—
IT FEELS LIKE WE'VE JUST KEPT REPEATING HISTORY.

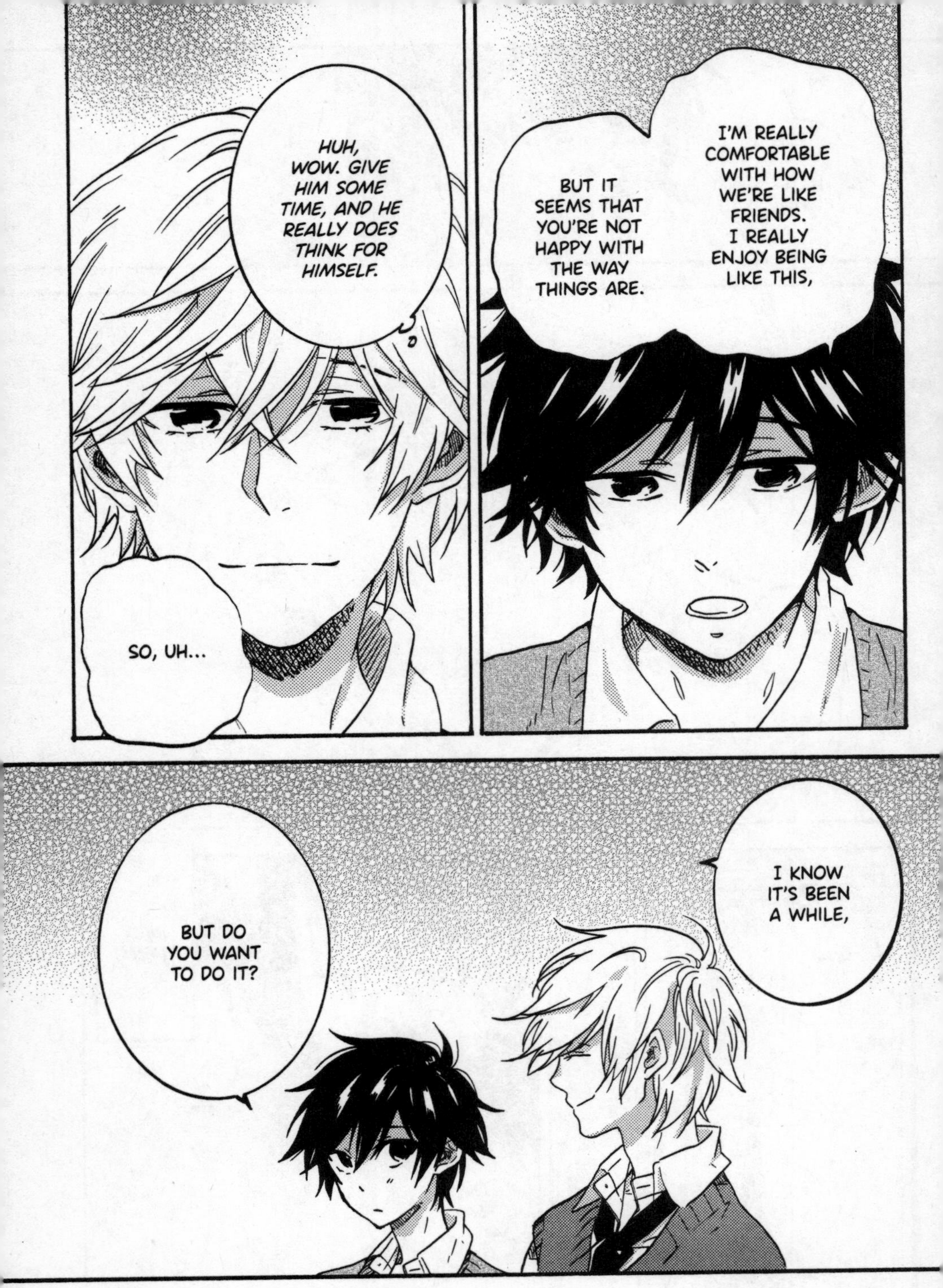
I'M REALLY COMFORTABLE WITH HOW WE'RE LIKE FRIENDS. I REALLY ENJOY BEING LIKE THIS,
BUT IT SEEMS THAT YOU'RE NOT HAPPY WITH THE WAY THINGS ARE.
HUH, WOW. GIVE HIM SOME TIME, AND HE REALLY DOES THINK FOR HIMSELF.
SO, UH...
I KNOW IT'S BEEN A WHILE,
BUT DO YOU WANT TO DO IT?

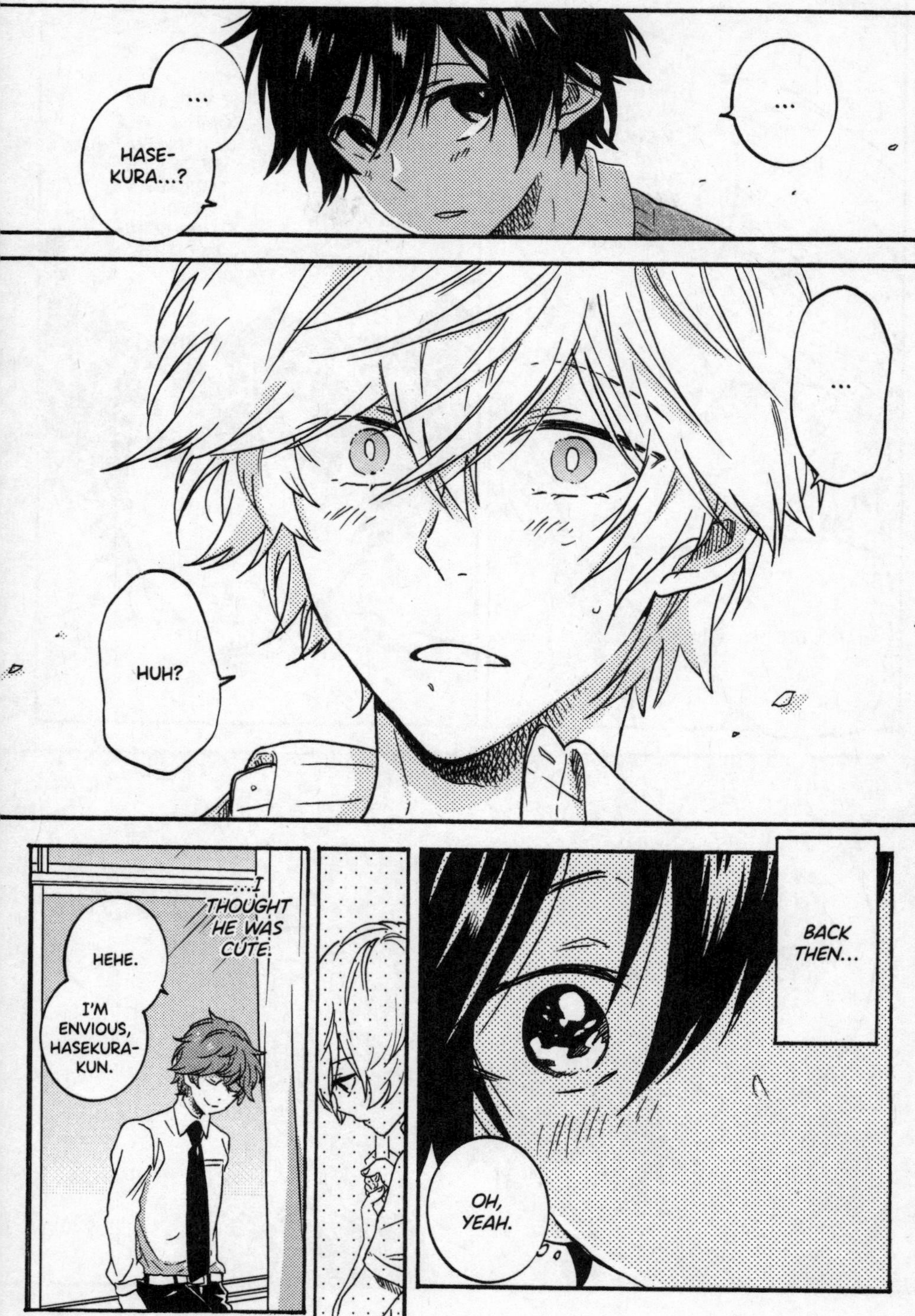
...
... HASE-KURA...?
...
HUH?
BACK THEN...
OH, YEAH.
...I THOUGHT HE WAS CUTE.
HEHE.
I'M ENVIOUS, HASEKURA-KUN.

Hitorijime
My Hero

Leading role

Rusanchi Yamakawa (28)

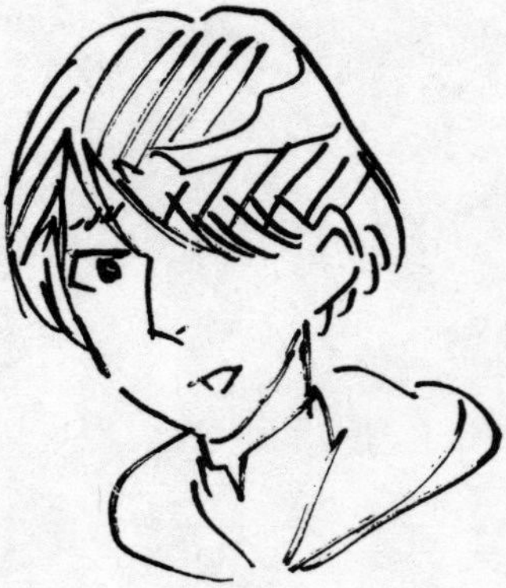

Interview

"The mystic arte
used on me
in the forest
was way too
terrifying,
wasn't it?
It actually hurt
my ribs (lol)"

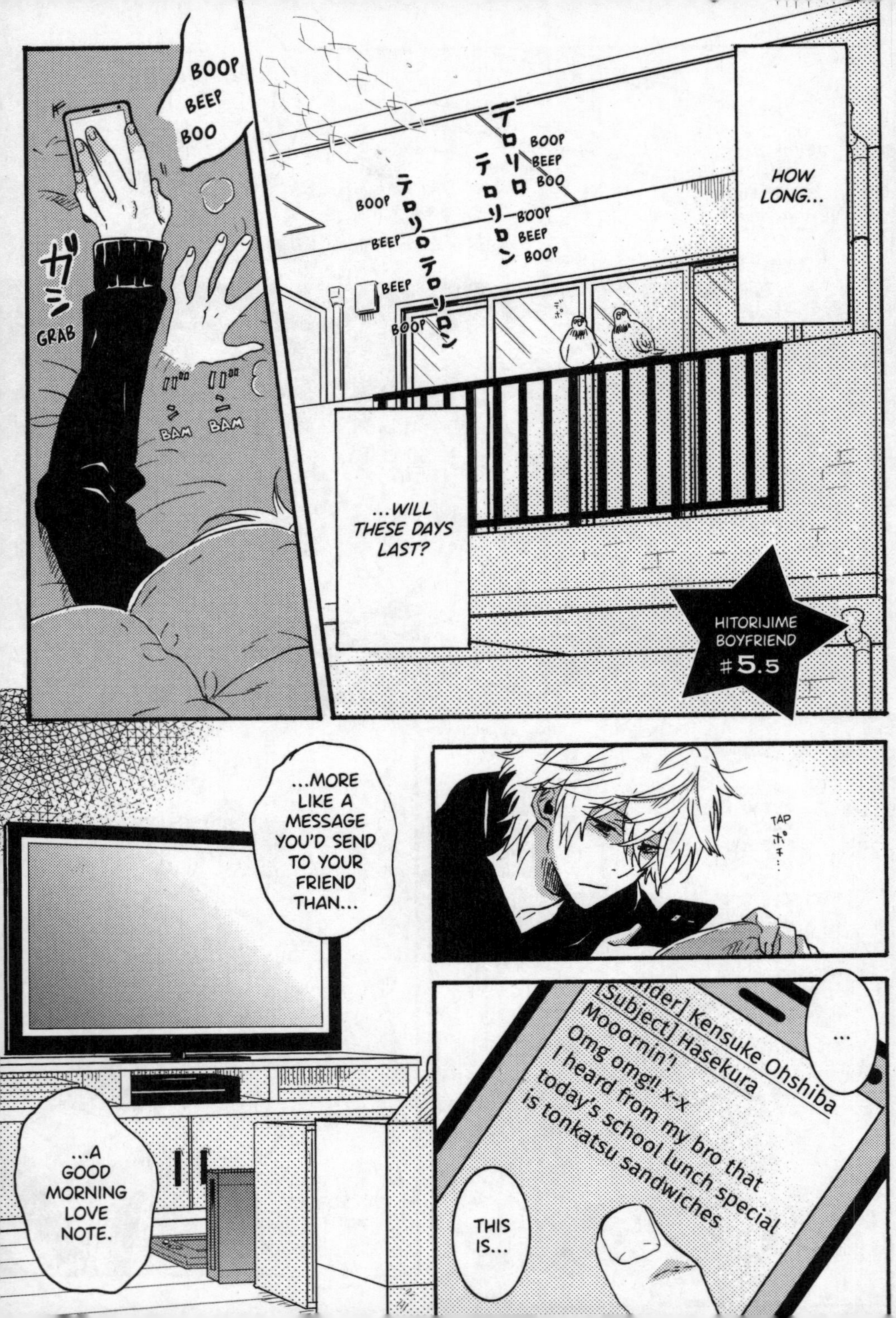
HOW LONG...
テロリロ テロリロン
BOOP BEEP BOO
BOOP BEEP BOOP
テロリロ テロリロン
BOOP BEEP BEEP BOOP
...WILL THESE DAYS LAST?
HITORIJIME BOYFRIEND #5.5
BOOP BEEP BOO
ガシ
GRAB
BAM BAM
TAP
ポチ...
nder] Kensuke Ohshiba
[Subject] Hasekura
Mooornin'!
Omg omg!! x-x
I heard from my bro that today's school lunch special is tonkatsu sandwiches
...
THIS IS...
...MORE LIKE A MESSAGE YOU'D SEND TO YOUR FRIEND THAN...
...A GOOD MORNING LOVE NOTE.

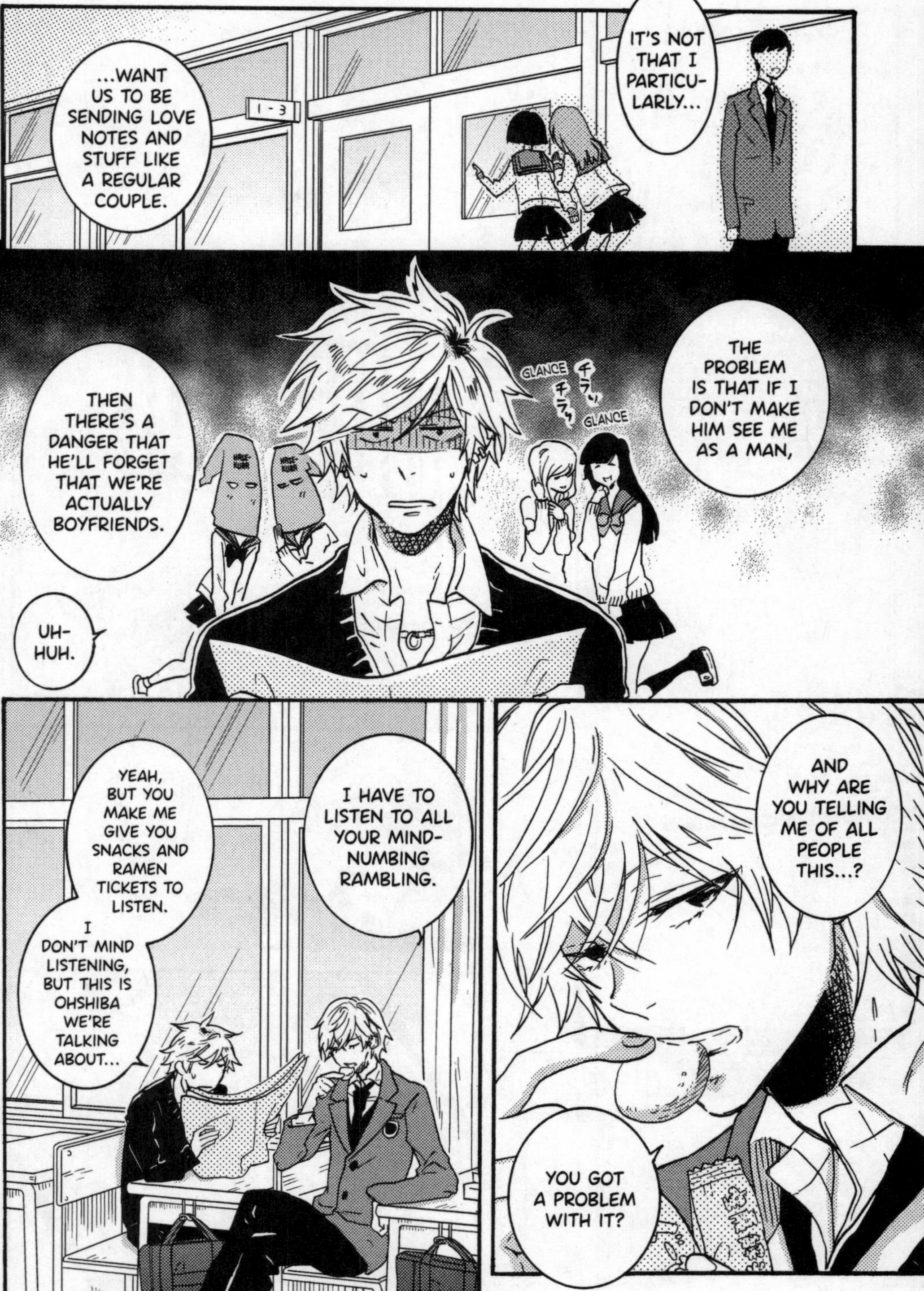
IT'S NOT THAT I PARTICU-LARLY...
...WANT US TO BE SENDING LOVE NOTES AND STUFF LIKE A REGULAR COUPLE.
THE PROBLEM IS THAT IF I DON'T MAKE HIM SEE ME AS A MAN,
GLANCE チラッ
チラッ GLANCE
THEN THERE'S A DANGER THAT HE'LL FORGET THAT WE'RE ACTUALLY BOYFRIENDS.
UH-HUH.
AND WHY ARE YOU TELLING ME OF ALL PEOPLE THIS...?
YOU GOT A PROBLEM WITH IT?
I HAVE TO LISTEN TO ALL YOUR MIND-NUMBING RAMBLING.
YEAH, BUT YOU MAKE ME GIVE YOU SNACKS AND RAMEN TICKETS TO LISTEN.
I DON'T MIND LISTENING, BUT THIS IS OHSHIBA WE'RE TALKING ABOUT...

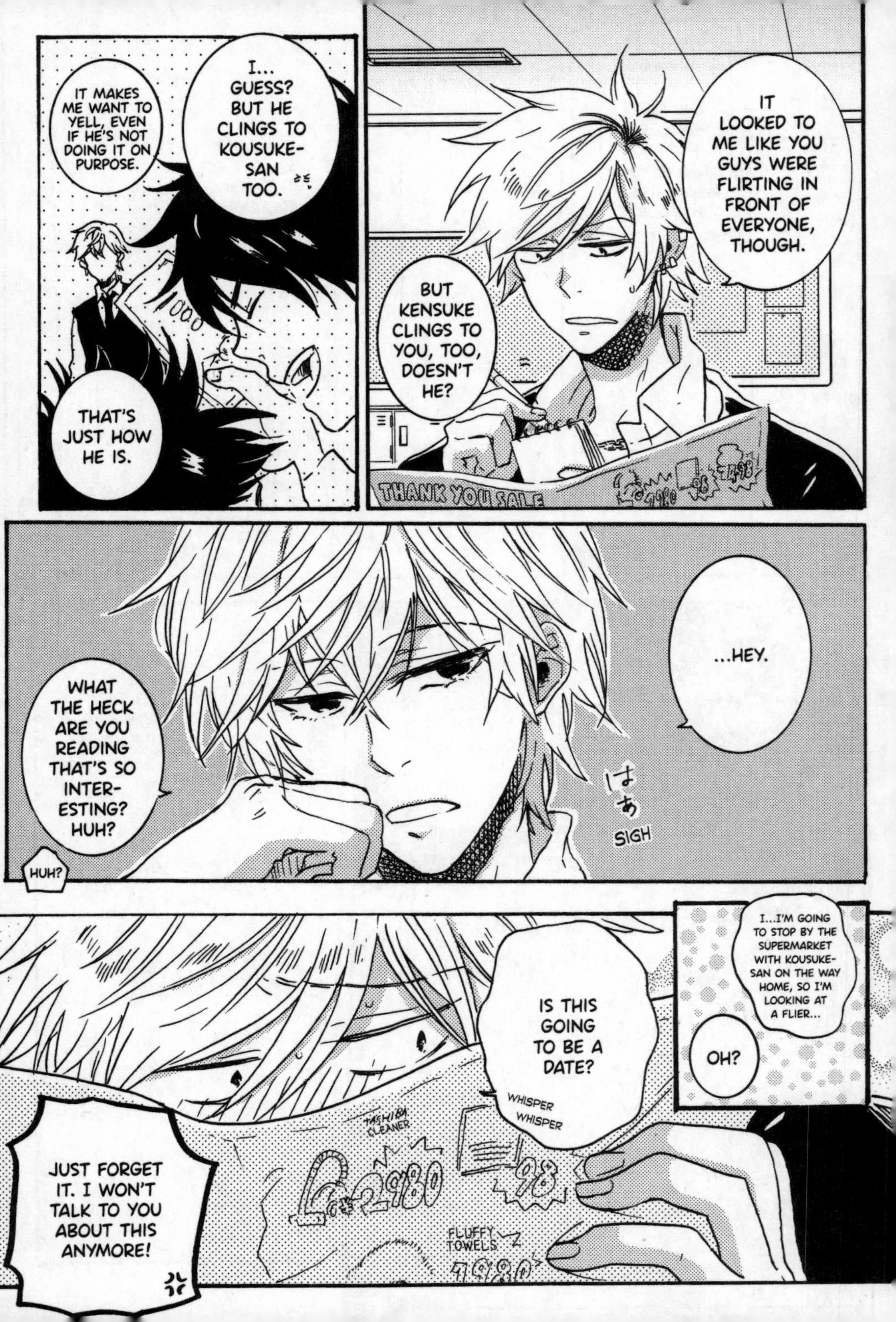
IT LOOKED TO ME LIKE YOU GUYS WERE FLIRTING IN FRONT OF EVERYONE, THOUGH.
BUT KENSUKE CLINGS TO YOU, TOO, DOESN'T HE?
THANK YOU SALE
I... GUESS? BUT HE CLINGS TO KOUSUKE-SAN TOO.
IT MAKES ME WANT TO YELL, EVEN IF HE'S NOT DOING IT ON PURPOSE.
THAT'S JUST HOW HE IS.
...HEY.
はあ
SIGH
WHAT THE HECK ARE YOU READING THAT'S SO INTERESTING? HUH?
HUH?
I...I'M GOING TO STOP BY THE SUPERMARKET WITH KOUSUKE-SAN ON THE WAY HOME, SO I'M LOOKING AT A FLIER...
OH?
IS THIS GOING TO BE A DATE?
WHISPER WHISPER
TASHIRA CLEANER
FLUFFY TOWELS
JUST FORGET IT. I WON'T TALK TO YOU ABOUT THIS ANYMORE!

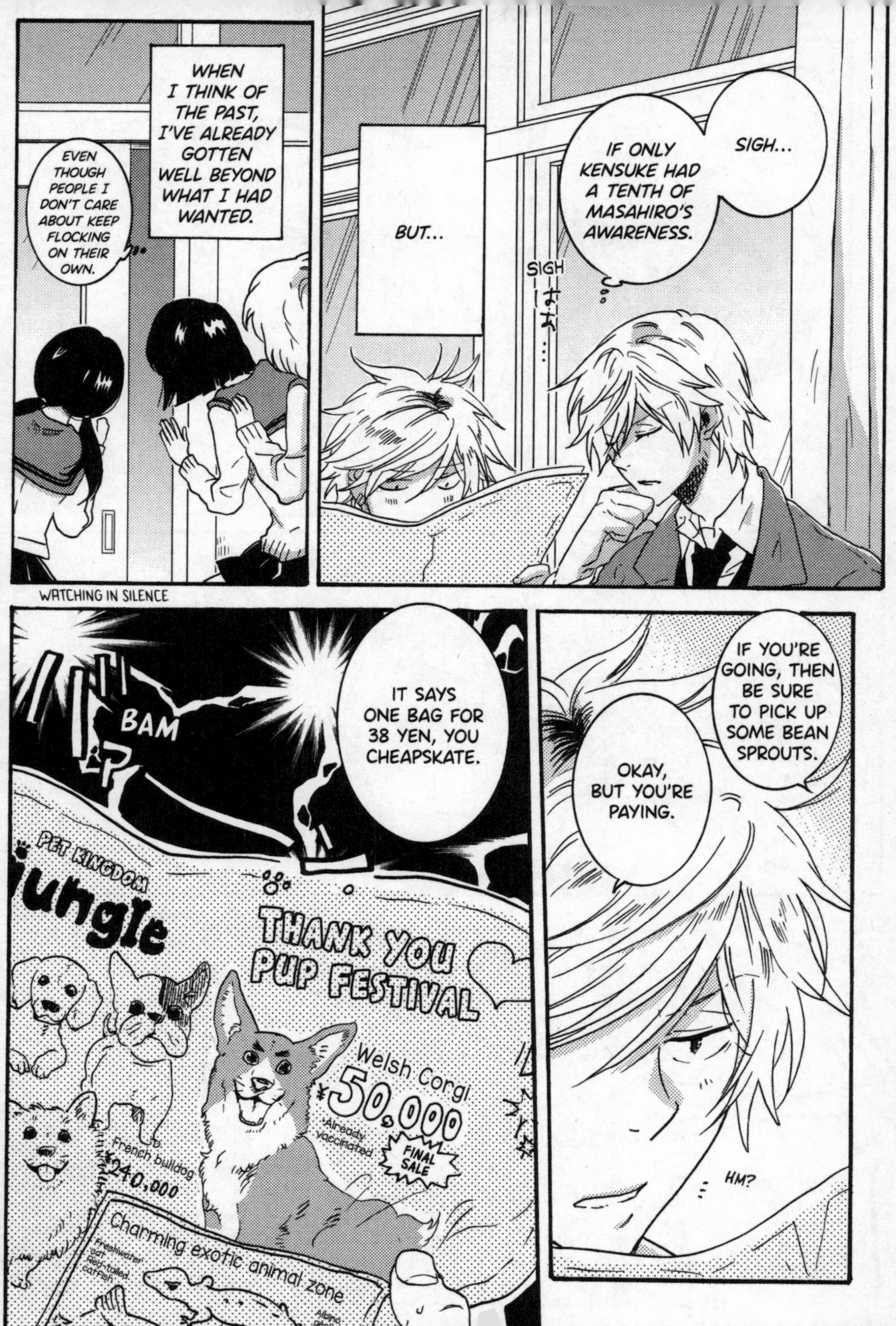
SIGH...
IF ONLY KENSUKE HAD A TENTH OF MASAHIRO'S AWARENESS.
BUT...
SIGH
はぁ…
WHEN I THINK OF THE PAST, I'VE ALREADY GOTTEN WELL BEYOND WHAT I HAD WANTED.
EVEN THOUGH PEOPLE I DON'T CARE ABOUT KEEP FLOCKING ON THEIR OWN.
WATCHING IN SILENCE
IF YOU'RE GOING, THEN BE SURE TO PICK UP SOME BEAN SPROUTS.
OKAY, BUT YOU'RE PAYING.
HM?
IT SAYS ONE BAG FOR 38 YEN, YOU CHEAPSKATE.
BAM
PET KINGDOM
Jungle
THANK YOU PUP FESTIVAL
Welsh Corgi
¥50,000
Already vaccinated
FINAL SALE
French bulldog
¥240,000
Charming exotic animal zone
Freshwater cat
Red-tailed catfish
Albino gecko

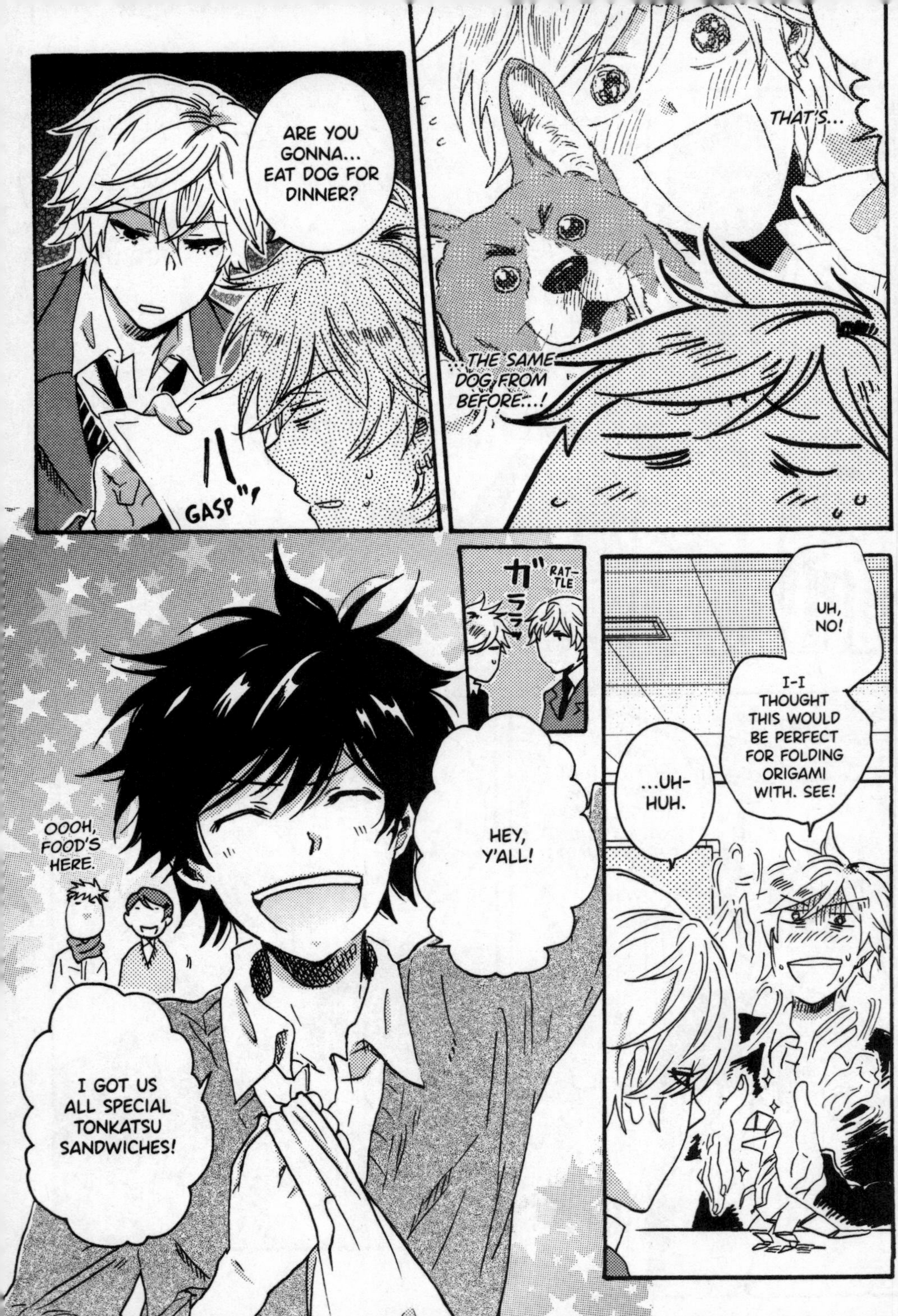
THAT'S...
...THE SAME DOG FROM BEFORE...!
ARE YOU GONNA... EAT DOG FOR DINNER?
GASP
UH, NO!
I-I THOUGHT THIS WOULD BE PERFECT FOR FOLDING ORIGAMI WITH. SEE!
...UH-HUH.
ガララ
RATTLE
HEY, Y'ALL!
OOOH, FOOD'S HERE.
I GOT US ALL SPECIAL TONKATSU SANDWICHES!

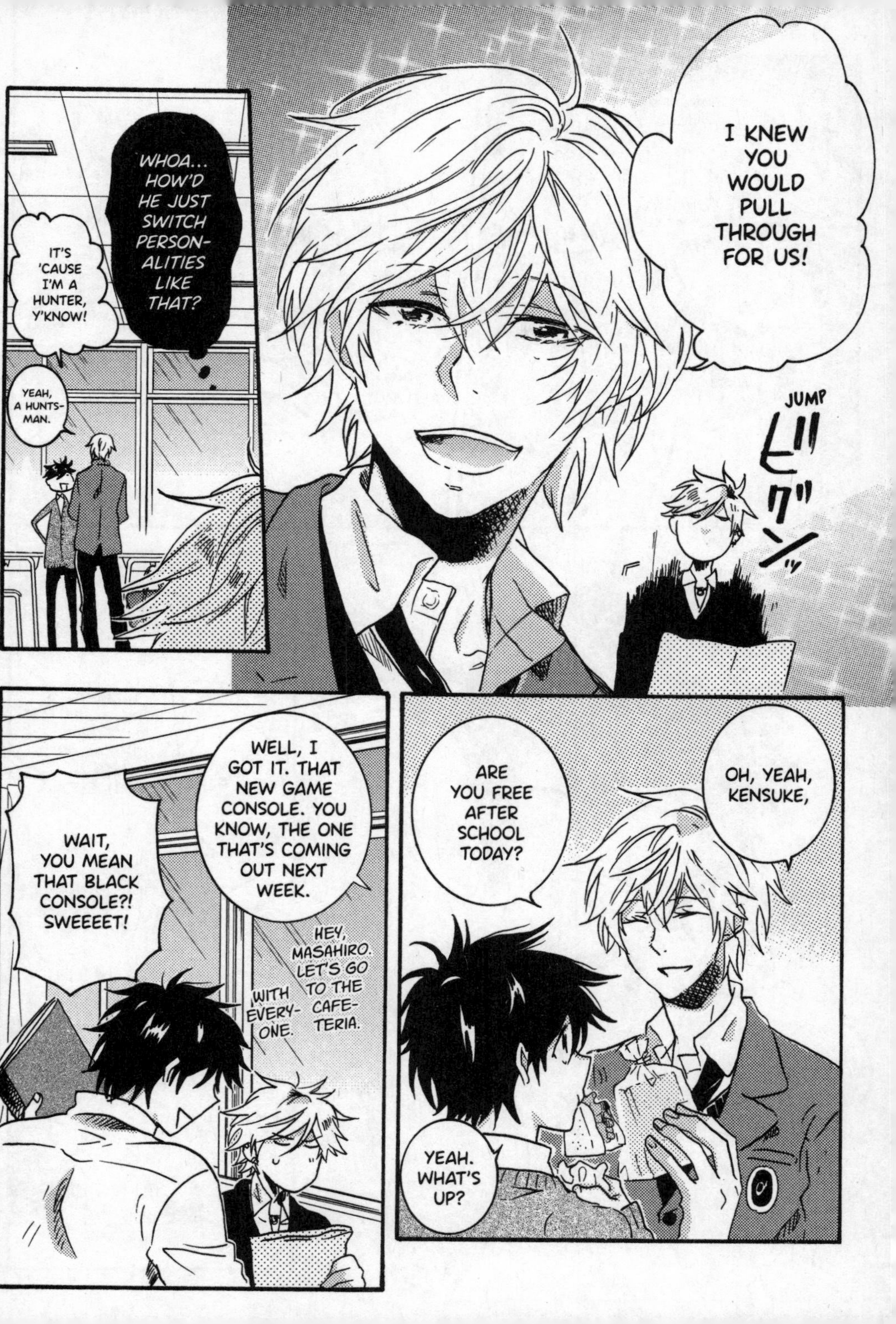
I KNEW YOU WOULD PULL THROUGH FOR US!
JUMP
WHOA... HOW'D HE JUST SWITCH PERSONALITIES LIKE THAT?
IT'S 'CAUSE I'M A HUNTER, Y'KNOW!
YEAH, A HUNTSMAN.
OH, YEAH, KENSUKE,
ARE YOU FREE AFTER SCHOOL TODAY?
YEAH. WHAT'S UP?
WELL, I GOT IT. THAT NEW GAME CONSOLE. YOU KNOW, THE ONE THAT'S COMING OUT NEXT WEEK.
WAIT, YOU MEAN THAT BLACK CONSOLE?! SWEEEET!
HEY, MASAHIRO. LET'S GO TO THE CAFETERIA.
WITH EVERYONE.

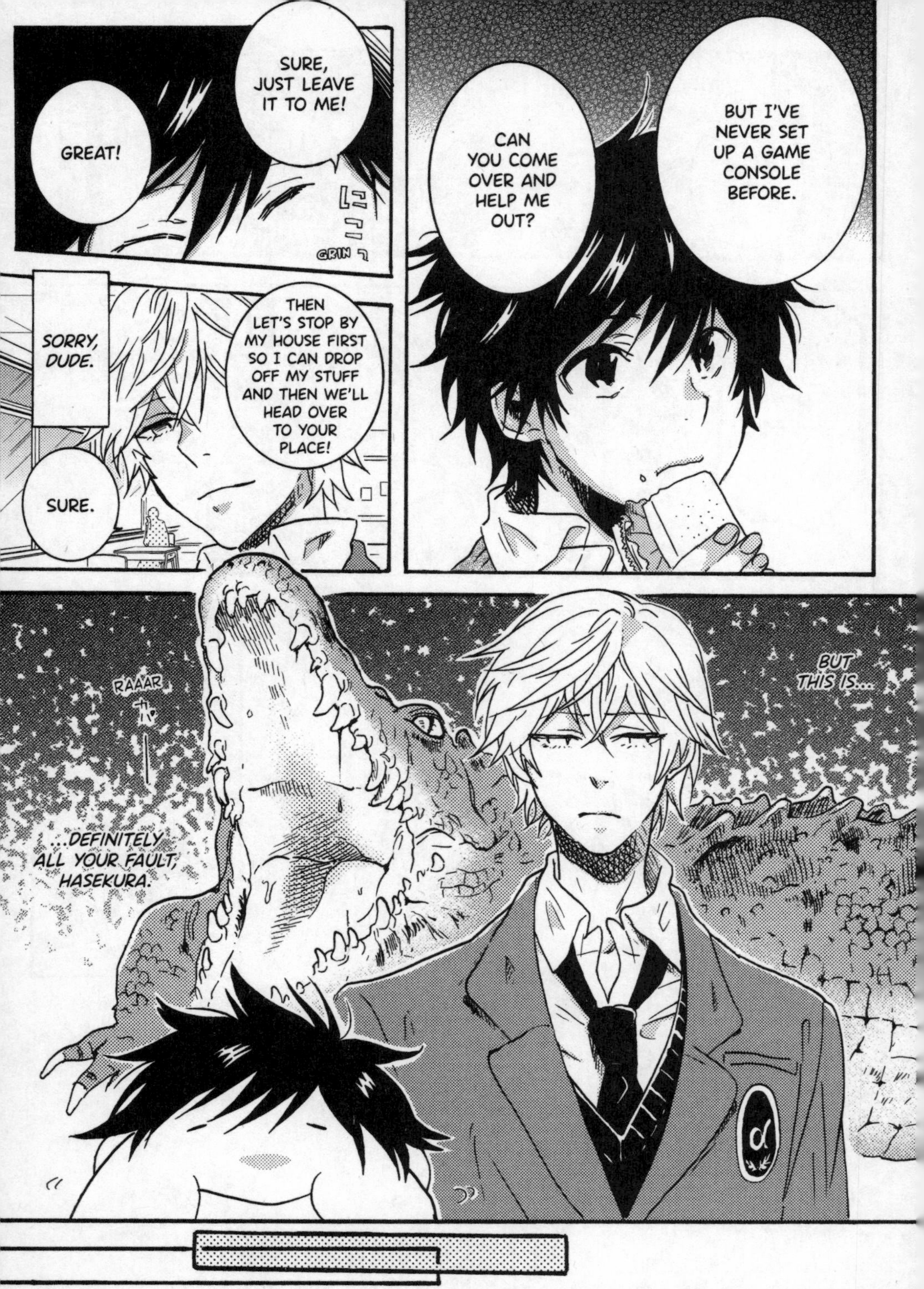
BUT I'VE NEVER SET UP A GAME CONSOLE BEFORE.
CAN YOU COME OVER AND HELP ME OUT?
SURE, JUST LEAVE IT TO ME!
GREAT!
GRIN
THEN LET'S STOP BY MY HOUSE FIRST SO I CAN DROP OFF MY STUFF AND THEN WE'LL HEAD OVER TO YOUR PLACE!
SORRY, DUDE.
SURE.
BUT THIS IS...
RAAAR
...DEFINITELY ALL YOUR FAULT, HASEKURA.

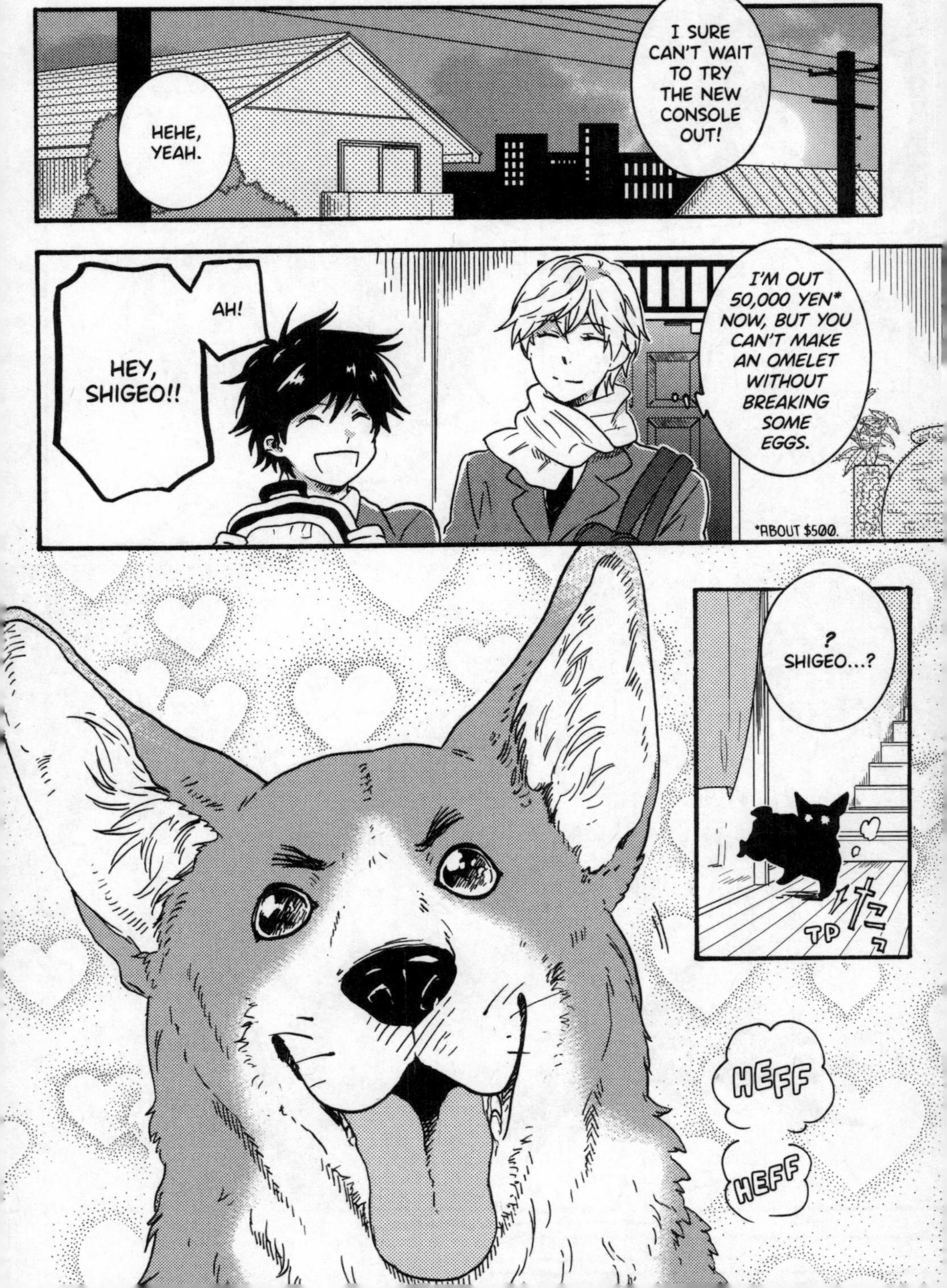
I SURE CAN'T WAIT TO TRY THE NEW CONSOLE OUT!
HEHE, YEAH.
I'M OUT 50,000 YEN* NOW, BUT YOU CAN'T MAKE AN OMELET WITHOUT BREAKING SOME EGGS.
*ABOUT $500.
AH!
HEY, SHIGEO!!
? SHIGEO...?
TP
HEFF
HEFF

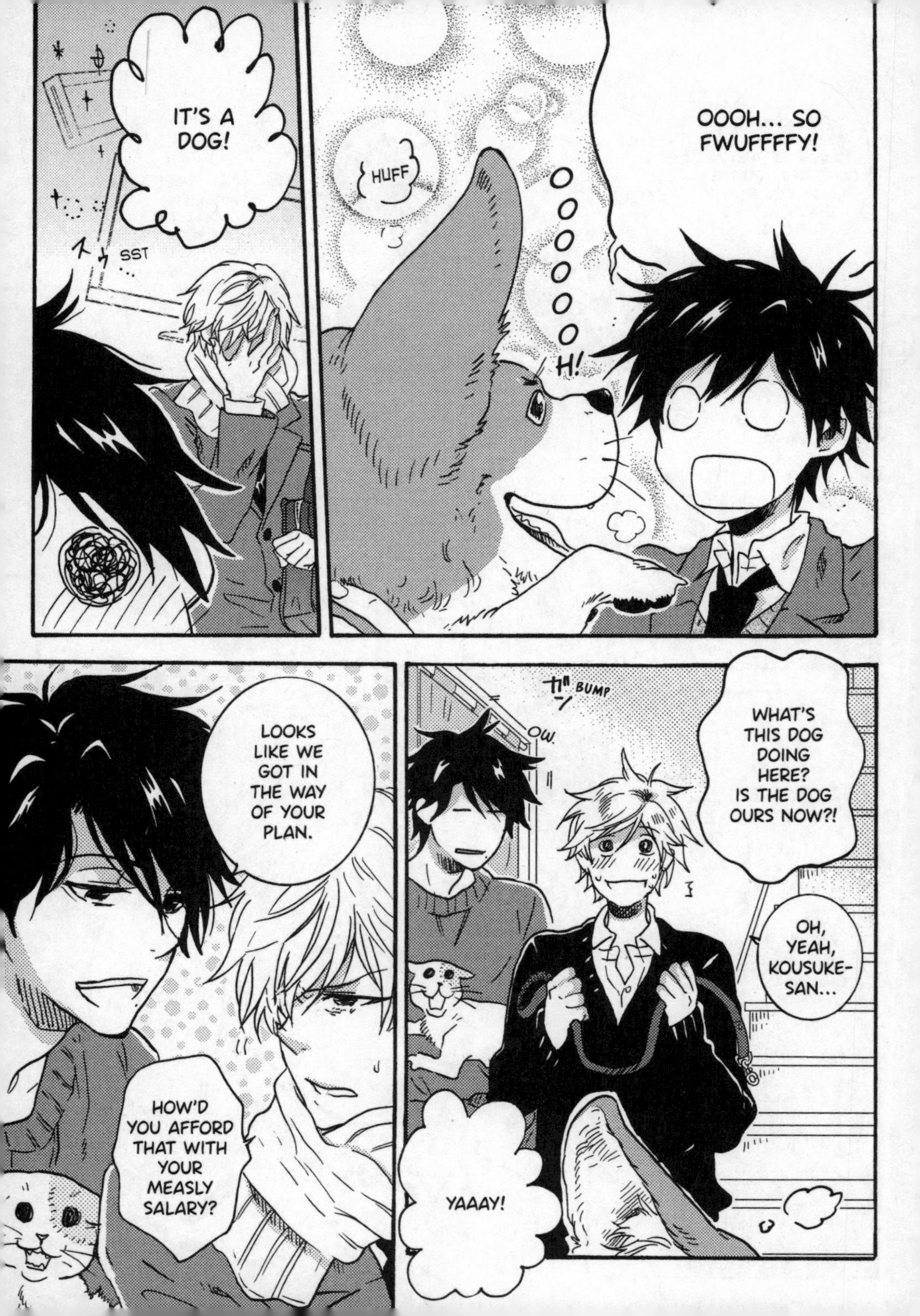
OOOH... SO FWUFFFFY!
HUFF
OOOOOOH!
IT'S A DOG!
SST
BUMP
OW.
WHAT'S THIS DOG DOING HERE? IS THE DOG OURS NOW?!
OH, YEAH, KOUSUKE-SAN...
YAAAY!
LOOKS LIKE WE GOT IN THE WAY OF YOUR PLAN.
HOW'D YOU AFFORD THAT WITH YOUR MEASLY SALARY?

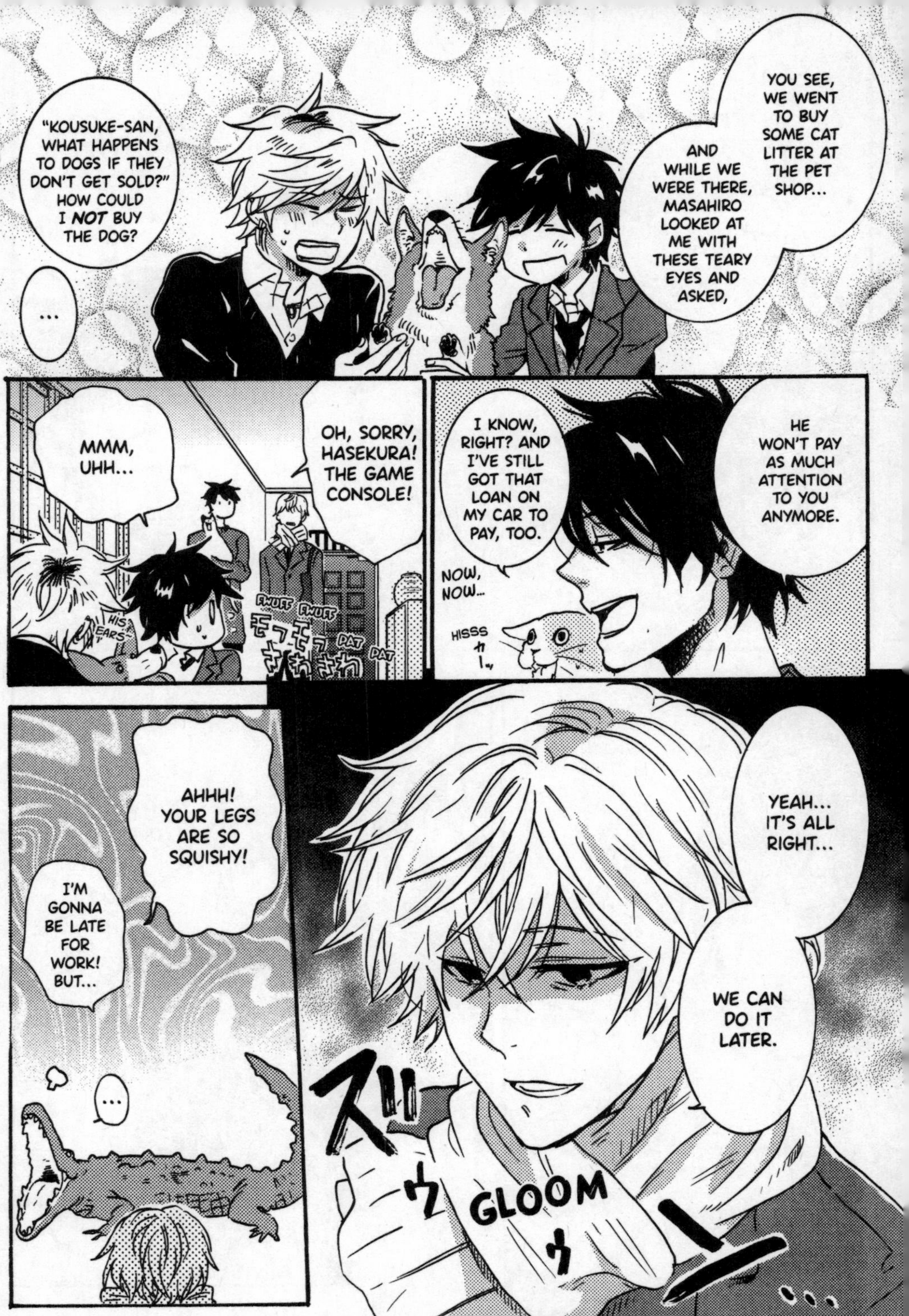
YOU SEE, WE WENT TO BUY SOME CAT LITTER AT THE PET SHOP...
AND WHILE WE WERE THERE, MASAHIRO LOOKED AT ME WITH THESE TEARY EYES AND ASKED,
"KOUSUKE-SAN, WHAT HAPPENS TO DOGS IF THEY DON'T GET SOLD?" HOW COULD I *NOT* BUY THE DOG?
...
HE WON'T PAY AS MUCH ATTENTION TO YOU ANYMORE.
I KNOW, RIGHT? AND I'VE STILL GOT THAT LOAN ON MY CAR TO PAY, TOO.
NOW, NOW...
HISSS
OH, SORRY, HASEKURA! THE GAME CONSOLE!
MMM, UHH...
HIS EARS
FWUFF FWUFF
PAT PAT
YEAH... IT'S ALL RIGHT...
WE CAN DO IT LATER.
GLOOM
...
AHHH! YOUR LEGS ARE SO SQUISHY!
I'M GONNA BE LATE FOR WORK! BUT...
...

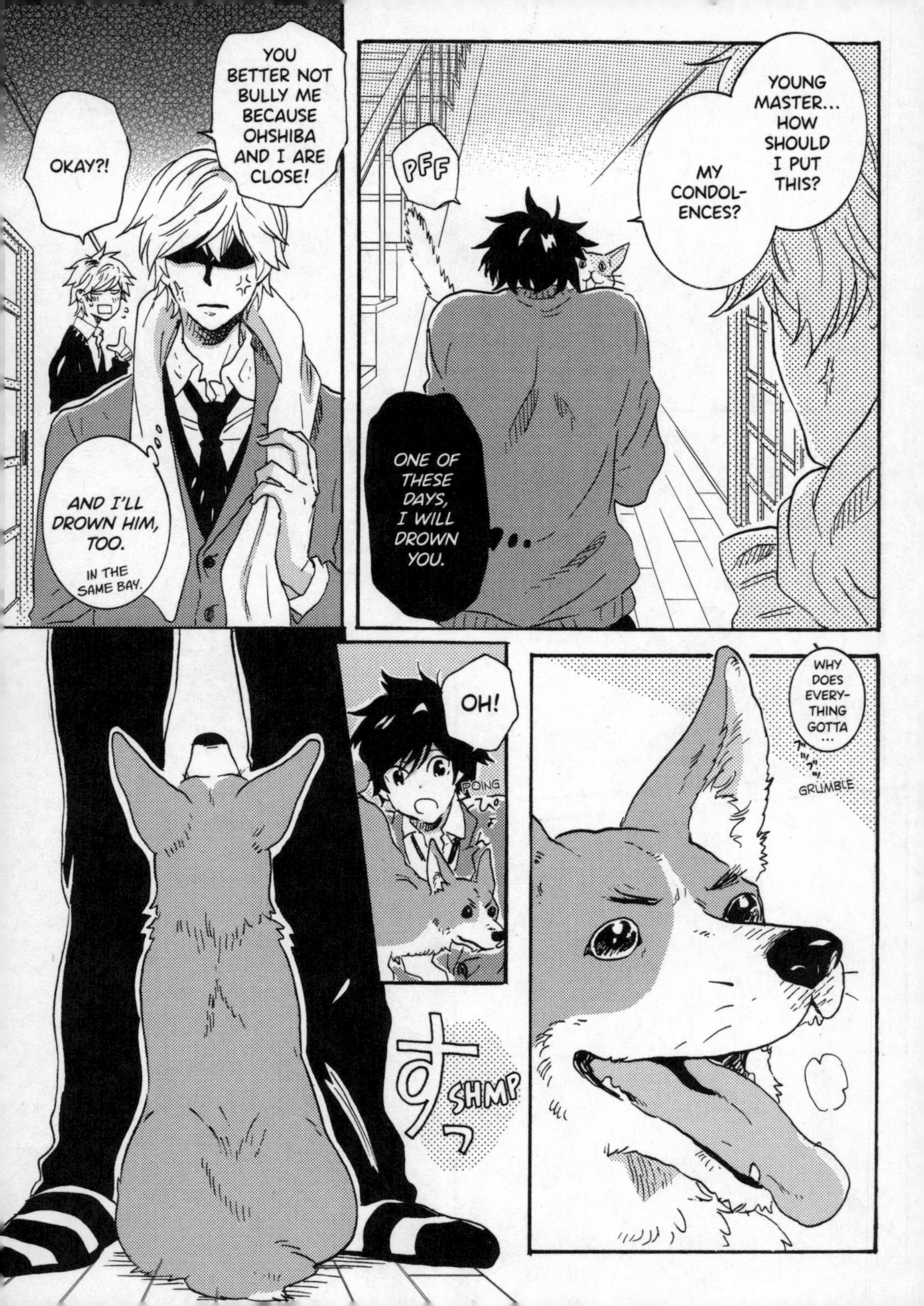
YOUNG MASTER... HOW SHOULD I PUT THIS?
MY CONDOLENCES?
PFF
ONE OF THESE DAYS, I WILL DROWN YOU.
YOU BETTER NOT BULLY ME BECAUSE OHSHIBA AND I ARE CLOSE!
OKAY?!
AND I'LL DROWN HIM, TOO.
IN THE SAME BAY.
WHY DOES EVERYTHING GOTTA...
GRUMBLE
OH!
POING
SHMP

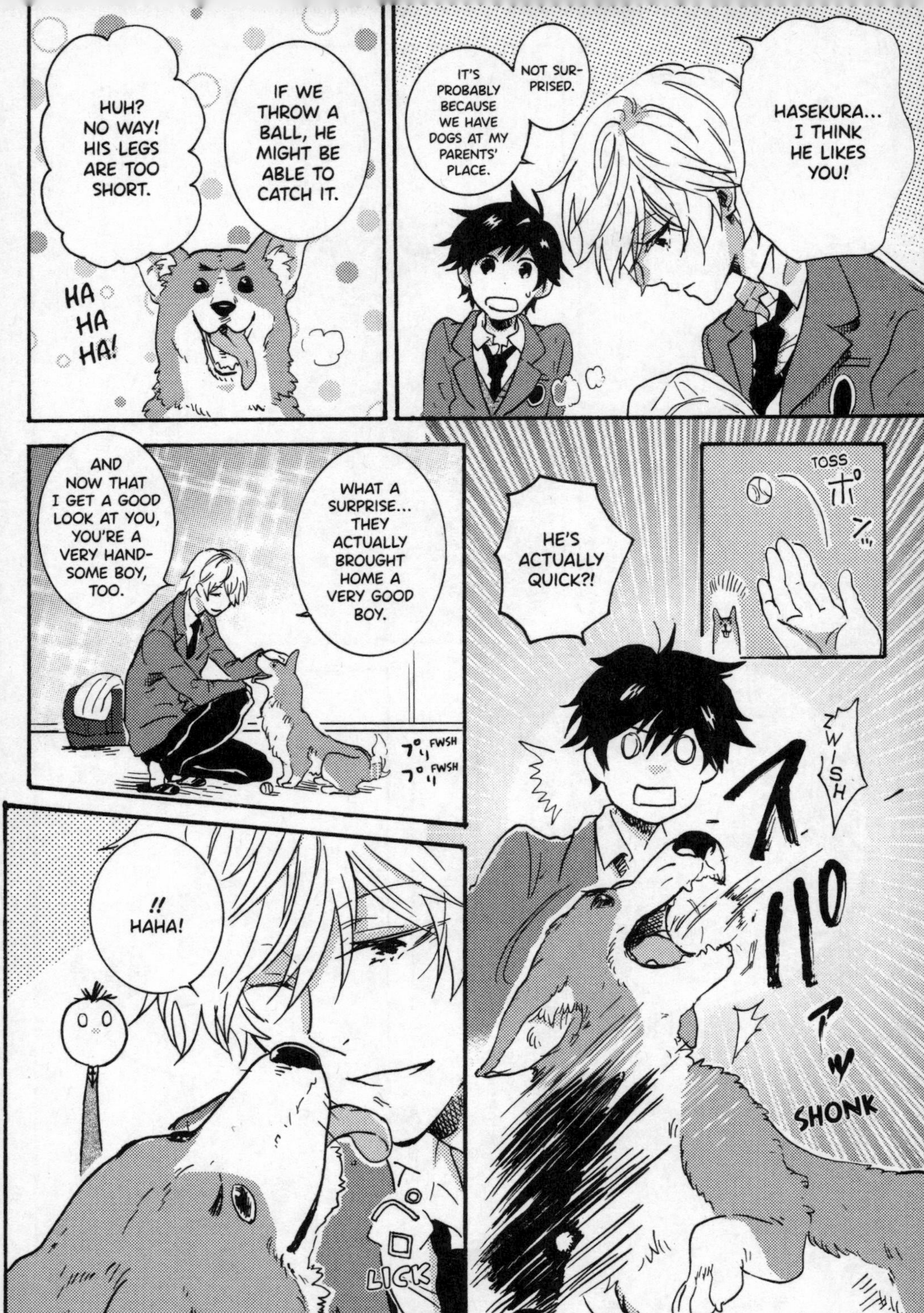
HASEKURA... I THINK HE LIKES YOU!
NOT SURPRISED.
IT'S PROBABLY BECAUSE WE HAVE DOGS AT MY PARENTS' PLACE.
IF WE THROW A BALL, HE MIGHT BE ABLE TO CATCH IT.
HUH? NO WAY! HIS LEGS ARE TOO SHORT.
HA HA HA!
TOSS
HE'S ACTUALLY QUICK?!
ZWISH
SHONK
WHAT A SURPRISE... THEY ACTUALLY BROUGHT HOME A VERY GOOD BOY.
AND NOW THAT I GET A GOOD LOOK AT YOU, YOU'RE A VERY HANDSOME BOY, TOO.
FWSH
FWSH
!! HAHA!
LICK

C'MERE.
HA HA HA!
ぺろ LICK
ぺろ LICK
ぺろ LICK
ぺろ LICK
HASEKURA!
DROP ぽと
YOU KNOW, I'M A...
...PRETTY GOOD HUNTER, TOO.
...?
YOU WANT ME TO THROW IT?
YEP.
TOSS

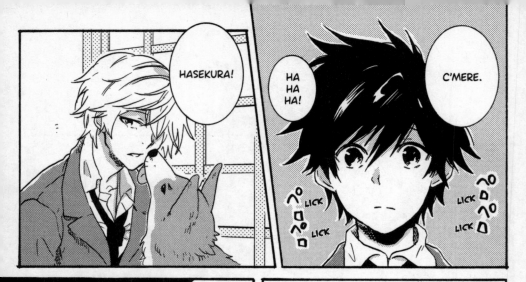

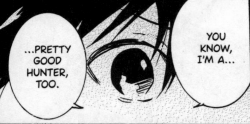

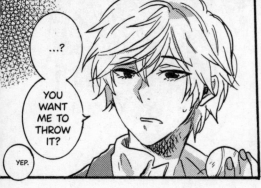

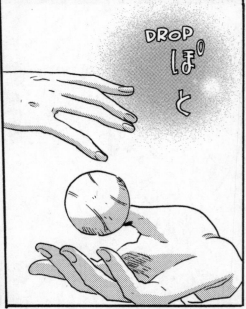

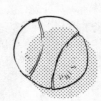

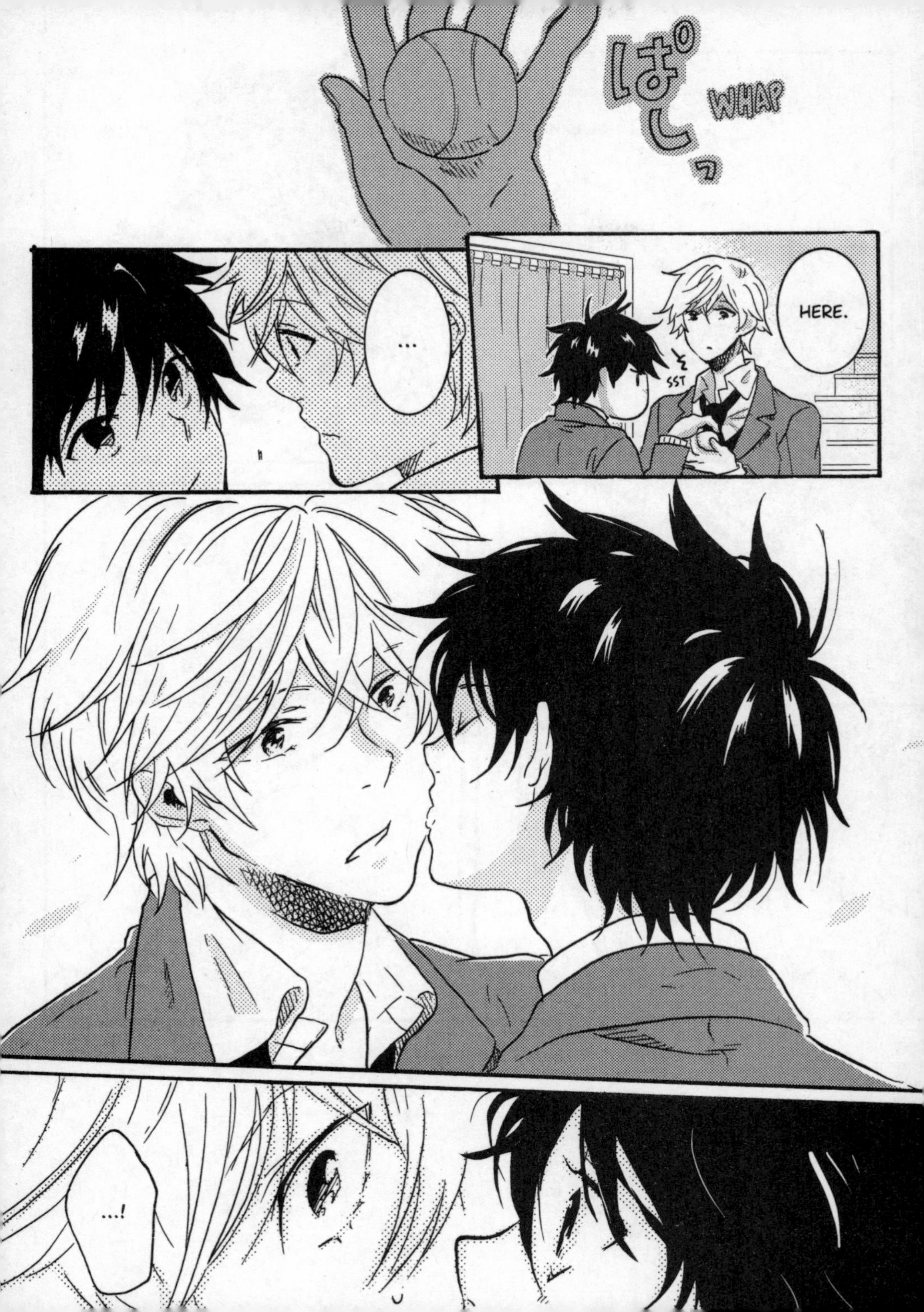
ぱしっ
WHAP
HERE.
SST
...
...!

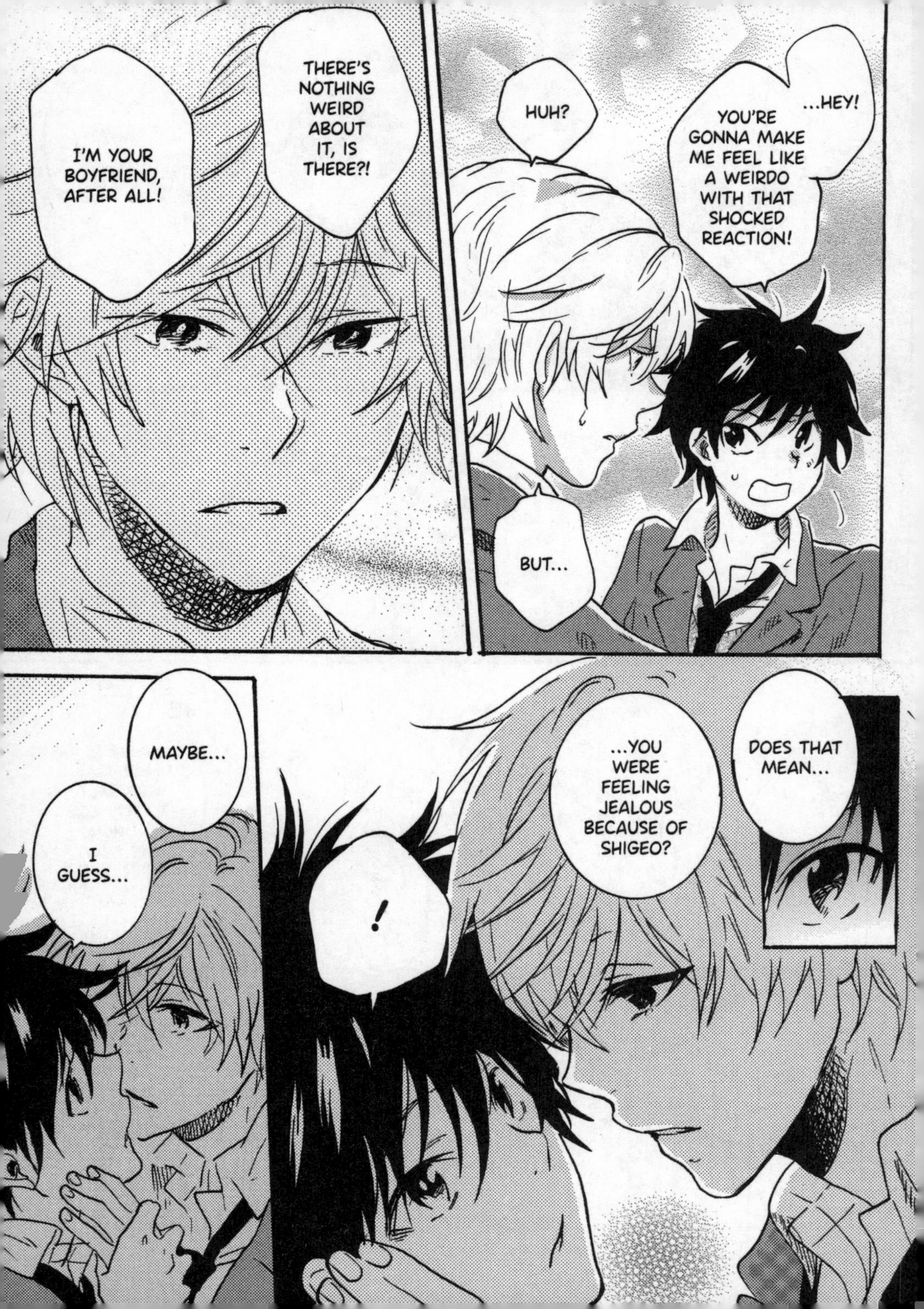
...HEY!
YOU'RE GONNA MAKE ME FEEL LIKE A WEIRDO WITH THAT SHOCKED REACTION!
HUH?
BUT...
THERE'S NOTHING WEIRD ABOUT IT, IS THERE?!
I'M YOUR BOYFRIEND, AFTER ALL!
DOES THAT MEAN...
...YOU WERE FEELING JEALOUS BECAUSE OF SHIGEO?
!
MAYBE...
I GUESS...

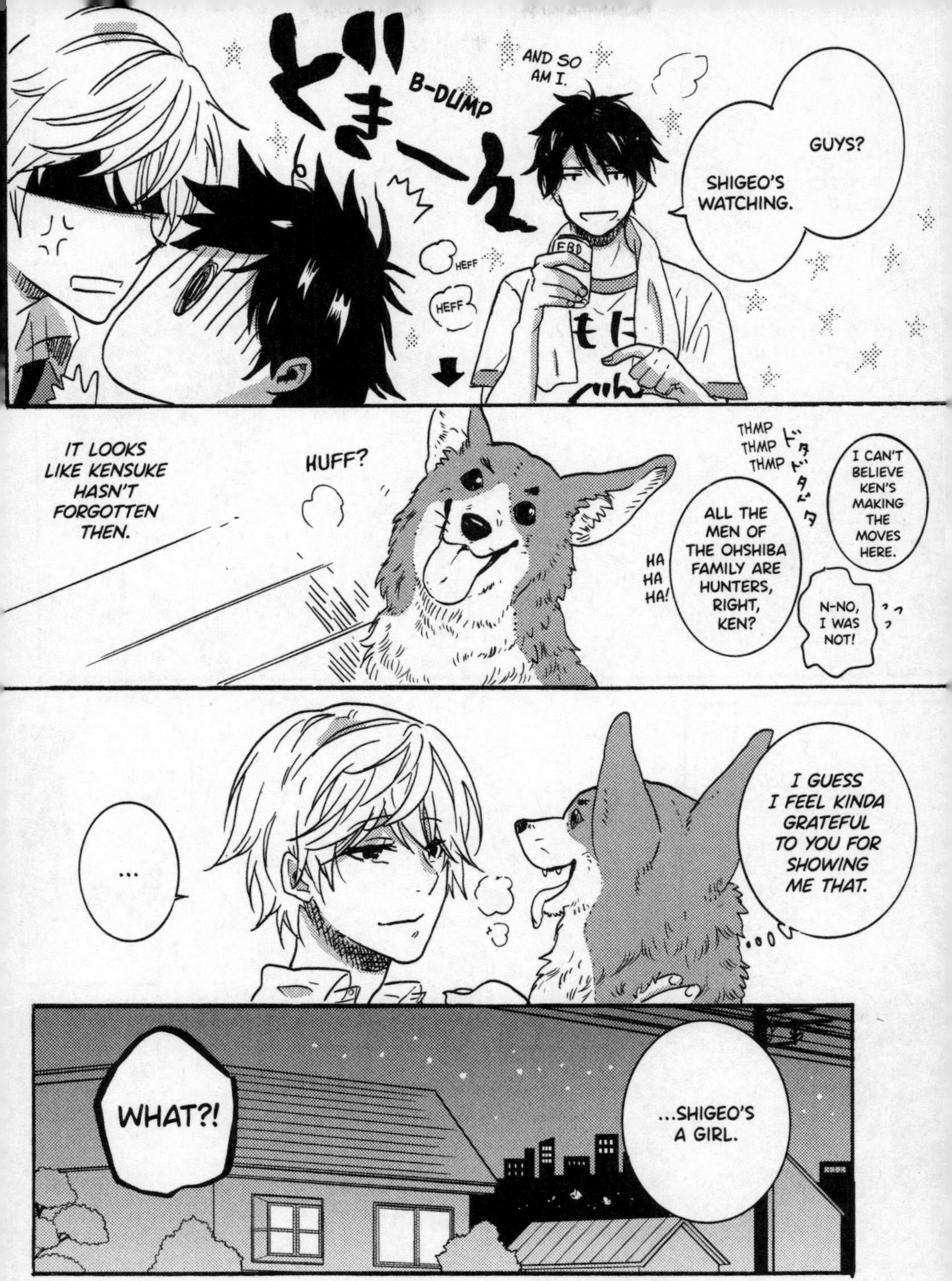
GUYS?
SHIGEO'S WATCHING.
AND SO AM I.
どきーん
B-DUMP
HEFF
HEFF
I CAN'T BELIEVE KEN'S MAKING THE MOVES HERE.
N-NO, I WAS NOT!
THMP THMP THMP
ドタドタ
ALL THE MEN OF THE OHSHIBA FAMILY ARE HUNTERS, RIGHT, KEN?
HA HA HA!
HUFF?
IT LOOKS LIKE KENSUKE HASN'T FORGOTTEN THEN.
I GUESS I FEEL KINDA GRATEFUL TO YOU FOR SHOWING ME THAT.
...
...SHIGEO'S A GIRL.
WHAT?!

Hitorijime
My Hero

~The Story of How Shigeo Joined the Family~
Boyfriend #5.5
Although the *Hitorijime My Boyfriend* story came first, Setagawa and Kousuke were there, too!
FWP
FWP

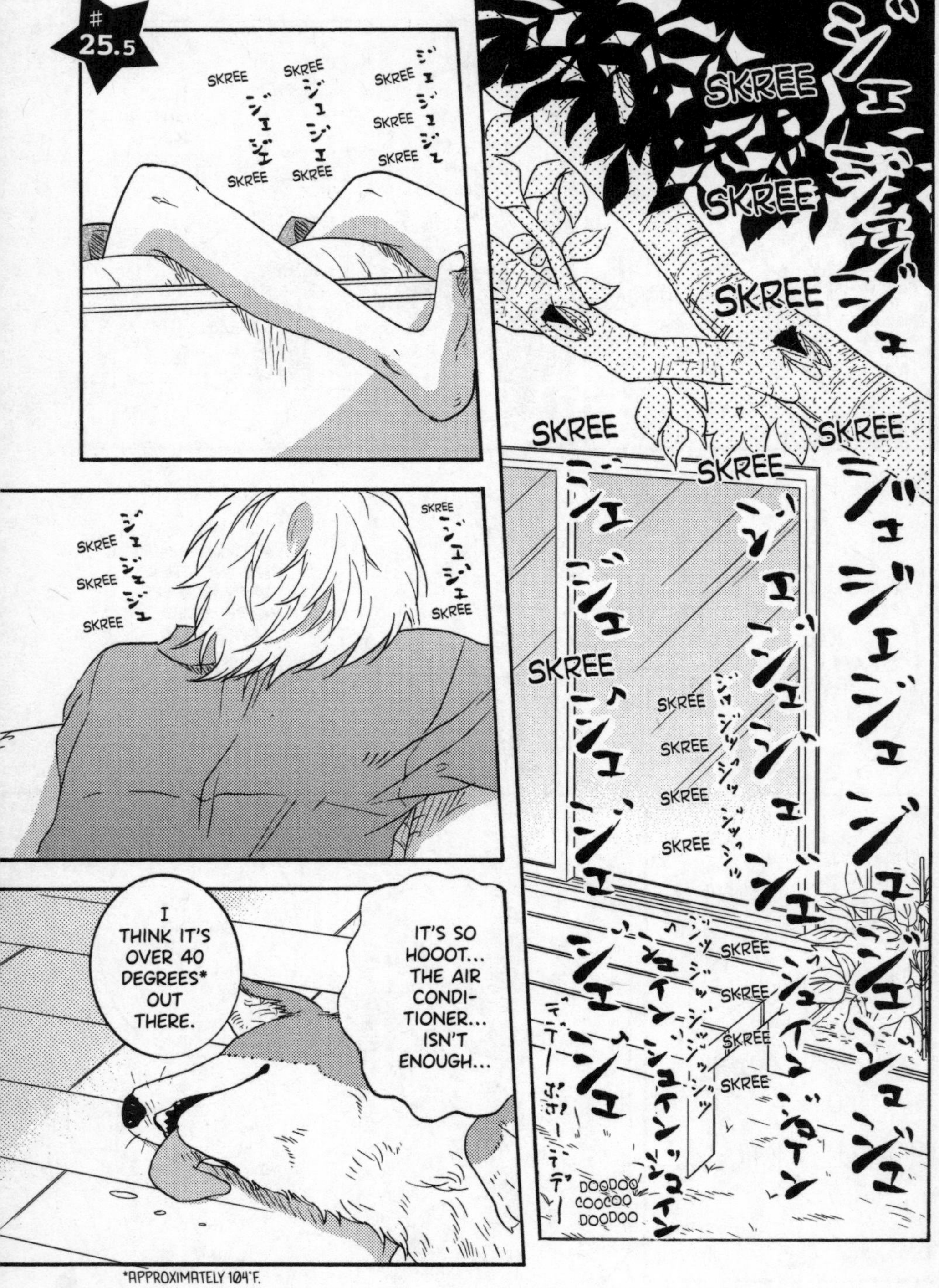

25.5
SKREE
SKREE
SKREE
SKREE
SKREE
SKREE
SKREE
SKREE
SKREE
SKREE
SKREE
SKREE
SKREE
SKREE
SKREE
SKREE
DOODOO COOCOO DOODOO
SKREE
SKREE
SKREE
SKREE
SKREE
SKREE
SKREE
SKREE
SKREE
SKREE
SKREE
SKREE
SKREE
SKREE
IT'S SO HOOOT... THE AIR CONDITIONER... ISN'T ENOUGH...
I THINK IT'S OVER 40 DEGREES* OUT THERE.

*APPROXIMATELY 104°F.

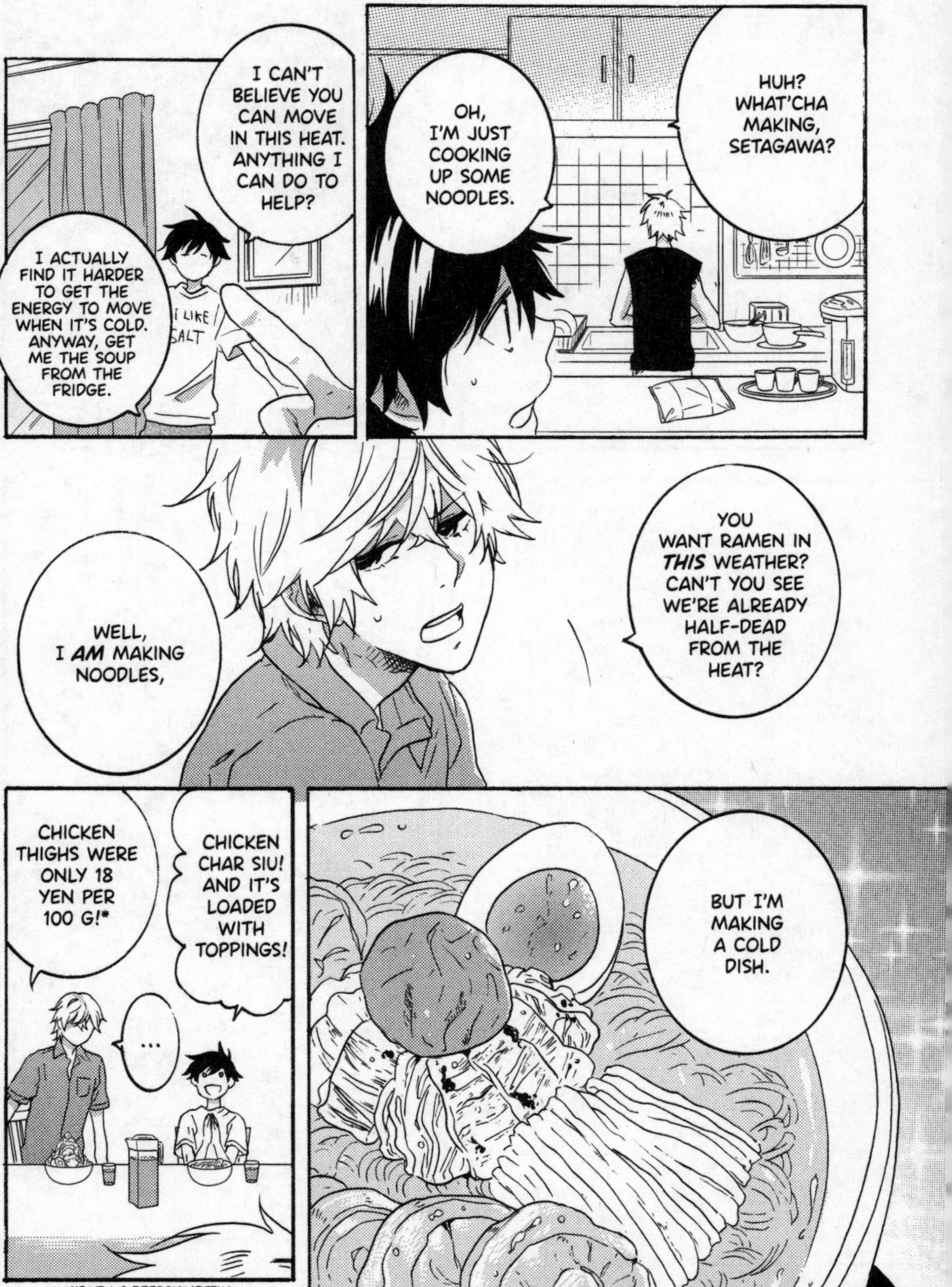
HUH? WHAT'CHA MAKING, SETAGAWA?
OH, I'M JUST COOKING UP SOME NOODLES.
I CAN'T BELIEVE YOU CAN MOVE IN THIS HEAT. ANYTHING I CAN DO TO HELP?
I ACTUALLY FIND IT HARDER TO GET THE ENERGY TO MOVE WHEN IT'S COLD. ANYWAY, GET ME THE SOUP FROM THE FRIDGE.
I LIKE SALT
YOU WANT RAMEN IN *THIS* WEATHER? CAN'T YOU SEE WE'RE ALREADY HALF-DEAD FROM THE HEAT?
WELL, I *AM* MAKING NOODLES,
BUT I'M MAKING A COLD DISH.
CHICKEN CHAR SIU! AND IT'S LOADED WITH TOPPINGS!
CHICKEN THIGHS WERE ONLY 18 YEN PER 100 G!*
...

*18 YEN IS APPROXIMATELY 18 CENTS AND 100 G IS 3.5 OZ.

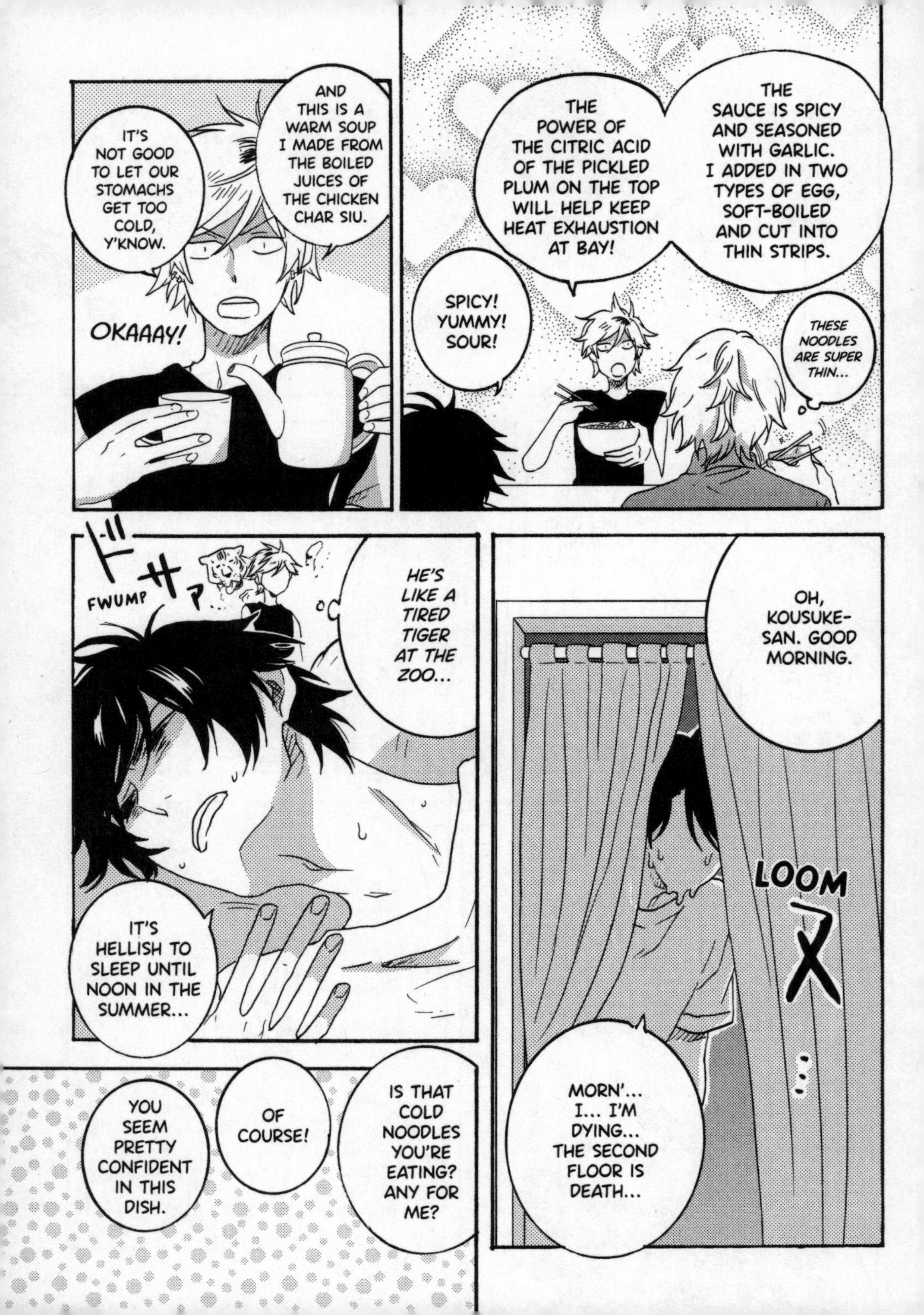
THE SAUCE IS SPICY AND SEASONED WITH GARLIC. I ADDED IN TWO TYPES OF EGG, SOFT-BOILED AND CUT INTO THIN STRIPS.
THE POWER OF THE CITRIC ACID OF THE PICKLED PLUM ON THE TOP WILL HELP KEEP HEAT EXHAUSTION AT BAY!
SPICY! YUMMY! SOUR!
THESE NOODLES ARE SUPER THIN...
AND THIS IS A WARM SOUP I MADE FROM THE BOILED JUICES OF THE CHICKEN CHAR SIU.
IT'S NOT GOOD TO LET OUR STOMACHS GET TOO COLD, Y'KNOW.
OKAAAY!
OH, KOUSUKE-SAN. GOOD MORNING.
LOOM
...
MORN'... I... I'M DYING... THE SECOND FLOOR IS DEATH...
HE'S LIKE A TIRED TIGER AT THE ZOO...
FWUMP
IT'S HELLISH TO SLEEP UNTIL NOON IN THE SUMMER...
IS THAT COLD NOODLES YOU'RE EATING? ANY FOR ME?
OF COURSE!
YOU SEEM PRETTY CONFIDENT IN THIS DISH.

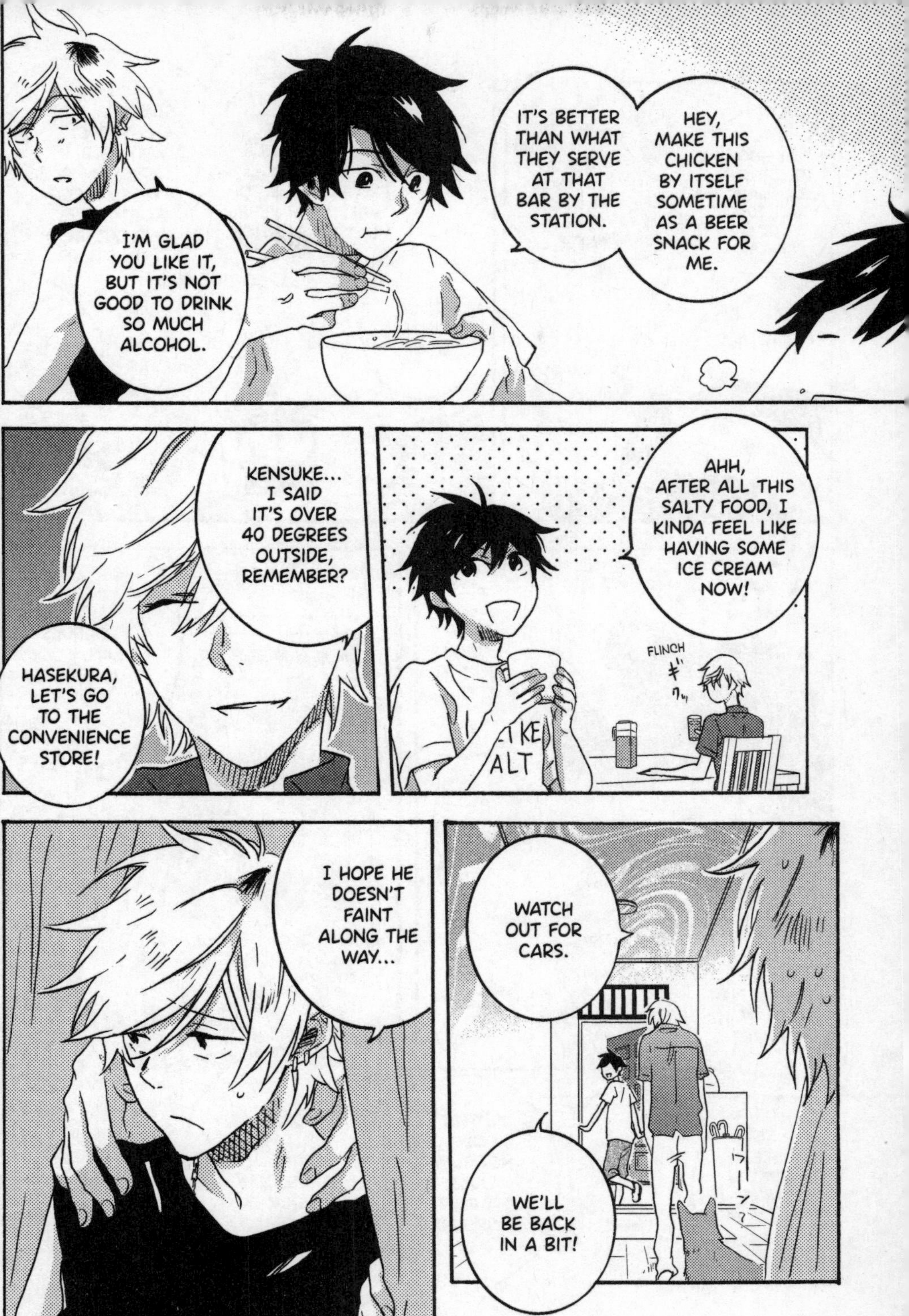
HEY, MAKE THIS CHICKEN BY ITSELF SOMETIME AS A BEER SNACK FOR ME.
IT'S BETTER THAN WHAT THEY SERVE AT THAT BAR BY THE STATION.
I'M GLAD YOU LIKE IT, BUT IT'S NOT GOOD TO DRINK SO MUCH ALCOHOL.
AHH, AFTER ALL THIS SALTY FOOD, I KINDA FEEL LIKE HAVING SOME ICE CREAM NOW!
FLINCH
KENSUKE... I SAID IT'S OVER 40 DEGREES OUTSIDE, REMEMBER?
HASEKURA, LET'S GO TO THE CONVENIENCE STORE!
WATCH OUT FOR CARS.
WE'LL BE BACK IN A BIT!
I HOPE HE DOESN'T FAINT ALONG THE WAY...

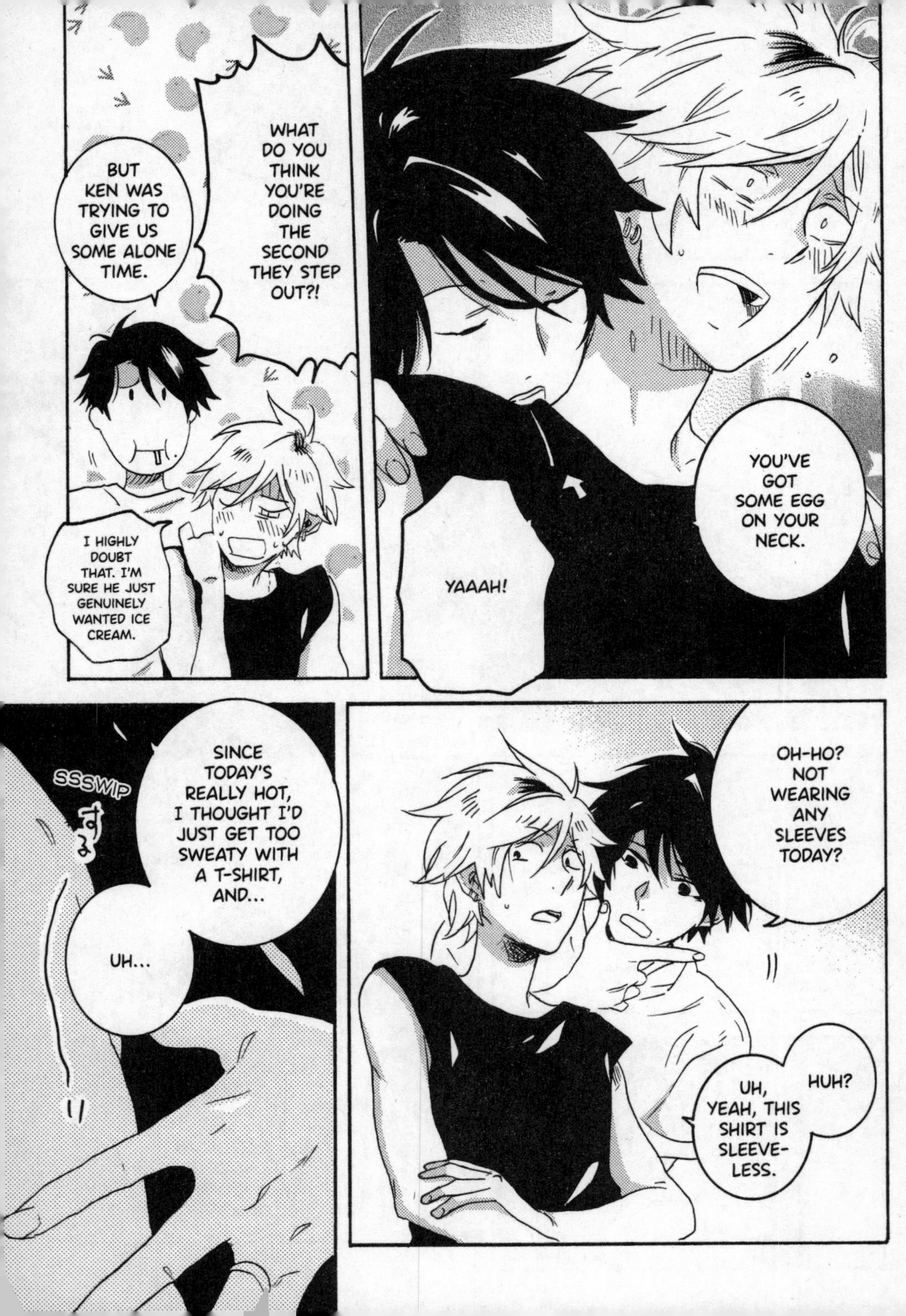
YOU'VE GOT SOME EGG ON YOUR NECK.
YAAAH!
WHAT DO YOU THINK YOU'RE DOING THE SECOND THEY STEP OUT?!
BUT KEN WAS TRYING TO GIVE US SOME ALONE TIME.
I HIGHLY DOUBT THAT. I'M SURE HE JUST GENUINELY WANTED ICE CREAM.
OH-HO? NOT WEARING ANY SLEEVES TODAY?
HUH?
UH, YEAH, THIS SHIRT IS SLEEVE-LESS.
SINCE TODAY'S REALLY HOT, I THOUGHT I'D JUST GET TOO SWEATY WITH A T-SHIRT, AND...
SSSWIP
する
UH...

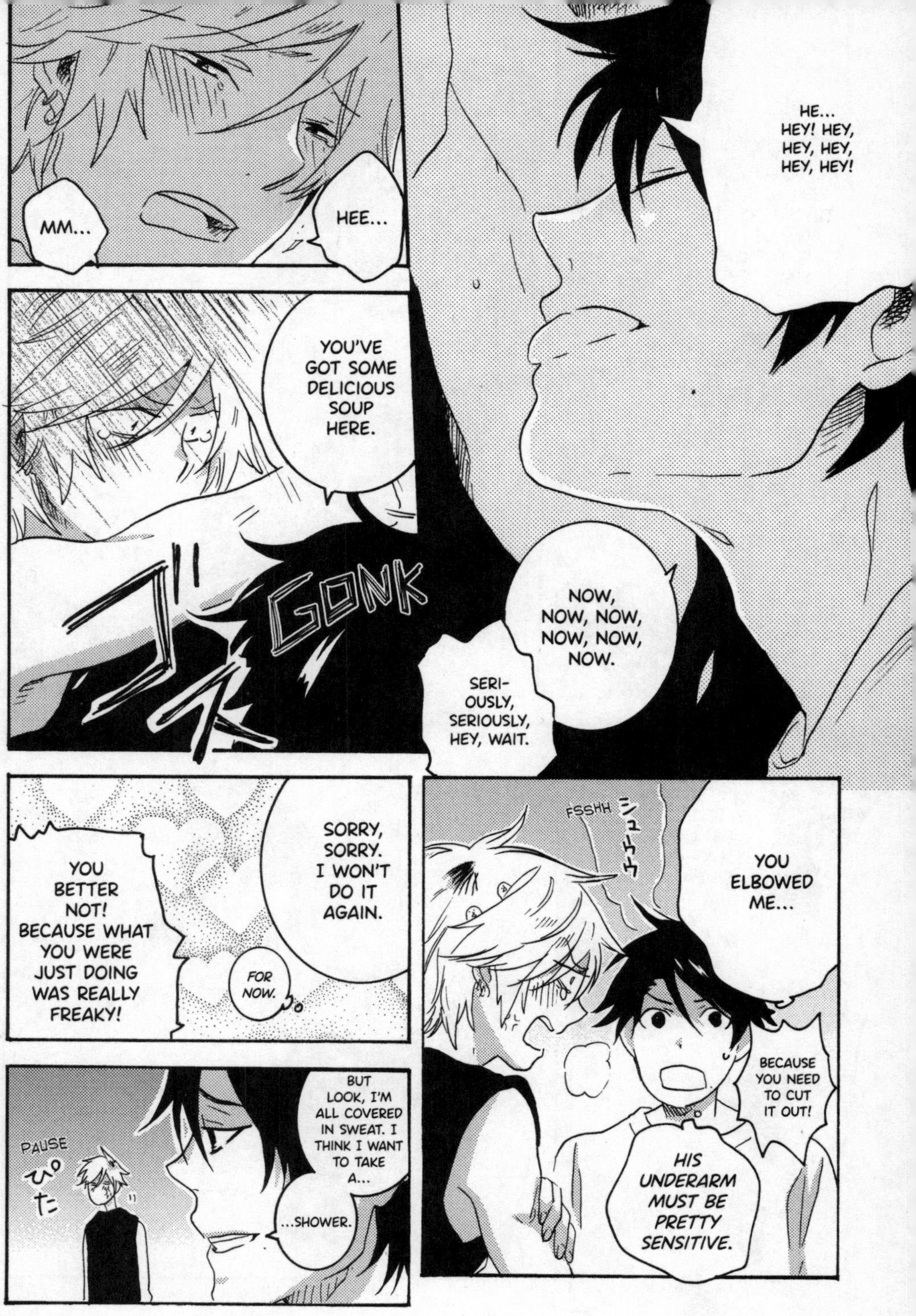
HE... HEY! HEY, HEY, HEY, HEY, HEY!
NOW, NOW, NOW, NOW, NOW, NOW.
SERI- OUSLY, SERIOUSLY, HEY, WAIT.
HEE...
MM...
YOU'VE GOT SOME DELICIOUS SOUP HERE.
GONK
FSSHH シュゥゥ
YOU ELBOWED ME...
BECAUSE YOU NEED TO CUT IT OUT!
HIS UNDERARM MUST BE PRETTY SENSITIVE.
SORRY, SORRY. I WON'T DO IT AGAIN.
FOR NOW.
YOU BETTER NOT! BECAUSE WHAT YOU WERE JUST DOING WAS REALLY FREAKY!
BUT LOOK, I'M ALL COVERED IN SWEAT. I THINK I WANT TO TAKE A...
...SHOWER.
PAUSE ぴた

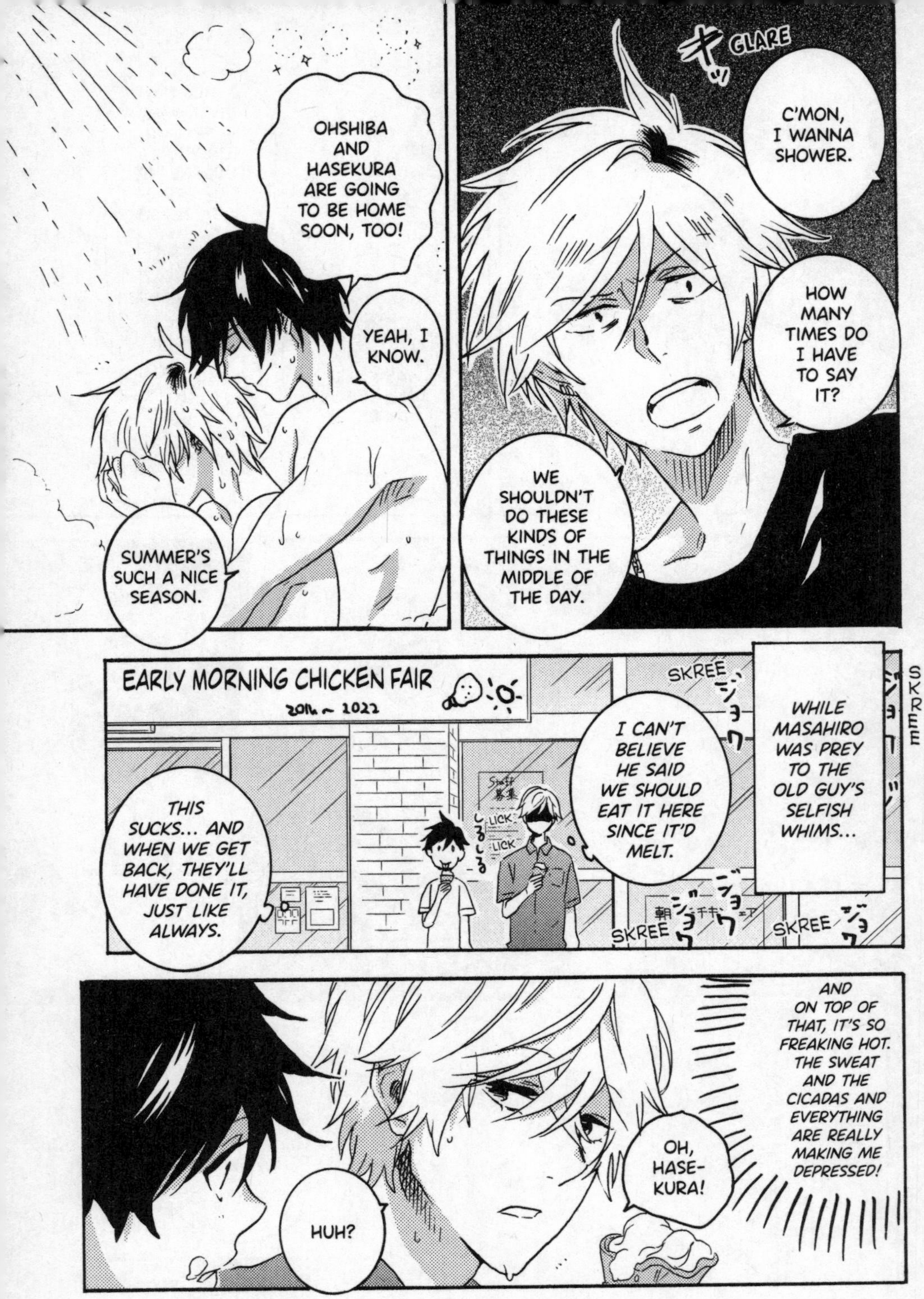
ギッ GLARE
C'MON, I WANNA SHOWER.
HOW MANY TIMES DO I HAVE TO SAY IT?
WE SHOULDN'T DO THESE KINDS OF THINGS IN THE MIDDLE OF THE DAY.
OHSHIBA AND HASEKURA ARE GOING TO BE HOME SOON, TOO!
YEAH, I KNOW.
SUMMER'S SUCH A NICE SEASON.
SKREE
WHILE MASAHIRO WAS PREY TO THE OLD GUY'S SELFISH WHIMS...
SKREE
I CAN'T BELIEVE HE SAID WE SHOULD EAT IT HERE SINCE IT'D MELT.
LICK LICK
THIS SUCKS... AND WHEN WE GET BACK, THEY'LL HAVE DONE IT, JUST LIKE ALWAYS.
EARLY MORNING CHICKEN FAIR
2014 ~ 2022
SKREE
SKREE
AND ON TOP OF THAT, IT'S SO FREAKING HOT. THE SWEAT AND THE CICADAS AND EVERYTHING ARE REALLY MAKING ME DEPRESSED!
OH, HASE-KURA!
HUH?

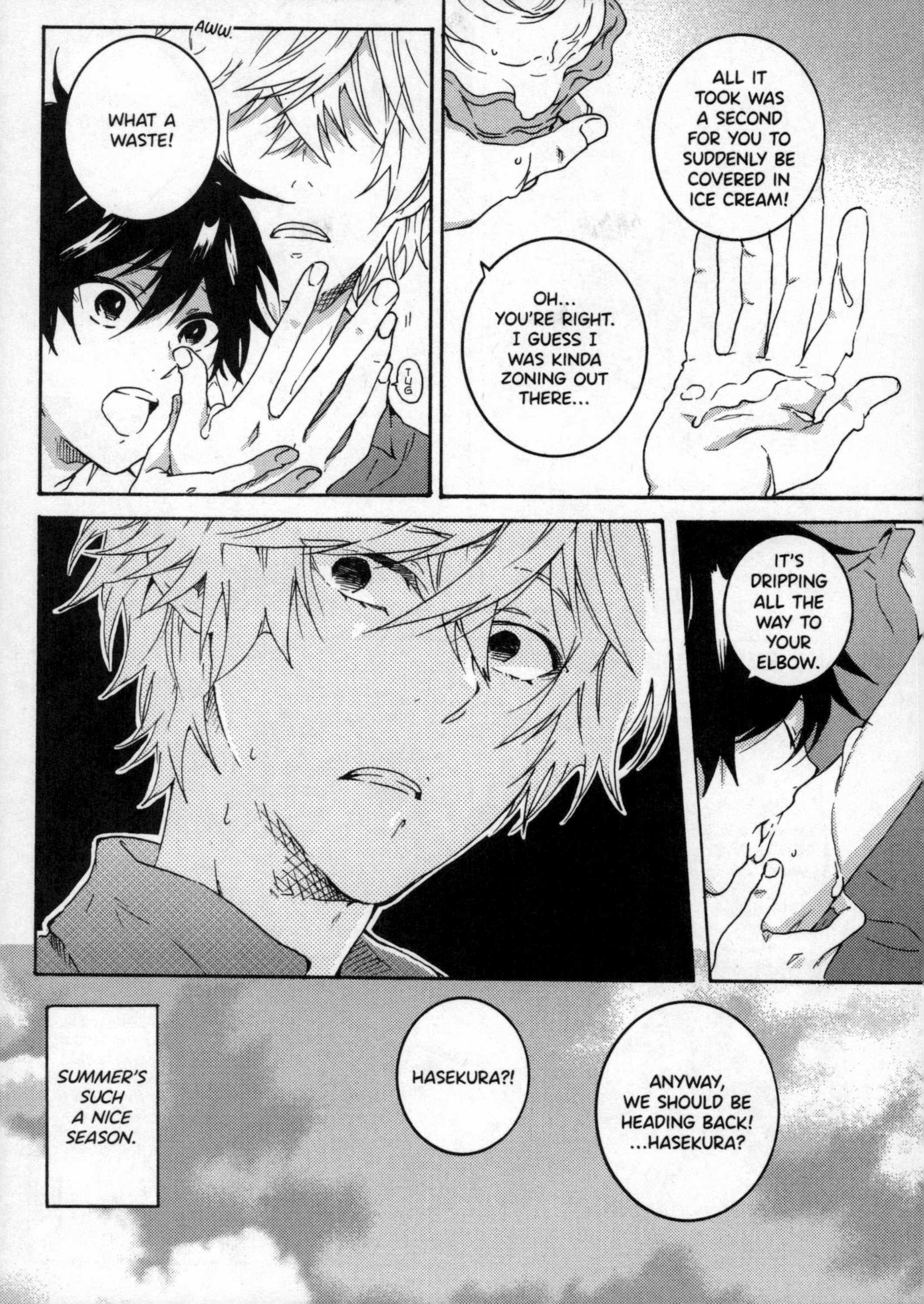
ALL IT TOOK WAS A SECOND FOR YOU TO SUDDENLY BE COVERED IN ICE CREAM!
OH... YOU'RE RIGHT. I GUESS I WAS KINDA ZONING OUT THERE...
AWW.
WHAT A WASTE!
TUG
IT'S DRIPPING ALL THE WAY TO YOUR ELBOW.
ANYWAY, WE SHOULD BE HEADING BACK! ...HASEKURA?
HASEKURA?!
SUMMER'S SUCH A NICE SEASON.

Hitorijime
My Hero

Cryptotympana
cicada

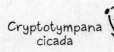

SKREE SKREE SKREE
SKREE SKREE SKREE

Translation:
It hates how
there's two
stupid couples.

Apparently, there
are less *large brown
cicadas* now and more
Cryptotympana cicadas
than compared
to before...

The ones that make the
"chirrup chirrup" sound.

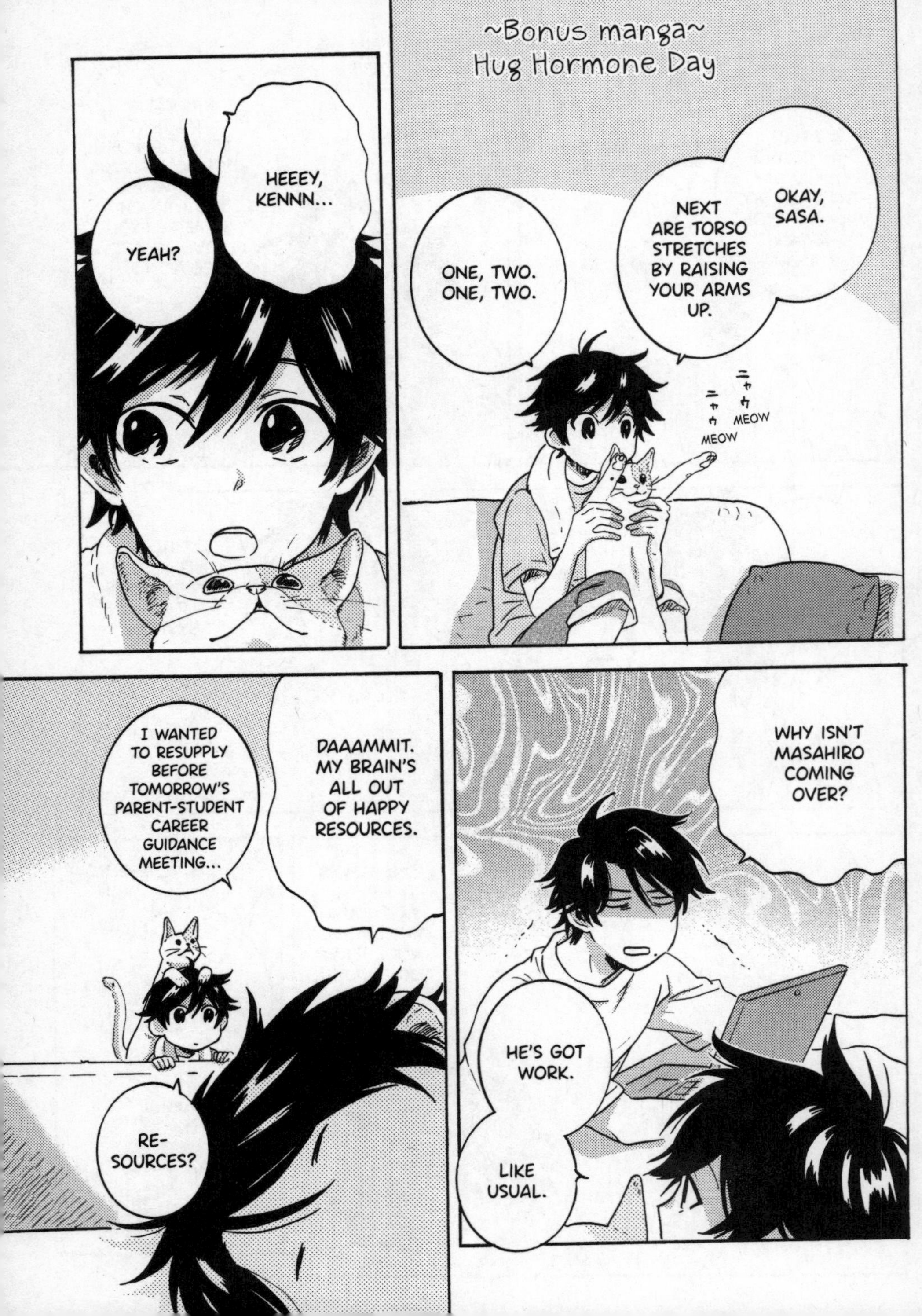
~Bonus manga~
Hug Hormone Day
OKAY, SASA.
NEXT ARE TORSO STRETCHES BY RAISING YOUR ARMS UP.
ONE, TWO. ONE, TWO.
ニャウ MEOW
ニャウ MEOW
HEEEY, KENNN...
YEAH?
WHY ISN'T MASAHIRO COMING OVER?
HE'S GOT WORK.
LIKE USUAL.
DAAAMMIT. MY BRAIN'S ALL OUT OF HAPPY RESOURCES.
I WANTED TO RESUPPLY BEFORE TOMORROW'S PARENT-STUDENT CAREER GUIDANCE MEETING...
RE-SOURCES?

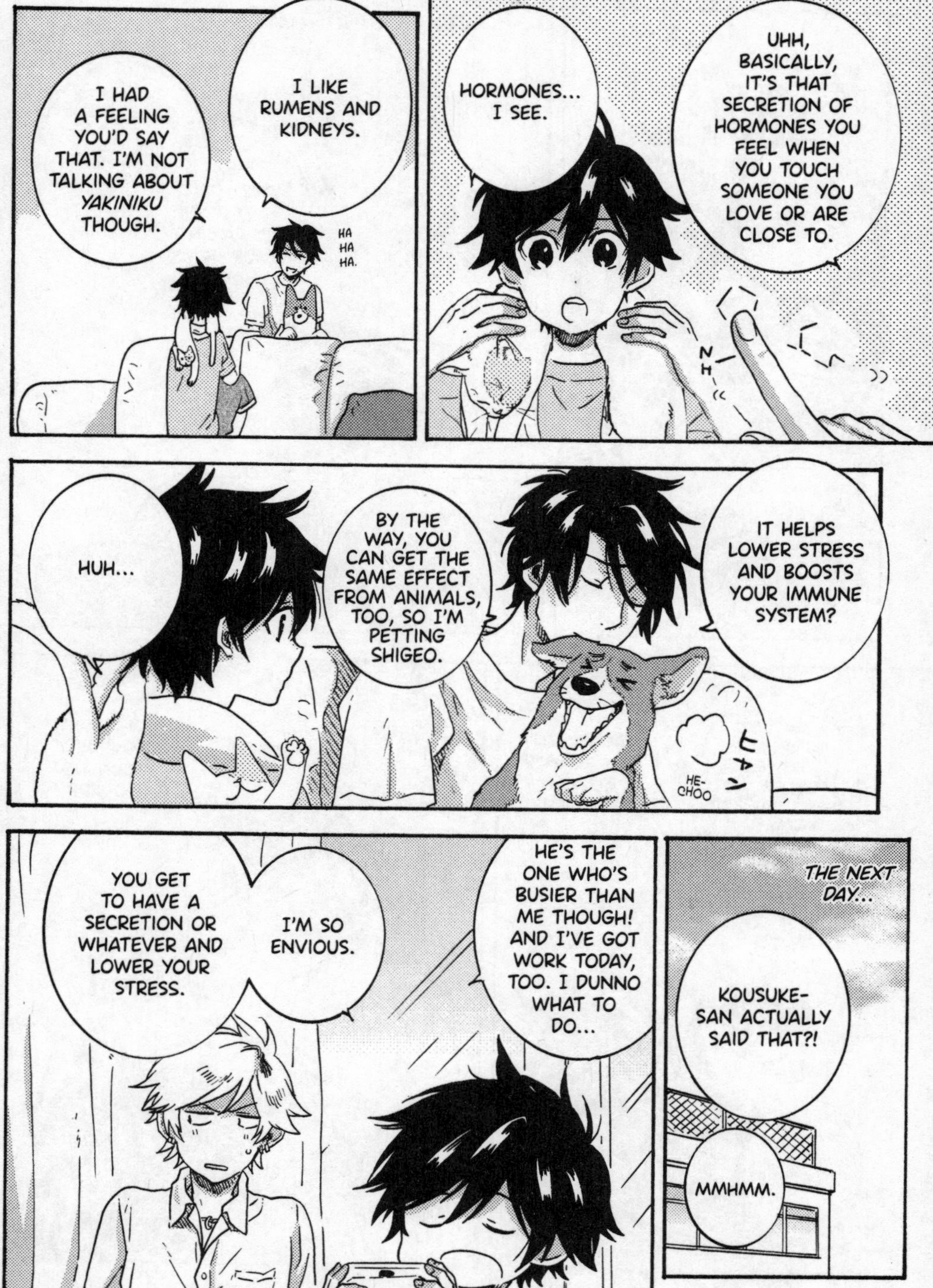
UHH, BASICALLY, IT'S THAT SECRETION OF HORMONES YOU FEEL WHEN YOU TOUCH SOMEONE YOU LOVE OR ARE CLOSE TO.
HORMONES... I SEE.
NH...
I LIKE RUMENS AND KIDNEYS.
I HAD A FEELING YOU'D SAY THAT. I'M NOT TALKING ABOUT *YAKINIKU* THOUGH.
HA HA HA.
IT HELPS LOWER STRESS AND BOOSTS YOUR IMMUNE SYSTEM?
BY THE WAY, YOU CAN GET THE SAME EFFECT FROM ANIMALS, TOO, SO I'M PETTING SHIGEO.
HUH...
HE-CHOO
THE NEXT DAY...
KOUSUKE-SAN ACTUALLY SAID THAT?!
MMHMM.
YOU GET TO HAVE A SECRETION OR WHATEVER AND LOWER YOUR STRESS.
I'M SO ENVIOUS.
HE'S THE ONE WHO'S BUSIER THAN ME THOUGH! AND I'VE GOT WORK TODAY, TOO. I DUNNO WHAT TO DO...

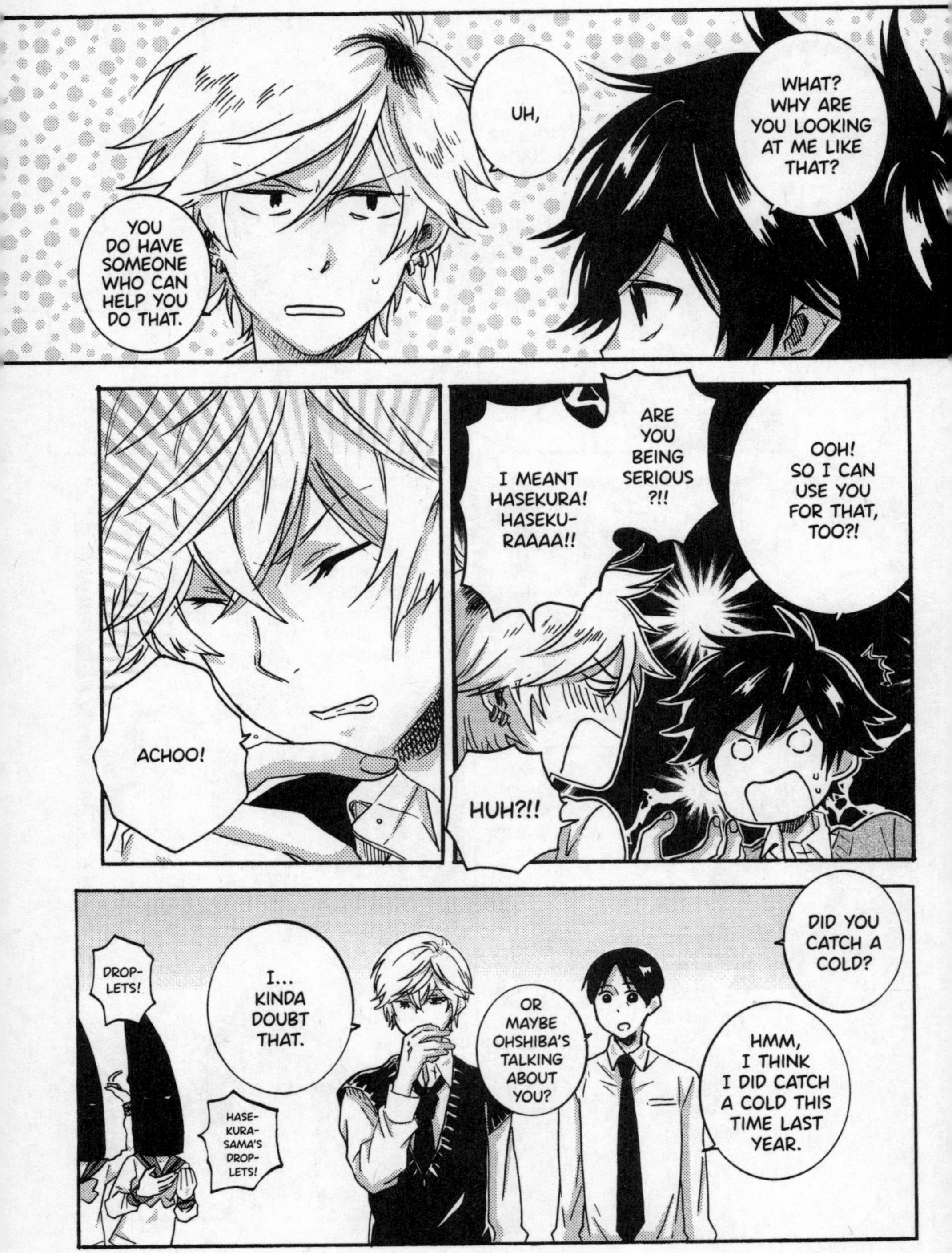
WHAT? WHY ARE YOU LOOKING AT ME LIKE THAT?
UH,
YOU DO HAVE SOMEONE WHO CAN HELP YOU DO THAT.
OOH! SO I CAN USE YOU FOR THAT, TOO?!
ARE YOU BEING SERIOUS?!!
I MEANT HASEKURA! HASEKU-RAAAA!!
HUH?!!
ACHOO!
DID YOU CATCH A COLD?
HMM, I THINK I DID CATCH A COLD THIS TIME LAST YEAR.
OR MAYBE OHSHIBA'S TALKING ABOUT YOU?
I... KINDA DOUBT THAT.
DROP-LETS!
HASE-KURA-SAMA'S DROP-LETS!

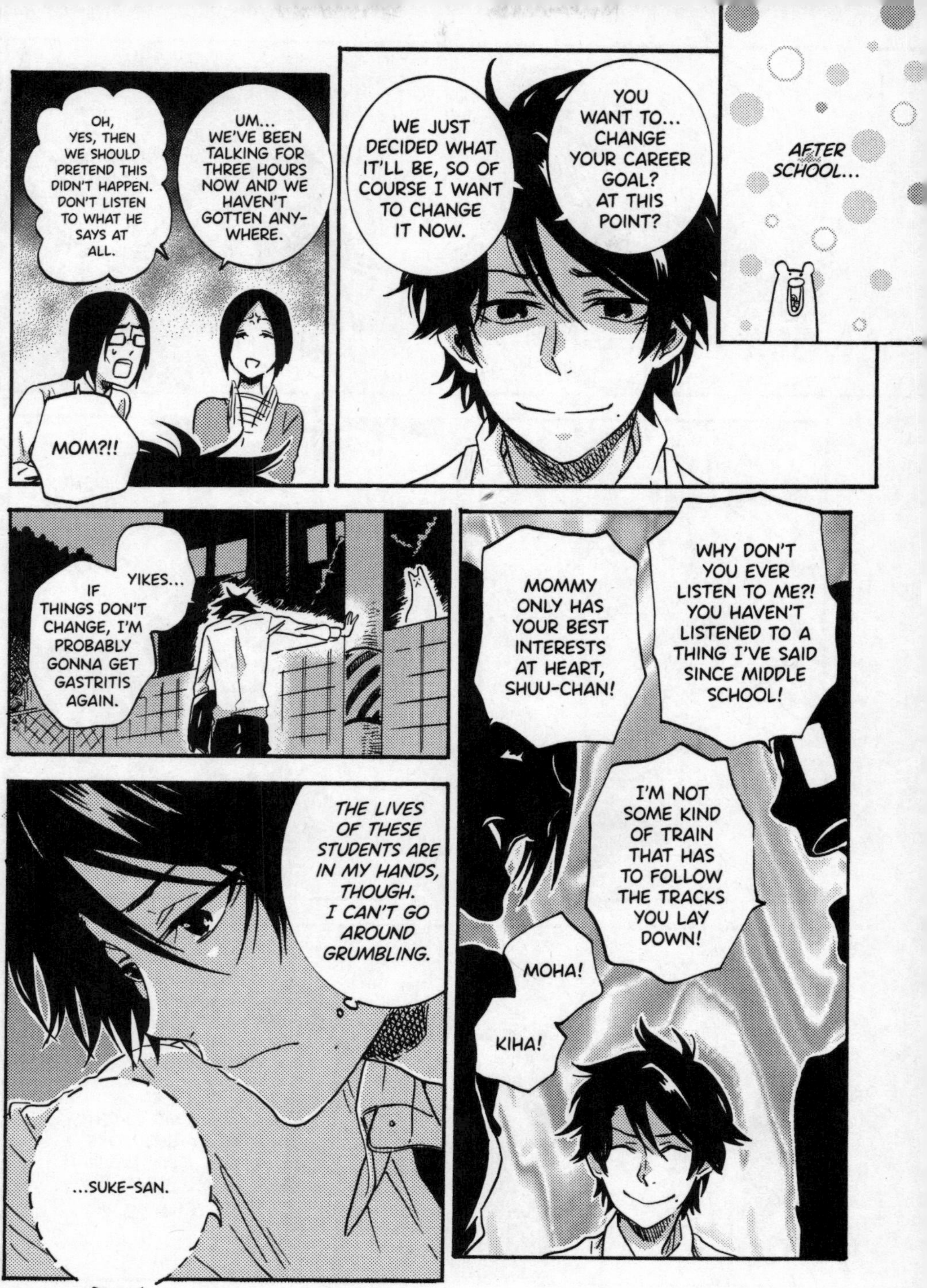
AFTER SCHOOL...
YOU WANT TO... CHANGE YOUR CAREER GOAL? AT THIS POINT?
WE JUST DECIDED WHAT IT'LL BE, SO OF COURSE I WANT TO CHANGE IT NOW.
UM... WE'VE BEEN TALKING FOR THREE HOURS NOW AND WE HAVEN'T GOTTEN ANYWHERE.
OH, YES, THEN WE SHOULD PRETEND THIS DIDN'T HAPPEN. DON'T LISTEN TO WHAT HE SAYS AT ALL.
MOM?!!
WHY DON'T YOU EVER LISTEN TO ME?! YOU HAVEN'T LISTENED TO A THING I'VE SAID SINCE MIDDLE SCHOOL!
MOMMY ONLY HAS YOUR BEST INTERESTS AT HEART, SHUU-CHAN!
I'M NOT SOME KIND OF TRAIN THAT HAS TO FOLLOW THE TRACKS YOU LAY DOWN!
MOHA!
KIHA!
YIKES...
IF THINGS DON'T CHANGE, I'M PROBABLY GONNA GET GASTRITIS AGAIN.
THE LIVES OF THESE STUDENTS ARE IN MY HANDS, THOUGH. I CAN'T GO AROUND GRUMBLING.
...SUKE-SAN.

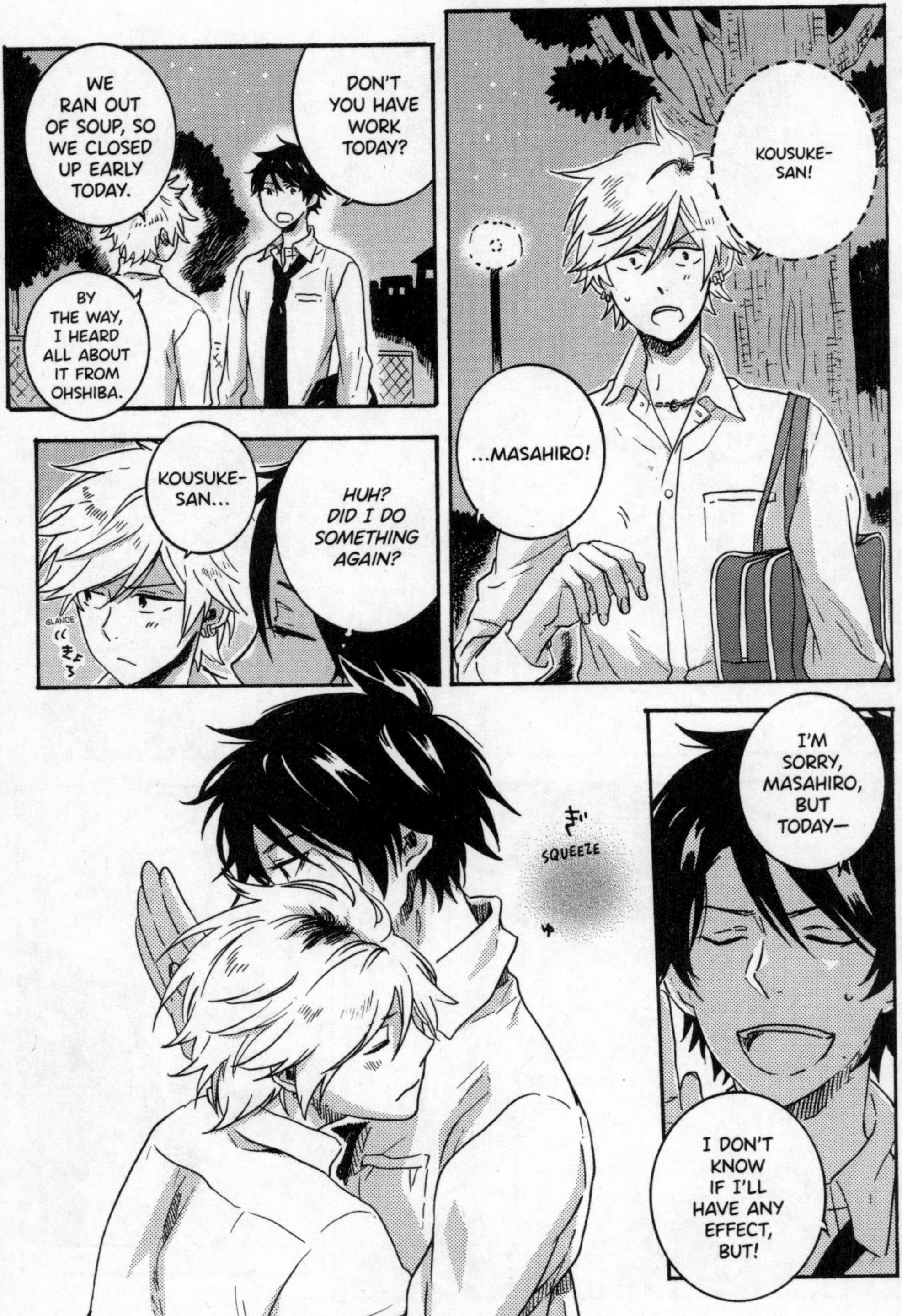
KOUSUKE-SAN!
...MASAHIRO!
DON'T YOU HAVE WORK TODAY?
WE RAN OUT OF SOUP, SO WE CLOSED UP EARLY TODAY.
BY THE WAY, I HEARD ALL ABOUT IT FROM OHSHIBA.
HUH? DID I DO SOMETHING AGAIN?
KOUSUKE-SAN...
GLANCE
I'M SORRY, MASAHIRO, BUT TODAY—
I DON'T KNOW IF I'LL HAVE ANY EFFECT, BUT!
SQUEEZE

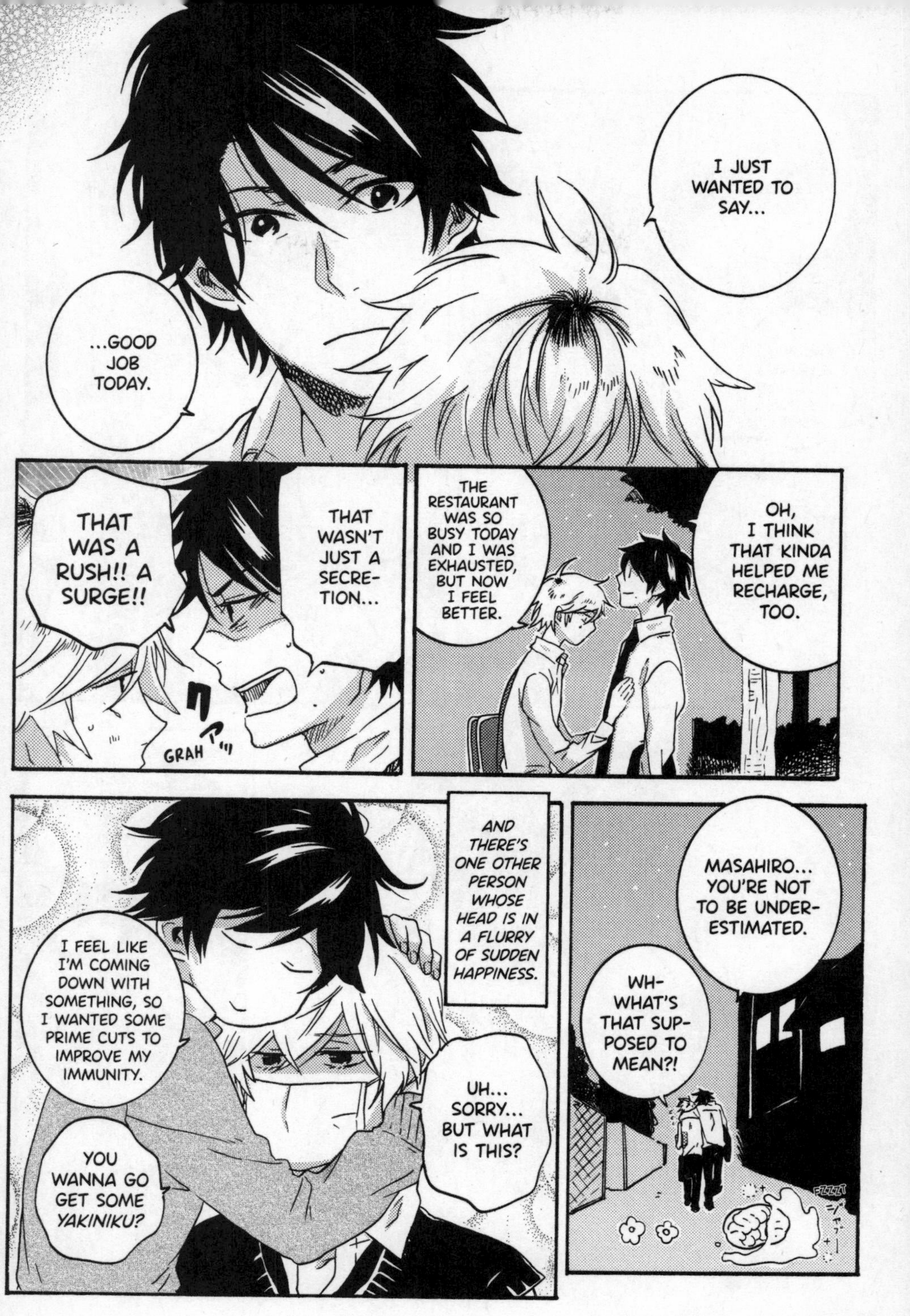
I JUST WANTED TO SAY...
...GOOD JOB TODAY.
OH, I THINK THAT KINDA HELPED ME RECHARGE, TOO.
THE RESTAURANT WAS SO BUSY TODAY AND I WAS EXHAUSTED, BUT NOW I FEEL BETTER.
THAT WASN'T JUST A SECRETION...
THAT WAS A RUSH!! A SURGE!!
GRAH
MASAHIRO... YOU'RE NOT TO BE UNDERESTIMATED.
WH-WHAT'S THAT SUPPOSED TO MEAN?!
FZZZT
AND THERE'S ONE OTHER PERSON WHOSE HEAD IS IN A FLURRY OF SUDDEN HAPPINESS.
I FEEL LIKE I'M COMING DOWN WITH SOMETHING, SO I WANTED SOME PRIME CUTS TO IMPROVE MY IMMUNITY.
UH... SORRY... BUT WHAT IS THIS?
YOU WANNA GO GET SOME *YAKINIKU*?

FIRST RUN

Hitorijime My Hero #25	gateau magazine June 2016 issue
Hitorijime My Hero #25.5	gateau magazine September 2016 issue
Hitorijime My Hero #26	gateau magazine October 2016 issue
Hitorijime My Hero #27	gateau magazine January 2017 issue
Hitorijime My Hero #28	gateau magazine January 2017 issue
Hitorijime My Hero #29	gateau magazine May 2017 issue
Hitorijime My Hero #30	gateau magazine June 2017 issue
Hitorijime Boyfriend #5.5	gateau magazine Vol.17

After word

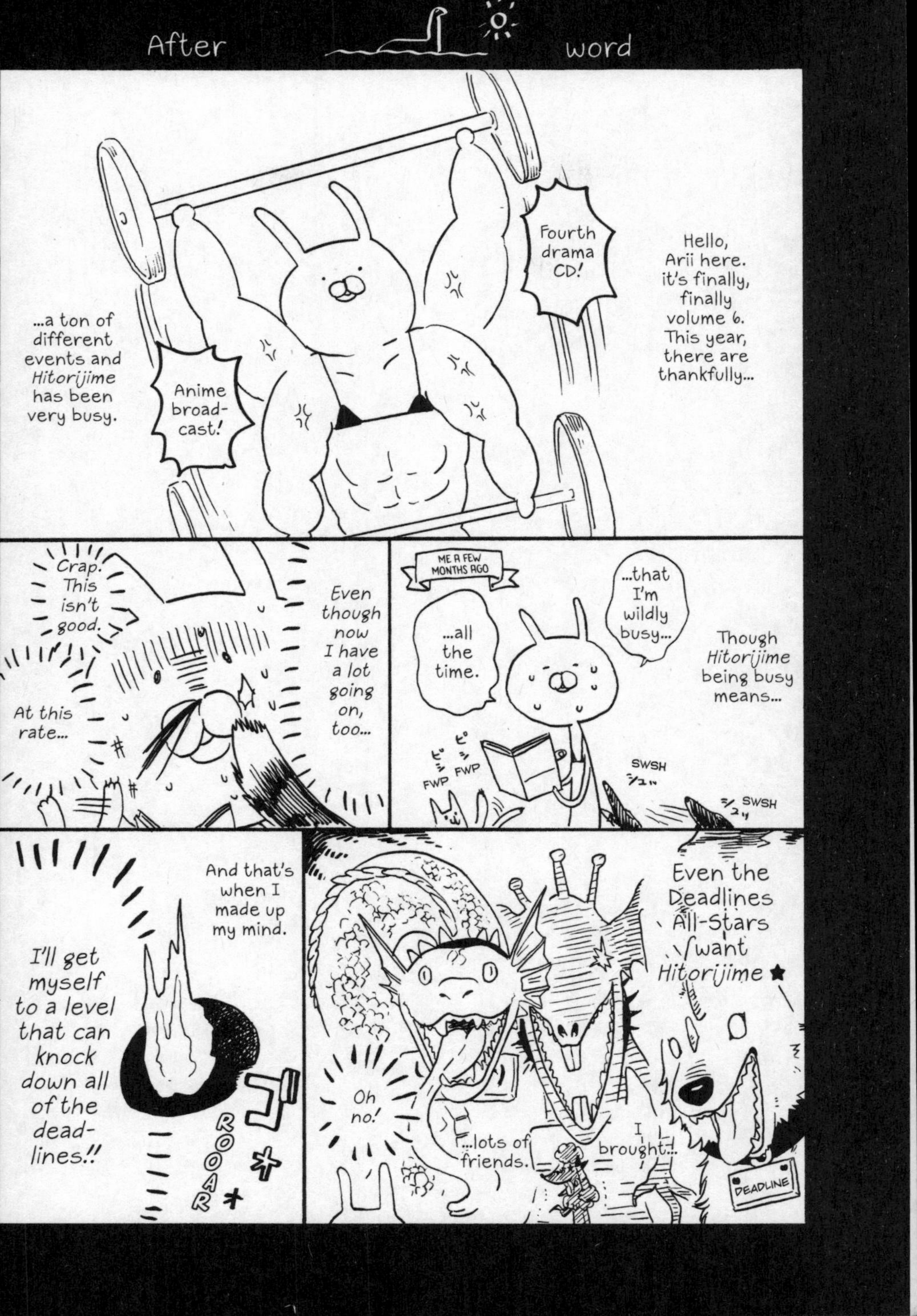
Hello, Arii here. it's finally, finally volume 6. This year, there are thankfully...
Fourth drama CD!
Anime broad-cast!
...a ton of different events and Hitorijime has been very busy.
ME A FEW MONTHS AGO
Though Hitorijime being busy means...
...that I'm wildly busy...
...all the time.
SWSH
SWSH
FWP
FWP
Even though now I have a lot going on, too...
Crap. This isn't good.
At this rate...
Even the Deadlines All-Stars want Hitorijime★
I brought...
...lots of friends.
Oh no!
DEADLINE
And that's when I made up my mind.
I'll get myself to a level that can knock down all of the dead-lines!!
ROOOAR

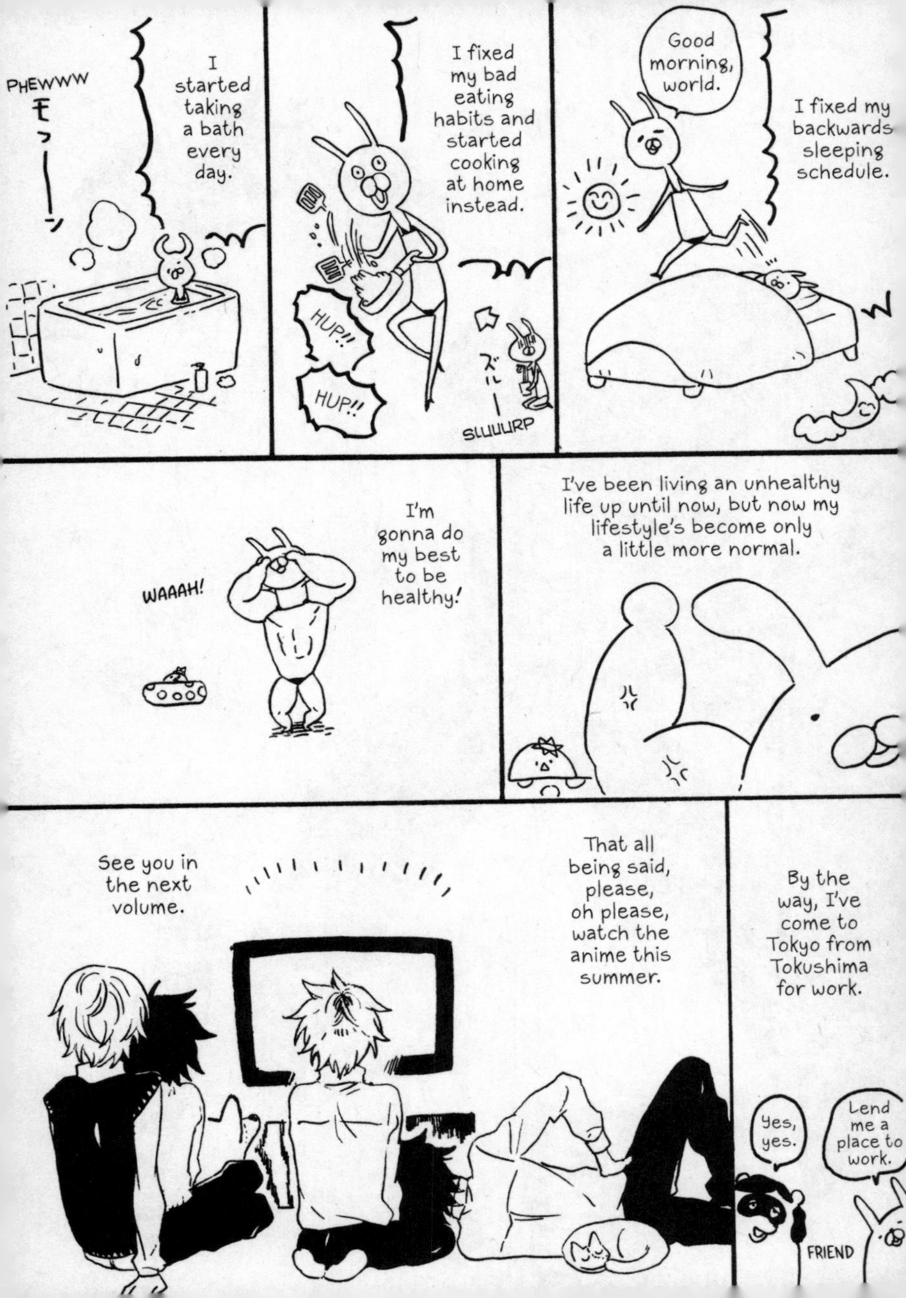
Good morning, world.
I fixed my backwards sleeping schedule.
I fixed my bad eating habits and started cooking at home instead.
HUP!!
HUP!!
SLUUURP
I started taking a bath every day.
PHEWWW
I've been living an unhealthy life up until now, but now my lifestyle's become only a little more normal.
I'm gonna do my best to be healthy!
WAAAH!
By the way, I've come to Tokyo from Tokushima for work.
Lend me a place to work.
Yes, yes.
FRIEND
That all being said, please, oh please, watch the anime this summer.
See you in the next volume.

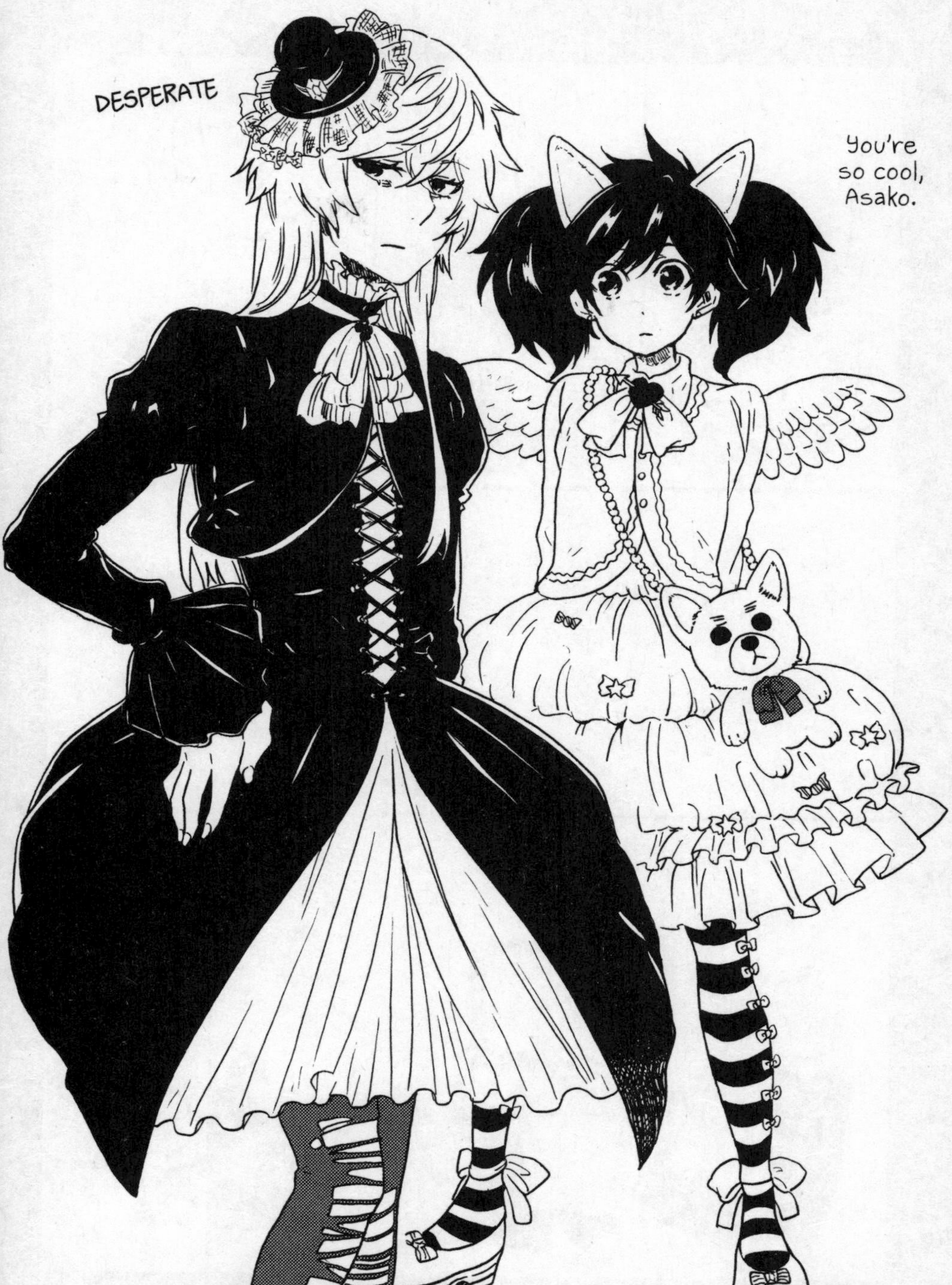
You're so cool, Asako.
DESPERATE

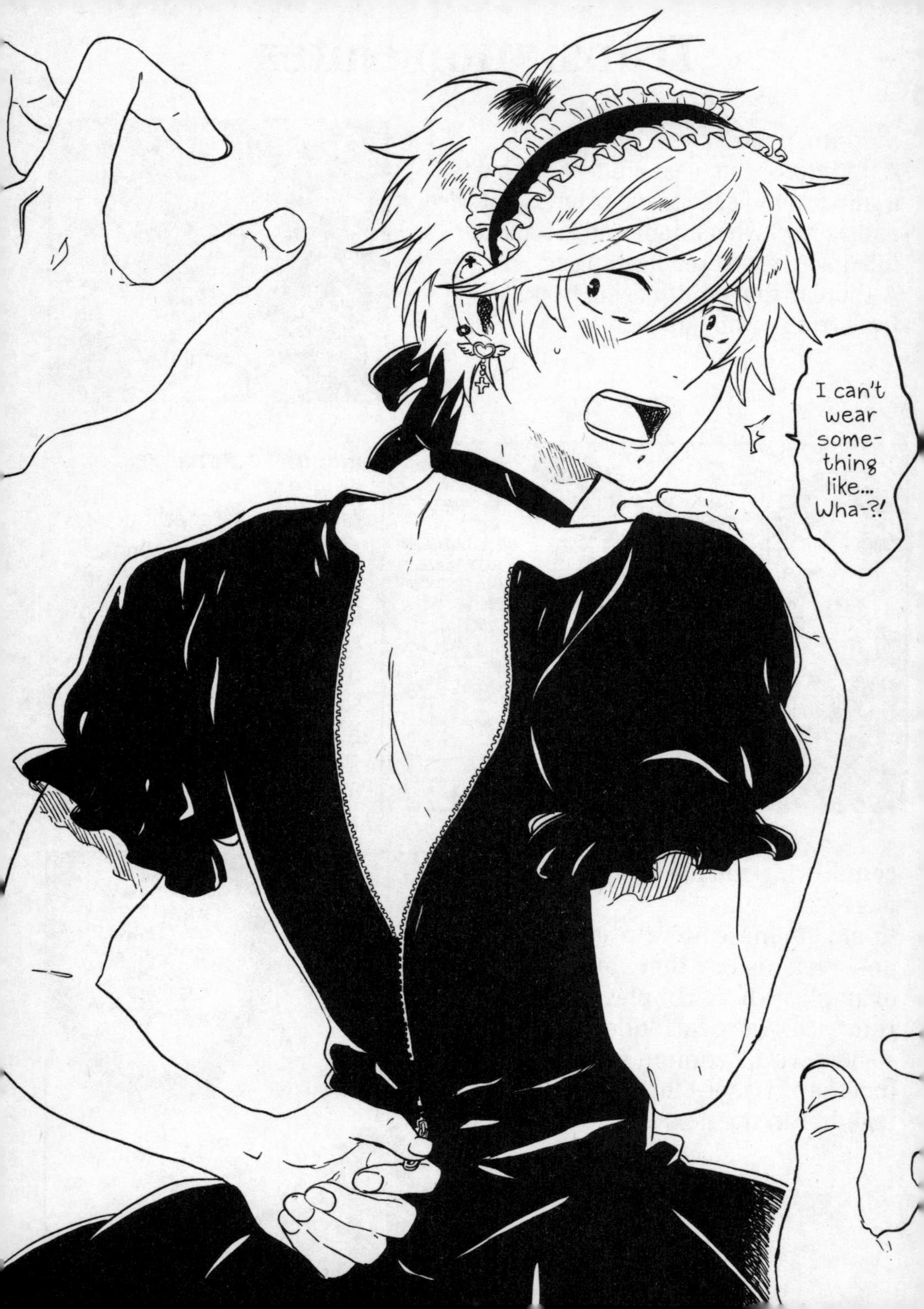
I can't wear some-thing like... Wha-?!

Translation Notes

***manjuu,* page 3**
A traditional Japanese confection that is a small round cake made from wheat, rice, and/or buckwheat flour and is typically filled with sweet red bean paste. A popular souvenir to bring back from trips within Japan.

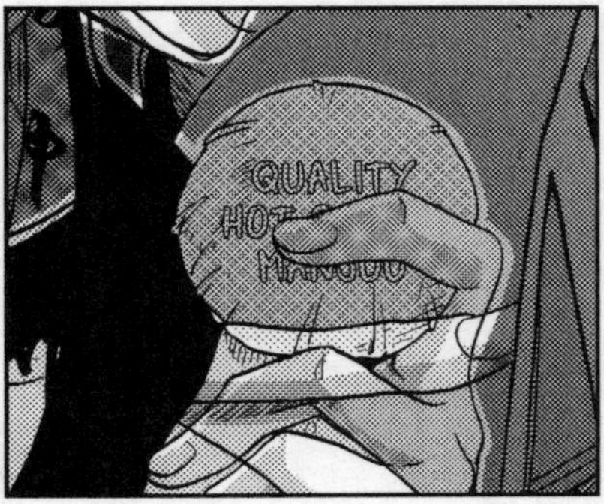
QUALITY

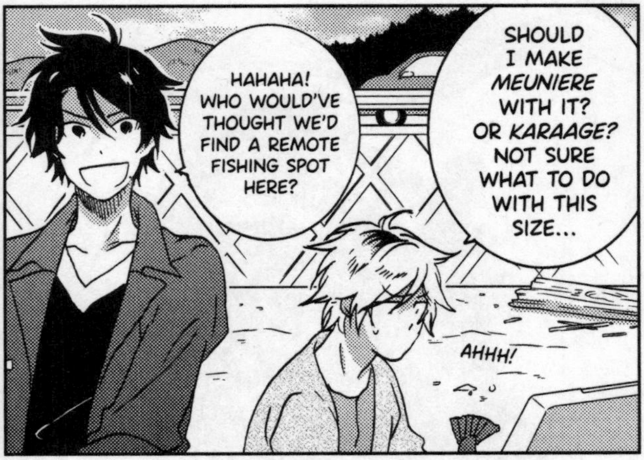
SHOULD I MAKE *MEUNIERE* WITH IT? OR *KARAAGE?* NOT SURE WHAT TO DO WITH THIS SIZE...
HAHAHA! WHO WOULD'VE THOUGHT WE'D FIND A REMOTE FISHING SPOT HERE?
AHHH!

***meuniere, karaage,* page 34**
Meuniere is a method of preparing fish which involves first dredging it in flour, then cooking it in oil and butter, and then adding a sauce made of soy sauce, *mirin* (sweet sake), butter, and lemon juice. *Karaage* is a method of deep-frying.

committing suicide by drowning, page 36
In old Japanese literature, theater, and even history, there are examples where couples whose romances were forbidden by society would commit suicide together in hopes that they can be together in the next life.

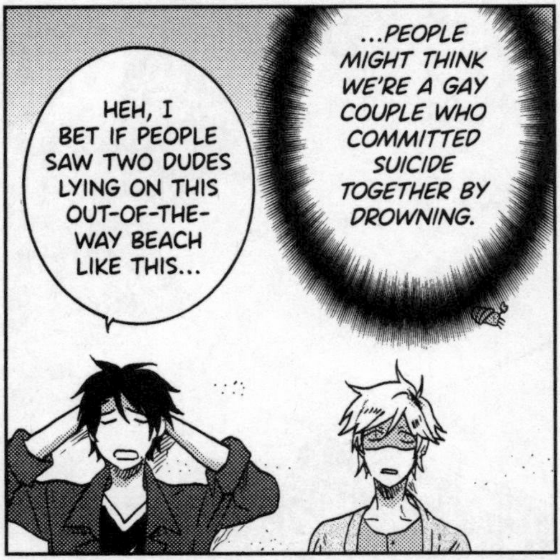
HEH, I BET IF PEOPLE SAW TWO DUDES LYING ON THIS OUT-OF-THE-WAY BEACH LIKE THIS...
...PEOPLE MIGHT THINK WE'RE A GAY COUPLE WHO COMMITTED SUICIDE TOGETHER BY DROWNING.

Natsuo's name, page 53
The first kanji in Natsuo's name means "summer" (*natsu*).

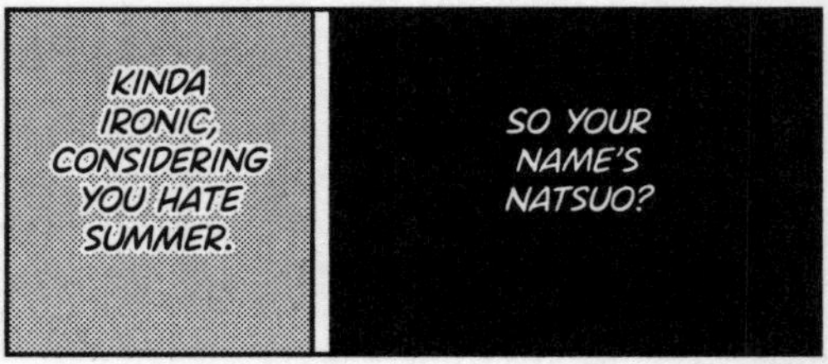
SO YOUR NAME'S NATSUO?
KINDA IRONIC, CONSIDERING YOU HATE SUMMER.

hormones, *yakiniku,* and rumen, page 151
Horumon (hormones) is in the name of a style of *yakiniku* (meat and vegetables cooked on a grill) called *horumonyaki,* which is why Kensuke starts thinking about meat and lists his favorite parts to eat. *Horumonyaki* uses intestines and other offal. Rumen is the first of the four compartments of a cow's stomach.

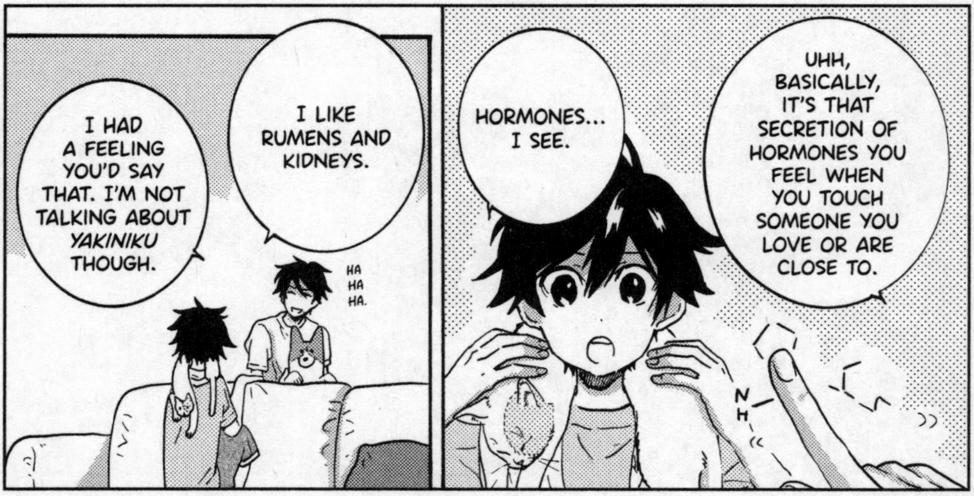
UHH, BASICALLY, IT'S THAT SECRETION OF HORMONES YOU FEEL WHEN YOU TOUCH SOMEONE YOU LOVE OR ARE CLOSE TO.
HORMONES... I SEE.
I LIKE RUMENS AND KIDNEYS.
HA HA HA.
I HAD A FEELING YOU'D SAY THAT. I'M NOT TALKING ABOUT *YAKINIKU* THOUGH.

Moha and Kiha, page 153
"Moha" and "Kiha" are the first part of the train code names for Japan Railway (JR) trains. "Mo" designates that the train has motors packed under the flooring. "Ki" (from '*kidousha*') designates that the train is powered by diesel or another kind of heat engine. "-ha" designates that the train is a regular train without any special cars such as ones with beds or travelers seats like on the bullet trains.

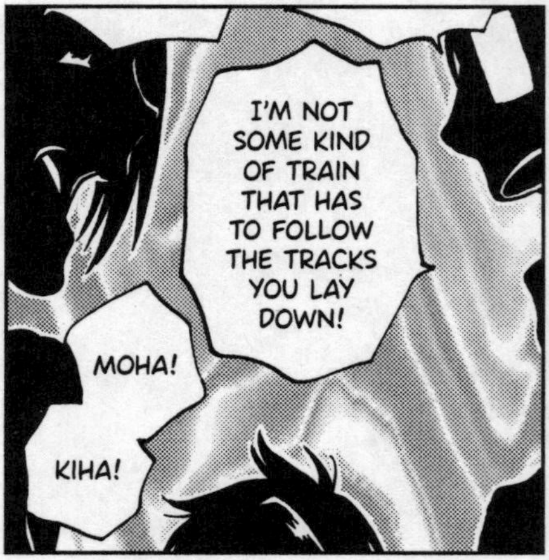
I'M NOT SOME KIND OF TRAIN THAT HAS TO FOLLOW THE TRACKS YOU LAY DOWN!
MOHA!
KIHA!

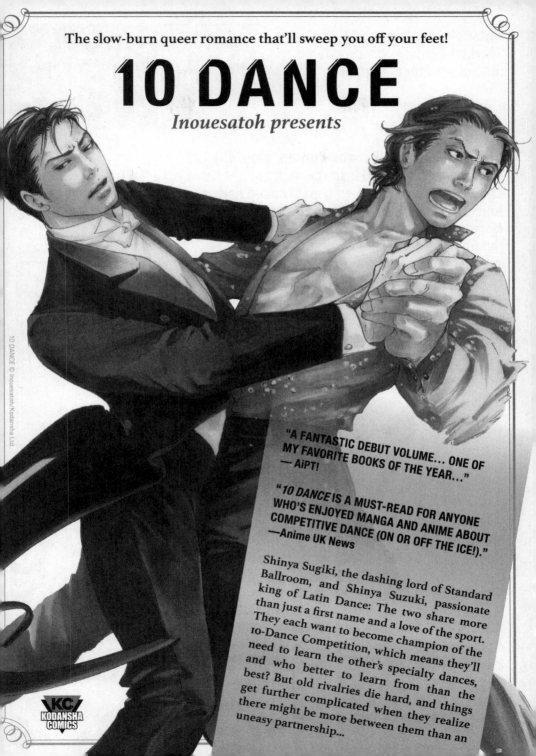

The slow-burn queer romance that'll sweep you off your feet!

10 DANCE

Inouesatoh presents

"A FANTASTIC DEBUT VOLUME... ONE OF MY FAVORITE BOOKS OF THE YEAR..."
— AiPT!

"10 DANCE IS A MUST-READ FOR ANYONE WHO'S ENJOYED MANGA AND ANIME ABOUT COMPETITIVE DANCE (ON OR OFF THE ICE!)."
—Anime UK News

Shinya Sugiki, the dashing lord of Standard Ballroom, and Shinya Suzuki, passionate king of Latin Dance: The two share more than just a first name and a love of the sport. They each want to become champion of the 10-Dance Competition, which means they'll need to learn the other's specialty dances, and who better to learn from than the best? But old rivalries die hard, and things get further complicated when they realize there might be more between them than an uneasy partnership...

KC
KODANSHA
COMICS